All About Pascal

Enhanced Edition

Produced by:

Brian Wiser & Bill Martens

All About Pascal: Enhanced Edition

Published by Apple Pugetsound Program Library Exchange (A.P.P.L.E.)

www.callapple.org

Paperback ISBN: 978-0-359-73994-3
Hardback ISBN: 978-1-71657-350-7

ACKNOWLEDGEMENTS

First and foremost, we would like to thank the original contributors:

Alan J. Nayer, Allen W. Todd, Chris Wilson, Dana Schwartz, David Geddes, David Lieberman, David Miller, David N. Jones, David Paul McCarthy, Dean Rosenhain, Dr. Wo, Keith McLauren, Michael Christensen, Mike Rosing, Paul W. Mosher, Philip Ender, Ron DeGroat, Roy Bollinger, Val J. Golding, and William Janes.

Special thanks to Steve Wozniak – just because. Thanks to everyone who joined the A.P.P.L.E. user group, read *Call-A.P.P.L.E.* magazine, made contributions, and supported our endeavors.

Cartoons by Jim Hilger and modified by Brian Wiser.

The Cover and Book were designed by Brian Wiser.

PRODUCTION

Brian Wiser → Design, Layout, Art, Editing
Bill Martens → Scanning, Disk Updates

DISCLAIMER

About the Producers

Brian Wiser

Brian Wiser is a producer of books, films, games, and events, as well as a long-time consultant, enthusiast and historian of Apple, the Apple II and Macintosh. Steve Wozniak and Steve Jobs, as well as *Creative Computing*, *Nibble*, *InCider*, and *A+* magazines were early influences.

Brian designed, edited, and co-produced dozens of books including: *Nibble Viewpoints: Business Insights From The Computing Revolution*, *Cyber Jack: The Adventures of Robert Clardy and Synergistic Software*, *Synergistic Software: The Early Games*, *The Colossal Computer Cartoon Book: Enhanced Edition*, *All About Applesoft: Enhanced Edition*, *Graphically Speaking: Enhanced Edition*, *What's Where in the Apple: Enhanced Edition*, and *The WOZPAK: Special Edition* – an important Apple II historical book with Steve Wozniak's restored original, technical handwritten notes. Brian is also the author of *The Etch-a-Sketch and Other Fun Programs*.

He passionately preserves and archives all facets of Apple's history, and noteworthy companies such as Beagle Bros and Applied Engineering, featured on AppleArchives.com. His writing, interviews and books are featured on the technology news site CallApple.org and in *Call-A.P.P.L.E.* magazine that he co-produces as an A.P.P.L.E. board member. Brian also co-produced the retro iOS game *Structris*.

In 2005, Brian was cast as an extra in Joss Whedon's movie *Serenity*, leading him to being a producer and director for the documentary film *Done The Impossible: The Fans' Tale of Firefly & Serenity*. He brought some of the *Firefly* cast aboard his Browncoat Cruise and recruited several of the *Firefly* cast to appear in a film for charity. Throughout these experiences, he develops close personal relationships with many actors, authors, and computer industry luminaries. Brian speaks about his adventures to large audiences at conventions around the country.

Bill Martens

Bill Martens is a systems engineer specializing in office infrastructures and has been programming since 1976. The DEC PDP 11/40 with ASR-33 Teletypes and CRT's were his first computing platforms with his first forays in the Apple world coming with the Apple II computer.

Influences in Bill's computing life came from *Byte* magazine, *Creative Computing* magazine, and *Call-A.P.P.L.E.* magazine as well as his mentors Samuel Perkins, Don Williams, Joff Morgan, and Mike Christensen.

Bill is the author of *ApPilot/W1*, *The Anatomy of an EAMON*, and multiple EAMon adventure games, as well as a co-producer of many books including *What's Where in the Apple: Enhanced Edition*, *The WOZPAK: Special Edition*, *Nibble Viewpoints: Business Insights From The Computing Revolution*, and co-programmer for the iOS version of the retro game *Structris*. He has written many articles which have appeared in user group newsletters and magazines such as *Call-A.P.P.L.E.*.

Bill worked for Apple Pugetsound Program Library Exchange (A.P.P.L.E.) under Val Golding and Dick Hubert as a data manager and programmer in the 1980s, and is the current president of the A.P.P.L.E. user group established in 1978. He reorganized A.P.P.L.E. and restarted *Call-A.P.P.L.E.* magazine in 2002. He is the production editor for the A.P.P.L.E. website CallApple.org, writes science fiction novels in his spare time, and is a retired semi-pro football player.

Contents

In Depth Charge – *Val J. Golding* ix

The Pascal + BASIC System – *Ron DeGroat* 1

a hybrid system that allows Pascal to operate concurrently with DOS 3.3 and the ROM-resident BASIC of your Apple II

An Apple Pascal Supplement – *Ron DeGroat*

The Structure of Pascal 13

Avoiding Unnecessary Frustration 17

A Guide to Better Pascal Programs 18

Getting Started (for the beginner) 19

System Utilities

A P-Code Decoder – *Chris Wilson* 21

for those who want to explore the inner workings of the so-called p-machine

Code Map – *David N. Jones* 31

a utility for reading the segment dictionary

Non-Present Boot Disk Patch – *Chris Wilson* 35

a simple patch which waits for you to insert the boot disk

Huffin – *Dana J. Schwartz* 37

(rhymes with "muffin") ... a utility to copy Pascal .TEXT files to DOS 3.3

Puffin – *Dr. Wo* 41

(rhymes with "muffin") ... a utility to copy DOS 3.3 text files to a Pascal environment

Memory Utility

Pascal Memory Utility – *Ron DeGroat* 57

expanded to include a very fast and useful search mode

Disk Utilities

Pascal Text Recovery – *William Janes* 69

when your directory is damaged, don't give up hope

Pascal Zap – *Philip B. Ender and Ron DeGroat* 73

an improved block-oriented disk utility

Pascal Information

Pascal 1.1 Memory Map – *Chris Wilson* 75
an extensive compilation of Pascal 1.1 memory locations

Pascal Internals – *Mike Rosing and Keith McLauren* 79
specific details about Apple Pascal

Pascal Bibliography '82 – *David Paul McCarthy* 87
a comprehensive, updated version of the Pascal Bibliography

Software Tools

Highly Interactive, Goof-proof Keyboard Input – *Ron DeGroat* 101
improving your input error checking

Terminal Independent Screen Control – *Roy Bollinger* 107
implementing full screen cursor control

Pascal Disk Directory Structure – *Allen W. Todd* 111
accessing the Pascal directory from within a program

Text File Header Page – *Alan J. Nayer* 113
a description of Pascal text file header data

Pascal Date Procedure – *David A. Geddes and Ron DeGroat* 117
a procedure to date files without going to the filer to change dates

Enhanced Console Driver – *Chris Wilson* 119
generating additional characters and improved lowercase from the keyboard

A Structured Record for the DOS *VTOC* – *Paul W. Mosher* 123
reading the DOS VTOC as an example of using a structured record to simplify programming

Hardware

Pascal Techniques for Hardware Interfacing – *Chris Wilson* 129
a modem unit and terminal program for the D.C. Hayes Micromodem

Pascal Speed-Up Software for The Mill 6809 Board – *Michael Christensen* 139
an extensive review of the Mill as used with Pascal

Inverse, Flash and Lowercase Display – *David Lieberman* 143
for those with a lowercase adapter

Graphics

A Pascal Character Editor – *Dean Rosenhain* 145
a user-oriented graphics utility

Artillery – *David Miller* 151

Word Processing

Pascal Text Formatter – *Chris Wilson* 163
makes the Editor into a bona fide word processor

Glossary

Now you'll always know the correct definitions for Apple, Nibble, VAL, and WOZ 181

EXPLORING THE
WORLD OF
APPLE

In Depth Charge

by Val J. Golding

written in 1982

What a blast! Working half way across the country with an associate by phone and mail. We are referring, of course, to Ron DeGroat, Pascal editor for *Call-A.P.P.L.E.* and editor of *All About Pascal,* our second volume of *Call-A.P.P.L.E. in Depth.* We would like to go on record, here and now, and express our thanks for his tremendous (and unpaid) contribution to the success of this book. Ron spent many hours reviewing stories, testing programs and correcting proofs.

All About Pascal has been a long time coming. Our original planning was for early spring, 1982. We obviously did not make that deadline. Many new developments came to light along the way, new methods, new tools, all vital information to make Apple Pascal programming easier and more informative for the beginner. Articles were rewritten and set in type a second time. Others were updated to reflect the very latest in state-of-the-art and information.

We believe you will find the long wait worthwhile, and we think *All About Pascal* will become a reference standard for Apple Pascal, just as *All About Applesoft* has for Applesoft BASIC.

This column is being written on August 4, 1982, and the material within this volume is current as of that date. A special thanks must be extended to David Paul McCarthy, whose constant efforts in updating his *Pascal Bibliography,* the most recent of which was received just a day or two ago, should not go unnoticed.

In addition to the two individuals we have already mentioned, we should also point out that this book could never have been as complete as it is without the six or so major features by Chris Wilson, whose patience was worn justifiably thin.

Two disk images of programs from this book can be downloaded from: www.callapple.org. Included in this set is the Applesoft BASIC program *Huffin,* sharing diskette space with Pascal files, another *Call-A.P.P.L.E.* first.

Looking at the other volumes of *Call-A.P.P.L.E. in Depth, such as All About Applesoft* and *All About DOS,* would be well worth your time. Accompanying articles found in *Call-A.P.P.L.E.* magazine can be accessed via a subscription to Call-A.P.P.L.E. at: www.callapple.org.

Now it's time to devour our table of contents – we suspect there is something for everyone there. Try it, you'll like it!

Enjoy,

Val J. Golding

MAKING BASIC BEHAVE!
COACH
PO
PRINT
GOTO
FOR
IF
GR

The Pascal + Basic System

Ron DeGroat

Until now, Pascal and BASIC have not been compatible with one another. But with the routines described in this article, you can make Pascal operate and interact with the ROM-resident BASIC of your Apple computer. Some of the things that you can do with the PASCAL+BASIC system are listed below:

- Perform any Pascal, BASIC or DOS operation without having to reboot.
- Save BASIC programs onto Pascal disks.
- Run BASIC programs from Pascal.
- Call BASIC programs under Pascal program control.
- Save machine code written under the BASIC system onto Pascal disks.
- Call machine code written under BASIC from Pascal.
- Call BASIC and monitor ROM subroutines from Pascal.
- Use BASIC's monitor from Pascal.
- Use the UCSD Adaptable Assembler to create machine code which can be saved onto DOS 3.3 disks and used with BASIC.
- Easily create your own PASCAL +BASIC hybrid programs.

***SYSTEM REQUIREMENTS:**

- Apple Pascal (II.1 or 1.1)
- DOS 3.3

```
(**********************************************)
(* LISTING #1 : PBMENU, A PASCAL+BASIC HYBRID *)
(*                                            *)
(* WRITTEN BY RON DEGROAT    3/81             *)
(**********************************************)

(*$S+,V-*)
PROGRAM PBMENU;

USES BASICSTUFF;

CONST BAS='.BAS';   (*FILENAME SUFFIXES*)
      BIN='.BIN';
      NOTHING='';

      STARTOFHEAP=3072; (* WITH 80 COL BOARD *)
                        (* STARTS AT $800     *)

VAR HOME,ERASEOL,BELL,CH      :CHAR;
    F                         :FILE;
    TESTNAME,FILENAME         :STRING[25];
    SUFFIX                    :STRING[5];
    ADDR,CODELEN,NUMBLKS,I    :INTEGER;
    DONE                      :BOOLEAN;

PROCEDURE DOIT(CHOICE:INTEGER); FORWARD;

PROCEDURE PROMPTAT(LINE:INTEGER; MESSAGE:STRING);
BEGIN
  GOTOXY(0,LINE);
  WRITE(MESSAGE,ERASEOL);
END; (*PROMPTAT*)


PROCEDURE IOERRCHK;
VAR IOERR:INTEGER;
BEGIN
 IOERR:=IORESULT;
 IF IOERR<>0 THEN BEGIN
  CLOSE(F);
  WRITELN(BELL);
  WRITELN('IO ERROR #',IOERR);
  IF IOERR=10 THEN
   WRITELN('CAN''T FIND ',TESTNAME);
  WRITE('PRESS <SP> TO CONTINUE');
  READ(CH); EXIT(DOIT);
 END;
END; (*IOERRCHK*)

PROCEDURE FILECHK;
BEGIN
 TESTNAME:=CONCAT(FILENAME,SUFFIX);
(*$I-*)
 RESET(F,TESTNAME); IOERRCHK;
(*$I+*)
 CLOSE(F);
END;

PROCEDURE GETFILENAME;
BEGIN
```

```
PROCEDURE GETADDR(PROMPT:STRING);
BEGIN
 PROMPTAT(2,PROMPT);
 READLN(ADDR);
END;

PROCEDURE BINLOAD;
BEGIN
   PROMPTAT(22,'REQUIRES COMPLETE FILE NAME');
   PROMPTAT(23,'INCLUDING SUFFIX (BAS,BIN,CODE)');
   GETFILENAME;
   SUFFIX:=NOTHING; FILECHK;
   GETADDR('LOADADDR ==> ');
   BLOAD(FILENAME,ADDR);
END; (*BINLOAD*)


PROCEDURE BINSAVE;
BEGIN
 GETFILENAME;
 GETADDR('STARTADDR ==> ');
 PROMPTAT(4,'LENGTH IN BYTES ==> ');
 READLN(CODELEN);
 BSAVE(FILENAME,ADDR,CODELEN);
END; (*BINSAVE*)


PROCEDURE BASICSAVE;
BEGIN
 GETFILENAME;
 SAVE(FILENAME);
END; (*SAVE*)


PROCEDURE BASICRUN;
BEGIN
 SUFFIX:=BAS;
 GETFILENAME; FILECHK;
 RUN(FILENAME);
END; (*RUN*)


PROCEDURE BINRUN;
BEGIN
   SUFFIX:=BIN;
   GETFILENAME; FILECHK;
   BRUN(FILENAME);
END; (*BRUN*)


PROCEDURE CALLIT;
BEGIN
   GETADDR('ADDR TO CALL ==> ');
   CALL(ADDR);
END; (*CALL*)


PROCEDURE ROMCALLIT;
BEGIN
   GETADDR('ROM ADDR TO CALL ==> ');
   ROMCALL(ADDR);
END; (*ROMCALL*)

PROCEDURE DOS;
BEGIN
 FILENAME:='DOS.3.3'; SUFFIX:=BIN;
 FILECHK;
 WRITE('NOW LOADING DOS...');
 LOADDOS;
END;
```

With the PASCAL+BASIC system you don't have to recreate everything that has already been done for BASIC. Many of these things can be saved onto Pascal disks and used with the Pascal system. For example, I have saved three dimensional hires graphics routines created under BASIC onto Pascal disks and then used them in Pascal programs.

The heart of the PASCAL+BASIC system consists of the UNIT BASICSTUFF and the hybrid program PBMENU which 'USES BASICSTUFF.'

GLOSSARY OF LISTINGS

Listing #1: PBMENU—A Pascal hybrid program that allows interactive use of almost every routine available in BASICSTUFF.

Listing #2: BASICSTUFF—A UNIT which when installed in the SYSTEM. LIBRARY, allows the Pascal system to interact with the co-resident, ROM-resident BASIC system.

Listing #3: PBPROC—External procedures used by BASICSTUFF.

Listing #4: DOS32K—A Pascal program which converts DOS 3.3 Master disks into 32K disks (so that PBMENU won't get over-written when DOS is loaded).

Listing #5: HYBRID—A short example of hybrid programming.

HOW TO USE PBMENU

PBMENU (shown in Listing #1) is easy to use because the command options are either self-explanatory or equivalent to BASIC commands.

VIDEO DISPLAY OF PBMENU:

PASCAL + BASIC: COMMAND OPTIONS

BRUN
BSAVE
BLOAD
RUN
SAVE
LOAD DOS
CALL
ROM CALL
QUIT

LEFT & RIGHT ARROWS MOVE CURSOR

[SP] OR [RET] EXECUTES SELECTION

LOAD DOS—simply loads DOS into memory from a Pascal file, connects DOS and enters whichever BASIC is ROM-resident. This option assumes that DOS has already been saved onto a Pascal disk with the filename 'DOS.3.3.BIN' (more about this later). When this option is selected, DOS is loaded into memory from $5600-7FFF and HIMEM is automatically set to protect it.

ROM CALL—is like a normal CALL except that it enables the onboard ROM's just before the jump is made. It also saves certain Pascal information that might get over-written, swaps the Pascal zero page for a Basic zero page and restores everthing upon return.

SAVE and BSAVE automatically append a suffix ('.BAS' or '.BIN') to the filename given by the user. RUN and BRUN automatically supply the appropriate suffix. All other command options act just like their BASIC counterparts.

Files created with the SAVE and BSAVE commands contain a header block which holds relevant information in a record called PBCODEINFO (see Listing #2). This information is used by RUN and BRUN and includes such things as the starting address of the routine, the code length and a copy of the entire zero page at the time of saving.

```
PROCEDURE DOIT;
BEGIN
 CASE CHOICE OF
   0:BINRUN;
   1:BINLOAD;
   2:BINSAVE;
   3:BASICRUN;
   4:BASICSAVE;
   5:DOS;
   6:CALLIT;
   7:ROMCALLIT;
   8:DONE:=TRUE;
 END; (*CASE*)
END; (*DOIT*)

PROCEDURE MENUOPTIONS;

CONST NUMOPTIONS=9;
      STARTMENU=3;
      SP=' ';

TYPE OPTIONS=STRING[10];

VAR MENU:PACKED ARRAY[0..NUMOPTIONS]
          OF OPTIONS;

    NEXT,SELECTION:INTEGER;

    INVERSE,NORMAL,
    LEFT,RIGHT:CHAR;

PROCEDURE INITMENU;
BEGIN
  MENU[0]:='BRUN';
  MENU[1]:='BLOAD';
  MENU[2]:='BSAVE';
  MENU[3]:='RUN';
  MENU[4]:='SAVE';
  MENU[5]:='LOAD DOS';
  MENU[6]:='CALL';
  MENU[7]:='ROM CALL';
  MENU[8]:='QUIT';
  SELECTION:=0;
END; (*INITMENU*)

PROCEDURE DISPLAYMENU;
BEGIN
  WRITE(HOME);
  WRITE('PASCAL+BASIC: COMMAND OPTIONS');
  GOTOXY(0,STARTMENU);
  FOR I:=0 TO NUMOPTIONS-1 DO
    BEGIN
      WRITELN(SP:14,MENU[I]);
      WRITELN;
    END;
  PROMPTAT(22,'LEFT & RIGHT ARROWS MOVE CURSOR');
  PROMPTAT(23,'<SP> OR <RET> EXECUTES SELECTION');
END;

PROCEDURE MAKESELECTION;
BEGIN
  REPEAT
   GOTOXY(0,STARTMENU+2*SELECTION);
   WRITE(SP:14,INVERSE,MENU[SELECTION]);
   READ(KEYBOARD,CH);
   IF (CH=LEFT) OR (CH=RIGHT) THEN
    BEGIN
     GOTOXY(0,STARTMENU+2*SELECTION);
     WRITELN(NORMAL,SP:14,MENU[SELECTION]);
     IF CH=RIGHT THEN NEXT:=1
      ELSE NEXT:=-1;
       NEXT:=NEXT+NUMOPTIONS;
     SELECTION:=(SELECTION+NEXT) MOD NUMOPTIONS;
    END
  UNTIL CH=SP;
  WRITE(NORMAL,HOME);
END;
```

```
BEGIN (*MENUOPTIONS*)

 INVERSE:=CHR(18);          (*CTL-R*)
 NORMAL:=CHR(20);           (*CTL-T*)
 RIGHT:=CHR(21);            (*CTL-U, -> *)
 LEFT:=CHR(8);              (*CTL-H, <- *)
 DONE:=FALSE;

 INITMENU;

 REPEAT
   DISPLAYMENU;
   MAKESELECTION;
   DOIT(SELECTION);
 UNTIL DONE;
END; (*MENU*)

BEGIN (*MAIN PROGRAM*)

(*CTL CHARS USED HERE MAY DIFFER FOR*)
(*EXT. TERMINALS, VIDEO BOARDS, ETC.*)

  BELL:=CHR(7);              (*CTL-G*)
  HOME:=CHR(12);             (*CTL-L*)
  ERASEOL:=CHR(29);          (*CTL-]*)

(*DISPLAY ONLY LEFT HALF OF SCREEN*)

  DISPLAY40;

(*MOVE HEAP FROM $C00 TO $8001*)

  MOVEHEAP(STARTOFHEAP,-32767);

  MENUOPTIONS;

  DISPLAY80;

  MOVEHEAP(-32767,STARTOFHEAP);

END.
```

```
(************************************)
(* LISTING #2: THE UNIT BASICSTUFF *)
(*                                  *)
(* WRITTEN BY RON DEGROAT    3/81   *)
(************************************)

(*$S+,V-*)
UNIT BASICSTUFF; INTRINSIC CODE 25 DATA 26;

(*REMOVE 'INTRINSIC CODE 25 DATA 26' TO *)
(*MAKE BASICSTUFF A REGULAR UNIT.       *)

(* THIS UNIT SHOULD BE COMPILED, THEN *)
(* LINKED TO THE EXTERNAL PROCEDURES  *)
(* SHOWN IN LISTING #3, AND INSTALLED *)
(* IN THE SYSTEM.LIBRARY.             *)

INTERFACE

TYPE UNITSTR=STRING[25];

VAR BASZERPG:PACKED ARRAY[0..255] OF 0..255;
    UNITFID:FILE;
```

With the PROGRAM PBMENU, memory is partitioned so that the BASIC part of the system is equivalent to a 32K machine. Because of this memory constraint, some programs may be too large to run under the PASCAL+BASIC system. A little experimentation will show which programs should be avoided.

With the PASCAL+BASIC system, there a several ways of getting to BASIC and back again to Pascal.

WAYS TO GO TO BASIC:

- ROMCALL -8192 to enter ROM-resident BASIC.
- ROMCALL -155 or -151 to enter the monitor.
- LOADDOS to load DOS and enter BASIC

WAYS TO RETURN TO PASCAL:

- CALL 7 from BASIC
- CALL 1016 from BASIC
- 'Ctrl-Y [RET]' from the monitor
- '7G[RET]' or '3F8G[RET]' from the monitor.

HOW IT WORKS

The idea is simple: move Pascal up and BASIC down so that the two do not interfere with one another (see diagram).

Actually, the two systems share memory above $D000, but this sharing of memory space is made non-interfering by switching on only that bank of memory which is currently needed. The RAM on the Language card contains Pascal and the ROM's on the motherboard contain BASIC. Selection between the two is made with the control codes ($C088 and $C08A) as described in the APPLE LANGUAGE SYSTEM INSTALLATION AND OPERATING MANUAL.

MEMORY MAP OF PBMENU

BASICSTUFF—Without BASICSTUFF, PBMENU would be useless. All of the routines necessary for hybrid programming have been placed in the UNIT BASICSTUFF which when installed in the SYSTEM.LIBRARY become available to any Pascal program with a USES BASICSTUFF declaration. A brief summary of each procedure in BASICSTUFF not already described is given below:

MOVEHEAP—allows you to configure your PASCAL + BASIC system to suit whatever conditions might arise. For example, if you have a large Pascal program which calls a short BASIC or binary routine, the heap should only be moved up a little. On the other hand, a small Pascal program running a large BASIC program may require the heap to be pushed way up. Of course, the heap should always be returned to its normal starting position of $C00 (3072) before returning to the Pascal command level. If you really want to get fancy, you could move the heap up a little to run a large Pascal segment and a short BASIC program, then go to a smaller Pascal segment, move the heap up some more and run a large BASIC program. In order to protect Pascal, HIMEM is automatically set to the bottom of the heap unless DOS (which must be located below the heap) is protected.

DISPLAY40—suppresses the display of the right half of the Pascal text screen. Most BASIC programs use this area of memory ($800-BFF, the second text page).

DISPLAY80—is used to restore the right half of the Pascal text screen. Normally used just before the termination of a Pascal (hybrid) program.

FPBASIC—is a function which returns a value of true if Applesoft is in ROM. If Integer BASIC is in ROM, the value returned is false.

```
PROCEDURE LOADDOS;
PROCEDURE DOSRESET;
PROCEDURE DISPLAY40;
PROCEDURE DISPLAY80;
FUNCTION  FPBASIC:BOOLEAN;
PROCEDURE RUN(FILENAME:UNITSTR);
PROCEDURE SAVE(FILENAME:UNITSTR);
PROCEDURE BRUN(FILENAME:UNITSTR);
PROCEDURE CALL(ADDR:INTEGER);
PROCEDURE ROMCALL(ADDR:INTEGER);
PROCEDURE MOVEHEAP(OLDLOC,NEWLOC:INTEGER);
PROCEDURE BLOAD(FILENAMEE:UNITSTR; BEGINADDR:INTEGER);
PROCEDURE BSAVE(FILENAME:UNITSTR; BEGINADDR,CODELEN:INTEGER);

IMPLEMENTATION

CONST DOSLOADADDR=22016;
      DOSINIT=23940;        (* $5D84 *)

TYPE MAGIC=RECORD CASE BOOLEAN OF
             TRUE:(INTPART:INTEGER);
             FALSE:(PTRPART:^INTEGER);
           END;

     BYTE=0..255;
     PAGEOFMEM=PACKED ARRAY[0..255] OF BYTE;

VAR CHEAT,SOURCE,DEST:MAGIC;

    SUFFIX:STRING[5];

    NUMBLKS,I,IO,
    HIMEM,HIMEMADDR,
    ENDADDR,RUNADDR,LOADADDR:INTEGER;

    DOSLOADED:BOOLEAN;

    PBCODEINFO:PACKED RECORD
                 CODELENG,CODEADDR:INTEGER;
                 NAME:STRING[25];
                 STARTADDR:INTEGER;
                 BASICZERPG:PAGEOFMEM;
                 COMMENT:STRING;
                 FILLER:ARRAY[0..71] OF INTEGER;
               END;
```

DIFFERENCES BETWEEN REGULAR AND INTRINSIC UNITS:

REGULAR UNIT	INTRINSIC UNIT
UNIT's code is inserted into each hosts codefile at Link time.	UNIT's code is loaded into memory at Run time.
Host is self-contained and independent of original UNIT.	Host is dependent on UNIT being on-line and in the SYSTEM.LIBRARY.
UNIT may waste disk space because UNIT's code is duplicated in each host's codefile.	UNIT may save disk space because UNIT's code is stored only once in the SYSTEM.LIBRARY.

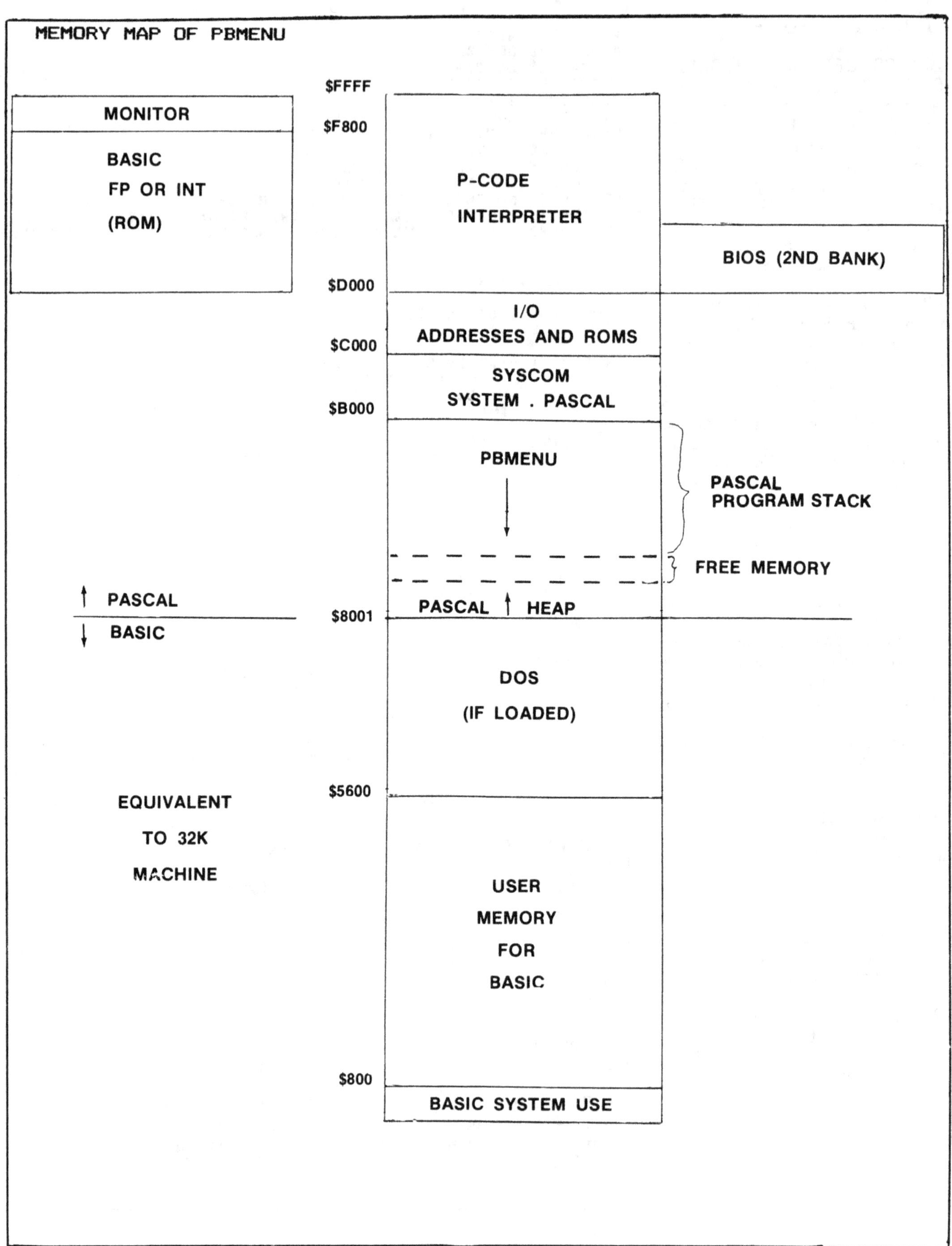
MEMORY MAP OF PBMENU
$FFFF
MONITOR
$F800
BASIC
FP OR INT
(ROM)
P-CODE
INTERPRETER
BIOS (2ND BANK)
$D000
I/O
ADDRESSES AND ROMS
$C000
SYSCOM
SYSTEM . PASCAL
$B000
PBMENU
PASCAL
PROGRAM STACK
FREE MEMORY
PASCAL
BASIC
PASCAL HEAP
$8001
DOS
(IF LOADED)
$5600
EQUIVALENT
TO 32K
MACHINE
USER
MEMORY
FOR
BASIC
$800
BASIC SYSTEM USE

```
PROCEDURE CALL; EXTERNAL;
PROCEDURE ROMCALL; EXTERNAL;
PROCEDURE DOSRESET; EXTERNAL;
PROCEDURE DISPLAY40; EXTERNAL;
PROCEDURE DISPLAY80; EXTERNAL;
PROCEDURE INITBASZERPG; EXTERNAL;
FUNCTION  FPBASIC; EXTERNAL;

PROCEDURE POKEWORD(ADDR,DATA:INTEGER);
BEGIN
  CHEAT.INTPART:=ADDR;
  CHEAT.PTRPART^:=DATA;
END; (*POKE*)

FUNCTION PEEKWORD(ADDR:INTEGER):INTEGER;
BEGIN
  CHEAT.INTPART:=ADDR;
  PEEKWORD:=CHEAT.PTRPART^;
END; (*PEEK*)

PROCEDURE MOVEHEAP;
(*HEAP NORMALLY STARTS AT $C00 (3072) *)

CONST NP=90;           (* TOP OF HEAP *)

VAR HEAPINFO,HPSTOP,HEAPPTR,LEN,
     DISPLACEMENT:INTEGER;
     HEAP:^INTEGER;

BEGIN
  HEAPINFO:=PEEKWORD(98)+14;
  HPSTOP:=HEAPINFO+112;
  DISPLACEMENT:=NEWLOC-OLDLOC;
  HIMEM:=NEWLOC;

(*DETERMINE LENGTH OF HEAP*)
  MARK(HEAP);    (*MAKE HEAP AS SMALL*)
  RELEASE(HEAP);   (*AS POSSIBLE*)
  LEN:=PEEKWORD(NP)-OLDLOC;

(*FIX NP (THE TOP OF HEAP)  *)
  POKEWORD(NP,PEEKWORD(NP)+DISPLACEMENT);

(*CHANGE POINTERS*)
  FOR I:=0 TO 2 DO  (*SYSTEM HEAP PTRS*)
    BEGIN
      HEAPPTR:=PEEKWORD(HEAPINFO+I*2);
      POKEWORD(HEAPPTR,PEEKWORD(HEAPPTR)+DISPLACEMENT);
    END;

  HEAPPTR:=PEEKWORD(HEAPINFO); (*MORE PTRS*)
  REPEAT
    POKEWORD(HEAPINFO,HEAPPTR+DISPLACEMENT);
    HEAPINFO:=HEAPINFO+2;
    HEAPPTR:=PEEKWORD(HEAPINFO);
  UNTIL (HEAPINFO>HPSTOP);

(*MOVE HEAP*)
  SOURCE.INTPART:=OLDLOC;
  DEST.INTPART:=NEWLOC;
  MOVELEFT(SOURCE.PTRPART^,DEST.PTRPART^,LEN);
END; (*MOVEHEAP*)

PROCEDURE SAVEFILE(FILENAME:UNITSTR;
                   BEGINADDR,CODELEN:INTEGER);
BEGIN
  CHEAT.INTPART:=BEGINADDR;
  PBCODEINFO.BASICZERPG:=BASZERPG;
  NUMBLKS:=(CODELEN + 511) DIV 512;
  REWRITE(UNITFID,FILENAME);
  IO:=BLOCKWRITE(UNITFID,PBCODEINFO,1,0);
  FOR I:=1 TO NUMBLKS DO BEGIN
   IO:=BLOCKWRITE(UNITFID,CHEAT.PTRPART^,1,I);
   CHEAT.INTPART:=CHEAT.INTPART+512;
  END;
  CLOSE(UNITFID,LOCK);
END; (*SAVEFILE*)
```

MORE ABOUT UNITS

Apple Pascal supports two kinds of UNITS. Each kind has certain advantages and disadvantages.

When a REGULAR UNIT is linked to a host program, the UNIT's code is actually inserted into the host's codefile so that the UNIT becomes a part of the program. This is good because the program is no longer dependent on the original UNIT. But, if the UNIT is used very often, it's code is duplicated in each host program's codefile resulting in a useless waste of disk space.

The INTRINSIC UNIT, on the other hand, eliminates this wasteful duplication of code by storing only one copy of the UNIT's code in the SYSTEM. LIBRARY. Then when a host program is run, the UNIT's code is automatically loaded into memory. The host program will not run unless the UNIT is on-line and in the SYSTEM.LIBRARY.

Each UNIT consists of three parts—INTERFACE, IMPLEMENTATION and INITIALIZATION.

The INTERFACE part is the only part of the UNIT that is visible to a host program. The CONST's, TYPE's, VAR's, PROCEDURE's and FUNCTION's declared in the INTERFACE portion of the UNIT act as if they were a part of the host program (i.e., they are public).

The IMPLEMENTATION part is private to the UNIT and cannot be accessed by the host.

The INITIALIZATION part is run when the host is executed, before the host program itself is run.

GETTING DOS ONTO PASCAL DISKS

1) Make a copy of your DOS 3.3 System Master diskette using a disk copy program (i.e., don't INIT the disk and use FID).

2) Delete the language which is not in ROM from the diskette you just copied (INTBASIC if you have an APPLE][PLUS, FPBASIC otherwise). This prevents Pascal from being overwritten in the boot process.

3) Convert the DOS 3.3 Master diskette to a 32K disk by running the Pascal program DOS32K on it.

4) Execute PBMENU (make sure you have at least 22 blocks of contiguous free space available on the disk).

5) 'ROM CALL' -8192 to enter BASIC.

6) Place the 32K Master diskette in the boot drive.

7) Type 'PR#6 [RET]' to boot the disk and load DOS into memory.

8) 'CALL 7' to get back to Pascal.

9) Re-insert your Pascal disk in the boot drive.

10) Use the 'BSAVE' command option with the following parameters:

FILENAME = 'DOS.3.3'

STARTADDR = 22016

LENGTH = 10751

11) Re-initialize the system by hitting the RESET key.

At this point, you should have DOS 3.3 on your Pascal disk.

It is now possible (if you have a two drive system) for drive one to contain a Pascal disk, while drive two contains a BASIC disk. Of course, you should not try to CATALOG a Pascal disk so remember to use 'CATALOGD2' if your BASIC disk is in drive two.

NOTES ON HYBRID PROGRAMMING

To avoid conflicts between the two systems, the following processes must occur in almost every hybrid program.

1) Usually the first thing is to move the heap up to make room for your BASIC program or machine code routines (moving the heap up could also be used for hiding machine code patches to the Pascal system, but there are better and easier ways to do that which I hope to publish in the near future).

2) It is also important to display only 40 columns on the video screen if memory in the range of $800-$BFF (the second page of the text screen) is to be used.

```
PROCEDURE BSAVE;
BEGIN
 WITH PBCODEINFOR DO BEGIN
  NAME:=CONCAT(FILENAME,'.BIN');
  STARTADDR:=BEGINADDR;
  CODELENG:=CODELEN;
  SAVEFILE(NAME,BEGINADDR,CODELEN);
 END;
END; (*BSAVE*)

PROCEDURE SAVE;
BEGIN
 WITH PBCODEINFO DO BEGIN
  NAME:=CONCAT(FILENAME,'.BAS');
  STARTADDR:=BASZERPG[104]*256+BASZERPG[103];
  ENDADDR:=BASZERPG[176]*256+BASZERPG[175];
  CODELENG:=ENDADDR-STARTADDR+1;
  SAVEFILE(NAME,STARTADDR,CODELENG);
 END;
END; (*SAVE*)

PROCEDURE BLOAD;
BEGIN
 CHEAT.INTPART:=BEGINADDR;
 I:=1;
 RESET(UNITFID,FILENAME);
 WHILE NOT EOF(UNITFID) DO
  BEGIN
   IO:=BLOCKREAD(UNITFID,CHEAT.PTRPART^,1,I);
   I:=I+1;
   CHEAT.INTPART:=CHEAT.INTPART+512;
  END;
 CLOSE(UNITFID,LOCK);
END; (*BLOAD*)

PROCEDURE SETHIMEM;
VAR HM:PACKED ARRAY[0..1] OF BYTE;
BEGIN
(*CONVERT INTEGER TO ARRAY OF BYTES*)
 MOVELEFT(HIMEM,HM,2);
 BASZERPG[HIMEMADDR]:=HM[0];
 BASZERPG[HIMEMADDR+1]:=HM[1];
END;

PROCEDURE CONNECT(CSWL,CSWH,KSWL,KSWH:BYTE);
BEGIN
 BASZERPG[54]:=CSWL; BASZERPG[55]:=CSWH;
 BASZERPG[56]:=KSWL; BASZERPG[57]:=KSWH;
END;

PROCEDURE LOADFILE(FILENAME:UNITSTR);
BEGIN
 FILENAME:=CONCAT(FILENAME,SUFFIX);
(*GET PBCODEINFO*)
 RESET(UNITFID,FILENAME);
 IO:=BLOCKREAD(UNITFID,PBCODEINFO,1,0);
 CLOSE(UNITFID,LOCK);
 BASZERPG:=PBCODEINFO.BASICZERPG;
 LOADADDR:=PBCODEINFO.STARTADDR;
 IF DOSLOADED THEN CONNECT(189,94,129,94)
  ELSE CONNECT(240,253,27,253);
 IF SUFFIX='.BAS' THEN (*CLEAR ERR BYTE*)
  POKEWORD(LOADADDR-1,0);
 BLOAD(FILENAME,LOADADDR);
END; (*LOADFILE*)

PROCEDURE RUN;
BEGIN
  SUFFIX:='.BAS';
  LOADFILE(FILENAME);;
  SETHIMEM;
  ROMCALL(RUNADDR);
END; (*RUN*)
```

```
PROCEDURE BRUN;
BEGIN
   SUFFIX:='.BIN';
   LOADFILE(FILENAME);
   ROMCALL(LOADADDR);
END; (*BRUN*)

PROCEDURE LOADDOS;
BEGIN
   BLOAD('DOS.3.3.BIN',DOSLOADADDR);
   DOSLOADED:=TRUE;
   HIMEM:=DOSLOADADDR;       (* $$5600 *)
   SETHIMEM;
(* SET UP PAGE 3 DOS VECTORS *)
   SOURCE.INTPART:=24145; (* $5E51  *)
   DEST.INTPART:=976;      (* $3D0   *)
   MOVELEFT(SOURCE.PTRPART^,DEST.PTRPART^,47);
   DOSRESET; (*CHANGE SOFT ENTRY VEC*)
   ROMCALL(DOSINIT);
END; (*DOS*)

PROCEDURE INITPBCODEINFO;
BEGIN
 WITH PBCODEINFO DO
   BEGIN
    CODELENG:=0;CODEADDR:=1;
    FILLCHAR(NAME,25,' ');
    STARTADDR:=0;
    FOR I:=0 TO 255 DO BASICZERPG[I]:=0;
    FOR I:=0 TO 71 DO FILLER[I]:=0;
    COMMENT:='P+B BY RON DEGROAT 2/81';
   END;
END; (*INITPB*)

BEGIN                    (*MAIN PROGRAM*)
 DOSLOADED:=FALSE;
 HIMEM:=3072; (* $C00, BOTTOM OF HEAP*)
 INITPBCODEINFO; INITBASZERPG;
 IF FPBASIC THEN BEGIN
   RUNADDR:=-10906; (* $D566 *)
   HIMEMADDR:=115;  (* $73-74*)
 END
   ELSE BEGIN
    RUNADDR:=-4116; (* $EFEC *)
    HIMEMADDR:=76;  (* $4C-4D*)
   END;
END.  (*CHANGE '.' TO ';' FOR COMBINED *)
      (*UNIT/HOST COMPILATION.          *)
```

```
;----------------------------------------------
;LISTING #3: PBPROC, ROUTINES USED BY BASICSTUFF
;
;WRITTEN BY RON DEGROAT          3/81
;----------------------------------------------

;POP ADDR FROM STACK

        .MACRO POP    ;FORMAT: POP ADDR
        PLA
        STA %1
        PLA
        STA %1+1
        .ENDM

;PUSH ADDR ONTO STACK

        .MACRO PUSH   ;FORMAT: PUSH ADDR
        LDA %1+1
        PHA
        LDA %1
        PHA
        .ENDM
```

3) Last but not least, you must move the heap back to its original location when the hybrid program is through or there may not be enough room for such things as the SYSTEM.EDITOR, etc.

The PROGRAM PBMENU (Listing #1) provides a good model for patterning your own creations after.

Another short example is given in Listing #5. The PROGRAM HYBRID demonstrates how easy hybrid programming can be once the UNIT BASICSTUFF is functioning. The program starts off in Pascal, RUN's a BASIC program named DEMO, returns to the Pascal program, BRUN's a machine code routine called MUSIC, returns to the Pascal program, ROMCALL's a monitor subroutine, then returns for the last time to the Pascal program—a truly hybrid program. Before a program like HYBRID can run, the BASIC and the machine code routines to be used must be previously saved onto a Pascal disk with a program like PBMENU. Incidentally, the WRITE statements must be included in HYBRID, or the program will hang.

GETTING IT ALL TOGETHER

If you want to use the old version of Pascal (II.1), two addresses (MAXCOL and SCR2) must be changed as indicated in Listing #3. If an external terminal or video board is used, the Pascal system reconfigures itself slightly, so some modification will be required (e.g., screen control codes may differ, starting the heap at $800 instead of the normal $C00, etc.).

There are two ways to get the PASCAL + BASIC system up and running. The first method uses BASICSTUFF in the form of a REGULAR UNIT and is good for debugging. The second method uses BASICSTUFF as an INTRINSIC UNIT stored in the SYSTEM.LIBRARY and is more appropriate for normal hybrid programming.

FIRST METHOD: For test purposes, compile the UNIT BASICSTUFF as part of the host program PBMENU. This is easily accomplished by placing a copy of the entire unit right after the program heading. Only two minor changes are necessary: First, the unit must be changed to a REGULAR UNIT by deleting 'INTRINSIC CODE 25 DATA 26;' from the unit heading. And second, the '.' at the end of the UNIT must be changed to a ';' (so the compiler will not stop compiling before it gets to the host program). With these changes made, you may compile the host/unit combination and link it to the external procedures (PBPROC). Then when all the routines in BASICSTUFF have been tested and everything is working properly, the UNIT can be converted back into an INTRINSIC UNIT, compiled separately from the host, linked to the external procedures, and installed in the SYSTEM. LIBRARY.

SECOND METHOD: Ultimately, you will want to install BASICSTUFF in the SYSTEM.LIBRARY. For this, the UNIT BASICSTUFF shown in Listing #2 must be compiled and linked to the properly assembled procedures of Listing #3. Then the properly compiled and linked UNIT must be installed in the SYSTEM.LIBRARY with the APPLE3:LIBRARY utility. Now any hybrid program (such as PBMENU) may be compiled separately from the UNIT and used to explore the fascinating world of PASCAL+BASIC. For specific details on the use of the Compiler, Assembler, Linker or Library consult your Apple Pascal Reference manuals.

If you would like to avoid keying in the routines given in this article, the complete PASCAL+BASIC package along with some examples of hybrid programming is available on the Call A.P.P.L.E. in Depth 2 diskettes.

CONCLUSION

Getting the PASCAL+BASIC system up and running may take a little time, but once you have the system operating, you will not only have learned a lot about your computer, but you will also have the unusual capabilities of a hybrid system with which you can discover many new and interesting things.

```
;CALL TO ROM SUBROUTINE

        .MACRO RCALL  ;FORMAT: RCALL ADDRESS
        STA 0C08A     ;ENABLE ROM
        JSR %1
        STA 0C088     ;RE-ENABLE RAM
        .ENDM

;LOAD DATA OR ROUTINE (NO MORE THAN 256 BYTES)

        .MACRO LOAD   ;FORMAT:
        LDY #00       ;LOAD SOURCE,DEST,LEN
$1      LDA %1,Y
        STA %2,Y
        INY
        CPY #%3
        BNE $1
        .ENDM

        .PUBLIC BASZERPG

SETNORM .EQU 0FE84
INIT    .EQU 0FB2F
SETVID  .EQU 0FE93
SETKBD  .EQU 0FE89
FPCHRGET.EQU 0F10A
CHRGET  .EQU 0B0

MONVEC  .EQU 03F0
ZERPAG  .EQU 0000
STK     .EQU 0100
DBUF    .EQU 03A0     ;DISK INFO

MAXCOL  .EQU 0DB7C    ;0D9B9 FOR VER II.1
SCR2    .EQU 0DBA6    ;0D9CB FOR VER II.1


        .PROC INITBASZERPG

        .REF ZERTEMP,STKTEMP

        LOAD ZERPAG,ZERTEMP,000
        LOAD STKTEMP,ZERPAG,000 ;ZERO IT
        RCALL INITZPG
        LOAD ZERPAG,BASZERPG,000
        LOAD ZERTEMP,ZERPAG,000
        RTS
INITZPG JSR SETNORM
        JSR INIT
        JSR SETVID
        JSR SETKBD
        LOAD FPCHRGET,CHRGET,01C
        RTS


        .FUNC FPBASIC

;IF APPLESOFT IN ROM, FPBASIC = TRUE

        .REF RETPAS

        STA 0C08A   ;ENABLE ROM
        POP RETPAS  ;SAVE PASCAL RET ADDR
        PLA         ;DISCARD OFFSET
        PLA
        PLA
        PLA
        LDY #00
        LDA 0E000   ;CHECK FOR INT OR FP
        CMP #04C
        BNE FALSE   ;BRANCH IF INT BASIC
        INY
```

```
FALSE   TYA          ;LSB = 1 IF FP
        PHA          ;LSB = 0 IF INT
        PHA
        PUSH RETPAS
        STA 0C088   ;SELECT RAM
        RTS

        .PROC ROMCALL,1

;SWAP ZERO PGS, SAVE PASCAL STUFF, ENABLE ROMS
;THEN JSR AND RESTORE EVERYTHING ON RETURN

        .DEF ZERTEMP,STKTEMP,DEST,RETPAS
        .DEF SOFTEV,PWREDUP

        LOAD ZERPAG,ZERTEMP,000
        LOAD BASZERPG,ZERPAG,000
        LOAD DBUF,BUFTEMP,012

        LOAD MVEC,MONVEC,010
        LOAD RETJMP,007,003

        POP RETPAS     ;SAVE PASCAL RETURN
        POP DEST       ;GET DESTINATION ADDR
        RCALL ENTRY    ;CALL DEST INDIRECTLY
        PUSH RETPAS    ;RESTORE PASCAL RETURN

;RESTORE DISK INFO, SWAP PASCAL ZERO PG FOR
;BASIC'S AND MESS PWR UP BYTE

        LOAD BUFTEMP,DBUF,012
        LOAD ZERPAG,BASZERPG,000
        LOAD ZERTEMP,ZERPAG,000
        STY 03F4       ;MESS PWR UP BYTE
        RTS

;SAVE STACK AND JUMP TO DEST

ENTRY   TSX
        STX SAVESP
        LOAD STK,STKTEMP,000
        JMP @DEST

RESTORE LOAD STKTEMP,STK,000
        LDX SAVESP
        TXS
        RTS

MVEC    .WORD 0FA59   ;BRK
SOFTEV  .WORD 0E003
PWREDUP .BYTE 045
        JMP 0FF59     ;RESET
RETJMP  JMP RESTORE
        JMP RESTORE
        .WORD 0FF65

DEST    .WORD 00
RETPAS  .WORD 00
SAVESP  .BYTE 00
ZERTEMP .BLOCK 0100
STKTEMP .BLOCK 0100
BUFTEMP .BLOCK 012


        .PROC DOSRESET

        .REF SOFTEV,PWREDUP

        LDA #0BF
        STA SOFTEV     ;POINT RESET VECTOR
        LDA #05D       ;TO DOS
        STA SOFTEV+1
        LDA #0F8
        STA PWREDUP    ;FIX PWR UP BYTE
        RTS
```

```
.PROC CALL,1

.REF RETPAS,DEST

POP RETPAS
POP DEST
PUSH RETPAS
JMP @DEST

.PROC DISPLAY40

LDA 0C083   ;WRITE-ENABLE RAM
LDA 0C083   ;ON 2ND BANK
LDA #0EA    ;NOP
STA SCR2
STA SCR2+1
LDA #27     ;MAX COLUMN # = 39
STA MAXCOL
LDA 0C088   ;SELECT AND PROTECT
            ;1ST BANK
RTS

.PROC DISPLAY80

LDA 0C083
LDA 0C083
LDA #0B0    ;BCS
STA SCR2
LDA #011
STA SCR2+1
LDA #04F    ;MAX COLUMN # = 79
STA MAXCOL
LDA 0C088
RTS

 END
```

```
(**********************************)
(* LISTING #4: 32K DOS CONVERSION *)
(*                                *)
(* WRITTEN BY RON DEGROAT 3/81    *)
(**********************************)

PROGRAM DOS32K;

(*THIS PROGRAM MODIFIES A DOS 3.3    *)
(*MASTER DISK SO THAT IT LOADS AS IF *)
(*THE SYSTEM WERE 32K.               *)

VAR BLK:PACKED ARRAY[0..511] OF 0..255;
    BLT,BLN:INTEGER;
    S:FILE;

PROCEDURE WAITFORCR;
BEGIN
 WRITELN('PRESS <RET> TO CONTINUE');
 READLN;
END;

BEGIN
 WRITELN; WRITELN
 ('INSERT COPY OF DOS 3.3 MASTER DISK');
 WRITELN('INTO THE BOOT DRIVE (#4:)');
 WAITFORCR;
 RESET(S,'#4:');
 BLN:=2;
 BLT:=BLOCKREAD(S,BLK,1,BLN);
 IF (BLK[260]=191) THEN
  BLK[260]:=127
   ELSE
    WRITELN('CONVERSION NOT POSSIBLE');
 BLT:=BLOCKWRITE(S,BLK,1,BLN);
 WRITELN;WRITELN('RE-INSERT PASCAL DISK');
 WAITFORCR;
END.
```

```
(**************************************)
(* LISTING #5: EXAMPLE HYBRID PROGRAM *)
(**************************************)

PROGRAM HYBRID;
USES BASICSTUFF;    (*ASSUMES BASICSTUFF  *)
BEGIN               (*IS IN SYSTEM.LIBRARY*)
 DISPLAY40;
(*MOVE HEAP UP JUST A LITTLE*)
 MOVEHEAP(3072,8192);

 WRITE(CHR(12)); (*ERASE SCREEN*)

 WRITELN('NOW RUNNING DEMO.BAS...');
 RUN('DEMO');

 WRITE('NOW BRUNNING MUSIC.BIN...');
 BRUN('MUSIC');

 ROMCALL(-198);  (*BELL MONITOR S/R*)

 WRITE(CHR(12));
 GOTOXY(10,8);
 WRITE('THAT''S ALL FOLKS...');

 DISPLAY80;
 MOVEHEAP(8192,3072);
END.
```

AN APPLE PASCAL SUPPLEMENT:

The Structure of Pascal

Ron DeGroat

THE following collection of topics is intended to supplement the Apple Pascal manuals with some useful information that is not generally available elsewhere. It is hoped that this material will help the Apple user to use and apply Pascal on the Apple more effectively.

The Structure of Pascal

Pascal is a highly structured language with built-in "control," "block" and "data" structures that make program logic easy to follow and understand. Pascal encourages the methodical and systematic development of algorithms in a "structured" way. Features inherent in the language promote and sometimes even force program logic to be straight-forward.

A. Control Stuctures

The Pascal control structures make the coding of algorithms very natural. There are four types of control available in Pascal:

1) Sequential Flow
2) Conditional Flow
3) Repetitive Flow
4) Unconditional Branch

Sequential Flow

The most fundamental computer statement is the assignment. It specifies which value is to be assigned a variable and it is the only completely sequential type of flow possible. All computer languages have some sort of assignment statement. In Pascal, the assignment operator, ":=," is not to be confused with the relational operator, "=."

Ex. of sequential flow (assigements)

```
DONE:=(A=B);  (* BOOLEAN  *)
CHOICE:="Q";  (* CHAR     *)
NUMBLKS:-
 =10;         (* INTEGER  *)
```

Conditional Flow

There are three kinds of conditional statements:

1) IF-THEN
2) IF-THEN-ELSE
3) CASE statements

These three statements make conditional flow of control easy to understand and follow.

A frequent abuse of the IF statement is illustrated below:

```
IF X=0  THEN DONE:=TRUE
        ELSE DONE:=FALSE;
```

A simpler statement would be:

```
DONE:=(X=0);
```

Nested IF statements are allowed, but careless formulation can be costly in execution time. For example, assume four mutually exclusive conditions, each instigating a distinct action.;

```
IF CH="A" THEN ABORT
  ELSE IF CH="B" THEN BUILD
    ELSE IF CH="C" THEN COR-
RECT
      ELSE IF CH="D" THEN DELETE;
```

The fulfillment of a condition and execution of its statement completes the IF statement, by-passing the remaining tests. The most efficient formulation would place the most likely condition first and the least likely condition last. In our example, if the probabilities are in the order, $p(A) > p(B) > p(C) > p(D)$, then execution speed will be faster because fewer tests will have to be made on the average.

The CASE statement is used to select one of several mutually exclusive statements with similar probability of selection.

Ex. of the CASE statement

```
CASE CHOICE OF
  'D','d': DISPLAYRESULT;
  'P','p': PROCESSDATA;
  'S','s': SAVEDATA;
END;
```

Repetitive Flow

There are three kinds of statements that allow for repetitive flow:

1) FOR-DO
2) WHILE-DO
3) REPEAT-UNTIL

If the number of repetitions is known beforehand, the FOR statement is usually appropriate. The FOR statement exists in two forms:

```
FOR COUNT:=1 TO 10 DO
  STATEMENT;
FOR I:=30 DOWNTO 5 DO
  ANOTHERSTATEMENT;
```

If a possibility exists that no repetitions should be performed the WHILE loop is applicable:

```
WHILE LENGTH(HEXSTR) < 4 DO
  HEXSTR:=CONCAT('0',HEXSTR);
```

If at least one repetition is to be performed, the REPEAT statement may be useful:

```
REPEAT
  READ(CH);
UNTIL CH IN CHOICESET;
```

Unconditional Branch

In Pascal there are three kinds of unconditional branches:

1) Subroutine Calls
2) GOTO
3) EXIT

Subroutine calls are invoked when the name of a procedure of function is supplied in the text of a program. Descriptive identifier names make program logic natural and the action of the subroutine self–explanatory. (More discussion on subroutines may be found under BLOCK STRUCTURES: Procedures and Functions.)

The use of GOTO usually destroys the natural flow of logic and its use is therefore discouraged. Most newcomers to Pascal are so accustomed to using GOTO as a primary means of control that they often overlook the more natural means of control available in Pascal.

The EXIT procedure is a controlled form of GOTO that allows the program to exit a program or procedure. Exiting a function may leave the function result undefined. EXIT is useful for extricating oneself from a complex tangle of logic, but it, too, should be used sparingly.

```
Ex. GOTO 1; (* "1" is a label *)

EXIT(PROGRAM);
```

B. Block Structures

Pascal provides four basic block–like structures:

1) **SIMPLE BLOCK**
2) **PROCEDURES AND FUNCTIONS**
3) **UNITS**
4) **SEGMENTS**

Block structures encourage programmers to break complex tasks into collections of simpler tasks that are easier to understand and implement.

Simple Block

The simple block is primarily used for casting a series of statements into one compound statement with BEGIN and END serving as brackets. Ex. of Simple Block

```
IF DONE THEN
  BEGIN (* COMPOUND STATEMENT *)
    FINISHUP;
    WRITE('THAT'S IT...');
  END;
```

As one becomes more accustomed to Pascal programming techniques, he will naturally break his programming tasks into subtasks that perform distinct actions. Although it is possible to camouflage the resulting logical structure, it is not desirable.

Procedures and Functions

Procedures and functions should expose the logical structure of a program. Even when a procedure is used only once, one should not hesitate to formulate an action as a procedure if readability is enhanced.

Variables exist only within the block in which they are declared. "Global" variables are declared in the program block and exist everywhere in the program. "Local" variables are declared in a procedure and only apply to that procedure. The "scope" of a variable is the domain in which the variable is valid and accessible. It is good programming practice to declare every identifier that is not referenced outside the procedure as strictly local to the procedure. Not only is this good documentation, it provides added security against accidentally changing a variable that you didn't intend to change.

```
PROGRAM PARMDEMO;
VAR HEXSTR:STRING; (* GLOBAL VARIABLE *)
PROCEDURE DECTOHEX(DEC:INTEGER; VAR HEX:STRING);
VAR I:INTEGER; (* LOCAL VARIABLE *)
BEGIN
  (* PROCEDURE DEFINITION *)
  (* DEC is local, HEX is not *)
END;
BEGIN (* MAIN PROGRAM *)
  DECTOHEX(127, HEXSTR); (* PROCEDURE STATEMENT *)
  WRITE(HEXSTR); (* HEXSTR came out of the proc. *)
END.
```

Parameters provide a substitution mechanism that allows a process to be repeated with a variation of its arguments. "Formal" parameters are defined in the procedure declaration. "Actual" parameters are substituted for the corresponding formal parameters in a procedure statement.

There are two ways to pass parameters in Apple Pascal:

1) by reference
2) by value

Parameters called by value are local to the procedure called. The actual parameter may be constant, expression or variable. Parameters called by reference are preceded by VAR in the formal parameter list and only variables may be substituted as actual parameters. The user should avoid VAR parameters unless a string value is being returned (functions cannot return strings). VAR parameters act like global variables because changes made to a VAR parameter are carried outside the procedure.

Segments

When a SEGMENT procedure or function is no longer active, it is swapped out to make additional memory available for other uses such as dynamic variable allocation or another SEGMENT. With this "overlay" capability, programs larger than memory are possible through appropriate segmentation.

Units

Units allow groups of procedures and functions to be compiled separately and linked together with other programs in a simple and logical way. There are two kinds of UNITS in Apple Pascal:

1) Intrinsic
2) Regular

Intrinsic units must be found in the SYSTEM.LIBRARY to be of use. They are loaded and linked to the host program at run–time. Regular units do not have to be in the library, and their code is actually inserted into the host's codefile at link time prior to execution. This means that a Regular unit will occupy extra disk space by being repeated in every host program that uses the unit. Intrinsic units are only found once on the disk in the

SYSTEM.LIBRARY, but the host is dependent on the library. If the unit is not in the library, or the library is missing, the host will not be able to load the required intrinsics.

C. Data Structures

Pascal offers data structures that express program information in a meaningful and flexible way. There are five predefined types and seven categories of user-definable types which can be used to create a virtually unlimited number of new data types.

The five predefined data types are:

1) INTEGER
2) REAL
3) BOOLEAN
4) CHAR
5) STRING

The seven user-defined data types are:

```
A. SIMPLE DATA TYPES
   1) SCALARS       DAYS = (SUN, MON, TUE, WED, THU, FRI, SAT);
   2) SUBRANGES     MON..FRI
                    BYTE = 0..255;
   3) POINTERS      STRPTR = ^STRING;
   4) SETS          WEEK = SET OF DAYS;
B. STRUCTURED DATA TYPES
   1) ARRAYS        WORD :  PACKED ARRAY[0..1] OF BYTE;
                    PAY :   ARRAY(MON..FRI) OF REAL;
   2) RECORDS       PERSON = RECORD
                                NAME:STRING;
                                SEX :(MALE,FEMALE);
                                ID :INTEGER;
                                END;
   3) FILES         CLUB : FILE OF PERSON;
```

The record type is probably the most flexible data structure available. Records allow a collection of different data types to be logically associated with one another. Of course, all of the data structures are useful, but it takes time to become adept at using them.

Top–Down Design

The essence of good Pascal programming is good structured programming. And the best way to achieve good structured programming is through step-wise refinement (also called top-down design).

In step-wise refinement, the programmer starts by defining his objective (or task) in the broadest terms possible and through a series of steps gradually refines his overall objective into a collection of smaller tasks. The refinement continues until each task resolves into a single, clearly defined action which can be easily understood. Actual coding does not occur until the final level of refinement has been reached. At this level the programmer has reduced a large complex problem into a collection of small, easy-to-solve problems. The overall task has been broken down and a collection of well-defined modules (procedures and functions) has emerged. The programmer is then free to devote his full attention to each module individually.

A program developed in this way will be structured so that each of the separate modules (procedures and functions) will be easy to understand, modify and debug.

AN APPLE PASCAL SUPPLEMENT:

Avoiding Unnecessary Frustration

Ron DeGroat

Be Prepared for Differences

WHEN Pascal does not behave like BASIC, many potential Pascal users become frustrated. However, if the Pascal neophyte is psychologically prepared, this kind of frustration can be largely avoided. Most of the differences between Pascal and BASIC are reasonable and desirable. A few of the more significant ones are discussed below.

Be Prepared for a Compiler

Apple BASIC is an interpreted language with a lot of user interaction. Pascal, however, is a compiled language and although it may be less interactive, it is faster than it would be if interpreted. A Pascal beginner should be prepared to write, compile and edit a program several times before it can be executed. Program development will not be as interactive as BASIC, but program execution speed will usually be faster.

Be Prepared for Variable Declarations

Another problem BASIC (and FORTRAN) users have with Pascal is the requirement that all variables be declared by type. Those unaccustomed to this requirement may initially consider it a nuisance and a waste of time, but there are several good reasons why this "feature" is definitely advantageous.

By listing all variables at the beginning of a program or procedure block, the programmer avoids contradictory and confusing identifier names. The declarations also provide a quick review of all the variables. Such a review can be especially helpful in a lengthy program.

Besides avoiding confusion and contradiction, variable declarations cause typographical errors in variable names to be detected by the compiler and flagged as undeclared identifiers. In BASIC and FORTRAN, typographical errors may create new variables that go undetected until the program malfuctions. This kind of built-in safeguard is typical of Pascal. There are many such features and mechanisms in the language that tend to protect against errors and promote well-thought-out program logic.

Be Prepared for Modular Design

Another built-in mechanism that encourages good program development involves the 1200 byte maximum code length limit. Some people consider this constraint as unnecessarily restrictive, but it does force a programmer to break a long procedure (3–4 pages in length) into a collection of simpler modules. And simple, well-defined modules are easier to understand, modify and debug.

Be Prepared for Strong Data Typing

Every data object in a Pascal program has a type which defines its logical meaning and the operations that can be performed on it. There are five pre-defined types (INTEGER, REAL, BOOLEAN, CHAR and STRING) and an almost unlimited number of user defined types (consisting of scalars, subranges, arrays, records, sets, files and pointers). In general, Pascal does not allow different types to be mixed. This characteristic prevents the programmer from accidentally using the wrong variable. For example, a program that classifies various objects may have a COLOR variable whose type is RAINBOW=(RED, ORANGE, YELLOW, GREEN, BLUE, INDIGO, VIOLET) and a SIZE variable whose type is MAGNITUDE=(SMALL, MEDIUM, LARGE). Then, if the programmer accidentally uses SIZE instead of COLOR, the compiler will flag the improper use as an error. This syntactic feature minimizes the mistaking of one variable for another. Most other computer languages do not have comparable safeguards.

Be Prepared for some Nice Surprises

Pascal also provides set notation and operators. Set operations are relatively fast and can be used to eliminate more complicated tests, e.g.,

```
IF (CH = "A") OR (CH = "B") OR
(CH = "C") OR (CH = "D") OR
(CH = "Z") THEN...
```

is equivalent to,

```
IF CH IN ["A".."D","Z"] THEN...
```

Long, descriptive identifiers make self-documenting programs a possibility. Only the first eight characters are significant, but longer names are permitted. And if the underscore is available (see "Moving the Heap to get Special Characters" by R. DeGroat, June, 1981 *Call-A.P.P.L.E.*), program readability can be further enhanced.

THIS_IS_A_LONG_NAME and THISISALONGNAME look the same to the Pascal compiler (which ignores underscores), but to the human reader, the first rendering is much clearer.

With Apple Pascal you can:

- Run programs that are larger than memory.
- Save memory with dynamic variable allocation.
- Create your own data types, e.g., COLOR=(RED, WHITE, BLUE).
- Plot in Cartesian or relative polar coordinates with Turtlegraphics.
- Break complex programs into simple, easy-to-implement modules.
- Use the SYSTEM.EDITOR as a word processor.

These are just a few of the differences between Pascal and BASIC. As you begin to familiarize yourself with Pascal, you will discover many more new and interesting possibilities.

AN APPLE PASCAL SUPPLEMENT:

A Guide to Better Pascal Programs

Ron DeGroat

SINCE many Apple Pascal programmers are self-taught, it is not surprising that inappropriate programming practices show up in some Pascal programs. In fact, a large percentage of the Pascal programs sent to *Call —A.P.P.L.E.* share certain peculiarities which tend to diminish program clarity and usefulness. This section describes how to improve your Pascal style by avoiding these common pitfalls.

Some Tips On Writing Good Pascal Programs

Make the main program a general overview of what the program does. For example:

```
PROGRAM EARTH ORBIT
```

(procedures and functions go here)

```
BEGIN (main program)
  REPEAT
    PLOT AXES;
    GET INITIAL VALUES;
    PLOT ORBIT;
  UNTIL DONE;
END
```

Break the program into clearly definable, easy-to-understand modules. If a module (procedure or function) is longer than one page in length, break it down into smaller modules. This makes a program easier to understand, modify and debug.

Use descriptive identifiers so that programs are self-documenting. BLOCK NUMBER is better than BN, and NUM OF STUDENTS is better than N. Also, avoid names that are too much alike. BLOCKNUM and BLCKNUM are almost indistinguishable and could easily be mistaken for each other.

Use the built-in control structures of Pascal so that the flow of logic is easy to follow. Avoid using GOTO because GOTO usually makes the logic harder to follow (see examples below).

BAD FLOW OF CONTROL	GOOD FLOW OF CONTROL
IF DONE THEN GOTO 1;	IF DONE THEN FINISH UP
TRY AGAIN;	
GOTO 2;	ELSE
1:FINISH UP;	TRY AGAIN;
2:	
3:SOMETHING;	REPEAT
IF NOT FINISHED THEN	SOMETHING;
GOTO 3;	UNTIL FINISHED;

The EXIT statement is a controlled form of GOTO. Frequent use of EXIT indicates the flow of logic could be improved.

Use meaningful comments liberally. Some things may be obvious to you (the programmer), but to someone else an illuminating comment can make a big difference. At the same time, do not misuse comments by stating the obvious, for example, when self-documented.

Do not use recursion unless the recursive definition is the most straight-forward approach. A recursive definition is often more difficult to understand and usually takes more time and memory space than a non-recursive definition.

Make variables as local as possible; avoid global variables. The benefits of local variables are: 1)No side effects — the accidental reuse of a value that was unwittingly changed in some remote part of the program. 2)More memory space — local variables only exist (have space allocated) while the procedure is active. 3)Better modular design — plug-in modules are possible with self-contained, independently allocated local variables.

Make your program as general and versatile as possible. For example, program utility is greatly enhanced if the user is given the option of sending output to a disk, console or printer. On the other hand, if all output is sent to the printer, the usefulness of the program is unnecessarily restricted.

Rule of thumb: If your program/procedure/function cannot be easily understood by someone else, then change it so that it will be.

Test your program with the following checklist:

1) Is the main program a general overview of the whole program?

2) Are the modules simple and well defined?

3) Will other people understand the identifier names used?

4) Is it easy to follow the flow of control?

5) Are any explanatory comments needed?

6) Are there any unnecessary uses of recursion?

7) Can any variables be made more local?

8) Can the program be made more general or versatile for maximum utility.

If your program passes all of these tests, then it's probably a well-written program.

AN APPLE PASCAL SUPPLEMENT:

Getting Started (for the Beginner)

Ron DeGroat

Learning the SYSTEM

Before you can actually write a Pascal program, you must first learn a little about the operating environment. A minimal introduction to the system is provided in Appendices D and E of the Apple Pascal Language Reference Manual. Appendix D describes how to boot the system, make backup copies and write a simple Pascal program with one drive. Appendix E describes the same thing for two drives.

But once you have a basic knowledge, the best way to thoroughly learn the U.C.S.D. operating system is to become completely familiar with the manuals. Even though I have used Apple Pascal almost every day for the past year and a half, I still find it instructive to re-read the manuals from time to time. This method of review keeps me aware of all the options available. When a problem occurs, I know exactly where to look for a solution. In actual practise, I refer to the manuals almost every day. Most Pascal-related problems can be resolved this way.

Because of the size and complexity of the system, it will take some time to become completely familiar with all that is available. To help find your way around the system, beginners should refer to the command tree printed on the inside back cover of the Apple Pascal Operating System Reference Manual. Most of the time a "prompt line" at the top of the screen displays what command options are available at the moment. From the Command Tree diagram, it should be obvious that the Editor and the Filer are the most complex options. They are also used most often.

The best place to start learning the system is in the Editor. The Apple Pascal Editor is a powerful screen-oriented which can be used for program development as well as word processing. Most people only learn a few of the the essential commands (like Insert, Delete and Quit) and fail to exploit the Editor's full potential.

If you want maximum utility from the Editor, get your operating manual and look up the chapter dealing with the Editor. Then systematically work your way through the entire section until you have experimented with and understand how to use every command. Now that you know what's available you can avoid a lot of inefficient and frustrating work. In actual practice you may not use some of the options at first, but eventually they will come in handy. At least, when a need arises, you will be familiar enough with the manual to know where to look for the solution.

Now that you know what's available you can avoid a lot of inefficient and frustrating work. In actual practice you may not use some of the options at first, but eventually they will come in handy. At least, when a need arises, you will be familiar enough with the manual to know where to look for the solution.

Use the same systematic technique to learn the Filer. Since the Compiler, Assembler, Linker, etc. are not so interactive, it would be difficult to try out every option in a systematic way, but you should at least read about them in the manuals. You'll be amazed by the features available. It will take a fair amount of time to truly master all aspects of the system, so take it one step at a time. The system is too big and powerful to digest all at once. In the meantime, you can start learning the Pascal language.

Learning the Language

When you are somewhat familiar with the system, you can start learning the Pascal language. But like the operating system, Pascal is too powerful to understand all at once.

The Apple Pascal manuals are good references and a source of basic information, but you should not try to learn Pascal from them. It would be a worthwhile investment to get a book specifically designed for learning Pascal. There are several good books available, although most of them are written for standard Pascal. Apple Pascal is an extension of U.C.S.D. Pascal II.1 which is an extension of standard Pascal as defined by Jensen and Wirth in the *Pascal User's Manual and Report.*

Despite the fact that Apple Pascal is twice removed from standard Pascal, it is essentially the same except for the extensions (strings, graphics, units, segments, etc.). In effect, Apple Pascal is a superset of standard Pascal. This means that programs written in standard Pascal should compile and run without modification on most Pascal systems. And since U.C.S.D Pascal is a step closer to Apple Pascal, many of the extensions are compatible too. In other words, to get started, a book on standard or U.C.S.D. Pascal would be fine.

Some Useful Books for Learning Pascal:

(A more complete list may be found in the *Pascal Bibliography* by David McCarthy)

Standard Pascal

Programming in Pascal by Peter Grogono

A Primer on Pascal by Conway, Richard and James

U.C.S.D. Pascal

Introduction to Pascal (Including UCSD Pascal) by Rodnay Zaks

Apple Pascal

Pascal Programming for the Apple by T.G. Lewis

Apple Pascal: A Hands-on Approach by Arthur Luehrman and Herbert Peckham

Besides good books beginners can learn a lot by studying good examples. One good source of quality Pascal software is an organization called USUS.

"USUS" stands for the UCSD p-System User's Society, and is pronounced "Use Us." The UCSD Pascal System is a machine independent software system developed to facilitate software portability; Pascal was its principal language, but now other languages such as FORTRAN, COBOL and BASIC are becoming available. The Society was created to influence the development and information exchange of the UCSD p-System. USUS is an excellent source of Pascal programs (Currently, at least 8 diskettes are available to members for a nominal reproduction charge). Special Interest Groups (SIGs) on topics including Apple Pascal, Word Processing, etc. have been or are being formed. For a USUS Membership Application or more information write to:

UCSD p-System Users" Society
Charles Chapin, Secretary
P.O. Box 1148
La Jolla, CA 92038

Pascal compatibility and portability is evidenced by the fact that USUS distributes Pascal source programs to Z80, 8080, PDP/LSI-11, 6502/Apple, 6800, 6809, 9900, 8086, z8000, GA-16, 68000 and MicroEngine based systems as well as others.

The most important thing to remember in learning Pascal is that Pascal is a highly structured language. Good Pascal programming style is quite unlike BASIC. To take full advantage of Pascal's potential, you must retrain yourself to effectively use the built-in control, data and block structures of Pascal.

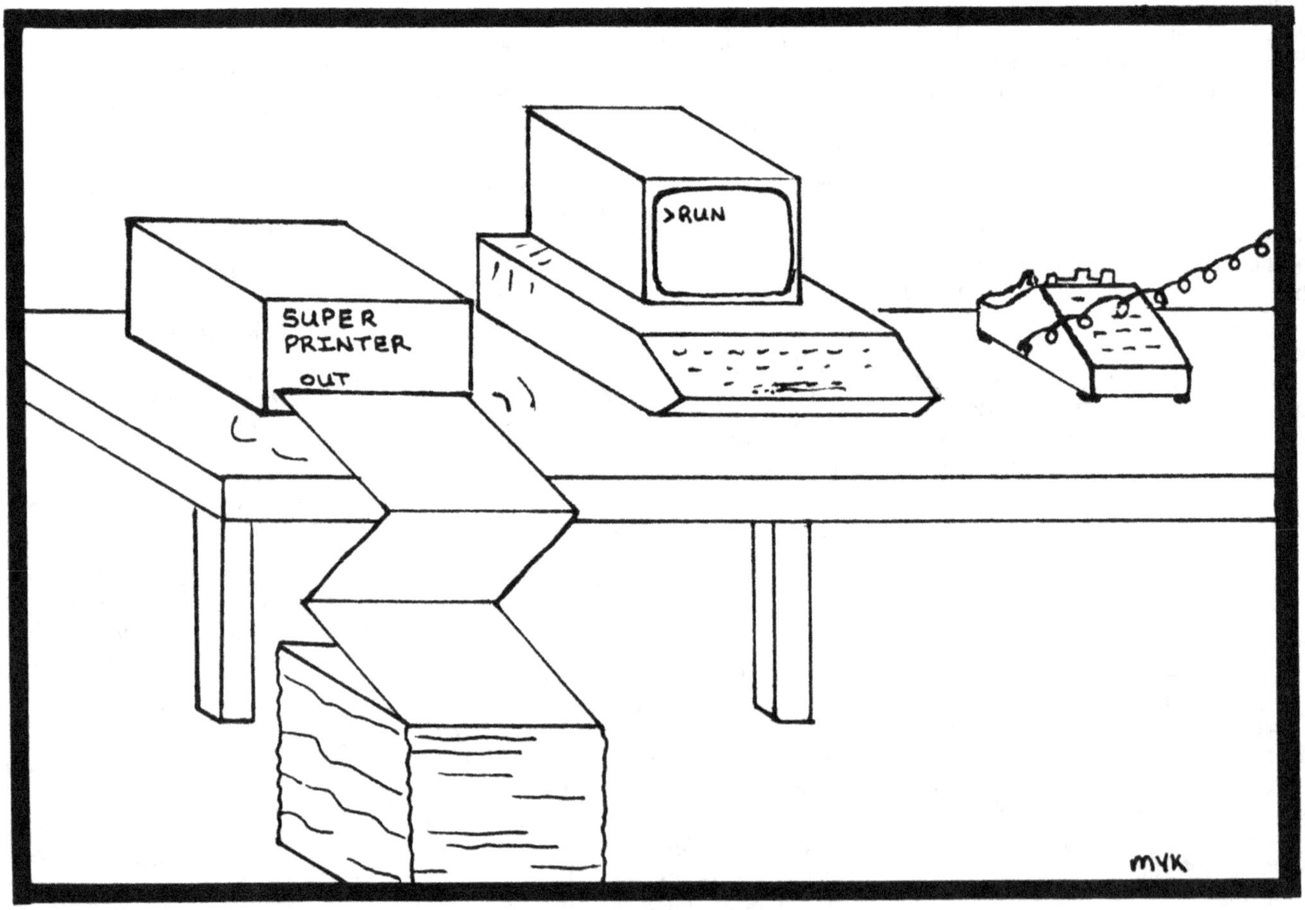

. . . HELLO, VAL? I THINK I'M IN A LOOP.

SYSTEM UTILITIES:

A P-Code Decoder

Chris Wilson

```
(*$C COPYRIGHT 1981 BY CHRIS WILSON *)

(* USE COMMAND-LEVEL SWAPPING OPTION TO EDIT & COMPILE *)

PROGRAM DECODE;

TYPE
  WORD = PACKED RECORD
    CASE INTEGER OF
    0: (B: PACKED ARRAY [0..1] OF 0..255);
    1: (C: PACKED ARRAY [0..1] OF CHAR);
    2: (H: PACKED ARRAY [0..3] OF 0..15);
    3: (I: INTEGER)
    4: (P: ^ WORD)
    END;
  MTYPES = (UNDEF, PCODEMOST, PCODELEAST, PDP11, M8080,
    Z80, GA440, M6502, M6800, TI9900);
  SDRECORD = RECORD
    DISKINFO: ARRAY [0..15] OF
      RECORD
      CODELENG,
      CODEADDR: INTEGER
      END;
    SEGNAME: ARRAY [0..15] OF
      PACKED ARRAY [0..7] OF CHAR;
    SEGKIND: ARRAY [0..15] OF
      (LINKED, HOSTSEG, SEGPROC, UNITSEG,
       SEPRTSEG, UNLINKEDINTRINS,
       LINKEDINTRINS, DATASEG);
    TEXTADDR: ARRAY[0..15] OF INTEGER;
    SEGINFO: PACKED ARRAY [0..15] OF
      PACKED RECORD
      SEGNUM: 0..255;
      MTYPE: MTYPES;
      UNUSED: 0..1;
      VERSION: 0..7
      END;
    (* AND OTHER GOOD STUFF *)
    END;
  FREEUNION = RECORD
    CASE INTEGER OF
    1: (BUF: PACKED ARRAY [0..511] OF 0..255);
    2: (DICT: SDRECORD);
    END;
  STRING1 = PACKED ARRAY [0..1] OF CHAR;
  STRING3 = PACKED ARRAY [0..3] OF CHAR;
  STRING7 = STRING[7];
  PTYPE = (UB,SB,DB,B,W,X0,X1,X2,X3,X4,X5,X6,X7,XX);
  OPREC = RECORD
    MNEMONIC: STRING7;
    P1,
    P2: PTYPE;
    END;

VAR
  PDCOUNT,
  FIRSTADDR,
  FIRSTBLOCK,
  CURRENTBLOCK: INTEGER;
  ADDR: STRING3;
  F: TEXT;
  SOURCEFILE: FILE;
  SOURCENAME,
  DESTNAME: STRING;
  OPCODE: ARRAY [0..255] OF OPREC;
  BUF: PACKED ARRAY [0..511] OF 0..255;
  SD: FREEUNION;
  PD: ARRAY [0..149] OF INTEGER;
  HEXDIGIT: PACKED ARRAY [0..15] OF CHAR;
```

```
PROCEDURE WAIT;
        (*====*)

BEGIN
IF DESTNAME = 'CONSOLE:' THEN
  BEGIN
  WRITELN;
  WRITE('[RETURN TO CONTINUE]');
  READLN;
  END;
END;

PROCEDURE SKIP;
        (*====*)

BEGIN
IF DESTNAME = 'CONSOLE:' THEN
  PAGE(F)
ELSE
  WRITELN(F);
END;

PROCEDURE READBLOCK(LOC: INTEGER);
        (*=========*)

BEGIN
IF LOC < FIRSTADDR THEN
  REPEAT
    CURRENTBLOCK := PRED(CURRENTBLOCK);
    FIRSTADDR := FIRSTADDR-512;
  UNTIL LOC >= FIRSTADDR
ELSE IF LOC >= (FIRSTADDR+512) THEN
  REPEAT
    CURRENTBLOCK := SUCC(CURRENTBLOCK);
    FIRSTADDR := FIRSTADDR+512;
  UNTIL LOC < (FIRSTADDR+512);
IF BLOCKREAD(SOURCEFILE,BUF,1,CURRENTBLOCK) <> 1 THEN
  BEGIN
  WRITELN('BLOCKREAD: ERROR IN READING SOURCEFILE');
  EXIT(DECODE);
  END;
END;

FUNCTION BYTEVAL(LOC: INTEGER): INTEGER;
       (*=======*)

BEGIN
IF (LOC >= FIRSTADDR) AND (LOC < FIRSTADDR+512) THEN
  BYTEVAL := BUF[LOC-FIRSTADDR]
ELSE
  BEGIN
  READBLOCK(LOC);
  BYTEVAL := BYTEVAL(LOC);
  END;
END;

FUNCTION WORDVAL(LOC: INTEGER): INTEGER;
       (*=======*)

VAR
  W: WORD;

BEGIN
W.B[0] := BYTEVAL(LOC);
W.B[1] := BYTEVAL(SUCC(LOC));
WORDVAL := W.I;
END;

PROCEDURE HEXBYTE(VALUE: INTEGER; VAR HEX: STRING1);
        (*=======*)

VAR
  W: WORD;
```

```
BEGIN
W.I := VALUE;
HEX[0] := HEXDIGIT[W.H[1]];
HEX[1] := HEXDIGIT[W.H[0]];
END;

PROCEDURE HEXWORD(VALUE: INTEGER; VAR HEX: STRING3);
        (*=======*)

VAR
  W: WORD;

BEGIN
W.I := VALUE;
HEX[0] := HEXDIGIT[W.H[3]];
HEX[1] := HEXDIGIT[W.H[2]];
HEX[2] := HEXDIGIT[W.H[1]];
HEX[3] := HEXDIGIT[W.H[0]];
END;

PROCEDURE DECODEPROC(PROC: INTEGER);
        (*==========*)

VAR
  IPC,
  JTAB,
  LEXLEVEL,
  ENTERIC,
  EXITIC,
  PARAMSIZE,
  DATASIZE,
  LASTCODE: INTEGER;
  HEX: STRING3;

PROCEDURE ONEOP;
        (*=====*)

VAR
  I,
  MIN,
  MAX: INTEGER;
  BYTE: STRING1;
  HEX: STRING3;

PROCEDURE HANDLEDB;
  BEGIN
  IPC := SUCC(IPC);
  HEXBYTE(BYTEVAL(IPC),BYTE);
  WRITE(F, BYTE:3);
  END;

PROCEDURE HANDLEB;
  BEGIN
  IPC := SUCC(IPC);
  IF BYTEVAL(IPC) > 127 THEN
    BEGIN
    HEXBYTE(BYTEVAL(IPC)-128,BYTE);
    WRITE(F, BYTE:3);
    IPC := SUCC(IPC);
    HEXBYTE(BYTEVAL(IPC),BYTE);
    WRITE(F, BYTE);
    END
  ELSE
    BEGIN
    HEXBYTE(BYTEVAL(IPC),BYTE);
    WRITE(F, BYTE:3);
    END;
  END;

PROCEDURE HANDLEW;
  BEGIN
  HEXBYTE(BYTEVAL(IPC+2),BYTE);
  WRITE(F, BYTE:3);
  HEXBYTE(BYTEVAL(IPC+1),BYTE);
  WRITE(F, BYTE);
  IPC := IPC+2;
  END;

PROCEDURE HANDLECSP;
  VAR S: STRING;
  BEGIN
  S := '';
  CASE BYTEVAL(IPC) OF
   0: S := ' (IOCHECK)';
   1: S := ' (NEW)';
   2: S := ' (MOVELEFT)';
   3: S := ' (MOVERIGHT)';
   4: S := ' (EXIT)';
   5: S := ' (UNITREAD)';
   6: S := ' (UNITWRITE)';
   7: S := ' (IDSEARCH)';
   8: S := ' (TREESEARCH)';
   9: S := ' (TIME)';
  10: S := ' (FILLCHAR)';
  11: S := ' (SCAN)';
  21: S := ' (LOAD RESIDENT SEGMENT)';
  22: S := ' (UNLOAD RESIDENT SEGMENT)';
  23: S := ' (TRUNC)';
  24: S := ' (ROUND)';
  32: S := ' (MARK)';
  33: S := ' (RELEASE)';
  34: S := ' (IORESULT)';
  35: S := ' (UNITBUSY)';
  36: S := ' (PWROFTEN)';
  37: S := ' (UNITWAIT)';
  38: S := ' (UNITCLEAR)';
  39: S := ' (HALT)';
  40: S := ' (MEMAVAIL)';
  END; (* CASE *)
  WRITE(F, S);
  END;

PROCEDURE HANDLECXP;
  VAR S: STRING;
  BEGIN
  HANDLEDB;
  IF BYTEVAL(PRED(IPC)) = 0 THEN
    BEGIN
    S := '';
    CASE BYTEVAL(IPC) OF
     2: S := ' (EXECERROR)';
     3: S := ' (BUILD FIB)';
     5: S := ' (RESET/REWRITE)';
     6: S := ' (CLOSE)';
     7: S := ' (GET)';
     8: S := ' (PUT)';
    10: S := ' (EOF)';
    11: S := ' (EOLN)';
    12: S := ' (READ INTEGER)';
    13: S := ' (WRITE INTEGER)';
    16: S := ' (READ CHAR)';
    17: S := ' (WRITE CHAR)';
    18: S := ' (READ STRING)';
    19: S := ' (WRITE STRING)';
    20: S := ' (WRITE ARRAY OF CHAR)';
    21: S := ' (READLN)';
    22: S := ' (WRITELN)';
    23: S := ' (CONCAT)';
    24: S := ' (INSERT)';
    25: S := ' (COPY)';
    26: S := ' (DELETE)';
    27: S := ' (POS)';
    28: S := ' (BLOCK READ/WRITE)';
    29: S := ' (GOTOXY)';
    END; (* CASE *)
    WRITE(F, S);
    END;
  END;
```

```
BEGIN (* ONEOP *)
WITH OPCODE[BYTEVAL(IPC)] DO
  BEGIN
  HEXWORD(IPC,HEX);
  HEXBYTE(BYTEVAL(IPC),BYTE);
  WRITE(F, HEX, ' ', MNEMONIC, ' (', BYTE, ')', ' ':7-LENGTH(MNEMONIC));
  CASE P1 OF
  UB, SB, DB:
    HANDLEDB;
  B:
    HANDLEB;
  W:
    HANDLEW;
  XX:
    BEGIN
    END;
  END; (* CASE *)
  CASE P2 OF
  UB, SB, DB:
    HANDLEDB;
  B:
    HANDLEB;
  W:
    HANDLEW;
  X0:
    HANDLECSP;
  X1:
    BEGIN
    (* LSA, LSP *)
    WRITE(F, ' ''');
    FOR I := 1 TO BYTEVAL(IPC) DO
      BEGIN
      IPC := SUCC(IPC);
      IF I MOD 16 = 0 THEN
        BEGIN
        WRITELN(F, '''');
        WRITE(F, ' ':21, '''');
        END;
      IF BYTEVAL(IPC) > 31 THEN
        WRITE(F, CHR(BYTEVAL(IPC)))
      ELSE
        WRITE(F, '.');
      END;
    WRITE(F, '''');
    END;
  X2:
    BEGIN
    (* XJP *)
    IF NOT ODD(IPC) THEN
      (* MUST BE WORD ALIGNED *)
      IPC := SUCC(IPC);
    HANDLEW;
    HANDLEW;
    HANDLEW;
    MIN := WORDVAL(IPC-5);
    MAX := WORDVAL(IPC-3);
    FOR I := MIN TO MAX DO
      BEGIN
      WRITELN(F);
      WRITE(F, ' ':19);
      HANDLEW;
      HEXWORD(PRED(IPC)-WORDVAL(PRED(IPC)),HEX);
      WRITE(F, ' (', HEX, ')');
      END;
    END;
  X3:
    BEGIN
    (* EQU, ETC. *)
    CASE BYTEVAL(IPC) OF
      2: WRITE(F, ' (REAL)');
      4: WRITE(F, ' (STRING)');
      6: WRITE(F, ' (BOOLEAN)');
      8: WRITE(F, ' (SET)');
     10: BEGIN
         HANDLEB;
         WRITE(F, ' (BYTE ARRAY)');
         END;
     12: BEGIN
         HANDLEB;
         WRITE(F, ' (WORD)');
         END;
    END; (* CASE *)
    END;
  X4:
    BEGIN
    (* LDC *)
    MAX := BYTEVAL(IPC);
    IF NOT ODD(IPC) THEN
      (* MUST BE WORD ALIGNED *)
      IPC := SUCC(IPC);
    FOR I := 1 TO MAX DO
      BEGIN
      WRITELN(F);
      WRITE(F, ' ':19);
      HANDLEW;
      END;
    END;
  X5:
    HANDLECXP;
  X6:
    BEGIN
    (* FJP, UJP, EFJ, NFJ *)
    I := BYTEVAL(IPC);  (* JUMP OFFSET
    IF I < 128 THEN
      HEXWORD(SUCC(IPC)+I,HEX)
    ELSE
      BEGIN
      I := JTAB-(256-I);
      HEXWORD(I-WORDVAL(I),HEX);
      END;
    WRITE(F, ' (', HEX, ')');
    END;
  X7:
    BEGIN
    (* RNP, RBP *)
    IF IPC >= EXITIC THEN
      LASTCODE := IPC;
    END;
  XX:
    BEGIN
    END;
  END; (* CASE *)
  END; (* WITH *)
WRITELN(F);
END;
```

```
 BEGIN (* DECODEPROC *)
 JTAB := PD[PROC];
 IF JTAB < 0 THEN
   BEGIN
   WRITELN;
   WRITELN('>>> PROCEDURE ADDRESS BAD <<<');
   END
 ELSE
   BEGIN
   LEXLEVEL := BYTEVAL(SUCC(JTAB));
   IF LEXLEVEL > 127 THEN
     LEXLEVEL := LEXLEVEL-256;
   ENTERIC := (JTAB-2)-WORDVAL(JTAB-2);
   EXITIC := (JTAB-4)-WORDVAL(JTAB-4);
   PARAMSIZE := WORDVAL(JTAB-6);
   DATASIZE := WORDVAL(JTAB-8);
   LASTCODE := JTAB-9;
   SKIP;
   WRITELN(F, 'PROCEDURE CODE:');
   WRITELN(F, '---------------');
   WRITELN(F);
   WRITELN(F, 'LEX LEVEL ', LEXLEVEL, ', PROCEDURE ', BYTEVAL(JTAB));
   HEXWORD(ENTERIC,HEX);
   WRITELN(F, 'ENTER IC ', ENTERIC, ' (', HEX, ')');
   HEXWORD(EXITIC,HEX);
   WRITELN(F, 'EXIT IC ', EXITIC, ' (', HEX, ')');
   HEXWORD(PARAMSIZE,HEX);
   WRITELN(F, 'PARAMETER SIZE ', PARAMSIZE, ' (', HEX, ')');
   HEXWORD(DATASIZE,HEX);
   WRITELN(F, 'DATA SIZE ', DATASIZE, ' (', HEX, ')');
   WRITELN(F);
   IPC := ENTERIC;
   IF LEXLEVEL < -1 THEN
     WRITELN('>>> LEX LEVEL BAD <<<')
   ELSE IF ENTERIC < 0 THEN
     WRITELN('>>> ENTER IC BAD <<<')
   ELSE IF EXITIC < 0 THEN
     WRITELN('>>> EXIT IC BAD <<<')
   ELSE
     REPEAT
       ONEOP;
       IPC := SUCC(IPC);
     UNTIL IPC > LASTCODE;
   END;
WAIT;
END;

PROCEDURE CHOOSEPROC;
        (*==========*)

VAR
  I: INTEGER;
  DONE: BOOLEAN;

BEGIN
REPEAT
  PAGE(OUTPUT);
  WRITELN('PROCEDURE TO DECODE:');
  WRITELN;
  WRITELN('[1..', PDCOUNT, ']');
  WRITELN;
  WRITELN;
  WRITELN('-1 TO EXIT');
  WRITELN;
  WRITE('PROCEDURE: ');
  READLN(I);
  DONE := I < 0;
  IF I IN [1..PDCOUNT] THEN
    DECODEPROC(I);
UNTIL DONE;
END;

PROCEDURE READPROCDICT(SEG: INTEGER);
        (*============*)
```

```
VAR
  I,
  LOC,
  SEGLENGTH: INTEGER;
  HEX: STRING3;

BEGIN
WITH SD.DICT DO
  BEGIN
  FIRSTADDR := 0;
  FIRSTBLOCK := DISKINFO[SEG].CODEADDR;
  CURRENTBLOCK := FIRSTBLOCK;
  SEGLENGTH := DISKINFO[SEG].CODELENG;
  END;
LOC := PRED(SEGLENGTH);
READBLOCK(LOC);
PDCOUNT := BYTEVAL(LOC);
LOC := PRED(LOC);
SKIP;
WRITELN(F, 'PROCEDURE DICTIONARY:');
WRITELN(F, '---------------------');
WRITELN(F);
WRITELN(F, 'SEGMENT ', BYTEVAL(LOC));
WRITELN(F, 'PROCEDURE COUNT ', PDCOUNT);
WRITELN(F);
FOR I := 1 TO PDCOUNT DO
  BEGIN
  LOC := LOC-2;
  PD[I] := LOC-WORDVAL(LOC);
  HEXWORD(PD[I],HEX);
  WRITELN(F, 'PROCEDURE ', I:2, ', ADDRESS ', PD[I]:5, ' (', HEX, ')');
  END;
WAIT;
CHOOSEPROC;
END;

PROCEDURE CHOOSESEGMENT;
        (*=============*)

VAR
  I: INTEGER;
  ANSWER: CHAR;
  DONE: BOOLEAN;

BEGIN
WITH SD.DICT DO
  REPEAT
    PAGE(OUTPUT);
    WRITELN('SEGMENT TO ANALYZE:');
    WRITELN;
    FOR I := 0 TO 15 DO
      IF SEGNAME[I] <> '        ' THEN
        WRITELN(I:2, ' ', SEGNAME[I]);
    WRITELN;
    WRITELN('-1 TO EXIT');
    WRITELN;
    WRITE('SEGMENT: ');
    READLN(I);
    DONE := I < 0;
    IF I IN [0..15] THEN
      IF SEGINFO[I].MTYPE <> PCODELEAST THEN
        BEGIN
        WRITELN('SEGMENT NOT P-CODE (LEAST)');
        IF SEGINFO[I].MTYPE IN [UNDEF,PCODEMOST] THEN
          BEGIN
          WRITE('TRY TO DECODE ANYWAY (Y/N): ');
          READLN(ANSWER);
          IF ANSWER IN ['Y','y'] THEN
            READPROCDICT(I);
          END
        ELSE
          WAIT;
        END
      ELSE
        READPROCDICT(I);
  UNTIL DONE;
END;
```

```
PROCEDURE READSEGDICT;
          (*===========*)
VAR
  I: INTEGER;
  S: STRING;

BEGIN
IF BLOCKREAD(SOURCEFILE,SD.BUF,1,0) <> 1 THEN
  BEGIN
  WRITELN('ERROR IN READING SEGMENT DICTIONARY');
  EXIT(DECODE);
  END;
WITH SD.DICT DO
  BEGIN
  I := 0;
  SKIP;
  WRITELN(F, 'SEGMENT DICTIONARY:');
  WRITELN(F, '-------------------');
  REPEAT
    IF SEGNAME[I] <> '        ' THEN
      WITH SEGINFO[I] DO
        BEGIN
        WRITELN(F);
        WRITELN(F, 'SEGMENT #', SEGNUM);
        WITH DISKINFO[I] DO
          WRITELN(F, 'LENGTH ', CODELENG, ', ADDRESS ', CODEADDR);
        WRITELN(F, 'SYSTEM VERSION = ', VERSION);
        S := '';
        CASE MTYPE OF
        UNDEF:
          S := 'UNDEFINED';
        PCODEMOST:
          S := 'P-CODE (MOST SIG. 1ST)';
        PCODELEAST:
          S := 'P-CODE (LEAST SIG. 1ST)';
        PDP11:
          S := 'PDP11';
        M8080:
          S := '8080';
        Z80:
          S := 'Z80';
        GA440:
          S := 'GA440';
        M6502:
          S := '6502';
        M6800:
          S := '6800';
        TI9900:
          S := 'TI9900';
        END; (* CASE *)
        WRITELN(F, 'CODE TYPE IS ', S);
        S := '';
        CASE SEGKIND[I] OF
        LINKED:
          S := 'LINKED';
        HOSTSEG:
          S := 'HOST SEGMENT';
        SEGPROC:
          S := 'SEGMENT PROCEDURE';
        UNITSEG:
          S := 'UNIT SEGMENT';
        SEPRTSEG:
          S := 'SEPARATE SEGMENT';
        UNLINKEDINTRINS:
          S := 'UNLINKED INTRINSIC';
        LINKEDINTRINS:
          S := 'LINKED INTRINSIC';
        DATASEG:
          S := 'DATA SEGMENT';
        END; (* CASE *)
        WRITELN(F, SEGNAME[I], ' (', S, ')');
        END;
    I := SUCC(I);
  UNTIL I > 15;
  END;
WAIT;
CHOOSESEGMENT;
END;
```

```
PROCEDURE INITIALIZE;
        (*==========*)

VAR
  I: INTEGER;
  S: STRING7;

PROCEDURE INIT(OP: INTEGER; MNE:STRING7; X1, X2: PTYPE);
  BEGIN
  WITH OPCODE[OP] DO
    BEGIN
    MNEMONIC := MNE;
    P1  := X1;
    P2  := X2;
    END;
  END;

PROCEDURE INIT1;
  BEGIN
  INIT(128,'ABI'   ,XX,XX);  (* 80 *)
  INIT(129,'ABR'   ,XX,XX);  (* 81 *)
  INIT(130,'ADI'   ,XX,XX);  (* 82 *)
  INIT(131,'ADR'   ,XX,XX);  (* 83 *)
  INIT(132,'LAND'  ,XX,XX);  (* 84 *)
  INIT(133,'DIF'   ,XX,XX);  (* 85 *)
  INIT(134,'DVI'   ,XX,XX);  (* 86 *)
  INIT(135,'DVR'   ,XX,XX);  (* 87 *)
  INIT(136,'CHK'   ,XX,XX);  (* 88 *)
  INIT(137,'FLO'   ,XX,XX);  (* 89 *)
  INIT(138,'FLT'   ,XX,XX);  (* 8A *)
  INIT(139,'INN'   ,XX,XX);  (* 8B *)
  INIT(140,'INT'   ,XX,XX);  (* 8C *)
  INIT(141,'LOR'   ,XX,XX);  (* 8D *)
  INIT(142,'MODI'  ,XX,XX);  (* 8E *)
  INIT(143,'MPI'   ,XX,XX);  (* 8F *)
  INIT(144,'MPR'   ,XX,XX);  (* 90 *)
  INIT(145,'NGI'   ,XX,XX);  (* 91 *)
  INIT(146,'NGR'   ,XX,XX);  (* 92 *)
  INIT(147,'LNOT'  ,XX,XX);  (* 93 *)
  INIT(148,'SRS'   ,XX,XX);  (* 94 *)
  INIT(149,'SBI'   ,XX,XX);  (* 95 *)
  INIT(150,'SBR'   ,XX,XX);  (* 96 *)
  INIT(151,'SGS'   ,XX,XX);  (* 97 *)
  INIT(152,'SQI'   ,XX,XX);  (* 98 *)
  INIT(153,'SQR'   ,XX,XX);  (* 99 *)
  INIT(154,'STO'   ,XX,XX);  (* 9A *)
  INIT(155,'IXS'   ,XX,XX);  (* 9B *)
  INIT(156,'UNI'   ,XX,XX);  (* 9C *)
  INIT(157,'LDE'   ,UB, B);  (* 9D *)
  INIT(158,'CSP'   ,UB,X0);  (* 9E *)
  INIT(159,'LDCN'  ,XX,XX);  (* 9F *)
  INIT(160,'ADJ'   ,UB,XX);  (* A0 *)
  INIT(161,'FJP'   ,SB,X6);  (* A1 *)
  INIT(162,'INC'   , B,XX);  (* A2 *)
  INIT(163,'IND'   , B,XX);  (* A3 *)
  INIT(164,'IXA'   , B,XX);  (* A4 *)
  INIT(165,'LAO'   , B,XX);  (* A5 *)
  INIT(166,'LSA'   ,UB,X1);  (* A6 *)
  INIT(167,'LAE'   ,UB, B);  (* A7 *)
  INIT(168,'MOV'   , B,XX);  (* A8 *)
  INIT(169,'LDO'   , B,XX);  (* A9 *)
  INIT(170,'SAS'   ,UB,XX);  (* AA *)
  INIT(171,'SRO'   , B,XX);  (* AB *)
  INIT(172,'XJP'   ,XX,X2);  (* AC *)
  INIT(173,'RNP'   ,DB,X7);  (* AD *)
  INIT(174,'CIP'   ,UB,XX);  (* AE *)
  INIT(175,'EQU'   ,DB,X3);  (* AF *)
  END;

PROCEDURE INIT2;
  BEGIN
  INIT(176,'GEQ'   ,DB,X3);  (* B0 *)
  INIT(177,'GRT'   ,DB,X3);  (* B1 *)
  INIT(178,'LDA'   ,DB, B);  (* B2 *)
  INIT(179,'LDC'   ,UB,X4);  (* B3 *)
  INIT(180,'LEQ'   ,DB,X3);  (* B4 *)
  INIT(181,'LES'   ,DB,X3);  (* B5 *)
  INIT(182,'LOD'   ,DB, B);  (* B6 *)
  INIT(183,'NEQ'   ,DB,X3);  (* B7 *)
  INIT(184,'STR'   ,DB, B);  (* B8 *)
  INIT(185,'UJP'   ,SB,X6);  (* B9 *)
  INIT(186,'LDP'   ,XX,XX);  (* BA *)
  INIT(187,'STP'   ,XX,XX);  (* BB *)
  INIT(188,'LDM'   ,UB,XX);  (* BC *)
  INIT(189,'STM'   ,UB,XX);  (* BD *)
  INIT(190,'LDB'   ,XX,XX);  (* BE *)
  INIT(191,'STB'   ,XX,XX);  (* BF *)
  INIT(192,'IXP'   ,UB,UB);  (* C0 *)
  INIT(193,'RBP'   ,DB,X7);  (* C1 *)
  INIT(194,'CBP'   ,UB,XX);  (* C2 *)
  INIT(195,'EQUI'  ,XX,XX);  (* C3 *)
  INIT(196,'GEQI'  ,XX,XX);  (* C4 *)
  INIT(197,'GRTI'  ,XX,XX);  (* C5 *)
  INIT(198,'LLA'   , B,XX);  (* C6 *)
  INIT(199,'LDCI'  , W,XX);  (* C7 *)
  INIT(200,'LEQI'  ,XX,XX);  (* C8 *)
  INIT(201,'LESI'  ,XX,XX);  (* C9 *)
  INIT(202,'LDL'   , B,XX);  (* CA *)
  INIT(203,'NEQI'  ,XX,XX);  (* CB *)
  INIT(204,'STL'   , B,XX);  (* CC *)
  INIT(205,'CXP'   ,UB,X5);  (* CD *)
  INIT(206,'CLP'   ,UB,XX);  (* CE *)
  INIT(207,'CGP'   ,UB,XX);  (* CF *)
  INIT(208,'LPA'   ,UB,X1);  (* D0 *)
  INIT(209,'STE'   ,UB, B);  (* D1 *)
  INIT(210,'NOP'   ,XX,XX);  (* D2 *)
  INIT(211,'EFJ'   ,SB,X6);  (* D3 *)
  INIT(212,'NFJ'   ,SB,X6);  (* D4 *)
  INIT(213,'BPT'   , B,XX);  (* D5 *)
  INIT(214,'XIT'   ,XX,XX);  (* D6 *)
  INIT(215,'NOP'   ,XX,XX);  (* D7 *)
  END;

PROCEDURE INIT3;
  BEGIN
  INIT(216,'SLDL1' ,XX,XX);  (* D8 *)
  INIT(217,'SLDL2' ,XX,XX);  (* D9 *)
  INIT(218,'SLDL3' ,XX,XX);  (* DA *)
  INIT(219,'SLDL4' ,XX,XX);  (* DB *)
  INIT(220,'SLDL5' ,XX,XX);  (* DC *)
  INIT(221,'SLDL6' ,XX,XX);  (* DD *)
  INIT(222,'SLDL7' ,XX,XX);  (* DE *)
  INIT(223,'SLDL8' ,XX,XX);  (* DF *)
  INIT(224,'SLDL9' ,XX,XX);  (* E0 *)
  INIT(225,'SLDL10',XX,XX);  (* E1 *)
  INIT(226,'SLDL11',XX,XX);  (* E2 *)
  INIT(227,'SLDL12',XX,XX);  (* E3 *)
  INIT(228,'SLDL13',XX,XX);  (* E4 *)
  INIT(229,'SLDL14',XX,XX);  (* E5 *)
  INIT(230,'SLDL15',XX,XX);  (* E6 *)
  INIT(231,'SLDL16',XX,XX);  (* E7 *)
  INIT(232,'SLDO1' ,XX,XX);  (* E8 *)
  INIT(233,'SLDO2' ,XX,XX);  (* E9 *)
  INIT(234,'SLDO3' .XX.XX);  (* EA *)
```

```
   INIT(235,'SLDO4'  ,XX,XX);   (* EB *)
   INIT(236,'SLDO5'  ,XX,XX);   (* EC *)
   INIT(237,'SLDO6'  ,XX,XX);   (* ED *)
   INIT(238,'SLDO7'  ,XX,XX);   (* EE *)
   INIT(239,'SLDO8'  ,XX,XX);   (* EF *)
   INIT(240,'SLDO9'  ,XX,XX);   (* F0 *)
   INIT(241,'SLDO10' ,XX,XX);   (* F1 *)
   INIT(242,'SLDO11' ,XX,XX);   (* F2 *)
   INIT(243,'SLDO12' ,XX,XX);   (* F3 *)
   INIT(244,'SLDO13' ,XX,XX);   (* F4 *)
   INIT(245,'SLDO14' ,XX,XX);   (* F5 *)
   INIT(246,'SLDO15' ,XX,XX);   (* F6 *)
   INIT(247,'SLDO16' ,XX,XX);   (* F7 *)
   INIT(248,'SIND0'  ,XX,XX);   (* F8 *)
   INIT(249,'SIND1'  ,XX,XX);   (* F9 *)
   INIT(250,'SIND2'  ,XX,XX);   (* FA *)
   INIT(251,'SIND3'  ,XX,XX);   (* FB *)
   INIT(252,'SIND4'  ,XX,XX);   (* FC *)
   INIT(253,'SIND5'  ,XX,XX);   (* FD *)
   INIT(254,'SIND6'  ,XX,XX);   (* FE *)
   INIT(255,'SIND7'  ,XX,XX);   (* FF *)
   END;

BEGIN (* INITIALIZE *)
FOR I := 0 TO 127 DO
  BEGIN
  STR(I,S);
  S := CONCAT('SLDC',S);
  INIT(I,S,XX,XX);
  END;
INIT1;
INIT2;
INIT3;
END;

(* ========== MAIN BODY ========== *)

BEGIN
HEXDIGIT := '0123456789ABCDEF';
PAGE(OUTPUT);
WRITELN('DECODE (6/25/81, 7:48 PM)');
WRITELN('COPYRIGHT 1981 BY CHRIS WILSON');
WRITELN;
WRITELN('INITIALIZING...');
INITIALIZE;
WRITELN;
WRITE('SOURCE FILE: ');
READLN(SOURCENAME);
IF SOURCENAME = '' THEN
  EXIT(DECODE);
IF POS('.CODE',SOURCENAME) = 0 THEN
  IF POS('SYSTEM.',SOURCENAME) = 0 THEN
    IF SOURCENAME[LENGTH(SOURCENAME)] <> '.' THEN
      SOURCENAME := CONCAT(SOURCENAME,'.CODE')
    ELSE
      DELETE(SOURCENAME,LENGTH(SOURCENAME),1);
WRITE('DESTINATION FILE: ');
READLN(DESTNAME);
IF DESTNAME = '' THEN
  DESTNAME := 'CONSOLE:'
ELSE IF POS('.TEXT',DESTNAME) = 0 THEN
  IF DESTNAME[LENGTH(DESTNAME)] <> ':' THEN
    IF DESTNAME[LENGTH(DESTNAME)] <> '.' THEN
      DESTNAME := CONCAT(DESTNAME,'.TEXT')
    ELSE
      DELETE(DESTNAME,LENGTH(DESTNAME),1);
RESET(SOURCEFILE,SOURCENAME);
REWRITE(F,DESTNAME);
READSEGDICT;
CLOSE(F,LOCK);
END.
```

SYSTEM UTILITIES:

Code Map

David N. Jones

What is this code file?

Have you ever tried to run a Pascal program and failed, only to find out that the file had not been linked? Or that it required a UNIT you did not have in your SYSTEM.LIBRARY? Or found out it was not an executable program at all? This is usually not a problem if you wrote the program yourself and understand how it works, but with the wide range of programs becoming available to USCD Pascal users, interesting problems may arise. UCSD code files contain a 'Segment Dictionary' on block 0 that contains an assortment of interesting information. This leads to the CODEMAP program, which reads the segment dictionary and displays the answers to the above questions about a code file. Output from CODEMAP contains:

- THE NUMBER OF SEGMENTS IN A SEGMENTED PROGRAM
- THE CODEFILE NAME (OR THE NAMES OF SEGMENTS)
- THE SEGMENT KIND
- THE BLOCK ADDRESS AND LENGTH (IN BYTES) OF EACH SEGMENT
- THE SLOT NUMBER
- THE BLOCK ADDRESS OF THE INTERFACE PORTION OF A UNIT
- THE TYPE OF CODE CONTAINED (P•CODE OR MACHINE CODE)
- THE PASCAL VERSION THE PROGRAM WAS COMPILED UNDER
- THE SLOT NUMBER OF ANY REQUIRED UNITS FROM THE SYSTEM.LIBRARY

A number of items listed above may need some explanation. There are now two versions of APPLE Pascal (1.0 and 1.1) and it may be of interest to discover under which version the program was compiled. The code type is of interest if the program contains any machine dependent code. You should note that any segment labeled 6502 is not necessarily all in machine language; if any machine dependent code is linked in, then the whole segment is labeled with the machine code type. The Segment Kind indicates if the program is linked, unlinked, a UNIT, or a DATA segment for a UNIT. Each segment starts on a block boundary and the block address gives the location of that segment relative to the beginning of the file. If the segment happens to be a UNIT then the block address of the INTERFACE portion is given.

```
(*                                    Listing 1


                                       CODEMAP
                            A Code File Utility Program
                                      written by
*)                                  David N. Jones
                                      14 May 1981

(*$I-*)
PROGRAM CODEMAP;
CONST
   MAXSEG = 31;
   MAXSLOT= 15;
TYPE
   SEGRANGE    =0..MAXSEG;
   SEGDICRANGE=0..MAXSLOT;
   MTYPES=(UNDEF,PCODEMOST,PCODELEAST,PDP11,M8080,Z80,GA440,M6502,M6800,TI990);
   REVISIONS=(NONAPPLE,ONEZERO,ONEONE,FUTURE1,FUTURE2,FUTURE3,
              FUTURE4,FUTURE5);
   SEGSET = SET OF SEGRANGE;
   SEGDICREC = RECORD
                 DISKINFO:  ARRAY[0..15] OF
                             RECORD
                               CODELENG, CODEADDR:INTEGER
                             END;
                 SEGNAME:   ARRAY[0..15] OF PACKED ARRAY[0..7] OF CHAR;
                 SEGKIND:   ARRAY[0..15] OF (LINKED,HOSTSEG,SEGPROC,UNITSEG,
                                             SEPRTSEG,UNLINKED_INTRINS,
                                             LINKED_INTRINS,DATASEG);
                 TEXTADDR:  ARRAY[0..15] OF INTEGER;
                 SEGINFO:ARRAY[SEGDICRANGE] OF
                                             PACKED RECORD
                                               SEGNO:0..255;
                                               MACHTYPE:MTYPES;
                                               FILLER:0..1;
                                               MAJORREVISION:REVISIONS;
                                             END;
                 INTSEGSET:SEGSET;
                 FILLER2:ARRAY[0..109] OF INTEGER
               END  (* SEGDICREC *);
```

```
VAR
  SEGDIC:SEGDICREC;
  F:FILE;
  O:INTERACTIVE;
  SEGNOTREQ:BOOLEAN;

FUNCTION YESNO:BOOLEAN;
  VAR CH:CHAR;
BEGIN
  REPEAT
    WRITE(' Y(es or N(o:');
    READ(CH);
    WRITELN
  UNTIL   CH IN['Y','N','y','n'];
  YESNO:= CH IN['Y','y'];
END;

PROCEDURE ERROR(MESSAGE:STRING);
BEGIN
  WRITELN;
  WRITELN('==>ERROR ',MESSAGE);
  WRITE  ('    RETURN to abort:');
  READLN;
  EXIT(CODEMAP)
END;

PROCEDURE INIT;
  VAR FCFNAME,OFNAME:STRING;
BEGIN
  CLOSE(F);
  WRITE('Code file Name     ===>');
  READLN(FCFNAME);
  RESET(F,FCFNAME);
  IF IORESULT<>0 THEN
    ERROR('opening code file');
  IF BLOCKREAD(F,SEGDIC,1,0) <> 1 THEN
    ERROR('reading the segment dictionary');
  WRITELN('Output file Name ');
  WRITE('<cr> for CONSOLE: ===>');
  CLOSE(O);
  OFNAME :='';
  READLN(OFNAME);
  IF LENGTH(OFNAME) = 0 THEN OFNAME:='CONSOLE:';
  REWRITE(O,OFNAME);
  IF IORESULT<>0 THEN
    ERROR('opening output file');
  PAGE(O);
  WRITELN(O,'------- Code Map for ',FCFNAME,' -------');
  WRITELN(O,' Seg # Name      Segment Kind       Addr ',
            ' Len  Slot Intrf  Type    Revision      ');
  WRITELN(O,'________________________________________',
            '________________________________________');
END;

PROCEDURE MAP;
VAR I: INTEGER; J: SEGRANGE;

PROCEDURE MAP1;
BEGIN
 WITH SEGDIC DO
    BEGIN
       WRITE(O,' ',I:4,' ',SEGNAME[I]);
       CASE SEGKIND[I] OF
           LINKED            : WRITE(O,' Linked executable ');
           HOSTSEG           : WRITE(O,' Unlinked Host     ');
           SEGPROC           : WRITE(O,' Segment procedure ');
           UNITSEG           : WRITE(O,' Regular UNIT      ');
           SEPRTSEG          : WRITE(O,' Seperate procedure');
           UNLINKED_INTRINS  : WRITE(O,' Unlinked INTRINSIC');
           LINKED_INTRINS    : WRITE(O,' Linked INTRINSIC  ');
           DATASEG           : WRITE(O,' DATA segment      ');
       END; (* OF CASE *)
       WRITE(O,' ',DISKINFO[I].CODEADDR:4,DISKINFO[I].CODELENG:6);
    END; (* WITH SEGDIC *)
END; (* MAP1 *)
```

The slot number is of interest only for the system library. If you use CODEMAP on the SYSTEM.LIBRARY file the slot numbers will show which slots refer to which UNITS. CODEMAP lists the slot numbers of required intrinsic units. Comparing the slot numbers will show which units are used. (A more complex version of CODEMAP could be written to read the segment names from the system library and list the names of required units instead of numbers.)

More information describing the definitions and most of the data required to write the CODEMAP program can be found in the Operating System Reference Manual on pages 266-270. Some but not all of the above information is given by the LIBMAP program on the APPLE3: disk, and you can use LIBMAP on code files as well as libraries. Listing 1 gives the Pascal program for CODEMAP, and listing number 2 is a sample output for the system compiler.

```
PROCEDURE MAP2;
  BEGIN
    WITH SEGDIC DO
      BEGIN
        WRITE(O,SEGINFO[I].SEGNO:5,TEXTADDR[I]:5,'   ');
        CASE SEGINFO[I].MACHTYPE OF
          UNDEF      :WRITE(O,' Undefined ');
          PCODEMOST  :WRITE(O,' P-Code (+)');
          PCODELEAST :WRITE(O,' P-Code (-)');
          PDP11      :WRITE(O,' PDP11      ');
          M8080      :WRITE(O,' 8080       ');
          Z80        :WRITE(O,' Z80        ');
          GA440      :WRITE(O,' GA440      ');
          M6502      :WRITE(O,' 6502       ');
          M6800      :WRITE(O,' 6800       ');
          TI990      :WRITE(O,' TI990      ');
        END; (* OF CASE *)
        CASE SEGINFO[I].MAJORREVISION OF
          NONAPPLE  : WRITE(O,'Non-Apple');
          ONEZERO   : WRITE(O,'   1.0    ');
          ONEONE    : WRITE(O,'   1.1    ');
        END; (* OF CASE *)
     END; (* WITH SEGDIC *)
   END; (* MAP2 *)

BEGIN
  FOR I:= 0 TO MAXSLOT DO
    BEGIN
       MAP1;
       MAP2;
       WRITELN(O);
    END;
  WRITE(O,'Intrinsic Segments required: ');
  SEGNOTREQ:=TRUE;
  WITH SEGDIC DO
    BEGIN
     FOR J := 0 TO MAXSEG DO
      BEGIN
        IF J IN INTSEGSET THEN
        BEGIN
          WRITE(O,J:3);
          SEGNOTREQ:=FALSE;
        END;
      END;
     IF SEGNOTREQ THEN WRITE(O,' None');
    END;
  WRITELN(O);
 END;

BEGIN
  REPEAT
    INIT;
    MAP;
    WRITE('===) Another Code File ? ');
  UNTIL NOT YESNO;
  CLOSE(O,LOCK);
END.
```

LISTING #2:

------- Code Map for #5:SYSTEM.COMPILER -------

Seg #	Name	Segment Kind	Addr	Len	Slot	Intrf	Type	Revision
0		Linked executable	0	0	0	0	Undefined	Non-Apple
1	PASCALCO	Linked executable	1	4486	1	0	P-Code (-)	1.1
2	COMPINIT	Linked executable	10	3226	7	0	P-Code (-)	1.1
3	DECLARAT	Linked executable	17	7574	8	0	P-Code (-)	1.1
4	BODYPART	Linked executable	32	7208	9	0	P-Code (-)	1.1
5	ROUTINE	Linked executable	47	2902	10	0	P-Code (-)	1.1
6	STATEMEN	Linked executable	53	1598	11	0	P-Code (-)	1.1
7	CASESTAT	Linked executable	57	436	12	0	P-Code (-)	1.1
8	FORSTATE	Linked executable	58	512	13	0	P-Code (-)	1.1
9	BODY1	Linked executable	59	326	14	0	P-Code (-)	1.1
10	BODY3	Linked executable	60	858	15	0	P-Code (-)	1.1
11	WRITELIN	Linked executable	62	818	16	0	P-Code (-)	1.1
12	UNITPART	Linked executable	64	1600	17	0	P-Code (-)	1.1
13	COMPOPTI	Linked executable	68	1060	18	0	P-Code (-)	1.1
14	NUMSTRIN	Linked executable	71	864	19	0	P-Code (-)	1.1
15	FINISHUP	Linked executable	73	672	20	0	P-Code (-)	1.1

Intrinsic Segments required: None

Non-Present Boot Disk Patch

Chris Wilson

IN general Apple Pascal 1.1 is quite good about dealing with disk swapping. One unfortunate exception is the absence of the boot disk when a program finishes execution. In particular, Pascal displays a message asking you to insert the boot disk and then checks the boot drive every few seconds to see if the boot disk has been inserted. This loop is most annoying.

The small program in this article patches Pascal such that after it displays the message asking you to insert the boot disk, it will display the message:

Type [space] to continue

and patiently wait for you to insert the boot disk. If you type [space] without inserting the boot disk, it will merely repeat this sequence until you do.

```
PROGRAM PATCHOS;

{ Block 15 of SYSTEM.PASCAL is patched
  to replace the loop which checks the
  boot drive with a call on the space-
  wait procedure instead.

       old code                 new code
------------------*--------------------
LDCI  (C7)      0FA0  ! LOD  (B6)       02 03
STL  (CC)       01    ! CXP  (CD)       00 16
SLDO1  (E8)           ! SLDC1  (01)
SLDL1  (D8)           ! SLDC0  (00)
LEQI  (C8)            ! SLDC0  (00)
FJP  (A1)       07    ! CBP  (C2)       28
SLDO1  (E8)           ! STL  (CC)       01
SLDC1  (01)           !
ADI  (82)             !
SRO  (AB)       01    !
UJP  (B9)       F6    !

}

TYPE
  HEXSTRING = STRING[2];

VAR
  F: FILE;
  B: PACKED ARRAY [0..40,0..511] OF 0..255;
  CH: CHAR;
  I: INTEGER;


FUNCTION CONV(HEX: CHAR): INTEGER;

BEGIN
IF HEX IN ['A'..'F'] THEN
  CONV := 10+(ORD(HEX)-ORD('A'))
ELSE IF HEX IN ['0'..'9'] THEN
  CONV := ORD(HEX)-ORD('0')
ELSE
  CONV := 0;
END;

PROCEDURE FIX(BLK, BYTE: INTEGER; OLD, NEW: HEXSTRING);

VAR
  IOLD,
  INEW: INTEGER;

BEGIN
IOLD := CONV(OLD[2])+(CONV(OLD[1])*16);
INEW := CONV(NEW[2])+(CONV(NEW[1])*16);
IF B[BLK,BYTE] = IOLD THEN
  B[BLK,BYTE] := INEW
ELSE
  BEGIN
  WRITELN('Byte at block ',BLK,' offset ',BYTE);
  WRITELN('is ',B[BLK,BYTE],', should be ',IOLD);
  EXIT(PATCHOS);
  END;
END;
```

```
BEGIN
PAGE(OUTPUT);
WRITELN('Patchos (15-Feb-81, 9:26 pm)');
WRITELN;
WRITELN('Copyright (c) 1982 by Chris Wilson');
WRITELN;
WRITELN('Insert disk with original SYSTEM.PASCAL');
WRITELN('in unit 4');
WRITE('Type <space> to continue');
READ(KEYBOARD,CH);
WRITELN;
RESET(F,'#4:SYSTEM.PASCAL');
I := BLOCKREAD(F,B,41);
CLOSE(F);
FIX(15,369,'C7','B6');
FIX(15,370,'A0','02');
FIX(15,371,'0F','03');
FIX(15,372,'CC','CD');
FIX(15,373,'01','00');
FIX(15,374,'E8','16');
FIX(15,375,'D8','01');
FIX(15,376,'C8','00');
FIX(15,377,'A1','00');
FIX(15,378,'07','C2');
FIX(15,379,'E8','28');
FIX(15,380,'01','CC');
FIX(15,381,'82','01');
FIX(15,382,'AB','D7');
FIX(15,383,'01','D7');
FIX(15,384,'B9','D7');
FIX(15,385,'F6','D7');
REPEAT
  PAGE(OUTPUT);
  WRITELN('Insert disk to be modified in unit 4');
  WRITE('Type <space> to continue');
  READ(KEYBOARD,CH);
  WRITELN;
  RESET(F,'#4:SYSTEM.PASCAL');
  I := BLOCKWRITE(F,B,41);
  CLOSE(F,LOCK);
  WRITE('Update another disk (y/n): ');
  READ(CH);
  WRITELN
UNTIL (CH <> 'Y') AND (CH <> 'y');
END.
```

PASCAL TO DOS FILE CONVERTER:

Huffin

Dana J. Schwartz / Washington Apple Pi

AFTER discovering that the DOS 3.3 RWTS (Read or Write a Track and Sector) routines could access any of the blocks on a Pascal formatted disk, it became a simple task, knowing the Pascal directory and text file structures, to locate any such file and convert it to a DOS text file. This higher-level language MUFFIN type program HUFFIN is the implementation of that concept.

Line 100 reduces HIMEM: by 2100 bytes to reserve space for the RWTS access routine and the buffers for the Pascal disk blocks. Lines 120-190 POKE this general purpose RWTS routine, and the associated IOB and DCT. See the DOS 3.3 manual, pp. 94-98, for a description of these data structures.

The screen display is set up in lines 200-230, followed by a request to the user for the source and target slot and drive. Instructions are next issued to the user for disk insertion. Note that in a single drive system there will be several manual disk exchanges performed, and that to avoid possible human error the Pascal input disk should be write-protected (expecially during your early testing!).

```
]LIST

10  REM

         HUFFIN
   PASCAL/DOS CONVERTER

    BY DANA J. SCHWARTZ

    WASHINGTON APPLE PI

CALL -A.P.P.L.E. IN DEPTH 2

100 HI =  PEEK (115) +  PEEK (116
     ) * 256 - 2100: HIMEM: HI
110  ONERR  GOTO 9000
120  DEF  FN MOD(X) = (X / 256 -
      INT (X / 256)) * 256
130 RWTS = HI:ER = HI + 17:IOB =
     HI + 18:DCT = HI + 36:BUFF =
     HI + 40
140 TK = IOB + 4:SC = IOB + 5:HB =
     IOB + 9:G$ =  CHR$ (7):PA =
     0:DR = 0
150  POKE RWTS,169: POKE RWTS + 1
     , INT (IOB / 256): POKE RWTS
      + 2,160: POKE RWTS + 3, FN
     MOD(IOB): POKE RWTS + 4,32: POKE
     RWTS + 5,217: POKE RWTS + 6,
     3: POKE RWTS + 7,176: POKE R
     WTS + 8,1: POKE RWTS + 9,96
160  POKE RWTS + 10,173: POKE RWT
     S + 11, FN MOD(IOB + 13): POKE
     RWTS + 12, INT (IOB + 13) /
     256: POKE RWTS + 13,141: POKE
     RWTS + 14, FN MOD(ER): POKE
     RWTS + 15, INT (ER / 256): POKE
     RWTS + 16,96
170  POKE IOB,1: POKE IOB + 3,0: POKE
     IOB + 6, FN MOD(DCT): POKE I
     OB + 7, INT (DCT / 256): POKE
     IOB + 8, FN MOD(BUFF)
180  POKE IOB + 10,0: POKE IOB +
     11,0: POKE IOB + 12,1: POKE
     IOB + 13,0: POKE IOB + 14,0:
      POKE IOB + 15,96: POKE IOB +
     16,1:
190  POKE DCT,0: POKE DCT + 1,1: POKE
     DCT + 2,239: POKE DCT + 3,21
     6
200  HOME : VTAB 2: HTAB 16: PRINT
     "HUFFIN": VTAB 5: PRINT " PA
     SCAL TO DOS TEXT FILE CONVER
     SION"
210  VTAB 7: HTAB 10: PRINT "BY D
     ANA J. SCHWARTZ": HTAB 10: PRINT
     "WASHINGTON APPLE PI": VTAB
     10: INVERSE
220  FOR I = 1 TO 40: PRINT " ";:
      NEXT : VTAB 23: FOR I = 1 TO
     40: PRINT " ";: NEXT :
230  NORMAL : VTAB 11: POKE 34,10
     : POKE 35,22: ON DR > 0 GOTO
     270
240  ON I GOTO 250: PRINT "SOURCE
      DISK: ": HTAB 8: PRINT "SLO
     T: ";: GET I$: PRINT I$:SS =
      VAL (I$): HTAB 8: PRINT "DR
     IVE: ";: GET I$: PRINT I$:SD
      =  VAL (I$)
245  PRINT : PRINT "TARGET DISK:
     ": HTAB 8: PRINT "SLOT: ";: GET
     I$: PRINT I$:TS =  VAL (I$):
      HTAB 8: PRINT "DRIVE: ";: GET
     I$: PRINT I$:TD =  VAL (I$)
250  ON SS < 1 OR SS > 7 GOTO 240
     : ON TS < 1 OR TS > 7 GOTO 2
     40: ON SD < 1 OR SD > 2 GOTO
     240: ON TD < 1 OR TD > 2 GOTO
     240
260 SS = SS * 16: IF SS = TS * 16
      AND SD = TD THEN DR = 1
270  POKE IOB + 1,SS: POKE IOB +
     2,SD: IF DR = 1 THEN  PRINT
      CHR$ (7): PRINT "INSERT WRI
     TE PROTECTED PASCAL DISK": GOTO
     290
280  ON J GOTO 300: PRINT : PRINT
     "WRITE PROTECT PASCAL SOURCE
      DISK AND    INSERT IN SOURC
     E DRIVE": PRINT "INSERT DOS
     3.3 TARGET DISK IN TARGET DR
     "
    "
```

Line 290 asks for the name of the file on the Pascal disk to be copied (without a volume name appended, e.g. DJS.TEXT). If no name is given, an abbreviated directory is displayed (GOSUB 5000) and the user is queried again. If a name is given, the directory is searched (GOSUB 1000) and, if found, the file type and size are verified. Lines 310-320 subsequently initialize the buffers and the DOS output file.

The conversion is performed in lines 330-440, prompting the single drive user when necessary. Characters are simply appended onto an output string (A$) until a CR (13) is encountered, at which time the string is sent to DOS. Lower case characters are not converted to upper case. Special processing is required for the DLE (16) and the NULL (0) characters. (See the description of Text File Formats on p.266 of the Pascal Operating System Manual for an explanation of their use). In addition, in order to entertain the user while Applesoft manipulates strings and memory, a window is provided to view the Pascal lines as they are written to the disk.

Lines 450-470 wrap up the session, closing the output file and restoring HIMEM:.

The subroutine at 1000 reads the Pascal directory into memory and searches for the named file (N$). The top and bottom blocks of the file are returned in TP and BT, respectively, and the file type is returned in TY. TY is set to -1 if the file is not found. The directory structure was supplied by Apple and was reproduced on p.9 of the December 1980 Washington Apple Pi.

The subroutine at 2000 reads two Pascal blocks into memory (BK and BK+1). The subroutine at 3000 is used to place the corresponding Track/Sector pairs for each block (BL) in TR and S1/S2. Note that any given block is contained in two sectors on a single track.

The routine at 4000 is the BASIC level access to the RWTS routine which was POKEd earlier. The 256 bytes of track TR, sector SE are read into the buffer address with high order byte BF (the low order byte was previously stored and does not change during execution).

The subroutine at 5000 reads in the Pascal directory and displays the file names. It is followed by a general purpose error handler at 9000. This handler will attempt to CLOSE the output file if it is believed to be present, allowing an early CTRL-C to effect a partial file transfer.

```
290   ON J GOTO 300: PRINT : PRINT
      "(HIT [C/R] FOR DIRECTORY)":
       PRINT "FILE NAME: ";: INPUT
      N$: IF  NOT  LEN (N$) THEN  GOSUB
      5000: PRINT "FILENAME: ";:J =
      1: INPUT N$: ON N$ = "" GOTO
      470: GOTO 200
300   GOSUB 1000: IF TY <  > 3 OR
      BT - TP < 4 THEN  PRINT : INVERSE
      : PRINT G$"FILE EMPTY, NOT T
      EXT OR NOT FOUND": NORMAL :J
       = 0: GOTO 290
310   HOME :B1 =  INT (BUFF / 256)
      :B2 = B1 + 1:B3 = B2 + 1:B4 =
      B3 + 1:BK = TP + 2: GOSUB 20
      00
320 A$ = "": PRINT  CHR$ (4)"OPEN
      "N$",S"TS",D"TD:D$ =  CHR$ (
      4): PRINT D$"MONO"
330   PRINT D$"WRITE"N$
340   FOR I = BUFF TO BUFF + 1023
350 C =  PEEK (I): IF C > 16 THEN
      A$ = A$ +  CHR$ (C): GOTO 41
      0
360   IF C = 13 THEN  PRINT A$:A$ =
      "":Y =  FRE (0): GOTO 410
370   ON C <  > 16 GOTO 400
380 I = I + 1:SP =  PEEK (I): ON
      SP < 33 GOTO 410
390   FOR S = 1 TO SP - 32:A$ = A$
       + " ": NEXT S: GOTO 410
400   IF C = 0 THEN I = BUFF + 102
      3
410   NEXT I
420 BK = BK + 2: ON BK = BT GOTO
      450
430   IF DR = 1 THEN  PRINT D$"PR#
      0": HOME : PRINT  CHR$ (7)"I
      NSERT PASCAL DISK AND HIT RE
      TURN": GET I$: PRINT : HOME

440   GOSUB 2000: GOTO 330
450   TEXT : HOME
460   IF D$ =  CHR$ (4) THEN  PRINT
      D$"CLOSE": PRINT D$"NOMONO"
465   HOME : VTAB 4: PRINT "ANOTHE
      R FILE ? ";: GET I$:I = 1: ON
      I$ = "Y" GOTO 200
470   HIMEM: HI + 2100: END : REM


1000  REM

*** FIND PASCAL FILE ***

1010 BF =  INT (BUFF / 256):TR =
     0: FOR SE = 11 TO 4 STEP  -
     1: GOSUB 4000:BF = BF + 1: NEXT
     SE
1020 NU =  PEEK (BUFF + 16):PT =
     BUFF + 32:LN =  LEN (N$)
1030  ON  PEEK (PT) <  > LN GOTO
     1110
1040  FOR J = 1 TO LN
1050  ON  PEEK (PT + J) <  >  ASC
     ( MID$ (N$,J,1)) GOTO 1110
1060  NEXT J
1070 TP =  PEEK (PT - 6) +  PEEK
     (PT - 5) * 256
1080 BT =  PEEK (PT - 4) +  PEEK
     (PT - 3) * 256
1090 TY =  PEEK (PT - 2)
1100  RETURN
1110 PT = PT + 26:NU = NU - 1: ON
     NU > 0 GOTO 1030
1120 TY =  - 1: RETURN
2000  REM

*** READ 2 PASCAL BLOCKS ***

2010 BL = BK: GOSUB 3000
2020 BF = B1:SE = S1: GOSUB 4000
2030 BF = B2:SE = S2: GOSUB 4000
2040 BL = BK + 1  GOSUB 3000
2050 BF = B3:SE = S1  GOSUB 4000
2060 BF = B4:SE = S2  GOSUB 4000
```

```
2070  IF DR = 1 THEN  PRINT  CHR$
     (7)"INSERT DOS DISK AND HIT
     RETURN ": GET I$: PRINT : HOME

2080  RETURN
3000  REM

*** BLK -> TR/SE ***

3010 TR =  INT (BL / 8):TMP = (BL
      / 8 - TR) * 8
3020 S2 = 2 * (7 - TMP):S1 = S2 +
     1
3030  IF  NOT TMP THEN S1 = 0
3040  IF TMP = 7 THEN S2 = 15
3050  RETURN
4000  REM

*** CALL RWTS ***

4010  POKE TK,TR: POKE SC,SE: POKE
     HB,BF: POKE ER,0: CALL RWTS
4020  IF  NOT  PEEK (ER) THEN  RETURN

4030  IF D$ =  CHR$ (4) THEN  PRINT
     D$"PR#0": PRINT D$"NOMONO"
4040  TEXT : HOME : PRINT G$"RWTS
      DISK ERROR "; PEEK (ER): POP
     : POP : GOTO 9020
5000  REM

*** PASCAL DIRECTORY ***

5010  TEXT : HOME :BF =  INT (BUF
     F / 256):TR = 0: FOR SE = 11
      TO 4 STEP  - 1: GOSUB 4000:
     BF = BF + 1: NEXT SE
5020 V$ = "":NL = BUFF + 6: FOR I
      = 1 TO  PEEK (NL):V$ = V$ +
      CHR$ ( PEEK (NL + I)): NEXT
     I: PRINT V$":":L$ = "":Y =  FRE
     (0)
5030 LN = 1:NF =  PEEK (BUFF + 16
     ): IF  NOT NF THEN  PRINT G$
     ;: FLASH : PRINT "[NO FILES]
     ": NORMAL : PRINT : PRINT "H
     IT [C/R] TO CONTINUE ": GET
     I$: PRINT : HOME : RETURN
5040  FOR I = 1 TO NF:ST = BUFF +
     I * 26 + 6:NL =  PEEK (ST): ON
      NOT NL GOTO 5060
5050  FOR J = 1 TO NL:L$ = L$ +  CHR$
     ( PEEK (ST + J)): NEXT J: PRINT
     "  "L$:L$ = "":Y =  FRE (0):L
     N = LN + 1
5060  IF LN > 20 OR I = NF THEN  PRINT
     : PRINT "HIT [C/R] TO CONTIN
     UE ": GET I$: PRINT : PRINT
     V$": ";:LN = 1
5070  NEXT I: RETURN
9000  REM

ERROR HANDLER

9010  IF D$ =  CHR$ (4) THEN  PRINT
     D$"PR#0": PRINT D$"NOMONO"
9020  TEXT : PRINT : PRINT GS$"ER
     ROR "; PEEK (222);" AT LINE
     "; PEEK (218) +  PEEK (219) *
     256
9030  POKE 216,0: IF (DR = 2 OR P
     A = 0) AND D$ =  CHR$ (4) THEN
      PRINT D$"CLOSE"
9040  GOTO 470
9999  REM

MINOR MODS BY VAL J GOLDING
```

THE MULTI LINGUAL

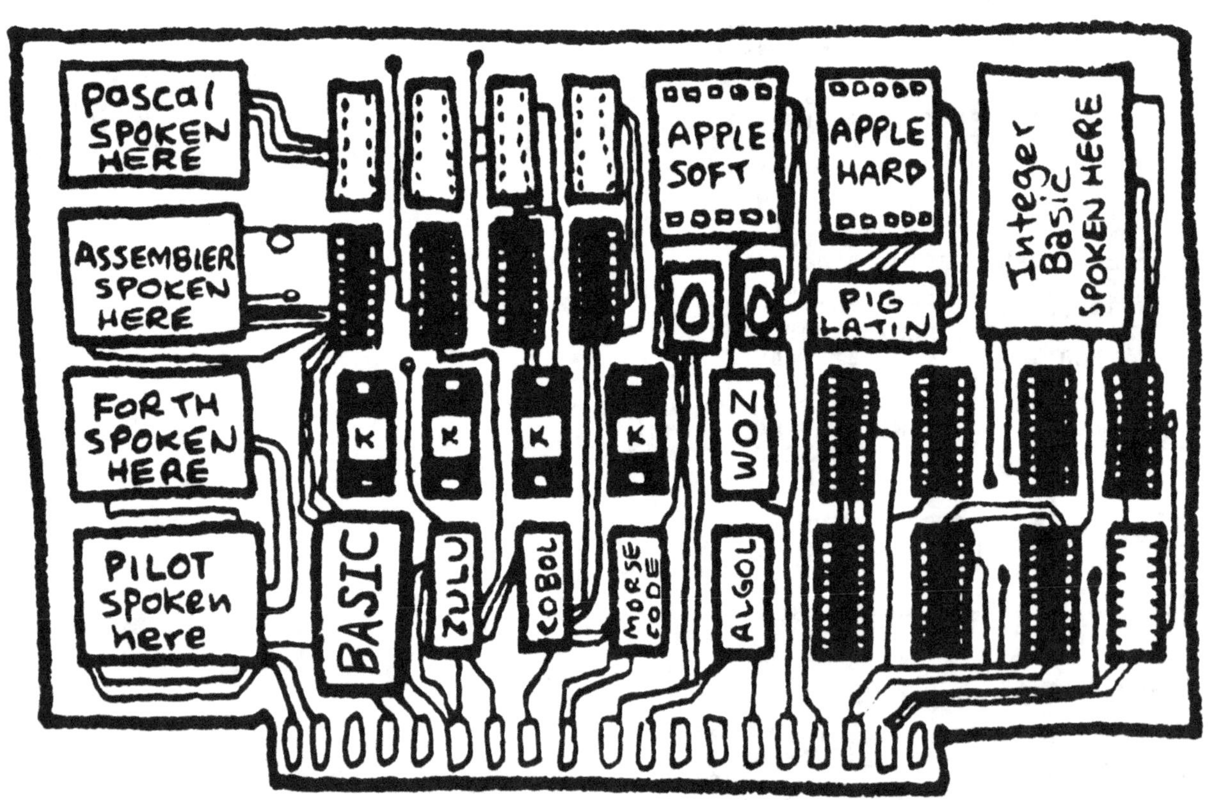

PASCAL TO DOS FILE CONVERTER:

Puffin

(Blaise Goes Both Ways)

Dr. Wo / Washington Apple Pi

A year or so ago some of my club mates who were introducing themselves to Pascal asked me about the possibility of swapping files between DOS 3.3 and Pascal. Given that both systems use 16 sector disks I replied "of course you can swap files!" One day I finally got 'round to proving it.

Being an inveterate, chauvinistic Pascal programmer, the project turned out to be both a little harder and a little easier than I first estimated. Harder, because I didn't know a whit about DOS, and had to learn how DOS keeps track of files. Easier, because I had (and still have) no desire to map Pascal files into DOS files, and dismissed that part of the project right off!

Of course, half of a suite of programs to communicate between operating systems is less than useless unless you really are a chauvinist. Fortunately, one of my club mates, Dana Schwartz, came to my rescue and supplied the other half.†

Actually, I owe Dana more than his half. It was he who came up with the names for the programs. Besides the reference to MUFFIN, the names allude to the translation from DOS's High-level language (the huff) to Pascal (the puff) and back again . . . or so he says. Sounds like a bit of fluff to me.

†See Huffin in this issue.

Like any good idea, or at least any idea for software, there turns out to be several variations on these programs. For example, our Pascal SIG is rife with home brew translation programs which are now in our library. In addition, the Carolina Apple Corps has a library disk with such programs on it ($10), and Lee Meador of Dallas had an article in the summer 1981 issue of the Apple Orchard on the topic. Also, there are several commercial versions, the BRIDGE ($90!!) from an outfit in North Carolina, and another program from Gryfon software in Silver Springs Md. Undoubtedly there are more.

What Good is it?

Any set of programs which maps between operating systems is, of course, interesting just for what it tells you about differences between the systems. But such programs go beyond that by increasing the utility of both systems. The programmer can select the best from two worlds.

From my point of view, the payoff from these mapping programs could be substantial for the BASIC programmer (but then I don't know why anybody programs in BASIC anyway).* Using the programs, you can transfer a DOS text file in which you have "listed" a BASIC program (see page 76 of the DOS manual) to a Pascal text file, edit the program using the Pascal editor, transfer it back, and EXEC it. Of course you could also originate the program text in the Pascal editor. Either way you can take advantage of the considerable power of the Pascal editor to build BASIC programs.

*You do now! . . .ed.

Going the other way, Pascal programmers can pick up high resolution graphics images created under DOS and transfer them to the Pascal operating system. The same is true of other DOS files, but there is likely to be some additional work to do on the Pascal end, for example formatting random access text files into a record structure to be used by a Pascal program. Given the need to observe word boundaries in Pascal, this could mean a custom program for each DOS file translated, unless you write a very flexible second stage formatting program. The need to observe word boundaries and dissassemble DOS's free use of single bytes is (unfortunately, he says) well illustrated in 'Puffin'.

Puffin: What Does it Do?

Puffin is a program to transfer arbitrary DOS files to Pascal files. Provision has been made for specifying the type of Pascal files to be created, independent of the type of DOS file selected. For example, it is possible to force a tokenized BASIC file into a Pascal file, even though the results will be virtually meaningless. More useful examples were mentioned above. The Pascal file types which can be created are text, foto and data.

Puffin presents a menu of four commands to the user: C)atalog, D)isplay, T)ransfer and Q)uit.

Catalog assembles and displays a DOS directory. Given the volume number of a disk drive as specified in Pascal (page 171 in the Language Manual, page 276 in the Operating System Manual), the procedure searches the designated disk for the sectors of a DOS directory, assembles the information, and displays the results on the console screen. The displayed information includes the filename, filetype, sector length, location of the first track sector list, and protection status of each file in the directory.

Display simply lists the contents of the last directory obtained by catalog. This is referred to as the current or working directory.

Transfer is the workhorse. It fetches the name of the DOS file to be transferred, the Pascal destination and the type of destination file. The transfer is initiated only if the DOS file is in the current directory and a valid Pascal file name is specified.

I/O error protection is used extensively to trap egregious keyboard blunders and disk I/O errors. The program will not run away from you, and control is always returned to the main menu in a disciplined way.

Globals and the Main Man

The global declarations for PUFFIN define the Pascal representation of a DOS directory and set the stage for the three working commands in the program.

Note that all strings are defined in terms of previously defined constants which determine their length, for example:

```
didleng=30;
did=STRING[didleng];
```

Also, note that all arrays are defined using constants which speify their bounds, types which specify the base type and sub-range types which are used to specify the range of an index into the array. For example:

```
TYPE
  blocksize=512;
  blockrange=0. .blocksize;
  blockbuffer=
    PACKED ARRAY[1. .blocksize]
      OF byte;
VAR
  block:blockbuffer;
  blockindex:blockrange;
```

work together to specify what a 'blockbuffer' is and a pointer, 'blockindex', into the variable 'block'.

The use of constants increases readability and facilitates program modification. The use of sub-range types increases the security of the program in the sense that violating the sub-range bounds will cause either a compilation or execution error — the language will not permit you to commit a range error. In more complicated programs this is a very definite plus, but even here the discipline is appropriate.

The declaration for a DOS directory entry, 'dosdirentry', should be familiar to DOS enthusiasts. Note that there are essentially two variations on a directory entry "tagged" by the field 'dfkind'. One variant, when dfkind = volinfo, occupies only the zeroth entry of the directory, and contains the unit number from which the directory was taken, and the number of entries in the directory. The other variant is used to describe an actual entry, and includes, of course, the field 'dfkind' denoting the type of DOS file.

The main program opens with an initialization of the directory The zeroeth entry is set up for the dfkind = volinfo variant, the number of entries is set to zero, and the associated unit number for the directory is also set to zero. After this, the program enters a loop which prints the command menus, fetches the desired command and executes it. The loop, and the program, terminates only upon selecting 'quit'.

Catalog

The structure of a DOS catalog is that of a linear linked list in which each node occupies one sector on diskette and consists of two fields, one a pointer to the location of the next sector; the other a list of up to seven directory entries. A Pascal declaration which describes this is:

```
dosnode=RECORD
          nextnode:link;
          entries: ARRAY[1. .7] OF
                          dosdirentry;
        END;
```

where 'link' and 'dosdirentry' are as actually declared in PUFFIN.

If only the layout of a DOS directory followed this declaration byte for byte, it would be a trivial matter to traverse the list, reading by turns each DOS directory sector and displaying them on the screen. Unfortunately, the layout does not so conform, and there arises the additional complication of having to reformat the information contained in a directory sector. Although not difficult, it is messy and involves moving bytes around. Moreover, the main idea of traversing a linked list is still at the core of the algorithm.

How then do we traverse the list and read the directory? We need only know where the list begins, when the last sector has been reached, and whether the entries are active or deleted. Following the information in the DOS manual, we assume the directory begins on track 17, sector 15, (decimal) and that the last sector has been reached when the link to the next sector points to track 0, sector 0. Furthermore, we assume that a directory entry is inactive when the pointer to the track number for the entry's track sector list (relative byte 0 of an entry) is either 0 or 255 ($FF).

'Catalog' begins by obtaining the number of the drive containing the DOS diskette to be cataloged. If drive 0 is selected, control is returned to the the main program. Otherwise initialization of the variables 'dirlink' and 'entrycount' is performed. Note that 'dirlink' now points to the first sector of the DOS directory.

The procedure now enters two nested WHILE loops which perform traversal of the DOS directory and transfer of the information to the variable 'dosdir'.

The outer loop is controlled by the BOOLEAN function 'eodir' which tests whether there is another directory sector to be read. The function returns FALSE if, and only if, the variable 'dirlink' points to track 0, sector 0.

Within the loop, the first task to be performed is to read into the variable 'dirsector', the disk sector pointed to by 'dirlink'. Assuming this is accomplished without error, the procedure initializes the variable 'sectorindex' and enters the inner loop of the traversal.

The inner loop is controlled by the BOOLEAN function 'eodirsector'. This function searches the current directory sector and returns FALSE if, and only if, it finds an active directory entry. The search begins at entry number 'sectorindex+l' and continues until an active entry is found, or the end of the sector is reached, whichever comes first. The end of sector is reached when all 7 (=maxindex) potential entries have been inspected. Note that initialization of the variable 'sectorindex' insures that inspection starts with entry 1.

In addition to updating 'sectorindex', 'eodirsector' also updates 'entrybase'. The latter points into the variable 'dirsector', marking the first byte of information for a directory entry.

At this point in the inner loop 'entrybase', points to the start of the next directory entry to be converted to Pascal format. This happens in three steps. First, the information to be converted (35=entrylength bytes long) is moved to the variable — 'nextentry'; second the variable 'entrycount' is updated; and third, the actual formatting is done by 'filldirentry'. Careful programmers will note that the variable 'nextentry', and the call to 'moveleft' which fills it, can be eliminated if appropriate changes are made to filldirentry.

After exhausting the current directory sector, the procedure updates 'dirlink' and the test controlling the outer loop is performed. Finally, upon exiting the outer loop, the zeroeth entry of the directory is updated, and a call to 'displaydir' is made to display the contents of the directory.

The procedure 'filldirentry' does the dirty work of formatting a DOS entry for Pascal. One important task it performs is to normalize the DOS file name to true ASCII, by setting low the high bit of each character. For program security, it also sets any non-printing characters to blanks. After that it finds the leftmost trailing blank in the name field, and sets the length of the name accordingly.

Displaydir

The procedure 'displaydir' is straightforward. A header is displayed, then entries are displayed one at a time. Provision is made for suspending the display when the screen is filled and even for escaping to the main program. A variable 'cumsectors' keeps a running total of the number of occupied sectors.

The procedures 'displayheader' and 'displayentry' are declared global to 'displaydir' because they are called by 'transfer'.

The directory display takes advantage of Pascal's 80 column format. Those who wish to avoid having to use CRTL-A for horizontal scrolling may wish to adjust the display procedures accordingly.

Transfer

The key to a DOS file is its track sector list, and like the DOS catalog, the list is a linear linked list. Nodes consist of two fields, a pointer to the next node (the continuation of the track sector list), and a list of pointers to the disk sectors allocated to the file, up to a maximum of 122 (=maxlink) in a node. The declarations

```
CONST
  maxlink=122;
TYPE
  byterange=0. .255;
  link=PACKED RECORD
         tracknum:byterange;
         sectnum:byterange;
       END;
  tslist=RECORD
         continuation:
          link;
         list:
          PACKED ARRAY[1. .max-
           link];
       END;
VAR
  currentlist:tslist;
```

correspond to this structure.

The structure of the track-sector list suggests the need for a traversal algorithm similar to that used in 'catalog', and appropriate tests for when the end of the list has been reached, and so on. These are explained below.

'Transfer' starts off with two loops to find out what to transfer and where to send it. It elicits the name of the DOS file to transfer. If none is given, control is returned to the main program; otherwise, a loop is entered which is controlled by the BOOLEAN function 'searchdir'. This function returns TRUE if, and only if, the designated DOS file is in the working directory; if it returns TRUE, it also returns the index number of the entry.

After this, the procedure conveniently displays the directory information for the selected file and initializes the variable 'nextnode' to point to the first node (sector) of the file's track-sector list.

At this point the procedure calls 'getfiletype' to elicit the type of Pascal file the DOS file is to be transferred to. Three choices are available: text, foto and data.

The procedure 'filetype' returns a string 'suffix' and a variable — 'filetype' of type 'pasfilekinds'. 'suffix' is appended to the name of the destination file, and 'filetype' controls the initialization and formatting to be performed.

Next the procedure elicits the name of the destination file, and enters a WHILE loop under control of 'openfile', which attempts to open the destination file. 'openfile' traps illegal file names and otherwise prevents the program from crashing while trying to open the file. Note that it is the user's responsibility to see to it that the destination file will be written on a diskette other than the DOS source. *The program is not protected against blunders of this type, and recovery cannot be guaranteed.* Take it from one who knows!

The procedure now initializes its key variables. The transfer buffers 'primpage' and 'sparepage' are filled with null characters; their associated position pointers are set to zero; the variable 'relblock' which keeps track of the number of blocks written, is set to zero. If the destination file is a 'fotofile', the BOOLEAN variable 'fotoflag' is set to TRUE. If the destination file is a text file, two blocks of nulls are written to the head of the file; these blocks are used by the editor, and are best set to nulls in operations such as this.

The buffers 'primpage' and 'sparepage' are each two blocks long to facilitate transferring to Pascal text files. Arranging other types of file transfers to fit within these declarations is easy to do.

At last we enter the nested WHILE loops which comprise the actual transfer of information.

The outer loop is controlled by the BOOLEAN function 'eolist' which tests whether there is a continuation to the track-sector list. The function returns TRUE if, and only if, 'nextlink' points to track zero, sector zero. Note that initialization of 'nextlist' insures that the transfer of information begins correctly.

Within this loop, the first task is to retrieve the node in the list pointed to by 'nextlink'. This is performed by the function 'get node' which returns FALSE if, and only if, the retrieval results in an I/O error; otherwise it returns TRUE and stores the sector it gets in the variable 'currentnode'.

Having obtained the current node, 'transfer' initializes the variable 'linkindex' and enters the inner WHILE loop controlled by the function 'eonode'. This variable-function pair is very similar to the pair 'sectorindex' and 'eodirsector' used by the catalog procedure. 'eonode' returns FALSE if, and only if, it finds an active file sector, and if it does, it also returns the location of the sector in 'nextlink'. Active sectors are indicated by track-sector pointers which do not point to track zero, sector zero.

Continuing through the inner loop, we make a call to 'readtrksec' which reads the file sector pointed to by 'nextlink', and stores the data in 'nextsector'. If all goes well, the information in 'nextsector' is stuffed into 'primpage', according to the format indicated by 'filetype'. If after exiting 'stuff', 'primpage' is full, the data contained therein are written to the destination file by 'writeblocks'. Control is then returned to the inner loop test. When the inner loop is exited, 'nextlink' is updated, and control reverts to the outer loop test.

Writeblocks

The task of writing the transfer buffer 'primpage' is isolated in 'writeblocks'. Upon entry, the variable 'pagepntr', which points to the last character placed in 'primpage', should be divisible by 'blocksize', and the variable 'blockcount' should contain the number of blocks to be written. If the call to the intrinsic 'blockwrite' fails to return a value equal to the number of blocks scheduled to be written, 'transfer' is aborted by a call to 'abortxfer'; otherwise 'relblock' is updated, and control is returned to 'transfer'.

Three Flavors of Stuffing

The details of converting from DOS to Pascal format are hidden in the procedure 'stuff'.

The simplest stuffing is that which converts a DOS file to a Pascal data file. In this situation the DOS file is transferred byte for byte, sector for sector to the Pascal destination.

The assumption when transferring to a foto file is that the DOS source file is a binary file, so that the first four bytes of file data are address and length information (presumably the address of one of the high res pages and the length of a hires image) which are important only to DOS. Consequently, the subprocedure 'stuffoto' is constructed to ignore the first four bytes of the first sector of file data, but transfer all succeeding sectors intact. The signal to ignore the first four bytes is relayed in the variable 'fotoflag'. Note that 'stuffoto' does not require a graphics image as input, only that it ignores four bytes.

'stuffoto' works as follows, except when dealing with the first sector of the source: It first moves whatever is in the spare page into 'primpage' since we only read a sector at a time this is guaranteed to be at most one full sector. It then moves as much of the current sector, 's', as is possible, into the primary page. If this is a complete sector, we exit 'stuffoto'; if it is less, the balance of 's' is moved to 'sparepage', and we exit 'stuffoto' with a full primary page, which is then cleared with a call to 'writeblocks'.

Converting to a text file is somewhat more complicated. We must make sure that the destination file follows the syntax for a text file if we expect to edit the file with the Pascal editor. 'Stufftext' insures compatibility with the system editor.

An editor compatible, Pascal text file can be defined from the top down as follows: A text file comprises two 512 byte blocks of header information followed by an arbitrary number of 1024 byte pages of text. Each page comprises a sequence of lines, and a line is a sequence of ASCII characters of the form

(DLE indent) (char) . . . (char) (CR)

where DLE and CR are ASCII 16 and 13 respectively, indent is the number of leading blanks+32 in the line, and 'char' denotes any printable ASCII character. Lines are not permitted to cross page boundaries, and the last line on a page is followed by a sequence of nulls to fill out the 1024 bytes. Note that this setup imposes the extremely mild condition that a Pascal line (but not an English sentence) can be a maximum of only 1024 bytes long.

'stufftext' transforms a DOS file into a Pascal file a sector at time, taking care to observe line to page boundaries, and converting all input characters to true ASCII.

The procedure begins with the conversion to ASCII, followed by conversion of all non-printing characters to nulls, followed by elimination of all null characters.

At this point, the input sector 's', comprising a total of 'lengindex' valid characters, is ready to be transferred to the buffer 'primpage'. If only we were willing to assume that no input line will ever contain more than 256 valid characters, we could transfer from 's' to 'primpage' directly. Unwilling to do this, we first transfer 's' to 'sparepage', which allows us to deal with input lines of up to 1024 characters, the Pascal maximum.

The procedure now enters a WHILE loop which scans 'sparepage' for successive lines and transfers them to 'primpage'. The variables 'leadindex' and 'lagindex' and the byte oriented function 'scan', are used to accomplish this. 'lagindex points to the end of the last line transferred and is set to zero at the outset. The function 'scan' is used to find the next carriage return starting at the location just past 'lagindex', and 'leadindex' is used to mark the location found by 'scan'. Thus leadindex-lagindex is the number of characters in the line, including the carriage return.

The WHILE loop is terminated when all characters in 'sparepage' have been scanned, or when it is known that the next line to be transferred will cross a page boundary. Upon exiting the loop, the balance of the information in 'sparepage' is shifted to the left to provide a clean start when 'stufftext' is reentered.

Bridging the Gap

Doing yeoman duty in support of the heavy players, is a small band of relatively low-level procedures and functions. Chief among these is 'readtrksec' which is the bridge from DOS to Pascal, and summarizes the different ways these two operating systems look at disk data.

DOS of course treats a 256 byte sector as the basic block of data, and looks at the disk as a collection of sectors within tracks, 16 sectors per track, 35 tracks to the disk. Pascal on the other hand, deals in 512 byte blocks, and organizes the disk into 280 blocks. Reading a DOS sector into Pascal entails reading the block which contains the desired sector and retaining the appropriate 256 bytes.

Interesting to me, was the discovery that DOS sectors do not logically map sequentially to Pascal blocks. For example, block 0 contains (track 0) sectors 0 and 14, block 1 contains sectors 12 and 13, and block 7 contains sectors 1 and 15.

The function 'writetrksec' maps from Pascal to DOS, but is not used here.

The Ultimate Perversion

Got your BASIC program up and running? OK, pass it over to Pascal using PUFFIN, compile it with your handy-dandy- BASIC-to-6502 compiler (written in Pascal, of course), and pass it back to DOS using Dana's program, HUFFIN. Off you go.

What's that you say? No such compiler?

Pour me another cup of coffee . . . BLAISE AWAY!!!!

```
(*$S+*)
(*$V-*)
PROGRAM puffin;
CONST
 maxunit   =12;  (* maximum number for a pascal unit *)
 maxdir    =105; (* maximum number of entries in a DOS diskette directory *)
 maxlink   =122; (* maximum number of entries in a track sector list *)
 didleng   =30;  (* maximum length of a DOS file name *)
 pidleng   =23;  (* maximum length of a Pascal file name *)
 sidleng   = 5;  (* maximum length of a Pascal file name suffix, e.g. ".TEXT" *)
 sectsize  =256; (* size of a DOS sector *)
 blocksize=512;
 pagesize  =1024; (* size of a pascal text page *)
 maxbyte   =255;

 dirtrack      =17; (* track number where a DOS directory resides *)
 firstdirsect=15;  (* first sector of a DOS directory *)

TYPE
 byterange =0..maxbyte;
 sectrange =0..sectsize;
 dirrange  =0..maxdir;
 linkrange =0..maxlink;
 unitrange =0..maxunit;
 blockrange=0..blocksize;
 pagerange =0..pagesize;

 sectbuffer =PACKED ARRAY[byterange] OF byterange;
 blockbuffer=PACKED ARRAY[1..blocksize] OF byterange;
 pagebuffer =PACKED ARRAY[1..pagesize] OF byterange;

 link=PACKED RECORD (* used to designate track/sector combinations *)
       tracknum:byterange;
       sectnum:byterange;
       END;
 tslist=(* track sector list *)
        RECORD
         continuation:link;
         list:PACKED ARRAY[1..maxlink] OF link;
        END;

 did=STRING[didleng];
 pid=STRING[pidleng];
 sid=STRING[sidleng];
```

```
 dosfilekinds= (* DOS file types *)
              (volinfo,unknown,dftext,dfinteger,applesoft,binary);
 pasfilekinds= (* some of the Pascal file types *)
              (textfile,fotofile,untyped);

 (* Pascal format for the information contained in a DOS directory entry *)
 dosdirentry=PACKED RECORD CASE dfkind:dosfilekinds OF
              volinfo: (* this is volume info *)
               (dunitnum:unitrange;
                dnumentries:dirrange);
              unknown,
              dftext,
              dfinteger,
              applesoft,
              binary:
               (file_tsl:link;      (* location of file's track-sector list*)
                locked:BOOLEAN;     (* designates whether file is locked *)
                name:did;
                sectorcount:byterange); (* number of diskette sectors allocated*)

             END;

 dosdirectory=ARRAY[dirrange] OF dosdirentry;
VAR
 dosdir:dosdirectory; (* current working DOS directory *)
 unitnum:unitrange;
 ioerror:INTEGER;
 ch:CHAR;

 FUNCTION readtrksec(unitnum:unitrange;
                     trksec:link;VAR sb:sectbuffer;VAR ioerror:INTEGER):BOOLEAN;

 (* reads sector number 'trksec.sectnum' from tracknumber 'trksec.tracknum'
    on disk drive nunber 'unitnum' *)
 VAR
  block:blockbuffer;
  blocknum,offset:INTEGER;
 BEGIN
  WITH trksec DO
   BEGIN
    (* compute half-block corresponding to desired sector  *)
     IF (sectnum IN [0,15]) THEN blocknum:=sectnum
      ELSE blocknum:=15-sectnum;
     IF (odd(blocknum)) THEN offset:=256
      ELSE offset:=0;
     (* now compte blocknum off set from track 0 *)
     blocknum:=(blocknum DIV 2)+8*tracknum;
   END; (* WITH trksec DO *)
  (*$I-*)
  unitread(unitnum,block,sizeof(block),blocknum);
  (*$I+*)
  ioerror:=ioresult;
  IF NOT (ioerror=0) THEN readtrksec:=FALSE
   ELSE BEGIN
    (* write into sector buffer *)
     moveleft(block[offset+1],sb,sizeof(sectbuffer));
     readtrksec:=TRUE;
   END; (* IF...THEN...ELSE *)
 END;

 FUNCTION writetrksec(unitnum:unitrange;
                      trksec:link;VAR sb:sectbuffer;VAR ioerror:INTEGER):BOOLEAN;

 VAR
  blocknum,offset:INTEGER;
  block:blockbuffer;
```

```
BEGIN
 (* see comments for 'readtrksec' *)
 WITH trksec DO
  BEGIN
   (* compute half-block corresponding to desired sector  *)
    IF (sectnum IN [0,15]) THEN blocknum:=sectnum
     ELSE blocknum:=15-sectnum;
    IF (odd(blocknum)) THEN offset:=256
     ELSE offset:=0;
    (* now compte blocknum off set from track 0 *)
    blocknum:=(blocknum DIV 2)+8*tracknum;
  END; (* WITH trksec DO *)
 (*$I-*)
 unitread(unitnum,block,sizeof(block),blocknum);
 (*$I+*)
 ioerror:=ioresult;
 IF NOT (ioerror=0) THEN writetrksec:=FALSE
  ELSE BEGIN
   moveleft(sb,block[offset+1],sizeof(sectbuffer));
   (*$I-*)
   unitwrite(unitnum,block,sizeof(block));
   (*$I+*)
   ioerror:=ioresult;
   writetrksec:=ioerror=0;
  END;
END;

FUNCTION searchdir(target:did;VAR index:dirrange):BOOLEAN;
VAR
 found:BOOLEAN;
BEGIN
 found:=FALSE;
 index:=dosdir[0].dnumentries;
 WHILE NOT (found OR (index=0)) DO
  BEGIN
   found:=target=dosdir[index].name;
   index:=index-1;
  END;
 IF found THEN index:=index+1;
 searchdir:=found;
END;

FUNCTION stoi:INTEGER;
VAR
 ch:CHAR;
 x:INTEGER;
BEGIN
 x:=0;
 read(ch);
 WHILE ch IN ['0'..'9'] DO
  BEGIN
   x:=10*x+(ord(ch)-ord('0'));
   read(ch);
  END;
 writeln;
 stoi:=x;
END;

FUNCTION get_unit_num(VAR unitnum:unitrange):BOOLEAN;
VAR
 un:INTEGER;
BEGIN
 REPEAT
  writeln;
  writeln('Enter the unitnum number [4,5,9..12] of the disk drive containing');

  writeln('the DOS diskette to be cataloged. Enter 0 to escape.');
  writeln;
  write(')) ');
  un:=stoi;
  IF NOT (un IN [0,4,5,9..12]) THEN writeln(chr(7));
 UNTIL un IN [0,4,5,9..12];
 unitnum:=un;
 get_unit_num:=(un<>0);
END;
```

```
PROCEDURE capitalize(VAR line:STRING);
CONST
 ordsmla=97;
 ordsmlz=122;
 shiftcase=32;
VAR
 index:0..maxbyte;
BEGIN
 FOR index:=1 TO length(line) DO
  IF line[index] IN [chr(ordsmla)..chr(ordsmlz)]
   THEN line[index]:=chr(ord(line[index])-shiftcase);
END;

FUNCTION getpasid(VAR name:pid):BOOLEAN;
BEGIN
 writeln;
 writeln('Enter the name of the Pascal destination file,');
 writeln('or enter <RET> to exit:');
 writeln;
 write('>>');
 readln(name);
 IF (length(name)=0) THEN getpasid:=FALSE
  ELSE BEGIN
   capitalize(name);
   getpasid:=TRUE;
  END;
END;

FUNCTION getdosid(VAR name:did):BOOLEAN;
BEGIN
 writeln;
 writeln('Enter the name of the DOS file to transfer,');
 writeln('or enter <RET> to exit:');
 writeln;
 write('>>');
 readln(name);
 IF (length(name)=0) THEN getdosid:=FALSE
  ELSE BEGIN
   capitalize(name);
   getdosid:=TRUE;
  END;
END;

PROCEDURE getfiletype(VAR suffix:sid;VAR filetype:pasfilekinds);
BEGIN
 writeln;
 writeln('Transfer to a:');
 writeln;
 writeln('T)ext file, F)oto file, or D)ata (binary) file?');
 writeln;
 write('>> ');
 read(keyboard,ch);
 WHILE NOT (ch IN ['t','f','d','T','F','D']) DO
  BEGIN write(chr(7));read(keyboard,ch); END;
 writeln(ch);
 CASE ch OF
  'T','t':BEGIN suffix:='.TEXT';filetype:=textfile; END;
  'F','f':BEGIN suffix:='.FOTO';filetype:=fotofile; END;
  'D','d':BEGIN suffix:='';filetype:=untyped; END;
 END;
END;

PROCEDURE printmenu;
CONST
 cleoln=29;
BEGIN
 gotoxy(0,0);
 write(chr(cleoln),'C)atalog, D)isplay, T)ransfer, Q)uit?');
END;
```

```
PROCEDURE readcommand(VAR ch:CHAR);
BEGIN
 read(keyboard,ch);
 WHILE NOT(ch IN ['C','c','D','d','T','t','Q','q']) DO
  BEGIN
   write(chr(7));
   read(keyboard,ch);
  END;
 writeln;
END;

PROCEDURE displayentry(de:dosdirentry);
BEGIN
 WITH de DO
  BEGIN
   write(name,' ':(didleng-length(name)+1));
   CASE dfkind OF
    dftext:write('text':6);
    dfinteger:write('int':6);
    applesoft:write('soft':6);
    binary:write('bnry':6);
    unknown:write('unkn':6);
    END;
   IF locked THEN write('yes':8)
    ELSE write('no':8);
   write(sectorcount:9);
   writeln(filetsl.tracknum:6,'-',filetsl.sectnum:3);
  END;
END;

PROCEDURE displayheader;
BEGIN
 write('File Name');
 write('Type':((didleng-length('file name'))+7));
 write('Locked':8);
 write('Sectors':9);
 writeln('TSL link':10);
END;

PROCEDURE displaydir;
CONST
 cleos=11;
 esc=27;
 maxlines=21;
VAR
 cumsectors:INTEGER;
 count:dirrange;

BEGIN
 page(output);
 gotoxy(0,1);
 cumsectors:=0;
 IF dosdir[0].dnumentries=0 THEN writeln('The working directory is empty!')
  ELSE BEGIN
    displayheader;
    FOR count:=1 TO dosdir[0].dnumentries DO
     BEGIN
      displayentry(dosdir[count]);
      cumsectors:=cumsectors+dosdir[count].sectorcount;
      IF (count MOD maxlines)=0 THEN
       BEGIN
        write('Type <RET> to continue, <ESC> to stop ');
        read(keyboard,ch);
        IF ch=chr(esc) THEN exit(displaydir)
         ELSE BEGIN gotoxy(0,2);write(chr(cleos)); END;
       END;
     END;
    write(dosdir[0].dnumentries,' files on disk, ',cumsectors,' sectors in use');

   END;
END;
```

```
PROCEDURE catalog;
CONST
 nextlink    = 1; (* relative byte 1 of directory sector is link to
                     next directory sector *)

 zerobase    =11; (* first byte of file info in a directory sector *)
 entrylength=35; (* DOS directory entries occupy 35 bytes *)
 mark        =maxbyte; (* directory entries which have been deleted are 'marked'
                     in (relative) byte zero *)
 maxindex    =  7; (* maximum of 7 directory entries in a sector *)

 space= 32; (* ASCII space *)
 tilde=126; (* ASCII tilde *)
TYPE
 indexrange=0..maxindex;
 entrybuffer=PACKED ARRAY[1..entrylength] OF byterange;

VAR
 sectorindex:indexrange;
 entrybase:byterange;
 dir_link:link;
 dir_sector:sectbuffer;
 nextentry:entrybuffer;
 entrycount:dirrange;

FUNCTION eodir(dirlink:link):BOOLEAN;
BEGIN
 WITH dirlink DO
  eodir:=(sectnum=0) AND (tracknum=0);
END;
```

```
PROCEDURE fill_dir_entry(VAR de:dosdirentry;VAR eb:entrybuffer);
CONST
 linkoffset = 1; (* relative byte zero for an entry gives the location of its
                    track-sector list *)
 kindoffset = 3; (* relative byte 2 designates the file type of the entry *)
 nameoffset = 4; (* relative byte 3 is the beginning of the file name *)
 countoffset=34; (* relative byte 33 is the sector count (MOD sectsize) for
                    the file *)
 lockbit   =128; (* locked files have the high bit of the file type byte set *)

VAR
 j,kind:byterange;
 nonblank:0..didleng;
BEGIN
 WITH de DO
  BEGIN
   filetsl.tracknum:=eb[linkoffset];
   filetsl.sectnum:=eb[linkoffset+1];
   kind:=eb[kindoffset];
   IF NOT ((kind MOD lockbit) IN [0,1,2,4]) THEN dfkind:=unknown
    ELSE CASE (kind MOD lockbit) OF
          0:dfkind:=dftext;
          1:dfkind:=dfinteger;
          2:dfkind:=applesoft;
          4:dfkind:=binary;
          END;
   IF ((kind DIV lockbit)=1) THEN locked:=TRUE
    ELSE locked:=FALSE;
   FOR j:=0 TO (didleng-1) DO
    BEGIN
     (* set the high bit low to get true ASCII *)
     eb[nameoffset+j]:=eb[nameoffset+j] MOD 128;
     (* eliminate any weird characters *)
     IF NOT (eb[nameoffset+j] IN [space..tilde]) THEN eb[nameoffset+j]:=space;
    END;
   (* find the leftmost trailing blank in the name field *)
   nonblank:=-scan(-didleng,<>' ',eb[nameoffset+didleng-1]);
   (* non_blank=0 if and only if no trailing blanks *)
   (* initialize the length of 'name' *)
   (*$R-*)
   name[0]:=chr(didleng-nonblank);
   (*$R+*)
   (* finally move in the name *)
   moveleft(eb[nameoffset],name[1],length(name));
   sectorcount:=eb[countoffset];
  END; (* WITH de DO *)
END; (* filldirentry *)

FUNCTION eodirsector(VAR index:indexrange;
                     VAR dirsector:sectbuffer;VAR entrybase:byterange):BOOLEAN;

VAR
 nofile:BOOLEAN;
BEGIN
 nofile:=TRUE;
 WHILE (nofile AND (index<maxindex)) DO
  BEGIN
   index:=index+1;
   entrybase:=zerobase+(index-1)*entrylength;
   nofile:=(dirsector[entrybase] IN [0,mark]);
  END;
 eodirsector:=nofile;
END;
```

```
BEGIN (* catalog *)
 page(output);
 IF NOT getunitnum(unitnum) THEN exit(catalog);
 WITH dir_link DO
  BEGIN
   tracknum:=dirtrack;
   sectnum:=firstdirsect;
  END;
 entrycount:=0;
 WHILE NOT eodir(dir_link) DO
  BEGIN
   IF NOT readtrksec(unitnum,dir_link,dir_sector,ioerror)
    THEN BEGIN writeln('ioerror ',ioerror,' reading directory');
              exit(catalog);
         END
    ELSE BEGIN
     sectorindex:=0;
     WHILE NOT eodirsector(sectorindex,dir_sector,entrybase) DO
     BEGIN
      moveleft(dir_sector[entrybase],nextentry,entrylength);
      entrycount:=entrycount+1;
      filldirentry(dosdir[entrycount],nextentry);
     END;
    END; (*IF...THEN...ELSE *)
   WITH dir_link DO
    BEGIN
     tracknum:=dir_sector[nextlink];
     sectnum:=dir_sector[nextlink+1];
    END;
  END;
 WITH dosdir[0] DO
  BEGIN
   dnumentries:=entrycount;
   dunitnum:=unitnum;
  END;
 displaydir;
END; (* catalog *)

(*$IPUFFIN:TRANSFER.TEXT*)
BEGIN
 WITH dosdir[0] DO
  BEGIN dfkind:=volinfo; dnumentries:=0; dunitnum:=0; END;
 page(output);
 gotoxy(0,5);
 writeln('Welcome to PUFFIN!');
 REPEAT
  printmenu;
  readcommand(ch);
  CASE ch OF
   'c','C':catalog;
   'd','D':displaydir;
   't','T':transfer;
   END;
 UNTIL ch IN ['Q','q'];
END.
```

```
PROCEDURE transfer;
TYPE
 ffile=FILE;
VAR
 dosname     :did;
 pasname     :pid;
 suffix      :sid;
 dirindex    :dirrange;
 linkindex   :linkrange;
 nextlink,
 nextnode    :link;
 nextsector  :sectbuffer;
 currentnode:tslist;
 ioerror     :INTEGER;
 pasfile     :ffile;
 primpage,
 sparepage   :pagebuffer;
 pagepntr,
 sparepntr   :pagerange;
 relblock    :INTEGER;
 filetype    :pasfilekinds;
 fotoflag    :BOOLEAN; (* flag for shifts of size 'binaryoffset' *)

 PROCEDURE abortxfer(ioerror:INTEGER);
 BEGIN
  writeln;
  writeln('IO ERROR ',ioerror);
  writeln('EXITING TRANSFER');
  (*$I-*)
   close(pasfile,purge);
  (*$I+*)
  exit(transfer);
 END;

 FUNCTION openfile(name:pid;VAR f:ffile;VAR ioerror:INTEGER):BOOLEAN;
 BEGIN
  (*$I-*)
  rewrite(f,name);
  ioerror:=ioresult;
  (*$I+*)
  openfile:=ioerror=0;
 END;

 FUNCTION eolist(next:link):BOOLEAN;
 BEGIN
  WITH next DO
   eolist:=((tracknum=0) AND (sectnum=0));
 END;

 FUNCTION get_node(location:link;VAR listdata:tslist):BOOLEAN;
 CONST
  contoffset=  1; (* beginning of continuation link *)
  contleng  =  2; (* length of continuation info *)
  listoffset= 12; (* beginning of list of track sector links *)
  listleng  =244; (* length of list data *)
 VAR
  sb:sectbuffer;
  i:linkrange;
 BEGIN
  IF NOT (readtrksec(dosdir[0].dunitnum,location,sb,ioerror)) THEN get_node:=FALSE

   ELSE WITH listdata DO
    BEGIN
     continuation.tracknum:=sb[contoffset];
     continuation.sectnum:=sb[contoffset+1];
     FOR i:=1 TO maxlink DO
     BEGIN
      list[i].tracknum:=sb[listoffset+(i-1)*contleng];
      list[i].sectnum:=sb[listoffset+(i-1)*contleng+1];
     END;
     get_node:=TRUE;
    END;
 END;
```

```
FUNCTION eonode(VAR linkindex:linkrange;VAR tslink:link):BOOLEAN;
VAR
 emptysector:BOOLEAN;
BEGIN
 emptysector:=TRUE;
 WHILE ((linkindex<maxlink) AND emptysector) DO
  BEGIN
   linkindex:=linkindex+1;
   WITH currentnode.list[linkindex] DO
    emptysector:=(tracknum=0) AND (sectnum=0)
  END;
 IF NOT emptysector THEN tslink:=currentnode.list[linkindex];
 eonode:=emptysector;
END;

PROCEDURE writeblocks(VAR pb:pagebuffer;pbpntr:pagerange;
                              blockcount:INTEGER;VAR relblock:INTEGER);
BEGIN
 (******* note: pbpntr should be divisible by blocksize upon entry *)
 (*$I-*)
 pbpntr:=pbpntr-(blockcount*blocksize)+1;
 IF (blockwrite(pasfile,pb[pbpntr],blockcount,relblock)=blockcount)
  THEN relblock:=relblock+blockcount
 (*$I+*)
  ELSE abortxfer(ioerror);
END;

PROCEDURE stuff(VAR s:sectbuffer;VAR p:pagebuffer;
                          VAR pagepntr:pagerange;filetype:pasfilekinds);
 PROCEDURE stufftext;
 CONST
  hibit=128;
  asciicr=13; (* ASCII carriage return *)
  space=32; (* ASCII space *)
  tilde=126; (* ASCII tilde *)
 VAR
  lengindex,nextnull:sectrange;
  leadindex,lagindex:pagerange;
  cr,null:CHAR;
  primfull,endofspare:BOOLEAN;
 BEGIN
  (* zero the high bits to get true ASCII *)
  FOR lengindex:=0 TO maxbyte DO
   BEGIN
    (* zero the high bit of s[lengindex] *)
    s[lengindex]:=s[lengindex] MOD hibit;
    (* eliminate weird characters by setting to null *)
    IF NOT (s[lengindex] IN [space..tilde,asciicr]) THEN s[lengindex]:=0;
   END;

  (* squeeze out the middle null characters *)
  null:=chr(0);
  lengindex:=sectsize;
  nextnull:=scan(lengindex,=null,s);
  WHILE (nextnull<lengindex) DO
   BEGIN
    moveleft(s[nextnull+1],s[nextnull],lengindex-nextnull-1);
    lengindex:=lengindex-1;
    nextnull:=scan(lengindex,=null,s);
   END;
```

```
  moveleft(s,sparepage[sparepntr+1],lengindex);
  sparepntr:=sparepntr+lengindex;
  endofspare:=FALSE;
  primfull:=FALSE;
  lagindex:=0;
  cr:=chr(asciicr);

  WHILE NOT (endofspare OR primfull) DO BEGIN
   leadindex:=scan((sparepntr-lagindex),=cr,sparepage[lagindex+1]);
   IF (leadindex=(sparepntr-lagindex)) THEN endofspare:=TRUE
    ELSE IF ((leadindex+pagepntr+1) > pagesize) THEN primfull:=TRUE
    ELSE BEGIN
     moveleft(sparepage[lagindex+1],primpage[pagepntr+1],leadindex+1);
     pagepntr:=pagepntr+leadindex+1;
     lagindex:=lagindex+leadindex+1;
     endofspare:=(lagindex=sparepntr);
    END;
   END;

  IF primfull THEN pagepntr:=pagesize;
  moveleft(sparepage[lagindex+1],sparepage,sparepntr-lagindex);
  sparepntr:=sparepntr-lagindex;

 END;(* stufftext *)

 PROCEDURE stuffoto;
 CONST
  fotoffset=4; (* four bytes of DOS address junk in the first sector *)
 BEGIN
  IF fotoflag (* first foto sector *)
   THEN BEGIN
         moveleft(s[fotoffset],primpage,sectsize-fotoffset);
         pagepntr:=sectsize-fotoffset;
         fotoflag:=FALSE;
        END
   ELSE BEGIN
    moveleft(sparepage,primpage[pagepntr+1],sparepntr);
    pagepntr:=sparepntr+pagepntr;
    sparepntr:=0;
    IF ((pagepntr+sectsize) <= pagesize) (* i.e., enough room for a sector *)
     THEN BEGIN
           moveleft(s,primpage[pagepntr+1],sectsize);
           pagepntr:=pagepntr+sectsize;
          END
     ELSE BEGIN
           (* move as much as possible into the primary page *)
           moveleft(s,primpage[pagepntr+1],pagesize-pagepntr);
           (* move the rest into the spare page *)
           (* begin by updating sparepntr *)
           sparepntr:=sectsize-(pagesize-pagepntr);
           moveleft(s[pagesize-pagepntr],sparepage,sparepntr);
           (* update pagepntr to end of page *)
           pagepntr:=pagesize;
          END;
   END;
  END;

 BEGIN
  IF (filetype=textfile) THEN stufftext
   ELSE IF (filetype=fotofile) THEN stuffoto
   ELSE BEGIN
    moveleft(s,p[pagepntr+1],sectsize);
    pagepntr:=pagepntr+sectsize;
   END;
 END;

BEGIN
 page(output);
 IF NOT (getdosid(dosname)) THEN exit(transfer);
 WHILE NOT (searchdir(dosname,dirindex)) DO
  BEGIN
   writeln;
   writeln(dosname,' not in current dosdir');
   IF NOT (getdosid(dosname)) THEN exit(transfer);
  END;
```

```
writeln;
displayheader;
displayentry(dosdir[dirindex]);
nextnode:=dosdir[dirindex].file_tsl;

getfiletype(suffix,filetype);
IF NOT (getpasid(pasname)) THEN exit(transfer);
WHILE NOT (openfile(concat(pasname,suffix),pasfile,ioerror)) DO
 BEGIN
  writeln;
  writeln('IO error ',ioerror,' opening ',concat(pasname,suffix));
  IF NOT (getpasid(pasname)) THEN exit(transfer);
 END;

(* initalize the page buffers and associated pointers *)
fillchar(primpage,pagesize,chr(0));
fillchar(sparepage,pagesize,chr(0));
pagepntr:=0;
sparepntr:=0;
relblock:=0;

IF (filetype=fotofile) THEN fotoflag:=TRUE
 ELSE IF (filetype=textfile) THEN
  (* write two header blocks of nulls *)
  BEGIN
   relblock:=blockwrite(pasfile,primpage,1,relblock)+relblock;
   relblock:=blockwrite(pasfile,primpage,1,relblock)+relblock;
  END;

WHILE NOT eolist(nextnode) DO
 IF NOT (get_node(nextnode,currentnode)) THEN abortxfer(ioerror)
  ELSE BEGIN
   linkindex:=0;
   WHILE NOT eonode(linkindex,nextlink) DO
    IF NOT (readtrksec(dosdir[0].dunitnum,nextlink,nextsector,ioerror))
     THEN abortxfer(ioerror)
     ELSE BEGIN
      stuff(nextsector,primpage,pagepntr,filetype);
      IF (pagepntr=pagesize) THEN
       BEGIN
        writeblocks(primpage,pagepntr,2,relblock);
        pagepntr:=0;
        fillchar(primpage,pagesize,chr(0));
       END;
     END;
   nextnode:=currentnode.continuation;
  END;

(* pick up anything in the spare page *)
moveleft(sparepage,primpage[pagepntr+1],sparepntr);
pagepntr:=pagepntr+sparepntr;
(* if page is partially full it needs to be written *)
IF (pagepntr>0) THEN (* note: pagepntr<pagesize will be true here *)
 BEGIN
  pagepntr:=blocksize*(1+(pagepntr DIV blocksize));
  writeblocks(primpage,pagepntr,(pagepntr DIV blocksize),relblock);
 END;

IF ((filetype=textfile) AND odd(relblock)) THEN
 BEGIN
  fillchar(primpage,pagesize,chr(0));
  relblock:=blockwrite(pasfile,primpage,1,relblock)+relblock;
 END;

writeln;
writeln(dosname,' transferred to ',concat(pasname,suffix));
writeln(relblock,' blocks transferred');
close(pasfile,lock);
END;
```

Pascal Memory Utility

Ron DeGroat

THE Pascal Memory Utility (PMU) is designed to help the user explore and investigate the inner workings of the Apple Pascal system. With PMU, all parts of the Pascal system are available for disassembly, examination or modification with numerous user options. The most unusual aspect of the utility is that monitor ROM subroutines perform most of the functions, including I/O operations. The Pascal part of the program serves mainly to display user options and call the appropriate ROM subroutines.

There are two big advantages in using ROM subroutines. First, most of the work is already done. And second, the machine code subroutines are very fast. Pascal purists may cringe at using ROM subroutines, but the practical programmer will gladly exploit the dormant code.

Before we can understand how PMU works, we must first understand how the Language Card works. The Language System requires that 48K of RAM ($0–BFFF) be available on the main circuit board of the Apple. An additional 4K of address space ($C000–CFFF) is dedicated to input/output devices and routines. This leaves only 12K of address space ($D000–FFFF) for the 16K of RAM on the Language Card. The problem is resolved by locating two 4K banks of RAM in the address space $D000–DFFF and switching between them with control codes. The control codes are special memory locations which act like switches that toggle when accessed (for more information, see the APPLE LANGUAGE SYSTEM manual, Appendix D: Language Card Control Codes). By using control codes to select which 4K bank is mapped into $D000–DFFF, 8K of memory can be addressed with 4K of address space. In addition to bank selection, the control codes can select or deselect RAM read as well as write–protect or write–enable the RAM on the Language Card. Deselecting RAM read enables the ROMs: the Autostart ROM ($F800-FFFF) on the Language Card, and the mother board ROM ($D000-F7FF) which contains the resident BASIC interpreter.

Most of the Pascal system is located in the Language Card RAM ($D000–FFFF). The BIOS (Basic Input/Output System) resides in the second 4K bank ($D000–DFFF). The P–code Interpreter occupies the first 4K bank ($D000–FFFF) and some of the remaining 8K section of the Language Card ($E000–FFFF). This presents a problem because the RAM of the Language Card cannot be read when the ROMs are enabled. Fortunately, most of the ROM subroutines used by PMU do not directly access the RAM of the Language Card. Part of the ROM disassembler, however, has to be copied into RAM so that certain modifications can be made (see PROC INITDISASSEM in Listing #2). These modifications make it possible to select and deselect RAM everytime a byte is needed by the ROM disassembler. The two 4K banks of RAM on the Language Card further complicate the process. The bank switching and RAM/ROM selection are automatically taken care of by the assembly language interface routines in Listing #2. Despite the complications, there is a bright side: 12K of ROM plus the second 4K bank of RAM makes the addressable memory space of the Language System effectively equivalent to 80K!!!

Another important feature of PMU is the chimpanzee–proof input. Illegal characters are not accepted, and a bell is immediately sounded to warn the user of an error. Legal length limits are also established. For example, if a hex address is expected, only hex digits (0..F) are allowed, and no more than four digits will be accepted.

The PMU command prompt line is given below:

PMU: D(ISASM E(XAMINE C(HANGE P(RINT[OFF] S(EARCH M(ONITOR B(ANK[1] Q(UIT

D(ISASM	Allows user to disassemble memory with the monitor disassembler.
E(XAMINE	Displays contents of memory in hex and ASCII formats.
C(HANGE	Allows user to change contents of memory.
P(RINT[ON]	If printer is "ON," all relevant output goes to the printer with an 80 column format. When "OFF", all output goes to the display console with a 40 column format. Depressing "P" switches to the opposite PRINT state.
S(EARCH	Allows user to easily find a sequence of two or three hex or ASCII values in memory.
M(ONITOR	Jumps to ROM–based monitor. RAM of Language Card is not accessible, but the rest of RAM may be operated on by any monitor command. Return to PMU with "Ctrl–Y [RET]".
B(ANK[2]	Allows user to select which 4K bank will be operated on by other options. Bank currently selected is indicated by number enclosed in square brackets. Depressing "B" selects the other 4K bank.

DISASM, EXAMINE and CHANGE have their own sub–options. For example:

DISASM: L(IST N(EXT R(ANGE B(ANK[1] Q(UIT

L(IST	**Disassembles 20 lines starting at user specified address.**
N(EXT	**Disassembles next 20 lines.**
R(ANGE	**Disassembles range of memory specified by user.**
B(ANK	**Same as BANK option in PMU Command line.**

EXAMINE has the same sub-options as DISASM, but instead of disassembling memory, it examines memory in a hex and ASCII format. The CHANGE prompt line with sample display is given below:

[ESC] TO TERMINATE,
[CR] TO SKIP)

STARTADDR 400
400- A0 A0
401- B1 EE
402- C3

The first column gives the memory address in hex, the second column shows the original contents of memory and the third column shows the new value. A carriage return leaves the current value unchanged and skips to the next location. Pressing the escape key aborts the CHANGE option and returns control to the PMU Command level. The escape key may also be used with any other option except the MONITOR. The SEARCH mode is good for finding a sequence of two or three byte values in hex or ASCII formats. Before the SEARCH is begun, the second bank of RAM ($D000-DFFF) is copied into the Hi-Res screen ($2000-2FFF) so that bank switching complications are avoided. The original search routine took a minimum of five minutes to search all 64 K of RAM. To improve speed, the critical loop of the Pascal routine was replaced with an assembly language routine that reduced search time to as little as 4.5 seconds. Search times may be longer than the minimum if a lot of matches are found.

SEARCH[3]: H(EX, C(HAR, Q(UIT

The three inside the square brackets indicates the search is set for a sequence of three values. Suppose the user only wants to look for a sequence of two hex values (such as C9F7, an address). He can change the search to look for two bytes by typing "2," which results in the following display:

SEARCH[2]: H(EX, D(EC, C(HAR, Q(UIT

Typing "H" will then lead to the following dialogue:

LOOK FOR THE SEQUENCE
FIRST F7 *(FOR ADDRESSES, LOBYTE COMES FIRST)*
SECOND C9

NOW SEARCHING MEMORY...

SEQUENCE F7 C9

FF84 FFA0 FFCC *(THE "FOUND" LOCATIONS ARE GIVEN IN HEX)*

A small portion of memory ($C030-C100) is purposely skipped over because it contains soft switches which activate different I/O functions which would otherwise result in a loss of normal text display.

The MONITOR option of PMU is not particularly useful for investigating the Pascal system because the monitor cannot directly operate on the Language Card (they both occupy the same address space). However, the MONITOR option can be used to aid in the development of other PMU options which might also use ROM subroutines. It can also help in debugging assembly language routines written with the UCSD Adaptable Assembler. Returning to the PMU program from the monitor is accomplished with a "Ctrl-Y [RET]." You can also enter BASIC from the monitor, but then returning to Pascal becomes impossible because BASIC has a nasty habit of messing up the stack.

To get PMU operational, the program in Listing #1 must be compiled and linked to the properly assembled routines in Listing #2.

Following are a few directions for exploring the system. A good reference may be found in the article entitled "Pascal Internals" by Mike Rosing and Keith McLauren which appeared in the March-April 1981 issue of *Call -A.P.P.L.E.* and is reprinted in this issue. This article contains a lot of useful information concerning the Pascal system.

A table of useful system locations is given below (a [1] or [2] in square brackets signifies BANK[1] or BANK[2], respectively):

PASCAL SYSTEM LOCATIONS

DESCRIPTION	PASCAL 1.1 ADDR	PASCAL II.1 ADDR
Keyboard input buffer	3B1-3FF	3B1-3FF
Beginning of heap (normally)	C00 .	C00
Last read directory	D72-155E	D72-155E
SYSCOM	BDDE	BDDE
P-code decoder	D253[1]	D243[1]
P-code jump table	D000[1]	D000[1]
Console input routine (CONCK)	D772[2]	D681[2]
Initialize console (CINIT)	D734[2]	D898[2]
Write to console (CWRITE)	D7D0[2]	D950[2]
Write to printer (PWRITE)	D830[2]	D9C3[2]
Initialize printer (PINIT)	D788[2]	D8EF[2]
Write to disk (DWRITE)	D038[2]	D028[2]
Read from disk (DREAD)	D03C[2]	D02C[2]
Initialize disk (DINIT)	D000[2]	D683[2]
Read remote (RREAD)	D84E[2]	D9E5[2]
Write remote (RWRITE)	D809[2]	D99C[2]
Initialize remote (RINIT)	D79C[2]	D91C[2]

With PMU it is easy to make small modifications to the system. For example, the text display mode may be changed by changing the location $DABO[2] in Pascal 1.1 or $D8ED[2] in Pascal II.1 from $80 for normal display to $40 for flashing and $00 for inverse. Certain key assignments may also be changed:

PASCAL CONTROL KEY ASSIGNMENTS

KEY	HEX VALUE	1.1 ADDR	II.1 ADDR
Ctrl–K	0B	D7A2[2]	D6A5[2]
Ctrl–A	01	7A8[2]	D6AB[2]
Ctrl–Z	1A	D7BA[2]	D6BD[2]
Ctrl–F	06	BE31	BE31
Ctrl–shft–P	00	BE32	BE32
Ctrl–S	14	BE33	BE33

Of course, be careful not to make key assignments that would conflict with previously established values. Since these changes are made in memory, they will only be good until the next initialization. However, any memory change can be made permanent by changing the corresponding locations on the SYSTEM.APPLE file of the boot diskette. This can be done in a straight-forward manner because there is a one-to-one mapping of the memory locations, $D000[2]-DFFF[2], $E000-FFFF, into blocks 0-23 of SYSTEM.APPLE, i.e., $D000[2] may be found at the zeroth byte of block #0 and $FFFF may be found at the last (511th) byte of block #23. The first bank, $D000[1]-DFFF[1], is mapped into blocks 24-32. Disk changes can be made with PASCALZAP in this issue; with PASCALZAP you must remember to use the correct absolute block number of the block you want to modify. Normally, the zeroth block of SYSTEM.APPLE is the sixth (absolute) block of the disk.

```
;---------------------------------
;LISTING #2: PMU.PROC
;
;WRITTEN BY RON DEGROAT        4/81
;---------------------------------

;MONITOR ROM ADDRS

SETNORM  .EQU 0FE84    ;I/O INIT
INIT     .EQU 0FB2F
SETVID   .EQU 0FE93
SETKBD   .EQU 0FE89

PRBYTE   .EQU 0FDDA    ;CHAR OUTPUT
COUT     .EQU 0FDED    ;SUBROUTINES
PRNTYX   .EQU 0F940

PCADJ    .EQU 0F953
PC       .EQU 0003A    ;PROG COUNTER
MON      .EQU 0FF65    ;MONITOR

RETURN   .EQU 00000    ;PASCAL RET ADDR
ADDR     .EQU 00002    ;PASSED PARAM.
VAL      .EQU 00004    ;PASSED PARAM.

;LOAD DATA OR ROUTINE (NO MORE THAN 256 BYTES)

         .MACRO LOAD   ;FORMAT:
         LDY #00       ;LOAD SOURCE,DEST,LEN
$1       LDA %1,Y
         STA %2,Y
         INY
         CPY #%3
         BNE $1
         .ENDM
```

Since disk modifications are more or less permanent, it is better to make system modifications in memory. If the routine that modifies memory is given the name SYSTEM. STARTUP, it will run everytime the disk is booted. System modification can then be defeated by changing the name of SYSTEM.STARTUP, and re-booting the disk.

In general, modification of the system should be avoided (for compatibility reasons). But for certain applications (lower case display, for example), modifying the system can provide the best (or cheapest, or easiest) solution to the problem. It is fairly easy to add new options to PMU. In fact, the hex/ASCII Search mode was added to PMU after its original publication in the July/August 1981 issue of *Call -A.P.P.L.E.* I would encourage readers to develop their own options or at least submit ideas for possible implementation. As new features are added, PMU's usefulness will be further enhanced.

With PMU, the Pascal system can be explored in depth. This utility is not intended to provide the user with the same peek/poke capabilities of BASIC. In fact, such usage is to be discouraged because it depends on the system being fixed to absolute memory locations — an extremely inflexible situation. The purpose of PMU is to allow the user direct access to the Pascal system. Hopefully, it will help satisfy the curiousity of those who want to know "how things work." More importantly, it can serve as a useful tool to those who want (or need) to exploit the full potential of their system.

```
;POP ADDR FROM STACK

         .MACRO POP   ;FORMAT: POP ADDR
         PLA
         STA %1
         PLA
         STA %1+1
         .ENDM

;PUSH ADDR ONTO STACK

         .MACRO PUSH ;FORMAT: PUSH ADDR
         LDA %1+1
         PHA
         LDA  %1
         PHA
         .ENDM

         .MACRO ROMSELECT
         STA 0C08A
         .ENDM

         .MACRO RAMSELECT
         JSR BANK
         .ENDM



         .PROC BANK1POKE,2

         .DEF POKE

         STA 0C089        ;WRITE-ENABLE
                          ;FIRST 4K BANK
POKE     POP RETURN
         POP VAL
         POP ADDR
         LDA VAL
         LDY #00
         STA (ADDR),Y     ;POKE VAL INTO ADDR
         STA 0C088        ;WRITE-PROTECT RAM
                          ;SELECT SECOND BANK
         PUSH RETURN
         RTS


         .PROC BANK2POKE,2

         .REF POKE

         STA 0C081        ;WRITE-ENABLE
                          ;SECOND 4K BANK
         JMP POKE


         .PROC MONITOR

         LOAD USER,03F8,03 ;CTL-Y JUMP
         ROMSELECT
         JMP MON
RET      PLA            ;REMOVE CTL-Y ADDR
         PLA
         STA 0C088  ;SWITCH ON RAM BANK1
         RTS
USER     JMP RET


         .PROC PRINTCR
         ROMSELECT
         LDA #8D      ;(RET)
         JSR COUT
         STA 0C088
         RTS
```

```
         .PROC PRINTXADDR,1

         POP RETURN
         PLA          ;GET ADDR
         TAX
         PLA
         TAY
         ROMSELECT
         JSR PRNTYX ;PRINT HEX ADDR
         LDA #0A0   ;PRINT ONE SPACE
         JSR COUT
         STA 0C088
         PUSH RETURN
         RTS


         .PROC PRINTHEXBYTE,1

         .REF BANK   ;USED BY RAMSELECT

         POP RETURN
         POP ADDR
         RAMSELECT
         LDY#00
         LDA (ADDR),Y ;GET HEX BYTE
         ROMSELECT
         JSR PRBYTE ;PRINT HEX BYTE
         LDA #0A0   ;PRINT SPACE
         JSR COUT
         STA 0C088
         PUSH RETURN
         RTS


         .PROC PRINTCHARBYTE,1

         .REF BANK

         POP RETURN
         POP ADDR
         RAMSELECT
         LDY #00
         LDA (ADDR),Y;GET CHAR BYTE
         ORA #80       ;SET HI BIT
         CMP #0A0      ;PRINT CONTROL
         BCS NORMAL    ;CHARS AS '.'
         LDA #0AE      ; '.'
NORMAL   ROMSELECT
         JSR COUT
         STA 0C088
         PUSH RETURN
         RTS


         .PROC SWITCHBANK

         .DEF BANK

         LDA BANK+1    ;CHANGE 0C088
         EOR #08       ;TO 0C080 AND
         STA BANK+1    ;VICE VERSA
         RTS
BANK     STA 0C088
         RTS


         .PROC DISASSEM

         .PUBLIC IC           ;INSTR COUNTER
         .REF INSTDSP,BANK
```

```
        LDA IC          ;TRANSFER IC
        STA PC          ;TO PC
        LDA IC+1
        STA PC+1
        ROMSELECT
        JSR INSTDSP     ;DISASM ONE INST
        JSR PCADJ       ;ADJUST PC
        STA PC
        STY PC+1
        STA IC          ;ADJUST IC
        STY IC+1
        STA 0C088       ;SWITCH BACK TO
        RTS             ;BANK1 BEFORE RET


        .PROC INITDISASSEM

        .DEF INSTDSP

        .REF BANK

        JMP BEGIN       ;SKIP COPY AREA

;COPY MAIN PART OF ROM DISASSEMBLER
;HERE IN RAM SO THAT IT CAN BE
;MODIFIED TO WORK WITH PASCAL

INSDS1  .BLOCK 0DF      ;COPY GOES HERE

BEGIN   ROMSELECT
        LOAD 0F882,INSDS1,0DF ;MAKE COPY

INSTDSP .EQU INSDS1+04E
PATCH1  .EQU INSDS1+00A
PATCH2  .EQU INSTDSP
PATCH3  .EQU INSDS1+0B0

;MAKE NECESSARY PATCHES & SET UP VIDEO

        LOAD CHANGE1,PATCH1,03
        LOAD CHANGE2,PATCH2,09
        LOAD CHANGE3,PATCH3,04
        JSR SETNORM
        JSR INIT
        JSR SETVID
        JSR SETKBD
        RAMSELECT     ;SWITCH ON LANG CARD
        RTS

CHANGE1 JSR DIS1

CHANGE2 JSR INSDS1
        PHA
        JSR DIS2
        NOP
        NOP

CHANGE3 JSR DIS3
        NOP

DIS1    RAMSELECT     ;SWITCH ON LANG CARD
        LDA (PC,X)    ;GET OPCODE BYTE
        ROMSELECT     ;SWITCH ON ROM
        TAY
        RTS

DIS2    RAMSELECT
        LDA(PC),Y
        ROMSELECT
        JMP PRBYTE

DIS3    CMP #0E8
        RAMSELECT
        LDA (PC),Y
        ROMSELECT
        RTS
```

```
;------------------------------------
;
; THE FOLLOWING EXTERNAL PROCEDURES AND
; FUNCTIONS ARE USED BY SEARCHMEMORY
;
;------------------------------------

;------------------------------------
;FUNCTION FOUND(ADDR:INTEGER; FIRST,
;               SECOND,THIRD:BYTE;
;               NOTHIRD:BOOLEAN):BOOLEAN;
;(BYTE:0..255)
;
;WRITTEN BY RON DEGROAT    15-JUN-80
;------------------------------------


         .FUNC FOUND,4

         .MACRO PULL ;PULL & STORE PARAMETER
         PLA
         STA %1
         PLA
         .ENDM

         .MACRO FIND
         LDA @SRCHADDR,Y
         CMP %1
         BNE NOMATCH
         INY            ;BUMP Y FOR NEXT BYTE
         .ENDM

THIRD    .EQU 12
SECOND   .EQU 13        ;SEQUENCE TO SEARCH FOR
FIRST    .EQU 15
NOTHIRD  .EQU 14        ;IS THERE A THIRD NO.?
SRCHADDR .EQU 16        ;SEARCH ADDR
ORIGIN   .EQU 18        ;STARTING ADDR OF SEARCH

         .PUBLIC SEARCHADDR

         POP RETURN ;PASCAL RETURN ADDR

         PLA            ;DISCARD OFFSET
         PLA
         PLA
         PLA

         PULL NOTHIRD ;GET PARAMETERS
         PULL THIRD   ;AND STORE VALUES
         PULL SECOND
         PULL FIRST

         LDA #00        ;PUSH MSB OF
         PHA            ;FUNCTION RESULT
         STA ORIGIN     ;START AT ZERO
         STA ORIGIN+1

         LDA SEARCHADDR    ;PUBLIC ADDR
         STA SRCHADDR      ;ZERO PG ADDR
         LDA SEARCHADDR+1
         STA SRCHADDR+1

LOOP     LDY #00        ;INIT Y EVERY TIME
         FIND FIRST     ;CHECK FOR MATCH
         FIND SECOND    ;ONLY IF 1ST MATCHES
         LDA NOTHIRD    ;IS THERE A 3RD?
         CMP #01
         BEQ MATCH      ;IF NOTHIRD THEN MATCH
         FIND THIRD     ;ELSE CHECK 3RD

MATCH    LDA #01        ;SET FOUND = TRUE
         CLC            ;AND GOTO END
         BCC END
```

```
NOMATCH  INC SRCHADDR  ;BUMP LSB OF SRCHADDR AND
         BNE NOBUMP    ;BRANCH IF NO CARRY

         INC SRCHADDR+1  ;BUMP MSB OF SRCHADDR

NOBUMP   LDA SRCHADDR+1  ;IF MSB OF SRCHADDR =
         CMP ORIGIN+1    ;MSB OF ORIGIN
         BNE NOTDONE
         LDA SRCHADDR    ;THEN CHECK LSB
         CMP ORIGIN
         BEQ ABORT       ;IF = THEN ABORT

NOTDONE  LDA SRCHADDR+1  ;SKIP SOFT SWITCHES
         CMP #0C0        ;FROM $C030 TO $C100
         BNE LOOP
         LDA SRCHADDR
         CMP #30
         BCC LOOP
         LDA #0C1
         STA SRCHADDR+1
         LDA #00
         STA SRCHADDR

         CLC
         BCC LOOP        ;DO IT AGAIN

ABORT    LDA #00         ;MAKE RESULT FALSE
END      PHA             ;PUSH LSB OF RESULT
         LDA SRCHADDR
         STA SEARCHADDR
         LDA SRCHADDR+1
         STA SEARCHADDR+1
         PUSH RETURN
         RTS             ;RETURN TO PASCAL HOST


         .PROC MOVEBANK2

         LDA #0D0    ;(0000) = D000
         STA 01
         LDA #20     ;(0002) = 2000
         STA 03
         LDA #00
         STA 00
         STA 02
         TAY
         TAX
         LDA 0C083   ;READ-ENABLE 2ND BANK
LOOP     LDA (00),Y  ;MOVE D000-DFFF
         STA (02),Y  ;TO 2000-2FFF
         INY
         BNE LOOP
         INC 01      ;SOURCE PAGE #
         INC 03      ;DESTINATION PAGE #
         INX
         CPX #10     ;TRANSFER SIXTEEN PAGES
         BNE LOOP
         LDA 0C088   ;WRITE-PROTECT RAM
         RTS

         .END
```

```
(****************************************)
(* LISTING #1: PASCAL MEMORY UTILITY *)
(*                                    *)
(* WRITTEN BY RON DEGROAT  15-APR-81 *)
(* SEARCH MODE ADDED       15-JUL-81 *)
(****************************************)

(*$S+*)
PROGRAM PMU;

CONST PRINTADDR=-16128;  (* $C100 *)
      COUT1=-528;        (* $FDF0 *)

TYPE MAGIC=RECORD CASE BOOLEAN OF
            TRUE: (ADDR:   INTEGER);
            FALSE:(VECTOR:^INTEGER);
           END;

     SETOFCHAR=SET OF CHAR;

     BYTE=0..255;


VAR ENDADDR,ADDR,VAL,BANK   :INTEGER;
    NUMOFCOLS,TEMP          :INTEGER;
    IC (*INST. COUNTER*)    :INTEGER;
    SEARCHADDR              :INTEGER;
    EOL,BELL,CH             :CHAR;
    ESC,BS,CR               :CHAR;
    DESET,HEXSET,PMUSET     :SETOFCHAR;
    CHRSET,OKSET            :SETOFCHAR;
    GOOD,ESCOK              :BOOLEAN;
    CSW                     :MAGIC;
    HEXADDR,HEXBYTE         :STRING;
    PSW                     :STRING[3];

PROCEDURE INITDISASSEM;                    EXTERNAL;
PROCEDURE DISASSEM; (* USES IC *)          EXTERNAL;
PROCEDURE MONITOR;                         EXTERNAL;
PROCEDURE PRINTCR;                         EXTERNAL;
PROCEDURE SWITCHBANK;                      EXTERNAL;
PROCEDURE PRINTXADDR(ADDR:INTEGER);        EXTERNAL;
PROCEDURE PRINTHEXBYTE(ADDR:INTEGER);      EXTERNAL;
PROCEDURE PRINTCHARBYTE(ADDR:INTEGER);     EXTERNAL;
PROCEDURE BANK1POKE(ADDR,VAL:INTEGER);     EXTERNAL;
PROCEDURE BANK2POKE(ADDR,VAL:INTEGER);     EXTERNAL;

PROCEDURE DOCHOICE;          FORWARD;

(* WARNING: The variable IC is public *)
(* to DISASSEM which automatically    *)
(* adjusts IC to point to the next    *)
(* instruction to be disassembled.    *)


PROCEDURE ABORT;

BEGIN
 PAGE(OUTPUT);
 ESCOK:=FALSE;
 EXIT(DOCHOICE);
END;


FUNCTION GETCHAR(OKSET:SETOFCHAR):CHAR;

VAR CH      :CHAR;
    GOOD    :BOOLEAN;

BEGIN
 REPEAT
  READ(KEYBOARD,CH);
  IF EOLN(KEYBOARD) THEN CH:=CR;
  IF (CH=ESC) AND ESCOK THEN ABORT;
  GOOD:=CH IN OKSET;
  IF NOT GOOD THEN WRITE(BELL)
   ELSE IF CH IN [' '..CHR(125)]
          THEN WRITE(CH);
 UNTIL GOOD;
 GETCHAR:=CH;
END;
```

```
PROCEDURE GETSTRING(VAR S:STRING;
    OKSET:SETOFCHAR; MAXLEN:INTEGER);

VAR S1         :STRING[1];
    STEMP      :STRING;
    LEN        :INTEGER;
    FIRSTCHAR  :BOOLEAN;
    LASTCHAR   :BOOLEAN;
    GETSET     :SETOFCHAR;

BEGIN
 S1:=' '; STEMP:='';
 REPEAT
  LEN:=LENGTH(STEMP);
  FIRSTCHAR:=(LEN=0);
  LASTCHAR:=(LEN=MAXLEN);

  IF FIRSTCHAR THEN GETSET:=OKSET
  ELSE IF LASTCHAR THEN GETSET:=[CR,BS]
       ELSE GETSET:=OKSET+[CR,BS];

  S1[1]:=GETCHAR(GETSET);

  IF S1[1] IN OKSET THEN
   STEMP:=CONCAT(STEMP,S1)
   ELSE IF S1[1]=BS THEN
    BEGIN
     WRITE(BS,' ',BS);
     DELETE(STEMP,LEN,1);
    END;
 UNTIL S1[1]=CR;
 S:=STEMP;
END; (*GETSTRING*)

PROCEDURE PROMPTAT(L:INTEGER;S:STRING);
BEGIN
 GOTOXY(0,L);
 WRITE(S,EOL);
END;

FUNCTION DEC(HEXSTR:STRING):INTEGER;

VAR DIGIT,NUM,
    STRPTR      :INTEGER;
    XDIGITS     :PACKED ARRAY[0..15] OF CHAR;

BEGIN
 NUM:=0;
 XDIGITS:='0123456789ABCDEF';
 FOR STRPTR:=1 TO LENGTH(HEXSTR) DO
  BEGIN
   DIGIT:=SCAN(16,=HEXSTR[STRPTR],XDIGITS);
   NUM:=NUM*16+DIGIT;
  END;
 DEC:=NUM;
END;


PROCEDURE GETADDR(STR:STRING);

BEGIN
  WRITELN;WRITELN;
  WRITE(STR);
  GETSTRING(HEXADDR,HEXSET,4);
  ADDR:=DEC(HEXADDR);
END;


PROCEDURE CHANGE;
BEGIN
 PROMPTAT(0,'CHANGE: <<ESC> ');
 WRITE('TO QUIT, <CR> TO SKIP)');
 GETADDR('STARTADDR ==> ');
 PAGE(OUTPUT);
 PRINTCR;  (*START PRINTING AT LEFT*)
 REPEAT
  PROMPTAT(1,'CHANGE: <<ESC> ');
  WRITE('TO QUIT, <CR> TO SKIP)');
  GOTOXY(79,0);
  IC:=ADDR;
  PRINTXADDR(ADDR);
  PRINTHEXBYTE(ADDR);
  GOTOXY(9,23);
  GETSTRING(HEXBYTE,HEXSET+[CR],2);
  GOTOXY(79,0);
  DELETE(HEXBYTE,LENGTH(HEXBYTE),1);
  IF LENGTH(HEXBYTE)<>0 THEN
    BEGIN
      VAL:=DEC(HEXBYTE);
      IF BANK=1 THEN BANK1POKE(ADDR,VAL)
                ELSE BANK2POKE(ADDR,VAL);
    END;
  PRINTHEXBYTE(ADDR);
  PRINTCR;
  ADDR:=ADDR+1;
 UNTIL FALSE;
END; (*CHANGE*)


PROCEDURE LINEOFBYTE(VAR ADDR:INTEGER);
VAR J :INTEGER;
BEGIN
 PRINTXADDR(ADDR);
 FOR J:=ADDR TO ADDR+NUMOFCOLS-1 DO
   PRINTHEXBYTE(J);
 FOR J:=ADDR TO ADDR+NUMOFCOLS-1 DO
   PRINTCHARBYTE(J);
 ADDR:=ADDR+NUMOFCOLS; (*ADJUST ADDR*)
 PRINTCR;
END;


PROCEDURE XNEXT;
VAR I :INTEGER;
BEGIN
 PRINTCR;
 FOR I:=1 TO 20 DO LINEOFBYTE(ADDR);
END;


PROCEDURE XLIST;

BEGIN
 PROMPTAT(0,'EXAMINE: LIST');
 GETADDR('STARTADDR ==> ');
 PAGE(OUTPUT);
 XNEXT;
END;


PROCEDURE XRANGE;

BEGIN
 GETADDR('STARTADDR ==> ');
 TEMP:=ADDR;
 GETADDR('ENDADDR ==> ');
 PAGE(OUTPUT);
 PRINTCR;
 ENDADDR:=ADDR;
 ADDR:=TEMP;
 WHILE ADDR<=ENDADDR DO LINEOFBYTE(ADDR);
END;
```

```
PROCEDURE BANKCHANGE;

BEGIN
  BANK:=(BANK MOD 2)+1;
  SWITCHBANK;
END;


PROCEDURE EXAMINE;

VAR CH:CHAR;

BEGIN
 REPEAT
  PROMPTAT(0,'EXAMINE: L(IST N(EXT ');
  WRITE('R(ANGE B(ANK[',BANK,'] Q(UIT');
  CH:=GETCHAR(DESET);
  PAGE(OUTPUT);
  CASE CH OF
   'L','l':XLIST;
   'N','n':XNEXT;
   'R','r':XRANGE;
   'B','b':BANKCHANGE;
  END;
 UNTIL CH='Q';
END; (*EXAMINE*)


PROCEDURE NEXT;
VAR I :INTEGER;
BEGIN
  FOR I:=1 TO 20 DO DISASSEM(* IC *);
  PRINTCR;
END;


PROCEDURE LIST;

BEGIN
 PROMPTAT(0,'DISASM: LIST');
 GETADDR('STARTADDR ==> ');
 PAGE(OUTPUT);
 IC:=ADDR;      (*IC (INSTR COUNTER)*)
 NEXT;          (*PUBLIC TO DISASSEM*)
END;


PROCEDURE RANGE;

BEGIN
  PAGE(OUTPUT);
  PROMPTAT(0,'DISASM: RANGE');
  GETADDR('STARTADDR ==> ');
  IC:=ADDR;
  GETADDR('ENDADDR ==> ');
  PAGE(OUTPUT);
  WHILE IC<=ADDR DO DISASSEM(* IC *);
  PRINTCR;
END;


PROCEDURE DISASM;

VAR CH:CHAR;

BEGIN
 REPEAT
  PROMPTAT(0,'DISASM: L(IST N(EXT ');
  WRITE('R(ANGE B(ANK[',BANK,'] Q(UIT');
  CH:=GETCHAR(DESET);
  PAGE(OUTPUT);
  CASE CH OF
   'L','l':LIST;
   'N','n':NEXT;
   'R','r':RANGE;
   'B','b':BANKCHANGE;
  END; (*CASE*)
 UNTIL CH IN ['Q','q'];
END;
```

```
PROCEDURE PRINT;

BEGIN

(*$I-*)
  UNITCLEAR(6);
  IF IORESULT<>0 THEN
   BEGIN
    PROMPTAT(3,'SORRY, NO PRINTER');
    WRITE(' ON-LINE');
    EXIT(PRINT);
   END;
(*$I+*)

  IF PSW='OFF' THEN
   BEGIN
    CSW.VECTOR^:=PRINTADDR;
    PSW:='ON';
    NUMOFCOLS:=16;
   END
  ELSE
   BEGIN
    CSW.VECTOR^:=COUT1;
    PSW:='OFF';
    NUMOFCOLS:=8;
   END;
END; (*PRINT*)


FUNCTION FOUND(FIRST,SECOND,THIRD:BYTE;
               NOTHIRD:BOOLEAN):BOOLEAN;
EXTERNAL;
PROCEDURE MOVEBANK2;
EXTERNAL;

(*******************************************)
(* SEARCH MEMORY FOR SEQUENCE OF 2 OR 3    *)
(* HEXADECIMAL OR CHARACTER VALUES         *)
(*******************************************)

PROCEDURE SEARCHMEM;

VAR FIRST,SECOND,THIRD      :BYTE;
    SFIRST,SSECOND,STHIRD  :STRING;
    SLEN,
    FOR2OR3,COLCOUNT        :INTEGER;
    NOTHIRD,
    SEQNOTFOUND,
    DONE                   :BOOLEAN;
    CH                     :CHAR;
    XADDR                  :STRING[4];


BEGIN
 NOTHIRD:=FALSE;
 THIRD:=0;
 STHIRD:='0';
 FOR2OR3:=3;

 REPEAT
 GOTOXY(0,0);
 WRITE('>SEARCH[',FOR2OR3,']: H(EX, C(HAR, Q(UIT');
 CH:=GETCHAR(['H','h','C','c','Q','q','2','3']);
 PAGE(OUTPUT);

 IF CH IN ['2','3'] THEN
  CASE CH OF
   '2':BEGIN
        NOTHIRD:=TRUE;
        FOR2OR3:=2;
       END;
   '3':BEGIN
        NOTHIRD:=FALSE;
        FOR2OR3:=3;
       END;
  END (*CASE*)
```

```
  ELSE
   IF NOT (CH IN ['Q','q']) THEN
    BEGIN

     CASE CH OF
      'H','h':BEGIN OKSET:=HEXSET; SLEN:=2; END;
      'C','c':BEGIN OKSET:=CHRSET; SLEN:=1; END;
     END; (*CASE*)

(*GET THE SEQUENCE*)

     WRITELN;
     WRITELN('LOOK FOR SEQUENCE');
     WRITE('FIRST  ==> ');
     GETSTRING(SFIRST,OKSET,SLEN);WRITELN;
     WRITE('SECOND ==> ');
     GETSTRING(SSECOND,OKSET,SLEN);WRITELN;
     IF NOTHIRD=FALSE THEN
      BEGIN
       WRITE('THIRD  ==> ');
       GETSTRING(STHIRD,OKSET,SLEN);WRITELN;
      END;

(*CONVERT TO INTEGER*)

     IF CH IN ['H','h'] THEN
      BEGIN
       FIRST  :=DEC(SFIRST);
       SECOND:=DEC(SSECOND);
       THIRD  :=DEC(STHIRD);
      END

     ELSE
      BEGIN
       FIRST  :=ORD(SFIRST[1]);
       SECOND:=ORD(SSECOND[1]);
       THIRD  :=ORD(STHIRD[1]);
      END;

     PROMPTAT(12,'NOW SEARCHING MEMORY...');WRITELN;
     WRITELN('SECOND BANK  (D000-DFFF) COPIED INTO');
     WRITE('HIRES SCREEN (2000-2FFF)');

(*ACTUAL SEARCHING PERFORMED IN EXTERNAL PROCEDURE FOUND*)

     MOVEBANK2;
     SEQNOTFOUND:=TRUE;
     SEARCHADDR:=0;            (*START SEARCH AT ZERO*)
     COLCOUNT   :=0;
     DONE:=FALSE;

     GOTOXY(0,20);
     WRITE('SEQUENCE',SFIRST:4,SSECOND:4);
     IF NOT NOTHIRD THEN
      WRITELN(STHIRD:4);

     GOTOXY(80,0); (*MOVE CURSOR OFF SCREEN*)
     PRINTCR;      (*START PRINTING AT LEFT*)

     REPEAT
      IF (FOUND(FIRST,SECOND,THIRD,NOTHIRD)) THEN
       BEGIN
        SEQNOTFOUND:=FALSE;
        PRINTXADDR(SEARCHADDR);
        SEARCHADDR:=SEARCHADDR+1;
        COLCOUNT:=(COLCOUNT+1) MOD NUMOFCOLS;
        IF (COLCOUNT=0) THEN
          IF (PSW='ON') THEN PRINTCR;
       END
      ELSE
        DONE:=TRUE;
     UNTIL DONE;

     IF SEQNOTFOUND THEN PROMPTAT(22,'NOT FOUND')
                    ELSE PRINTCR;
     WRITE(BELL);
    END;
```

```
 UNTIL CH IN ['Q','q'];
END; (*SEARCH*)


PROCEDURE DOCHOICE;

BEGIN
 PAGE(OUTPUT); ESCOK:=TRUE;
 CASE CH OF
  'D','d':DISASM;
  'E','e':EXAMINE;
  'C','c':CHANGE;
  'S','s':SEARCHMEM;
  'B','b':BANKCHANGE;
  'P','p':PRINT;
  'M','m':MONITOR;
 END;
 ESCOK:=FALSE;
END;


PROCEDURE INITIALIZE;

BEGIN
 BELL:=CHR(7);              (*CTL-G*)
 EOL:=CHR(29);              (*CTL-]*)
 ESC:=CHR(27);              (*CTL-[*)
 BS:=CHR(8);                (*CTL-H*)
 CR:=CHR(13);               (*CTL-M*)

 ESCOK:=FALSE;
 BANK:=1;
 PSW:='OFF';    (*PRINTER SWITCH*)
 NUMOFCOLS:=8;
 ADDR:=0;
 CSW.ADDR:=54; (*CHAR OUTPUT SWITCH*)

 DESET:=['L','l','N','n','R','r',
         'B','b','Q','q'];

 PMUSET:=['D','d','E','e','B','b','M','m',
          'S','s','C','c','P','p','Q','q'];

 CHRSET:=[' '..CHR(127)];

 HEXSET:=['0'..'9']+['A'..'F'];

 INITDISASSEM;

END; (*INIT*)

BEGIN (*MAIN PROGRAM*)

 INITIALIZE; (*EVERYTHING*)

 REPEAT
  PROMPTAT(0,'PMU: D(ISASM E(XAMINE ');
  WRITE('C(HANGE P(RINT[',PSW,'] M(ONITOR ');
  WRITE('S(EARCH B(ANK[',BANK,'] Q(UIT');
  CH:=GETCHAR(PMUSET);
  DOCHOICE;
 UNTIL CH IN ['Q','q'];

END.
```

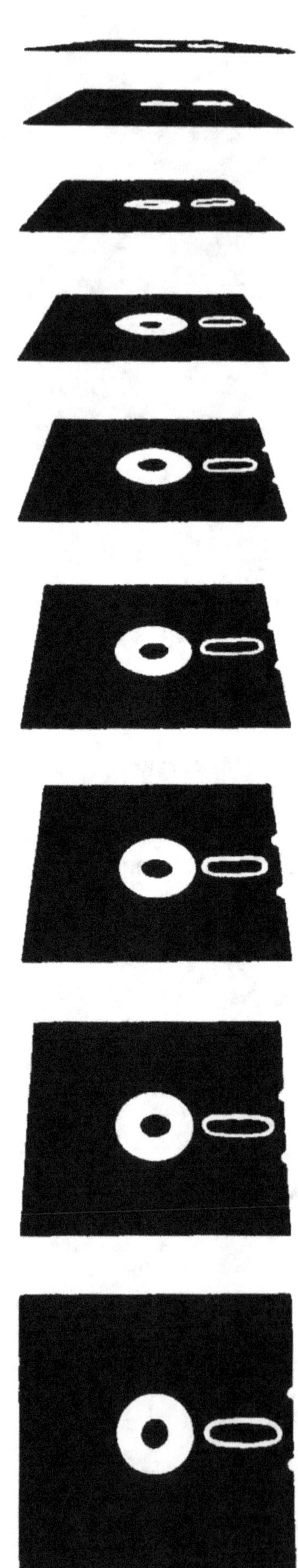

Pascal Text Recovery

William Janes

```
PROGRAM RECOVER;

(* BY W. JANES, DECEMBER 28, 1980                                        *)

(* THIS PROGRAM USES THE LOW LEVEL PROCEDURE UNITREAD TO READ FILES *)
(* WHOSE DIRECTORY HAS BEEN DESTROYED, AND IS DESIGNED MAINLY TO    *)
(* RECOVER TEXT FILES.  THE FILES SO RECOVERED MAY BE WRITTEN TO    *)
(* THE CONSOLE, PRINTER, OR A DISC FILE.  THE FILES ARE ACCESSED BY *)
(* INITIAL BLOCK NUMBER AND NUMBER OF BLOCKS TO BE READ.  NONPRINT- *)
(* ABLE CHARACTERS CAN EITHER BE SUPPRESSED OR WRITTEN AS THEIR     *)
(* ASCII VALUE IN BRACKETS.                                          *)


TYPE OUTMODE = (PRNTR, CONSL, DISC);
      INMODE  = 4..5;
      BLOCK   = PACKED ARRAY [0..511] OF CHAR;
      CHARSET = SET OF CHAR;

VAR START,STOP: INTEGER;
    AGAIN      : CHAR;
    FILTRATION: BOOLEAN;
    INDENTBYTE: BOOLEAN;
    OUTDEVICE : OUTMODE;
    INDEVICE  : INMODE;
    OUTFILE   : TEXT;
    PRINTSET  : SET OF CHAR;

FUNCTION PROMPT(S:STRING; OKSET:CHARSET):CHAR;

VAR GOOD: BOOLEAN;
      CH: CHAR;

BEGIN
  REPEAT
    WRITELN;
    WRITE(S);
    READ(CH);
    WRITELN;
    UNITCLEAR(1);
    GOOD:=CH IN OKSET;
    IF NOT GOOD THEN
      WRITE(CHR(7));
  UNTIL GOOD;
  PROMPT:=CH;
END;

PROCEDURE WRITEBLOCK(BLKNUM:INTEGER; BLOCKARRAY:BLOCK);

VAR I       :INTEGER;
    TEMP    :CHAR;
    NOSKIP  :BOOLEAN;

BEGIN
  IF OUTDEVICE <> DISC
    THEN BEGIN
          WRITELN(OUTFILE,CHR(13));
          WRITELN(OUTFILE,'BLOCKNUMBER ',BLKNUM);
          WRITELN(OUTFILE);
        END;

  FOR I:=0 TO 511 DO
    BEGIN
      TEMP:=BLOCKARRAY[I];
      IF (TEMP IN PRINTSET) AND NOT INDENTBYTE
        THEN WRITE(OUTFILE,TEMP)
        ELSE BEGIN
          IF FILTRATION
            THEN INDENTBYTE:=(TEMP=CHR(16))
            ELSE WRITE(OUTFILE,'[',ORD(TEMP),']')
        END
    END; (*I LOOP*)
```

```
  IF OUTDEVICE <> DISC
     THEN WRITELN(OUTFILE,CHR(13),'END OF BLOCKNUMBER ',BLKNUM);
END; (*WRITEBLOCK*)

PROCEDURE GETPRNTOPTION(VAR RSLT:BOOLEAN);

VAR CH: CHAR;

BEGIN
  WRITELN;
  WRITELN('THE OUTPUT PRINT OPTIONS ARE');
  WRITELN('              A)LL CHARACTERS PRINTED, USING ORD WHEN NEEDED');
  WRITELN('              F)ILTER OUT NONPRINTABLE CHARACTERS');
  CH:=PROMPT('SELECTION ? ',['A','F']);
  RSLT:=(CH='F');
END; (*GETPRINTOPTION*)

PROCEDURE INITIALIZE(VAR PRNTSET:CHARSET; VAR INDEV:INMODE;
                     VAR OUTDEV:OUTMODE; VAR FILTER:BOOLEAN);

VAR SELECTION, DEVICE: CHAR;

BEGIN
  DEVICE:=PROMPT('DISC UNIT TO BE READ (4..5)? ',['4','5']);
  IF DEVICE='4'
     THEN INDEV:=4
     ELSE INDEV:=5;
  SELECTION:=PROMPT('OUTPUT TO P)RINTER C)ONSOLE D)ISC ',
                    ['P','C','D']);
  CASE SELECTION OF
     'P':BEGIN
           PRNTSET:=[CHR(32)..CHR(127),CHR(13)];
           REWRITE(OUTFILE,'PRINTER:');
           OUTDEV:=PRNTR;
           GETPRNTOPTION(FILTER);
         END;
     'C':BEGIN
           PRNTSET:=[CHR(32)..CHR(127),CHR(13)];
           REWRITE(OUTFILE,'CONSOLE:');
           OUTDEV:=CONSL;
           GETPRNTOPTION(FILTER);
         END;
     'D':BEGIN
           PRNTSET:=[CHR(32)..CHR(127),CHR(13),CHR(16)];
           OUTDEV:=DISC;
           FILTER:=TRUE
         END
     END (*CASE*)
END; (*INITIALIZE*)

PROCEDURE PROCESSBLOCKS(FIRST,LAST:INTEGER);

VAR BLOCKNUM:INTEGER;
    BUFFER  :BLOCK;
    F       :STRING;

BEGIN
  IF OUTDEVICE = DISC
    THEN BEGIN
           WRITELN;
           WRITE('SAVE AS? ');
           READLN(F);
           F:=CONCAT(F,'.TEXT');
           REWRITE(OUTFILE,F);
         END;

   INDENTBYTE:=FALSE;  (*USED TO DELETE [INDENT] AFTER [DLE]*)

   FOR BLOCKNUM:=FIRST TO LAST DO
     BEGIN
       UNITREAD(INDEVICE,BUFFER,512,BLOCKNUM);
       WRITEBLOCK(BLOCKNUM,BUFFER);
     END; (*LOOP*)
   IF OUTDEVICE=DISC THEN CLOSE(OUTFILE,LOCK);
 END; (*PROCESSBLOCKS*)
```

```
PROCEDURE GETRANGE(VAR FIRST,LAST:INTEGER);

VAR MAX,NUM:INTEGER;

BEGIN
  WRITELN;
  WRITE('START AT BLOCK? ');
  READLN(FIRST);
  MAX:=280-FIRST;
  WRITELN;
  WRITE('NUMBER OF BLOCKS? (1..',MAX,') ');
  READLN(NUM);
  LAST:=FIRST+NUM-1;
END; (*GETRANGE*)

BEGIN (*MAIN PROGRAM*)
   INITIALIZE(PRINTSET,INDEVICE,OUTDEVICE,FILTRATION);
   REPEAT
     GETRANGE(START,STOP);
     PROCESSBLOCKS(START,STOP);
     AGAIN:=PROMPT('PROCESS ANOTHER RANGE OF BLOCKS? ',['Y','N']);
   UNTIL AGAIN = 'N';
END.
```

Call-
A.P.P.L.E.
SOFTWARE

DISK UTILITIES:

Pascal Zap

Philip B. Ender and Ron DeGroat

THIS program is an enchanced version of Pascal Zap which originally appeared in the January 1981 issue of *Call —A.P.P.L.E.* It is designed to read, modify and write any block of a 16 sector disk. When Pascal Zap is executed, the following options are displayed:

MENU OF OPTIONS

R(EAD BLOCK
W(RITE BLOCK
D(ISPLAY BUFFER
P(RINT BUFFER
A(SCII CHANGE
H(EX CHANGE
S(ET DRIVE[4]
Q(UIT

ENTER CHOICE:

The program will read and write to any disk drive the user chooses (the default is device #4, the boot drive). The options are fairly self-explanatory. From the menu, entering an "R" allows the user to read a block off the disk in the drive indicated by the S(ET DRIVE option. The block is placed in a buffer which can be displayed in hex and ASCII formats by typing "D" for D(ISPLAY BUFFER. Individual bytes in the buffer may be edited with H(EX or A(SCII CHANGEs. The changes can then be made permanent with W(RITE BLOCK.

WARNING: Pascal Zap can make irreparable changes to a disk. Be sure to make a backup copy before using this program. Pascal Zap may sometimes be helpful in file recovery (the Pascal directory begins at block two). But mostly, it's good for examining the blocks on your disk to learn more about the inner workings of Pascal.

```
PROGRAM PASCAL_ZAP;

(*****************************************************)
(*                                                   *)
(* Written by Philip B. Ender                        *)
(* Modified by Ron DeGroat      Jun 81               *)
(* Originally appeared in Jan 81 Call-A.P.P.L.E.     *)
(*                                                   *)
(*****************************************************)

CONST SP=' ';

VAR
   BUF            : PACKED ARRAY[0..511] OF 0..255;
   HEX_DIGIT      : PACKED ARRAY[0..15 ] OF CHAR;
   HEX_BYTE       : PACKED ARRAY[0..1  ] OF CHAR;
   HEX_STR        : STRING[5];
   BLK_NUM, BYTE,
   DEV_NUM, DEC,
   NUM_COLS       : INTEGER;
   CHOICE,CH      : CHAR;
   PRINTER_OFF    : BOOLEAN;
   F              : INTERACTIVE;

PROCEDURE DEC_TO_HEX_BYTE(DEC: INTEGER);
BEGIN
   HEX_BYTE[0]:=HEX_DIGIT[(DEC DIV 16)];
   HEX_BYTE[1]:=HEX_DIGIT[(DEC MOD 16)]
END;

PROCEDURE WRITE_BLOCK;
BEGIN
   WRITELN; WRITELN;
   WRITE('RESPOND YES TO WRITE TO BLOCK ',
            BLK_NUM:3,SP:2);
   READLN(CH);
   IF CH='Y' THEN
     UNITWRITE(DEV_NUM,BUF,512,BLK_NUM,0)
END;

PROCEDURE READ_BLOCK;
BEGIN
   WRITELN; WRITELN;
   WRITE('READ WHICH BLOCK?'); READLN(BLK_NUM);
   WRITELN;
   WRITE('READING BLOCK ',BLK_NUM:3);
   UNITREAD(DEV_NUM,BUF,512,BLK_NUM,0)
END;

PROCEDURE DISPLAY_BUFFER;

VAR ROW,COL: INTEGER;

BEGIN
   ROW:=0; BYTE:=0;
   REPEAT
     WRITE(F,BYTE:3,':');
     FOR COL:=0 TO NUM_COLS DO
       BEGIN
         DEC_TO_HEX_BYTE(BUF[BYTE+COL]);
         WRITE(F,HEX_BYTE:3)
       END;
     WRITE(F,SP);
     FOR COL:=0 TO NUM_COLS DO
       IF (BUF[BYTE+COL]>31) AND
          (BUF[BYTE+COL]<127)
          THEN
             WRITE(F,CHR(BUF[BYTE+COL]))
          ELSE
             WRITE(F,'.');
```

```
    WRITELN(F);
    BYTE:=BYTE+NUM_COLS+1; ROW:=ROW+1;
    IF (ROW MOD 22 = 0) AND PRINTER_OFF THEN
        BEGIN
          WRITE(F,'BLOCK ',BLK_NUM:3,
                 ': SP-CONT; E-EXIT');
          READ(KEYBOARD,CH); PAGE(F);
          IF CH='E' THEN EXIT(DISPLAY_BUFFER)
        END
  UNTIL BYTE>504;
  WRITELN(F,'BLOCK ',BLK_NUM:3);
  IF NOT PRINTER_OFF THEN GOTOXY(7,7);
  WRITE('HIT ANY KEY TO CONTINUE');
  READ(KEYBOARD,CH);
END;

PROCEDURE PRINT_BUFFER;
BEGIN
  CLOSE(F); (* CLOSE F BEFORE RESETTING *)
  RESET(F,'PRINTER:');
  NUM_COLS:=15;
  PRINTER_OFF:=FALSE;
  WRITE('PRINTING...');
  DISPLAY_BUFFER;
  PRINTER_OFF:=TRUE;
  CLOSE(F);
  RESET(F,'CONSOLE:');
  NUM_COLS:=7;
END; (*PRINT_BUFFER*)


PROCEDURE GET_BYTE;
BEGIN
  WRITE('BYTE TO BE CHANGED?');
  READLN(BYTE); WRITELN
END;

PROCEDURE ASCII_CHANGE;
BEGIN
 GET_BYTE;
 REPEAT
  IF (BUF[BYTE]>31) AND (BUF[BYTE]<127)
    THEN CH:=CHR(BUF[BYTE])
    ELSE CH:='.';
  WRITELN(BYTE:3,': ',CH,' = CHR(',BUF[BYTE],')');
  WRITE  (BYTE:3,': '); READ(CH);
  WRITELN;
  IF NOT EOLN THEN BUF[BYTE]:=ORD(CH);
  BYTE:=BYTE+1
 UNTIL EOLN
END;

PROCEDURE HEX_STR_TO_DEC;

VAR LO,HI: INTEGER;

BEGIN
  HI:=SCAN(16,=HEX_STR[1],HEX_DIGIT);
  LO:=SCAN(16,=HEX_STR[2],HEX_DIGIT);
  DEC:=HI*16+LO
END;

PROCEDURE HEX_CHANGE;

VAR LEN: INTEGER;

BEGIN
  GET_BYTE;
  REPEAT
    DEC_TO_HEX_BYTE(BUF[BYTE]);
    WRITELN(BYTE:3,': ',HEX_BYTE);
    WRITE  (BYTE:3,': ');
    READLN(HEX_STR);
    WRITELN;
    LEN:=LENGTH(HEX_STR);
    IF LEN<>0 THEN
      IF LEN>2 THEN
        WRITELN('HEX VALUE TOO LONG')
      ELSE
        BEGIN
          IF LEN=1 THEN
          HEX_STR:=CONCAT('0',HEX_STR);
          HEX_STR_TO_DEC;
          BUF[BYTE]:=DEC; BYTE:=BYTE+1
        END
   UNTIL LEN=0
END;

PROCEDURE SET_DRIVE;
BEGIN
  GOTOXY(0,8);
  WRITE('SPECIFY DRIVE (4..5, 9..12): ');
  READLN(DEV_NUM);
END;

PROCEDURE SHOWMENU;
BEGIN
  PAGE(OUTPUT);
  WRITELN; WRITELN;
  WRITELN(SP:5,'MENU OF OPTIONS');
  WRITELN;
  WRITELN(SP:5,'R(EAD BLOCK');
  WRITELN(SP:5,'W(RITE BLOCK');
  WRITELN(SP:5,'D(ISPLAY BUFFER');
  WRITELN(SP:5,'P(RINT BUFFER');
  WRITELN(SP:5,'A(SCII CHANGE');
  WRITELN(SP:5,'H(EX CHANGE');
  WRITELN(SP:5,'S(ET DRIVE[',DEV_NUM,']')
  WRITELN(SP:5,'Q(UIT');
  WRITELN; WRITELN;
  WRITE('ENTER CHOICE: ')
END;

PROCEDURE INITIALIZE;
BEGIN
  HEX_DIGIT:='0123456789ABCDEF';
  PRINTER_OFF:=TRUE;
  RESET(F,'CONSOLE:');
  NUM_COLS:=7;
  DEV_NUM:=4;
END;

BEGIN (*MAIN PROGRAM*)
  INITIALIZE;
  REPEAT
    SHOWMENU;
    READ(KEYBOARD,CHOICE);
    PAGE(OUTPUT);
    CASE CHOICE OF
      'R': READ_BLOCK;
      'W': WRITE_BLOCK;
      'D': DISPLAY_BUFFER;
      'P': PRINT_BUFFER;
      'A': ASCII_CHANGE;
      'H': HEX_CHANGE;
      'S': SET_DRIVE
    END;
  UNTIL CHOICE='Q';
  GOTOXY(8,8); WRITE('THAT''S ALL...');
END.
```

Pascal 1.1 Memory Map

Chris Wilson

THE information in the following table is grouped by major categories (such as page zero variables). Indentation is used to show the nesting of items within the various groups.

Location(s)	Meaning
0000-00FF	Page 0 interpreter & bios variables
0050/1	BASE (base procedure)
0052/3	MP (markstack pointer)
0054/5	JTAB (jump table pointer)
0056/7	SEG (segment pointer)
0058/9	IPC (interpreter program counter)
005A/B	NP (new pointer)
005C/D	KP (program stack pointer)
006E-0070	Indirect jump used by main interpreter loop (JMP @D0xx)
0071-0073	Indirect jump used by CSP instruction (JMP @D1xx)
007E	NOSPEC (from unitread/write control word)
0080	NOCRLF (from unitread/write control word)
0096-00A2	DLE expansion table used by unitread/write
00BD/E	ZEROL & ZEROH (used to clear memory at reset)
00BF/C0	JUMP1 & JUMP2 (used for control character case jump)
00C1/2	BXS1L & BXS1H
00C3/4	BXS2L & BXS2H
00C5/6	CKPTRL & CKPTRH
00D0/1	CHECKL & CHECKH
00D2	TT1
00D3	NT2
00D4	TT3
00E0	HSMODE (used by Hi-Res routines)
C0E1	HCMODE (used by Hi-Res routines)
00E2/3	ACJVAFLD (pointer to ATTACH copy of original bios jump vector)
00E4/5	RTPTR (pointer to character device read table)
00E6/7	WTPTR (pointer to character device write table)
00E8/9	UDJVP (pointer to user device jump vector)
00EA/B	DISKNUMP (pointer to disk number vector)
00EC/D	JVBFOLD (pointer to bios jump vector before fold)
00EE/F	JVAFOLD (pointer to bios jump vector after fold)
00F0/1	BAS1L & BAS1H (text screen one pointer)
00F2/3	BAS2L & BAS2H (text screen two pointer)
00F4	CH (cursor horizontal position)
00F5	CV (cursor vertical position)
00F6	TEMP1
00F7	TEMP2
00F8/9	SYSCOM (pointer to SYSCOM)
0100-01FF	Interpreter evaluation stack
0200-????	BUFFER (bios disk buffer)
03B1-03FF	Bios console type ahead buffer
0400-07FF	Apple text page one
0800-0BFF	Apple text page two
0C00-????	Heap
0C40-0C7D	INPUT file information block
0C7E-0CBB	OUTPUT file information block
0CBC-0CF9	KEYBOARD file information block
0CFA-0D35	SYSTEM.WRK.TEXT file information block (if present)
0D36-0D71	SYSTEM.WRK.CODE file information block (if present)
A988-AC99	Activation record for segment zero, procedure one of SYSTEM.PASCAL
A994/5	Pointer to SYSCOM
A996/7	Pointer to INPUT file information block
A998/9	Pointer to OUTPUT file information block
A99A/B	Pointer to KEYBOARD file information block
A9A2/3	Pointer to SYSTEM.WRK.CODE file information block
A9A4/5	Pointer to SYSTEM.WRK.TEXT file information block
A9AC/D	Student flag from MISCINFO
A9AE/F	Slow terminal flag from MISCINFO
A9B0/1	Editor escape key from MISCINFO
A9B2/3	SYSTEM.WRK.CODE present flag
A9B4/5	SYSTEM.WRK.TEXT present flag
A9B6-A9BD	SYSTEM.WRK.CODE volume id (STRING[7])
A9BE-A9C5	SYSTEM.WRK.TEXT volume id (STRING[7])
A9C6-A9CD	Permanent workfile volume id (STRING[7])
A9CE-A9DD	SYSTEM.WRK.CODE title id (STRING[15])
A9DE-A9ED	SYSTEM.WRK.TEXT title id (STRING[15])
A9EE-A9FD	Permanent workfile title id (STRING[15])
A9FE/F	Pointer to empty heap for user programs
AA02/3	Pointer to KEYBOARD file information block
AA04/5	Pointer to OUTPUT file information block

Address	Contents
AA06/7	Pointer to INPUT file information block
AA08-AA0F	Default (:) volume id (STRING[7])
AA10-AA17	System (*) volume id (STRING[7])
AA18/9	Current date (PACKED RECORD MONTH: 0..12; DAY: 0..31; YEAR: 0..100 END)
AA1E-AA6F	Command prompt line (STRING[80])
AA70-AA79	Integer powers of ten table (ARRAY [0..4] OF INTEGER)
AA7A-AA85	String of vertical-move-delay nulls from MISCINFO (STRING[11])
AA86-AA8D	Digits (SET OF "0".."9")
AA8E-AB29	Unit table (ARRAY [0..12] OF RECORD UNITVID: STRING[7]; (*Unit volume id*) CASE BLOCKED: BOOLEAN OF (*True if unit is blocked*) TRUE: (LAST-BLOCK: INTEGER) (*Last block if unit is blocked*) END)
AB2A-AB41	SYSTEM.ASSEMBLER file name (STRING[23])
AB42-AB59	SYSTEM.COMPILER file name (STRING[23])
AB5A-AB71	SYSTEM.EDITOR file name (STRING [23])
AB72-AB89	SYSTEM.FILER file name (STRING[23])
AB8A-ABA1	SYSTEM.LINKER file name (STRING [23])
ABA6-ABC5	Configuration characters from MISCINFO (SET OF CHAR)
ABC6-ABDD	Next file name from SETCHAIN in CHAINSTUFF (STRING[23])
ABDE-AC2F	Message from SETCVAL in CHAINSTUFF (STRING[80])
AC3A/B	Reading an exec file flag
AC3C/D	Writing an exec file flag
AC3E/F	System swapping flag
AC44/5	Just booted flag
AC5A-AC61	Exec file volume id (STRING[7])
AC70-AC7F	Exec file title id (STRING[15])
AC9A-BD1B	Code for segment zero, procedures 29-57 of SYSTEM. PASCAL
BD1E-BD5D	Interpreter segment usage count table
BD5E-BD9D	Interpreter segment location table
BD9E-BDDD	Interpreter segment procedure dictionary table
BDDE-BEBB	SYSCOM
BDDE/F	I/O result code
BDE0/1	Execution error code
BDE2/3	Boot unit
BDE4/5	Debugger state
BDE6/7	Pointer to last directory read in
BDE8/9	Pointer to EXEC-ERROR activation record
BDEA/B	Copy of interpreter BASE register
BDEC/D	Copy of interpreter MP register
BDEE/F	Copy of interpreter JTAB register
BDFO/1	Copy of interpreter SEG register
BDF2/3	Pointer to bottom of program stack (top of memory)
BDF4/5	Copy of IPC when an execution error occurs
BDF6/7	Breakpoint line number
BDF8-BDFF	Debugger breakpoint array (ARRAY [0..3] OF INTEGER)
BE1C-BE3D	Configuration information from MISCINFO
BE1C	Lead in to screen
BE1D	Move cursor home
BE1E	Erase to end of screen
BE1F	Erase to end of line
BE20	Move cursor right
BE21	Move cursor up
BE22	Backspace
BE23	Vertical move delay
BE24	Erase line
BE25	Erase screen
BE28/9	Screen height
BE2A/B	Screen width
BE2C	Key to move cursor up
BE2D	Key to move cursor down
BE2E	Key to move cursor left
BE2F	Key to move cursor right
BE30	Key to end file
BE31	Key for flush
BE32	Key for break
BE33	Key for stop
BE34	Key to delete character
BE35	Non printing character
BE36	Key to delete line
BE37	Editor escape key
BE38	Lead in from keyboard
BE39	Editor accept key
BE3A	Backspace
BE3E-BEFD	Segment table (ARRAY [0..31] OF RECORD UNITNUM: INTEGER; BLOCKNUM: INTEGER; CODELENG: INTEGER END)
BF00-BFFF	Interpreter & bios variables
BF0A-BF0D	CONCKVECTOR (vector to console keyboard check routine)
BF0E	SCRMODE (bit 2 set → external console)
BF0F	LFFLAG (bit 7 reset → send LFs to printer)
BF11	NLEFT (used in controlling horizontal screen scrolling)
BF12	ESCNT (count for escape sequences)
BF13/4	RANDL & RANDH (random number seed)

Address	Contents
BF15	CONFLGS (autofollow bit = 0, flush bit = 6, stop bit = 7)
BF16/7	BREAK (vector to user-break routine)
BF18	RPTR (console buffer read pointer)
BF19	WPTR (console buffer write pointer)
BF1A/B	RETL & RETH (interpreter return address on bios calls)
BF1C	SPCHAR (controls special character checking) bit 0 set → don't check for Ctrl A, Z, K, W, & E bit 1 set → don't check for Ctrl S & F
BF1D/E	IBREAK (vector to user-break routine)
BF1F/20	ISYSCOM (pointer to SYSCOM)
BF21	VERSION (02 = Apple 1.1, 00 = Apple 1.0)
BF22	FLAVOR (01 = regular system)
BF27-BF2E	SLTTYPS (slot types table)
BF2F/30	XITLOC (vector to XIT instruction)
BF56-BF7F	Used by Fortran protection
BFC0-BF7F	Available for non-Apple boot devices
C000-CFFF	Apple memory-mapped I/O
D000-DFFF	Bios code
D028	Disk write routine
D02C	Disk read routine
D683	Disk init routine
D69E	Hard reset initialization routine
D772	Console keyboard check routine
D898	Console init routine
D8C6	Console read routine
D8EF	Printer init routine
D907	Firmware card init routine
D918	Graphic init routine
D91C	Remote init routine
D923	Communications card init routine
D930	Serial card init routine
D950	Console write routine
D97B	Firmware card write routine
D98A	Serial card write routine
D99C	Remote write routine
D9A4	Printer card write routine
D9B2	Communications card write routine
D9C3	Printer write routine
D9E5	Remote read routine
D9F8	Communications card read routine
DA07	Firmware card read routine
DA15	Serial card read routine
DCA0	Remote status & printer status routines
DCB0	Console status routine
DCC5	Disk status routine
DCE4	IDSEARCH routine
DDF5-DE28	Index table by first letter for IDSEARC
DE29-DFF9	Table of identifiers for IDSEARCH
D000-F22D	Interpreter code
D000-D0FF	Main interpreter jump table
D100-D151	Call standard procedure (CSP) jump table
D253	Main interpreter loop
D25F	FJP (false jump)
D267	UJP (unconditional jump)
D296	LDCN (load constant NIL)
D29D	LDCI (load one-word constant)
D2A9	SLDL1..SLDL16 (short load local word)
D2B6	LDL (load local word)
D2D4	LLA (load local address)
D2FA	STL (store local word)
D318	SLDO1..SLDO16 (short load global word)
D325	LDO (load global word)
D343	LAO (load global address)
D369	SRO (store global word)
D387	LOD (load intermediate word)
D3AD	LDA (load intermediate address)
D3DB	STR (store intermediate word)
D401	LDE (load extended word)
D426	STE (store extended word)
D44B	LAE (load extended address)
D467	SIND1..SIND7 (short index and load word)
D46A	SIND0 (load indirect word)
D47B	STO (store indirect word)
D495	LDC (load multiple word constant)
D4C8	LDM (load multiple words)
D4F6	STM (store multiple words)
D523	LDB (load byte)
D53D	STB (store byte)
D557	MOV (move words)
D56B	LAND (logical and)
D57E	LOR (logical or)
D591	LNOT (logical not)
D59E	XJP (case jump)
D62F	NEW (CSP 1)
D66B	MARK (CSP 32)
D682	RELEASE (CSP 33)
D6A0	XIT (exit the operating system)
D6BB	ABI (absolute value of integer)
D6D9	ADI (add integers)
D6F1	NGI (negate integer)
D703	SBI (subtract integers)
D742	MPI (multiply integers)
D789	SQI (square integer)
D839	DVI (divide integers)
D866	MODI (modulo integers)
D87E	CHK (check against subrange bounds)
D8CD	LPA (load a packed array)
D8E5	LSA (load constant string address)
D907	SAS (string assign)
D948	IXS (index string array)
D96B	IND (static index and load word)
D987	INC (increment field pointer)
D99A	IXA (index array)
D9D9	IXP (index packed array)
DA1C	LDP (load a packed field)
DA72	STP (store into a packed field)
DB20	INT (set intersection)
DB57	DIF (set difference)
DB79	UNI (set union)
DBE5	ADJ (adjust set)
DC55	INN (set membership)
DCBA	SGS (build a singleton set)
DD92-DDD3	Table of masks for packed field manipulations

Address	Contents
DDD4	NEQ (not equal)
DDD8	GRT (greater than)
DDDC	LES (less than)
DDE0	GEQ (greater than or equal)
DDE4	LEQ (less than or equal)
DDE8	EQU (equal)
DF2B	LESI (integer less than)
DF2F	GRTI (integer greater than)
DF33	LEQI (integer less than or equal)
DF37	GEQI (integer greater than or equal)
DF3B	NEQI (integer not equal)
DF65	EQUI (integer equal)
E253	CIP (call intermediate procedure)
E2A1	CLP (call local procedure)
E2BD	CGP (call global procedure)
E2D4	CXP (call external procedure)
E2F9	CBP (call base procedure)
E32A	RBP (return from base procedure)
E33F	RNP (return from non-base procedure)
E417	Segment read routine
E61C	Load resident segment (CSP 21)
E626	Unload resident segment (CSP 22)
E630	CSP (call standard procedure)
E63A	IDSEARCH (CSP 7)
E640	TREESEARCH (CSP 8)
E6B2	FILLCHAR (CSP 10)
E6F7	SCAN (CSP 11)
E784	EXIT (CSP 4)
E82B	BPT (breakpoint)
E833	HALT (CSP 39)
E841	TIME (CSP 9)
E8A0	MOVELEFT (CSP 2) & MOVERIGHT (CSP 3)
E904	MEMAVAIL (CSP 40)
EAC2	ADR (add reals)
EB09	SBR (subtract reals)
EB5A	DVR (divide reals)
EC55	MPR (multiply reals)
EC7D	SQR (square real)
ECB2	ABR (absolute value of real)
ECC0	NGR (negate real)
ED3F	FLO (float next to top-of-stack)
ED62	FLT (float top-of-stack)
EDBB	ROUND (CSP 24)
EDD0	TRUNC (CSP 23)
EDE5	PWROFTEN (CSP 36)
EE0E-EEA9	Power of ten table
EEAD-EEBC	Character device write table
EEBD-EECC	Character device read table
EECD	Valid unit test
EEF9	IORESULT (CSP 34)
EF04	IOCHECK (CSP 0)
EF0F	UNITBUSY (CSP 35)
EF1D	UNITWAIT (CSP 37)
EF27	UNITSTATUS (CSP 12)
EFA5	UNITCLEAR (CSP 38)
F069	UNITREAD (CSP 5)
F06E	UNITWRITE (CSP 6)
F22E-FE7B	Code for segment zero, procedures 1-28 of SYSTEM. PASCAL
FE80-FEAF	User device jump vector
FEB0-FEC7	Disk number vector
FF00-FF41	Bios jump vector before fold
FF5C-FF9D	Bios jump vector after fold
FF5C-FF5E	Vector to console read routine
FFEF-FF61	Vector to console write routine
FF62-FF64	Vector to console init routine
FF65-FF67	Vector to printer write routine
FF68-FF6A	Vector to printer init routine
FF6B-FF6D	Vector to disk write routine
FF6E-FF70	Vector to disk read routine
FF71-FF73	Vector to disk init routine
FF74-FF76	Vector to remote read routine
FF77-FF79	Vector to remote write routine
FF7A-FF7C	Vector to remote init routine
FF7D-FF7F	Vector to graphic write routine
FF80-FF82	Vector to graphic init routine
FF83-FF85	Vector to printer read routine
FF86-FF88	Vector to console status routine
FF89-FF8B	Vector to printer status routine
FF8C-FF8E	Vector to disk status routine
FF8F-FF91	Vector to remote status routine
FF92-FF94	Vector to console keyboard check routine
FF95-FF97	Vector to routine to get an attached driver via user device jump vector
FF98-FF9A	Vector to routine to get an attached driver via disk number vector
FF9B-FF9D	Vector to IDSEARCH
FFF6/7	Version word (0 = Apple 1.1, 1 = Apple 1.0)
FFF8-FFFF	Vectors
FFF8/9	Start vector
FFFA/B	Non-maskable interrupt vector
FFFC/D	Reset vector
FFFE/F	Interrupt request & BRK vector

Pascal Internals

Mike Rosing and Keith McLauren

INTRODUCTION

THE USCD Pascal system used and modified by Apple Computer Inc. for the Apple II is a very sophisticated level of programming for the 6502 microcomputer. Unfortunately, using Pascal and machine language is not as simple as using BASIC and machine language on the Apple II.

The following information was found by trial and error. It is hoped that those computer fanatics who enjoy understanding their machines will correct errors found in this article.

Pascal is far too complex for any one individual to attempt to figure out in his spare time. The following information is certainly useful to machine language programmers who wish to have more control over their Pascal operating system.

Part one is an explanation of the Pascal booting process. It is by no means trivial. One can learn a lot about the Apple II just by following a boot from disk.

Part two is a detailed explanation of how to use the Pascal disk I/O routines.

Part three contains an explanation of the Pascal directory. This is useful for saving programs after I/O done as in part 2.

Part four is a simple explanation of how the 6502 machine code is used to understand p-code. The locations of each p-code are given in subsequent tables.

Part five is a description of how Pascal floats in memory. The differences between the manuals and actual implementation are noted.

Appendix one contains locations of pseudo-machine registers. One must have some manuals which explain what these mean. The manuals come with the Apple Pascal language card system.

For those seriously interested in the Apple Pascal it is a good idea to get hold of BIOS — the Basic Input/Output Subroutines which is pubished by Apple. The latest version is called SYSTEM.ATTACH and is available from International Apple Core, 910-A George St., Santa Clara, CA 95050 for $7.50.

Throughout this article, the "new" version is version 1.1 and the "old" version is the original Apple Pascal.

BOOT PROCESS

The Apple Pascal boot process is a 4-stage process. This is because part of the boot is done in Pascal. For comparison, read the March/April 1980 Apple Orchard: "Apple DOS Booting Process" by Ted Burns. The first stage is in ROM, so obviously it is exactly the same. The second stage boot loads SYSTEM.PASCAL into the 16K language card. The third stage boot folds in BIOS, and sets up initial p-code pointers. The third stage brings in Pascal code over itself, and does the fourth stage in p-code.

Upon disassembling blocks 0 and 1, you will find the following code:

```
08A9 6C F8 FF JMP @FFF8
```

Here 08A9 is the location in memory (hexadecimal), 6C F8 FF is the machine code, and JMP @FFF8 is the interpretation of the code in human terms. The syntax is as described in the Apple Pascal manuals under the assembler.

The jump begins the third stage boot process. The location pointed to is FEE9 (new version), or FF65 (old version). This location folds in BIOS, and sets the language card up with the Pascal operating system.

The third stage boot is written in machine code. It brings in the fourth stage, which is written in Pascal. In the new version, this fourth stage overwrites the third stage boot. The old version left the third stage in memory so that warm restarts were possible. The new version can only do cold restarts, since the third stage initializes important pointers.

The fourth stage is written in Pascal and has no name in the SYSTEM.PASCAL file. It is segment number 15 in SYSTEM.PASCAL.

The following is a detailed description of the boot process. It may or may not be accurate, so check it out for yourself!

1) Autostart ROM jumps to C600 ROM, reads track zero, sector 0 into $800.

2) Jumps to $801 and loads rest of second stage boot.

3) Looks for SYSTEM.APPLE in block 2 (start of directory). If not there puts message NO FILE SYSTEM. APPLE on screen and does

```
0869 F0 FE BEQ 869
```

which is a very nice infinite loop!

4) Finds SYSTEM.APPLE in directory. Write enables RAM. Loads BIOS in second 4K bank and E000 thru FFFF. Switches in first 4K bank and writes in p-code interpreter. See Apple language card owners manual for explanation of bank switching.

5) Read/write enables language card, selects second 4K bank, and jumps to BIOS Reset location D69E (new), D5DD (old).

6) Clears all memory from 0 to BFFF.

7) Checks all slots for ROMs. Puts result in location BF27 (new), or BFF8 (old). The codes are:

0 no ROM
1 unrecognizable ROM
2 disk card
3 com card
4 serial card

5 printer
6 Smart term 80 column board (new version only)

Lcoation + slot number gives code.
EXAMPLE:

BF2D = 02 new version
BFFE = 02 old version

8) Clears screen, puts cursor on screen and initializes external consoles. Initializes disk and external consoles. Minor additions to new version.

9) Jumps to F275 (new), EF3F (old). New version moves F275 - F675 to 6800 - 6C00. This is the part which is overwritten.

10) Clears stack. New version sets reset vector to D6A0. Sets syscom to BDDE. Clears BDDE - BEFE (new), BDDE - BEDE (old). Does useless disk check for unit #4.

11) Reads directory into location $6000. Looks for SYSTEM. PASCAL 78 times. If not found, does console init and outputs:

nothing (old)
Insert boot disk with SYSTEM. PASCAL on it, then press RESET (new)

New version changes reset vectors. Both versions then do

D0 FE BNE 696E new
D0 FE BNE EF94 old

and waits for reset very patiently. After reset does jump to top of BIOS (step 5) and repeats the whole thing.

12) Finds SYSTEM.PASCAL in directory. Gets block 0 of SYSTEM. PASCAL and reads it into location $6000.

13) Reads unnamed file of length $1082 into locations AC9A to BD1B (new), or length $1258 into ABC3-BD1B (old). This is segment number F.

14) Gets SYSTEM.PASCAL segment #0 and loads it into F22E thru FE7C (new), or F104 - FEFC (old).

15) Creates first activation record for PASCALSY (segment #0) and points IPC to F22E (new) F104 (old).

16) Puts p-code jump instructions in 6E - 73.

17) Jumps to p-code decoder D253 (new), D243 (old).

18) Fourth stage boot is PASCALSY. From here on is p-code.

HOW TO USE DISK I/O

The old version requires 8 elements pushed on the system stack before a disk read/write takes place. The new version requires 10 elements.

There are two ways of getting to the disk I/O routines. The first is to use the jumps suggested by Apple in their BIOS. This way, the user's program will run on both the old and new versions with just a couple of extra pushes on the stack. The second method is to switch in the 4K bank of BIOS, and jump directly to the disk I/O routines.

The items which must be pushed on the system stack are: unit number, block number, buffer area, number of sectors or bytes to read/write, and stack marker. In the old version there is only one stack marker; the new version has three.

The order of parameters on the stack is:

1) stack marker(s)
   1 for old
   3 for new
2) unit number
3) buffer area
   high byte
   low byte
4) number of bytes
   high byte
   low byte
5) block number on disk
   high byte
   low byte

Example for saving a photofile on disk:

```
            .PROC SAVEFOTO
            JMP START
;Fotofl is the start of hires page 1
;Lngth is the length in bytes of the
;file to be saved
;Unit is pointing to drive 4
;Blknm is pointing to block 6, at least
;8 blocks needed to hold 8K of memory

 FOTOFL     .WORD   02000
 LNGTH      .WORD   01FFF
 UNIT       .BYTE   00
 BLKNM      .WORD   0006

 START      LDA     #00         ;Push stack
            PHA                 ;markers
            PHA                 ;for new
            PHA                 ;version
            LDA     UNIT        ;Drive to
            PHA                 ;write on
            LDA     FOTOFL+1    ;High byte
            PHA                 ;first
            LDA     FOTOFL      ;of buffer
            PHA                 ;location
            LDA     LNGTH+1     ;Same with
            PHA                 ;size of
            LDA     LNGTH       ;buffer
            PHA
            LDA     BLKNM+1     ;Put on
            PHA                 ;disk at
            LDA     BLKNM       ;safe
            PHA                 ;location
            JSR     0FF0F       ;I/O call
            RTS                 ;back to  Pascal
```

Alternatively one can push all the above on the stack and do

LDA 0C083 ;switch in BIOS
JSR 0D028 ;new version
LDA 0C08B ;fold back p-code

The location is D038 in the old version.

The same information is pushed for a disk read. The JSR's go to slightly different locations. Remember that the directory has not been changed when you do this, so don't be surprised if Pascal overwrites anything done this way. See the next section for information on the Pascal directory.

Disk read FF12,D02C new
Disk write FF0F,D028
Disk read FF12,D03C old
Disk write FF0F,D038

The D0XX locations are on the second 4K bank page. The FFXX locations will switch in the second 4K bank, do the disk I/O, and switch in the first 4K bank automatically.

The PASCAL Directory

UCSD Pascal uses a block structure for the disk, while BASIC uses a track/sector approach. The discs used by DOS 3.3 are of a 16 sector format which is compatible with Pascal with a few constraints. The two different languages share the same media format, and disks created on one system can be read by the other. A useful BASIC and machine language (assembly) program from DOS 3.3 is the COPY program. It will copy Pascal disks with one or two drives, and one does not need a formatted disk. Also, some of the BASIC utility programs for the disk will work on Pascal disks.

The major problem in using RWTS on Apple Pascal disks is understanding or calculating the track and sector address for a particular block. The track is obtained by dividing by eight and the sector from a lookup table (see sector assignment for Apple Pascal).

The directory is of particular interest, since one may be able to salvage programs and data from crashed disks or whatever. First, some very general information. The disk consists of 35 tracks with 16 sectors in each track. In Pascal, these sectors are grouped in two's to form blocks.

Table one

Decimal	Hex	Mnemonic	Location old	Location new
128	80	ABI	D698	D6BB
129	81	ABR	EAF2	ECB2
130	82	ADI	D6B6	D6D9
131	83	ADR	E902	EAC2
132	84	AND	D548	D56B
133	85	DIF	DB2C	DB57
134	86	DVI	D815	D839
135	87	DVR	E99A	EB5A
136	88	CHK	D85A	D87E
137	89	FLO	EB6F	ED3F
138	8A	FLT	EB92	ED62
139	8B	INN	DC2A	DC55
140	8C	INT	DAF5	DB20
141	8D	IOR	D55B	D57E
142	8E	MOD	D842	D866
143	8F	MPI	D71F	D742
144	90	MPR	EA95	EC55
145	91	NGI	D6CE	D6F1
146	92	NGR	EB00	ECC0
147	93	NOT	D56E	D591
148	94	SRS	DCA1	DCCC
149	95	SBI	D6E0	D703
150	96	SBR	E949	EB09
151	97	SGS	DC8F	DCBA
152	98	SQI	D766	D789
153	99	SQR	EABD	EC7D
154	9A	STO	D46B	D47B
155	9B	IXS	D924	D948
156	9C	UNI	DB4E	DB79
157	9D	S2P	D3F1	D401
158	9E	CSP	E5B1	E630
159	9F	LDCN	D286	D296
160	A0	ADJ	DBBA	DBE5
161	A1	FJP	D24F	D25F
162	A2	INC	D963	D987
163	A3	IND	D947	D96B
164	A4	IXA	D976	D99A
165	A5	LAO	D333	D343
166	A6	LSA	D8C1	D8E5
167	A7	LAE	D43B	D44B
168	A8	MOV	D534	D557
169	A9	LDO	D315	D325
170	AA	SAS	D8E3	D907
171	AB	SRO	D359	D369
172	AC	XJP	D57B	D59E
173	AD	RNP	E2FC	E33F
174	AE	CIP	E210	E253
175	AF	EQU	DDBD	DDE8
176	B0	GEQ	DDB5	DDE0
177	B1	GRT	DDAD	DDD8
178	B2	LDA	D39D	D3AD

Table one (continued)

Decimal	Hex	Mnemonic	Location old	Location new
179	B3	LDC	D485	D495
180	B4	LEQ	DDB9	DDE4
181	B5	LES	DDB1	DDDC
182	B6	LOD	D377	D387
183	B7	NEQ	DDA9	DDD4
184	B8	STR	D3CB	D3DB
185	B9	UJP	D257	D267
186	BA	LDP	D958	DA1C
187	BB	STP	DA4E	DA72
188	BC	LDM	D4B8	D4C8
189	BD	STM	D4D3	D4F6
190	BE	LDB	D500	D523
191	BF	STB	D51A	D53D
192	C0	IXP	D9B5	D9D9
193	C1	RBP	E2E7	E32A
194	C2	CBP	E2B6	E2F9
195	C3	EQUI	DF3A	DF65
196	C4	GEQI	DF0C	DF37
197	C5	GRTI	DF04	DF2F
198	C6	LLA	D2C4	D2D4
199	C7	LDCI	D28D	D29D
200	C8	LEQI	DF08	DF33
201	C9	LESI	DF00	DF2B
202	CA	LDL	D2A6	D2B6
203	CB	NEQI	DF10	DF3B
204	CC	STL	D2EA	D2FA
205	CD	CXP	E291	E2D4
206	CE	CLP	E25E	E2A1
207	CF	CGP	E27A	E2BD
208	D0	LPA	D8A9	D8CD
209	D1	STE	D416	D426
210	D2	NOP	D23D	D24D
211	D3	EFJ	D212	D1EF
212	D4	NFJ	D212	D1EF
213	D5	BPT	E67E	E82B
214	D6	XIT	D67D	D6A0
215	D7	NOP	D23D	D24D
216	D8	SLDL1		
:	:	:	D299	D2A9
231	E7	SLDL16		
232	E8	SLDO1		
:	:	:	D308	D318
247	F7	SLDO16		
248	F8	SINDO	D45A	D46A
249	F9	SIND1		
:	:	:	D457	D467
255	FF	SIND7		

Examination of the directory from BASIC reveals some information that may be useful in aiding salvage of crashed information. The directory starts in track 0, sector 11 and extends downward. Useful space is available in sectors 11 thru 2 (blocks 1 thru 5). Sectors 0, 14, 13 and 12 are reserved by the operating system for booting, which is only important for the disks containing SYSTEM.APPLE. The remaining blocks 6 and 7 are used by Pascal for file storage. The sequence of sectors or the sector numbers used by Pascal is almost sequential in a descending manner with minor corrections for blocks 0 and 7 or the first and last block on each track. Each track for Apple Pascal is composed of 8 blocks with the sector numbers as shown in the table of block to sector numbers applied to each block. This pattern repeats for each track on the disk.

Starting with block 2 or track 0 sector 11, the directory contains as its first entry the disk name and date.

Entries are added sequentially, following the disk name. In all names of files or disks, the character string is preceeded by a hexadecimal number representing its length. Dates are encoded in two bytes (20 and 21 for the current date used by the filer); from the start of each directory entry, bytes 25 and 26 contain the creation date for the program. The date is composed of 16 bits of data, by connecting byte 26 and 25 together. The year is formed from bits 7-1 of 26, and the day of the month from bit 0 of byte 26 and bits 7-4 of byte 25. The month is contained in bits 3-0 of byte 25. All the date information is encoded in binary numbers, with the months appearing as 0..12. Bytes 1 and 2 of each directory entry contain the block start number, and bytes 3 and 4 contain the block end number. Bytes 5 and 6 represent the file type as 2,3, and 5, which represent code, text, and data files respectively. The 7th byte contains the name string length, and the name string is in the following 15 bytes. Bytes 23 and 24 contain the number of bytes used in the last block of a file. These are followed by the file date in bytes 25 and 26, as explained previously. In all of the pairs of bytes, including the date code, the arrangement is least significant byte first and most significant byte last. (A "5" would appear as 05 00.) The first directory entry starts with byte 26 and contains 26 bytes of information. The next 26-byte group contains the 2nd directory entry and so on.

Files are removed by decreasing the number of active files and compressing the directory. If the file is removed from the end of the list then the directory cannot be compressed further and only the number of files is updated. It is possible to resurrect files in Pascal if they were at the end of the directory and the information on the disk has not been altered. The recovery of deleted files in Pascal is not always so simple when the entry is not the last one on the disk. The information pertaining to the location of the file on the disk is lost and must deducted from an extended directory listing or by direct examination of the blocks on the disk.

PASCAL DISK DIRECTORY STRUCTURE

BYTE #

0-25	Disk volume name and related information
26-51	First file entry
52-77	Second file entry
MOD 26	Subsequent files

DISK VOLUME

1,0	Start of directory
3,2	End of directory blocknumber
5,4	? always zero ?
6	Length of disk volume name
7-13	Disk volume name string
15,14	Number of blocks on disk
17,16	? always zero ?
19,18	? always zero ?
21,20	Current date as used by the Pascal system
23,22	? always zero?
25,26	? always zero?

INDIVIDUAL FILES

BYTE #

1,0	Block start number
3,2	Block end number
5,4	File type 2 = Code, 3 = Text, 5 = Data
6	Length of file name (15 maximum)
7-21	Filename string
23,22	number of bytes in last block
25,24	File date

FILE DATE

BYTE 25	BYTE 24	
(7654321)	(07654)	(3210)
Year	Day	Month
0..99	0..31	1..12

The directory structure can also be expressed as a Pascal Type using the record construct. The Pascal type construct on the following page illustrates the directory structure. A file indexing or Master Catalog program uses this information to catalog all of your Pascal disks (see BYTE May 1981).

HOW P-CODE INTERPRETER WORKS

The following is our interpretation of how the Pascal p-codes are executed by the 6502. I admire the people who wrote this code. It is very efficient and very compact.

The top line is D243 for the old version, and D253 for the new version.

```
LDY #00
LDA @58,Y ;get p-code
BPL PUSH  ;if no p-code
          ;push word on
          ;stack
ASL A     ;code times 2
STA 6F    ;alter indirect
          ;jump
JMP 006E  ;go to jump
```

Locations 58 and 59 are the IPC or Interpreter Program Counter. This is a pointer to the current byte of code to be worked on. If the number is less than 7F, it and the following byte are pushed on the system stack. If the number is $80 or greater, then this is multiplied by 2. This is because two bytes are required to created a 16-bit pointer. The result is stored in location 6F, which is the low byte of an indirect jump command. This jump command is reserved on zero page as

```
006E 6C XX D0 JMP @D0XX
```

where XX is the low byte of the instruction, and D0 is the page of the lookup table. Thus the p-code is just an index into a lookup table which interprets each p-code. It takes 24 microseconds for the 6502 to do it!

Table 1 lists the p-codes and where they reside in memory. For an explanation of p-code, see your Apple or UCSD manuals.

In addition to these op codes, there are additional special procedures (CSP =9E). These are listed in the second table. There are quite a few with no names. The new version has one new one — 9E 0C. I leave it to the reader to discover what it does!

SECTOR ASSIGNMENT FOR APPLE PASCAL

	BLOCK NUMBER	SECTOR NUMBERS
	0	0 , 14
	1	13 , 12
	2	11 , 10
	3	9 , 8
	4	7 , 6
	5	5 , 4
	6	3 , 2
	7	1 , 15
next track)	8	0 , 14

(repeat above 34 times)

```
type    date_record = packed record                  (*pack into 16 bits*)
                          month:1..12;               (*four bits for month*)
                          day:1..31;                 (*five bits for day*)
                          year: 0..99                (*seven bits for year*)
        end;
        vol_id = string[7]                  (*the disk name e.g. APPLE3*)
        file_id = string[15];               (*the file name in the directory*)
        (*the file types are expressed as an enumerated list of the 9 UCSD file types. Apple Pascal supports al
        but the info,graf,foto and secure directory file types. The filer recognizes all of the types and the use
        may implement his own info, foto and graf files. But do not expect future implementations from Appl
        to be compatible with your creation (e.g. the FOTO file example).*)
        file_type = (untyped,badblk,code,text,info,data,graf,foto,securedir);
        (*the actual directory record begins here and uses the above constructs for easier reading*)
        dir_record = record
                  first_block: integer;
                  last_block: integer;
        (*the two different directory parts are handled by a case statement*)
                  case dir_file_kind:file_type of
                    securedir,untyped: :     (*first case*)
                      (dir_vol_name:vol_id;
                       zero_block,num_of_files,total_blocks:integer;
                       last_boot:date_record);
                    badblk,code,text,info,data,graf,foto: (*second case*)
                      (dir_file_name:file_id;
                       lastbyte:1..512;
                       dir_file_date:date_record)
        end;
```

PASCAL STRUCTURE

After reading the Apple manuals on the USCD Pascal system about ten times I was left totally confused and completely lost. By following the machine code step by step however, the manuals now make sense and the major confusions are differences between UCSD and Apple implementations.

On page ?? is a picture of the Pascal memory for an arbitrary program. The major sections of a program are 1) SEGMENT DISK DICTIONARY and 2) the SEGMENT PROCEDURE DICTIONARY. The Segment Disk Dictionary is located in BE3E-BE6D and contains the drive, block-number and length of each segment of a program. The Segment Procedure Dictionary is located in BD9E-BDBD and contains self relative pointers to each segment's procedure dictionary table.

Why is this important? When a procedure is called via p-code, the pascal operating system has to find the specified procedure. It first checks the Invocation Table located in BD1E-BD3D to see if the desired segment is in memory. If not it goes to the Segment Disk Dictionary to find the segment on disk and load it into memory. If it is already in memory the Pascal operating system looks in the Segment Procedure Dictionary to find the Procedure Dictionary of the required segment.

The Procedure Dictionary in turn gives self-relative pointers to the Markstack of each procedure. The use of self-relative pointers gives Pascal its flexibility. The Procedure Dictionary structure contains the number of procedures in the dictionary, the segment number and the word list of self-relative pointers to all the procedures of a segment. This is in fact accurately described in the Apple manuals.

Each procedure has an associated JTAB or Jump Table. Here the manuals disagree with what one finds in memory. To the right is a more accurate description of Apple Pascal:

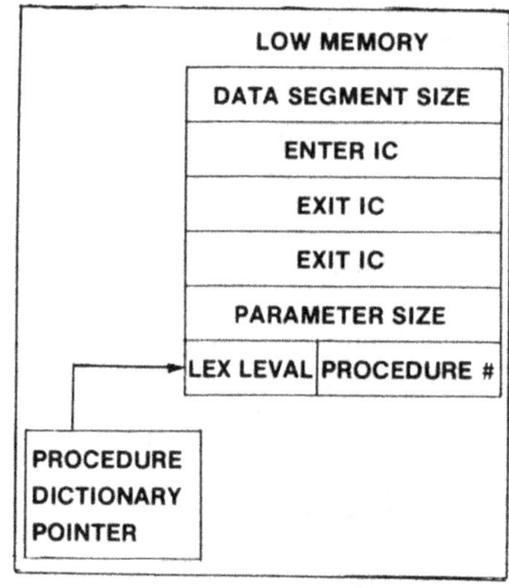

The enter and exit interpreter counters (IC) are self-relative pointers to the beginning and end of code respectively. The parameter size must be less than 255 but the data segment size is unlimited.

For an example of why all this is useful we will follow a single p-code instruction which calls a procedure.

Table 2 Special procedures
[all are preceded with 9E (CSP)]

Decimal	Hex	Mnemonic	Location old	Location new
0	0		ED26	EF04
1	1	NEW	D60C	D62F
2	2	MVL	E6F3	E8A0
3	3	MVR	E6F3	E8A0
4	4	EXIT	E5D9	E784
5	5		EDD9	F069
6	6		EDDE	F06E
7	7	IDS	E5BB	E63A
8	8	TRS	E5CD	E640
9	9	TIM	E694	E841
10	A	FLC	E5C1	E6B2
11	B	SCN	E5C7	E6F7
12	C		----	EF27
13	D			
:	:	UNUSED	----	----
20	14			
21	15		E59D	E61C
22	16	TNC	E5A7	E626
23	17	RND	EC00	EDD0
24	18	SIN	EBEB	EDBB
25	19			
:	:	MATH	D212	D1EF
31	1F			
32	20	MRK	D648	D66B
33	21	RLS	D65F	D682
34	22		ED1B	EEF9
35	23	POT	ED31	EF0F
36	24		EC15	EDE5
37	25		ED3F	EF1D
38	26		ED49	EFA5
39	27		E686	E833
40	28		E757	E904

The simplest example is CLP #P or Call Local Procedure #P. The instruction first saves P in zero page location 78. It then enters the BUILD AN ACTIVATION RECORD subroutine (E0A1 external procedures or E0BC local procedures).

This subroutine is probably the most important to Pascal because it sets up the Markstack for each called procedure. Since Pascal is written in itself every procedure calls another procedure until some base intrinsic is executed in machine code.

parameters,and jump table on the Base and then pointing the new Base to the bottom of the new pile. If the pile exceeds the top of heap then a STACK OVERFLOW error occurs.

The code which does all this takes slightly less than one block. Following it gives one an appreciation for the power of Pascal.

Another important subroutine is the Invocation Counter. This is located at E4A5. If a new segment is called and it has never been invoked before then this subroutine reads it in from disk and looks for the lex leval zero, procedure zero of the segment. If not there it could get stuck in an infinite loop, but then the segment is fairly useless anyway.

If the segment has already been invoked the Invocation Table is bumped by one for that segment to show that it is still in use and the level to which it is in use.

Appendix one gives a list of the zero page pointers and tables used by Pascal as understood so far. Because of the complexity of Pascal one is advised that these may not be entirely accurate so be careful when playing around with the Markstack!

Appendix One

Useful Pascal Locations

The following locations seem to fit in the description given of them in the Apple Pascal manuals. They are valid for both old and new versions.

Location	Meaning
BDDE-BDFF	SYSCOM
BDDE,BDDF	IORESULT
BDE0,BDE1	XEQERR
BDE2	SYSUNIT
BDE3	BUGSTATE
BDE4,BDE5	GDIRP
BDEA,BDEB	STKBASE
BDEC,BDED	LASTMP
BDEE,BDEF	JTAB
BDF0,BDF1	SEG
BDF2,BDF3	BOMBP
BDF4,BDF5	BOMIPC
BDF6,BDF7	HLTLN
BDF8-BDFF	BRKPTS

ZERO page pointers

50,51	Pointer to BASE activation record
52,53	Mark Stack pointer
54,55	JTAB Pointer
56,57	SEG pointer
58,59	IPC
5A,5B	Pascal stack pointer
5C,5D	Pointer to BASE-2
5E,5F	Word offset from stack
64,65	Duplicate of 50,51
6E-70	Jump table for p-codes
71-73	Jump table for special ops
74,75	temporary
78	procedure number for building activation record
7E,7F	MARKSTACK
80,81	disk buffer
86	segment number for activation record
8E,8F	return address storage
90,91	Pascal System
D0,DF	Disk temps

There is a lot more to zero page than this. Happy hunting!

BE3E-BE9D Code file buffer has the form drive blk# lnth

Where drive is the unit on which to find the segment, blk# is the block number on the disk where the segment starts, and lnth is the length of the segment. This is an array of 16 x 3 words, which is created after reading the first block of a code file. Each group of words is for one of the 16 possible segments in the file.

BD1E-BD5D Invocation count table

The invocation count tells the operating system how many times a particular segment has been called. There are two bytes for each segment so one can call a segment over 65,000 times before problems arise.

BD5E-BD9D Another file
BD9E-BDBD Segment Procedure Dictionary Table

The Segment Procedure Dictionary Table tells the operating system where each segment's Procedure Dictionary is to be found.

The above buffers are used in the segment read routine (E417 new, E3D7 old), which reads a specified segment (0-F) which has been stored in BE3E-BE9D.

Pages 2 and 3 ($200-$3FF) are used by disk I/O for error checking. Anything left there will be clobbered after a disk read or write.

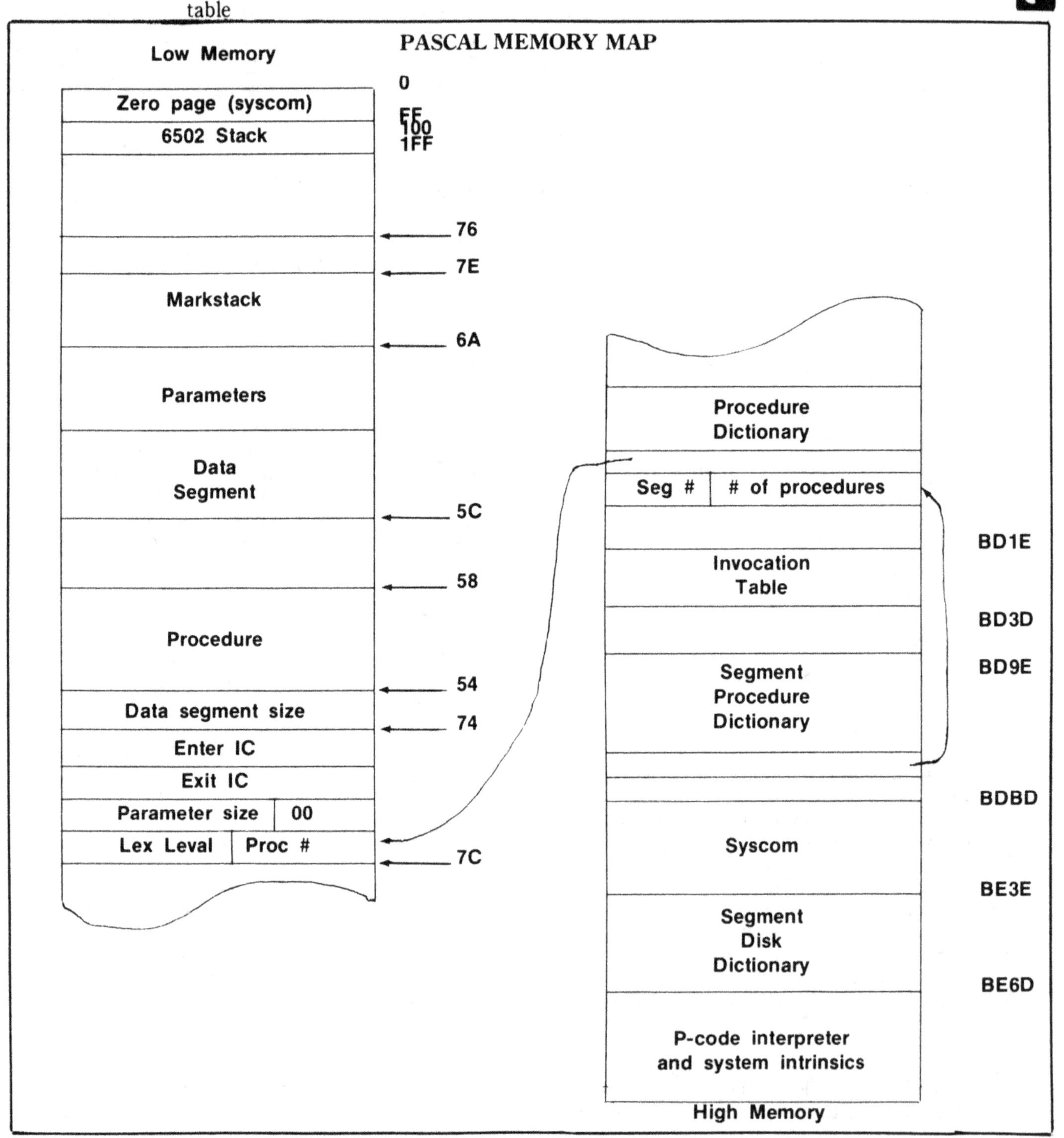

Pascal Bibliography

Compiled by David Paul McCarthy

A Bibliography of Pascal articles of general interest for and by the Adam & Eve Apple Users' Group Madison Wi. 53703

ACKERMAN, ROBERT. "LANGUAGE COMPARISON." CIDER PRESS, MAY 1980, p. 7. a speed comparison of his game of Mastermind in Integer (8 minutes), in Pascal (2 minutes), in Forth (1 minute), and in Assembly (1 second).

AHL, DAVID H. "PASCAL, ADA AND COMPUTER LITERACY." CREATIVE COMPUTING, NOVEMBER 1981, pp. 116 – 122 [4 pp.]. an interview with Art Luehrmann, writer, philosopher, and Renaissance man of the computer age.

ALLISON, DENNIS. "ALGORITHM (APR80)." DR. DOBB'S, APRIL 1980, pp. 44-45. a column...

AMROMIN, JOEL L. "PASCAL LINEFEED MOD FOR AIO, ETC." THE APPLE SHOPPE, MAY/JUNE 1980, pp. 23-24. with a program to modify the BIOS modules.

ANDERSON, ROBERT V. "PEACEFUL COEXISTENCE." NIBBLE, VOL. 3, NO. 2 1982, pp. 65-67 [2 pp.]. this program creates a diskette on which it is possible to save both DOS 3.3 and Pascal files.

ANDREWS, LAWRENCE C. "PASCAL VERSUS BASIC: ROUND 2 INCLUDES FORTRAN." BYTE, APRIL 1979, p. 239. a letter in answer to Schwartz's article.

ANSON, CHRISTOPHER p. "TRIX TO PEEK AND POKE IN PASCAL." CALL -A.P.P.L.E., JUI Y/AUGUST 1980, pp. 28-29. this program permits the examining of memory without an Assembly linkage.

APPLE CORPORATION. "THE PRELIMINARY APPLE PASCAL GUIDE TO INTERFACING FOREIGN HARDWARE." DECEMBER 10, 1979, pp. 1-30. gives the listing of the BIOS.

APPLE CORPORATION. "PASCAL II: AN APPLICATION AT UNIVERSITY OF CALIFORNIA, SAN DIEGO." APPLE EDUCATION NEWS, MAY 1980, pp. 4,9. a promo for Apple-Pascal.

APPLE CORPORATION. "SET 1100 BAUD." 1980. a procedure that sets the communications card to 1100 baud.

APPLE CORPORATION. "PROGRAM" this second part focuses on the streamlined version of TI Pascal.

APPLE CORPORATION. "PROGRAM FORTFIX." CALL -A.P.P.L.E., JUNE 1981, pp. 39-41. "user defined Pascal intrinsic units will not work with FORTRAN, nor will built-in Pascal intrinsic units work all of the time with FORTRAN, unless the following post-processor is applied to the code files."

ARCHER, ROWLAND. "PASCAL-80." BYTE, DECEMBER 1981, pp. 304-312 [6 pp.]. a description of FMG Corporations's version of UCSD Pascal for the TRS-80 computer

ARONSON, MIKE. "A REVIEW OF 'PROBLEM SOLVING AND STRUCTURED PROGRAMMING IN PASCAL' BY ELLIOT B. KOFFMAN." MICROCOMPUTING, JUNE 1982, pp. 154-155. 'Koffman's book is a good place to begin because of the emphasis on problem analysis and the large number (over 30) of complete example program.'

ASHKENAZI, DAVID. "HARDWARE COMES TO THE AID OF MODULAR HIGH-LEVEL LANGUAGES." ELECTRONICS, APRIL 21, 1981, pp. 175-177. "by defining a clean interface between separately compiled modules, 16-bit microprocessor architecture supports languages like Ada and Pascal."

BAKER, ROBERT. "PETPOURRI: KMMM PASCAL." MICROCOMPUTING, OCTOBER 1981, pp. 10-12 [2 pp.]. shares comments on KMMM Pascal for the Pet.

BARRUS, SCOTT. "APPLE PASCAL LISTER." COMPUTE!, JUNE 1982, pp. 116-118. the Pascal program puts headers and page numbers on listings.

BATE, ROGER R. AND JOHNSON, DOUGLAS S. "LANGUAGE EXTENSIONS, UTILITIES BOOST PASCAL'S PERFORMANCE." ELECTRONICS, JUNE 7, 1979, pp. 111-116. a two-part article that traces Pascal's three-year evolution at Texas Instruments. this first part focuses on the languag meeting the corporate goal.

BATE, ROGER R. AND JOHNSON, DOUGLAS S. "PASCAL SOFTWARE SUPPORTS REAL-TIME MULTIPROGRAMMING ON SMALL SYSTEMS." ELECTRONICS, JUNE 7, 1979, pp. 117-121. this second part focuses on the streamlined version of TI Pascal.

BERG, ARNIE. "BASIC "VAL" FUNCTION IN PASCAL." CALL -A.P.P.L.E., MAY 1981, p. 66. a Pascal unit that behave very much like its BASIC equivalent.

BEJAR, ISSAAC, I. "VIDEODISCS IN EDUCATION: INTEGRATING THE COMPUTER AND COMMUNICATION TECHNOLOGIES." BYTE, JUNE 1982, pp. 78-104 [12 pp.]. this discusses interactive videodiscs entering the classroom, with a Pascal program for controlling the DVA PR 7820-2.

BERGGREN, STEPHEN R. "DOZO IN PASCAL." RECREATIONAL COMPUTING, ISSUE 48, pp. 32-36. accepted the challenge of H. Kohl in the April 1980 Recreational Computing to write this Japanese board game; uses Turtlegraphics.

BIERMAN, PAUL. "THE INS AND OUTS OF HIGH-LEVEL LANGUAGES." PERSONAL COMPUTING, MAY 1981, pp. 10-73 [11 pp.]. a popular description of BASIC, COBOL, FORTRAN, ALGOL, Pascal, PL/1, PILOT, LISP

BILLARD, STEPHEN L. "LOWER CASE FOR APPLE PASCAL." CIDER PRESS, OCTOBER # 2 1980, pp. 15-16. lower case with the Paymar adapter.

BLANK, GEORGE. "A TOURIST'S GUIDE TO THE CYBERNETIC TOWER OF BABEL." CREATIVE COMPUTING, NOVEMBER 1981, pp. 94-103 [6 pp.]. describes BASIC, Pascal, APL, Forth, FORTRAN, COBOL, Tiny C, Logo, LISP, and Pilot—listing their availability for the more popular personal computers.

BOLTHOFF, GEORGE. "MORE GOTOXY (PASCAL CURSOR ADDRESSING)." BYTE, APRIL 1980, p. 110. routines (in answer to Helmer's Jan 1980 comments) to place the cursor at a specified address on the COPS-10 terminal and the SOROC 120; he uses the UNITWRITE.

BONDY, JON. "A MONITOR PROGRAM IN PASCAL." S-100 MICROSYSTEMS, JULY/AUGUST 1980, pp. 44-49 [4 pp.]. with 4 assembly routines, he goes on to present an extensive monitor program that dumps memory, modifies memory, and reads and writes ports.

BONDY, JON. "READING UCSD PASCAL DISK DIRECTORIES." MICROSYSTEMS, JANUARY 1981, pp. 49-52. an article...

BONDY, JON. "VIRTUAL SEGMENT PROCEDURES UNDER UCSD PASCAL." MICROSYSTEMS, NOVEMBER 1981, pp. 48-53. an article...

BONDY, JON. "VIRTUAL SEGMENTS ARTICLE." USUS NEWS, FEBRUARY 1982, pp. 31-36. explains the feature of UCSD segments procedure for Versions III and IV, which allow for a convenient form of overlay.

BOOCH, GRADY. "PROGRAMMING QUICKIES: IDIOT PROOF INPUT IN PASCAL." BYTE, JULY 1982, pp. 452-453. the program demonstrates a method for obtaining idiot-proof input in Pascal.

BORGERSON, MARK. "BEATING THE SYSTEM." INTERFACE AGE, SEPTEMBER 1980, pp. 76-78. an article.

BORGERSON, MARK J. "PASCAL MEANS BUSINESS." MICROCOMPUTING, APRIL 1981, pp. 46-54 [7 pp.]. makes a strong case for Pascal over BASIC. "the greatest strength of Pascal—the ability to create special types of variables."

BOWLES, KENNETH L. "STATUS OF THE UCSD PASCAL PROJECT." DR. DOBB'S, MARCH 1978, pp. 16-19. current R. and D., extensions, alterations and other questions that users have been asking.

BOWLES, KENNETH L. "THE UCSD PASCAL PROJECT." EDUCOM BULLETIN, VOL. 13, NO. 1, 1978, pp. 2-13. an article...

BOWLES, KENNETH L. "AN INTRODUCTION TO THE UCSD PASCAL SYSTEM." BEHAV. RES. METHODS AND INSTRUM., VOL. 10, NO. 4, 1978, pp. 531-534. an article...

BRENNAN, THOMAS. "PASCAL POINTERS & PRINCIPLES: PASCAL TEXT PAGING." NIBBLE, VOL. 3, NO. 3, 1982, pp. 151-152. this program prints out a listing with the lines numbered on the left.

BRODERICK, JOHN. "PASCAL NOTEBOOK." 1980, p. 1. published in the Apple Corps of Dallas.

BUCKLEY, JOEL. "WRITE -A.P.P.L.E." CALL -A.P.P.L.E., MAY 1982, pp. 85-86. a letter explaining how to split files that are too large for the Editor; he uses, Make, Transfer, and Krunch commands.

BUDGE, JOSEPH H. "PASCAL VISITS ANCIENT GREECE." COMPUTE, SEPTEMBER/OCTOBER, 1980, pp. 64-67. a full treatment of a maze search program.

BUDGE, JOSEPH H. "COPY-ONE AN IMPROVED PASCAL SINGLE DISK COPY." FROM THE CORE (CAROLINA APPLE CORE) DECEMBER 1980, p. 4. "in only three and one-half disk swaps you can have a complete 280 block verified copy with only one drive."

BUDGE, JOSEPH H. "UPPER/LOWER CASE PASCAL." FROM THE CORE (CAROLINA APPLE CORE), JANUARY, 1981, p. 8-9. a program to modify the BIOS modules of Pascal 1.1.

BUDGE, JOSEPH H. "A PASCAL DISASSEMBLER FOR SYSTEM.APPLE." FROM THE CORE (CAROLINA APPLE CORE), JANUARY 1981, pp. 10-13. this Disassembles System.Apple into 16 separate files on diskette, which may be re-assembled by the Apple supplied assembler.

BUDGE, JOSEPH H. "L/C SYSTEM STARTUP FOR PASCAL 1.1." FROM THE CORE (CAROLINA APPLE CORE), JANUARY 1981, p. 13. a permanent patch to System. Apple, which calls an Assembly language program to set various startup options.

BUDGE, JOSEPH H. "SOME USES FOR A DIS-ASSEMBLER." FROM THE CORE (CAROLINA APPLE CORE) FEBRUARY 1981, pp. 5-7 [2 pp.]. 'once the right tools are available, a little imagination goes a long way."

BURNS, NINA. "HELP FOR THE WEARY PASCAL PRINTER." SOFTALK, MAY 1982, p. 19. a letter on the use of SSM to run a printer under Pascal.

CARPENTER, CHUCK. "APPLE-CART." CREATIVE COMPUTING, DECEMBER 1979, pp. 141-144 [3 pp.]. gives a few details about Turtle-graphics.

CARPENTER, CHUCK. "APPLE-CART." CREATIVE COMPUTING, AUGUST 1980, pp. 150-152 [2 pp.]. gives a couple of routines by Ron DeGroat that allows the user to display text in flashing, inverse, and normal modes.

CARPENTER, CHUCK. "APPLE-CART." CREATIVE COMPUTING, APRIL 1981, p. 202. an assembly program by Jim Levin, which relates to the above August 1980 article on flashing, inverse, and normal modes.

CARPENTER, CHUCK. "APPLE-CART." CREATIVE COMPUTING, MARCH 1982, pp. 222-226 [3 pp.]. gives one program that writes out a table of ASCII characters to a printer and another that illustrates the shuffling algorithm of Moses and Oakford.

CASSERES, DAVID. "BITS AND BYTES IN PASCAL AND OTHER BINARY WONDERS." BYTE, OCTOBER 1981, pp. 448-457. the bitfiddler program uses the ODD and ORD functions to manipulate data types; the binary program employs free union to access the individual bits of a word; David works at Apple and relates other tricks, such as PEEKing and POKEing.

CAUDILL, PAT. "USING ASSEMBLY CODING OPTIMIZE HIGH-LEVEL LANGUAGE PROGRAMS." ELECTRONICS, FEBRUARY 1, 1979, pp. 121-124. coding critical sections by hand can trim microcomputers' storage needs and execution time.

CHAVEZ, FRANK. "PROGRAM OF THE MONTH." APPLE SHOPPE, VOL. 1 NO. 5, 1980, pp. 22-26. a full listing of the eight queens problem; compare with Wirth's 'Program Development by Stepwise Refinement'.

CICHELLI, RICHARD J. "A REVIEW OF BOWLES" PROBLEM SOLVING USING PASCAL." BYTE, NOVEMBER 1978, p. 134. 'the title sounds like a wish, but it is a fact.'

CICHELLI, RICHARD J. "PASCAL— PROGRAMMING FOR THE '80'S." SMALL SYSTEMS WORLD, JUNE 1980, p. 26-30. 'Pascal programming is ten times as cost effective as COBOL programming.'

CLIPPINGER, R. F. "LETTERS: LEARNING FROM PASCAL." BYTE, JULY 1982, pp. 23-26 [2 pp.]. some comments on Doyle's and Heyman's February Byte articles.

COLE, TOM AND JACKSON, GENE. "DOS TO PASCAL TRANSFER PROGRAM." FROM THE CORE (CAROLINA APPLE CORE) JANUARY 1981, pp. 8-9. this program transfers files from DOS to Pascal.

CONRAD, MARVIN. "PASCAL A HIGH-LEVEL LANGUAGE FOR MICROS AND MINIS." DATAMATION, JULY 1979, pp. 153-156. in praise of Pascal.

CORNELIUS, BARRY. "SUGGESTED CORRECTIONS TO GROGONO'S BOOK 'PROGRAMMING IN PASCAL'." NOTES FROM UNIVERSITY OF HULL, ENGLAND, 13 AUGUST 1980 pp. 1-8. this list contains the corrections suggested for the first printing of the first edition.

COTTON, GENE. "ABOUT SEARCHES: 3 TECHNIQUES (IN PASCAL)." INTERFACE AGE, MARCH 1981, p. 70. an article...

CRARY, FRED. "PASCAL PRECISION." BYTE, SEPTEMBER 1980, pp. 20-22 [2 pp.]. a program for determining the actual precison of floating-point routines.

CROW, FRANKLIN C. "THREE-DIMENSIONAL COMPUTER GRAPHICS, PART 1." BYTE, MARCH 1981, pp. 54-82 [12 pp.]. 'the procedures provide essentially everything needed to display three-dimensional line drawings representing solid objects modeled by polygons.'

CROW, FRANKLIN C. "THREE-DIMENSIONAL COMPUTER GRAPHICS, PART 2." BYTE, APRIL 1981, pp. 290-302 [7 pp.]. gives the complete Pascal program, which was discussed in part 1.

CURTIS, ROGER. "FILE BURP." CALL -A.P.P.L.E., SEPTEMBER 1980, pp. 30-33. this program will dump designated 512 byte blocks of data, from any kind of file, to your printer in a formatted 16 x 32 array.

DARR, ROBERT W. "PASCAL READABILITY ANALYZER." NIBBLE, VOL. 2, NO. 5, 1981, pp. 47-119 [2 pp.]. this program counts vowels, words, and sentences, in order to calculate the grade level of a piece of writing.

DARR, ROBERT W. "PASCAL IN SPACE." MICROCOMPUTING, FEBRUARY 1982, pp. 72-74. this orrery program shows the relative positions and motions of the members of the solar system.

DAVIS, HENRY. "THE PASCAL NOTEBOOK." INTERFACE AGE

1. JUNE 1979, pp. 106-109
2. JULY 1979, pp. 97-104 [7 pp.]
3. AUGUST/SEPTEMBER 1979,
1. JUNE 1979, pp. 106-109
2. JULY 1979, pp. 97-104 [7 pp.]
3. AUGUST/SEPTEMBER 1979, pp. 85-89 [4 pp.]
4. OCTOBER 1979, pp. 88-94 [4 pp.]
5. NOVEMBER 1979, pp. 148-152 [4 pp.]
6. DECEMBER 1979, pp. 117-126 [7 pp.]
7. JANUARY 1980, pp. 98-103 [4 pp.]
8. FEBRUARY 1980, pp. 118-123 [5 pp.]

9. APRIL 1980, pp. 115-117. topics presented: outer compiler structure and initialization; the scanner; blocks and declarations; constants, types, id search; parameter list, field list; code generation; type checking statements; expressions; control structure; intrinsic functions; interpreting the compiled code; native code generation.

DEGROAT, RON. "INVERSE & FLASHING MODES FOR APPLE PASCAL TEXT DISPLAY." CALL -A.P.P.L.E., JULY/AUGUST 1980, p. 46. gives Assembly language procedures.

DEGROAT, RON. "SEEING DOUBLE WITH PASCAL GRAPHICS." CALL -A.P.P.L.E., FEBRUARY 1981, pp. 30-33. a program to make Turtlegraphics work on the primary and secondary pages of the Hi-Res screen.

DEGROAT, RON. "INVERSE TEXT DISPLAY WITH PASCAL 1.1." CALL -A.P.P.L.E., MARCH/APRIL 1981, p. 63. a [Ctrl-R] in a write statement will display upper case letters as inverse text on the video screen. [Ctrl-T] returns the text to normal.

DEGROAT, RON. "LOWER CASE DISPLAY FOR PASCAL 1.1." CALL -A.P.P.L.E., MARCH/ APRIL 1981, p. 67. Craig Vaughan's February Call -A.P.P.L.E fix will not work with Version 1.1.

DEGROAT, RON. "CORRECTIONS AND ENHANCEMENTS FOR PASCAL ZAP." CALL -A.P.P.L.E., MAY 1981, p. 60. Jill David has a correction for both Pascal Zap by Philip Ender and program File Burp by Roger Curtis. David Geddes adds a print option to Pascal Zap.

DEGROAT, RON. "ROSA PASCAL SEZ." CREATIVE COMPUTING, MAY 1981, p. 204. a program that would randomly generate all 26 alpha characters without repetition.

DEGROAT, RON. "MOVING THE HEAP TO GET SPECIAL CHARACTERS." CALL -A.P.P.L.E., JUNE 1981, pp. 35-38. this article is a tutorial to help understand how the underscore, left and right curly brackets, the backslash, the vertical bar, and the squiggle can become available.

DEGROAT, RON. "PASCAL MEMORY UTILITY." CALL -A.P.P.L.E., JULY/AUGUST 1981, pp. 43-51. this program is designed to help the user explore and investigate the inner workings of the Apple Pascal system.

DEGROAT, RON. "WRITING THE WRONGS." CALL -A.P.P.L.E., SEPTEMBER 1981, p. 16. notes a layout error in the Pascal memory utility of CALL -A.P.P.L.E., July/August 1981.

DEGROAT, RON. "PASCAL COMPUTER SIMULATIONS." CALL -A.P.P.L.E., SEPTEMBER 1981, pp. 31-38 [6 pp.]. gives a program for earth orbits and another for ionic scattering expriments; these include goof-proof input routines.

DEGROAT, RON. "PASCAL LOW RESOLUTION GRAPHICS." NIBBLE, VOL. 2, NO. 6, 1981, pp. 53-59 [2 pp.]. the Lo-Res ROM subroutines are made available to Apple Pascal.

DEGROOT, DOUG. "PASCAL PROGRAMMING." DR. DOBBS JOURNAL, MAY 1981, pp. 18-19. an article.

DIJKSTRA, EDSGER W. "THE HUMBLE PROGRAMMER." COMMUNICATIONS OF THE ACM, VOL. 15, NO. 10, OCTOBER 1972, pp. 859-866. 'the sooner we can forget that Fortran ever existed, the better, for as a vehicle of thought it is no longer adequate: it wastes our brainpower.'

DOGGETT, W. O. "HOW TO SPLIT LONG TEXT FILES INTO SMALLER FILES FOR THE APPLE PASCAL EDITOR." FROM THE CORE (CAROLINA APPLE CORE), MAY 1981, p. 7. his method is to use the Krunch and Make commands in the filer.

DOTY, KEITH L. "A TOP-DOWN EVALUATION OF PASCAL." COMPUTER DESIGN, MAY 1980, pp. 167-177. a fine discussion of Pascal and its capabilities.

DOYLE, THOMAS E. "PASCAL NOW: LET PASCAL BALANCE YOUR NOW ACCOUNT." BYTE, FEBRUARY 1982, pp. 290-322 [16 pp.]. this program is designed to manage a NOW account and provides some hints to think in Pascal.

EDITOR. "PASCAL WHO?" THE BEST OF CIDER PRESS 1978-1979, p. 32. gives a few sentences introducing Messrs. Pascal, Wirth, and Bowles.

EDITOR. "C LANGUAGE BEFRIENDS MICROPROCESSORS." ELECTRONICS, FEBRUARY 15, 1979, pp. 41-42. 'I think Pascal is just a stepping-stone to C.'

EDITOR. "PRINTOUT." NEWSLETTER, NO. 13, OCTOBER 1979, pp. 1-3. this short program outputs to a printer from within a program.

EDITOR. "SOUTHEASTERN SOFTWARE EL CHEAPO PASCAL LOWER/UPPER CASE WRITER." NEWSLETTER, NO. 14, NOVEMBER 1979, pp. 5-7. this program brings lower case to the printer.

EDITOR. "QUICK REFERENCE INDEX FOR FILER COMMANDS." APPLE COOKBOOK, VOL. 1, NO. 1, 1979, p. 4. some may find this type of index to the Apple Manual handy.

EDITOR. "APPLE PASCAL REVEALED." APPLE SHOPPE, VOL. 1, NO. 2, 1979, pp. 16-17. the announcement of the specs of the system.

EDITOR. "THE CHINA SYNDROME." APPLE SHOPPE, VOL. 1, NO. 3, 1979, pp. 17-19. to be an ongoing problem in future projects.

EDITOR. "THE CHINA SYNDROME." APPLE SHOPPE, VOL. 1, NO. 4, 1979, p. 26. beginning to sep up the simulation in a Pascal algorithm.

EDITOR. "TINY PASCAL FOR THE APPLE II." NIBBLE, NO. 5, 1980, pp. 52-53. an announcement.

EDITOR. "PASCAL OWNERS..." APPLE SHOPPE, VOL. 1, NO. 5, 1980, p. 11. a digression explaining that both monitor ROMS can be active with the language card.

EDITOR. "PASCAL I & II COMPUTER INFORMATION." 80 MICROCOMPUTING, MAY 1980, pp. 38-42. a software review...

EDITOR. "A REVIEW OF 'PASCAL: AN INTRODUCTION TO METHODICAL PROGRAMMING' BY WILLIAM FINDLAY AND DAVID A. WATT." 80 MICROCOMPUTING, MAY 1980, p. 13. a review...

EDITOR. "CIRCUIT THEORY." THE APPLE SHOPPE, MAY/JUNE 1980, pp. 7-8. an intro to the area of circuit theory with a program to do the necessary math.

EDITOR. "A REVIEW OF 'PASCAL WITH STYLE: PROGRAMMING PROVERBS' BY HENRY F. LEDGARD, JOHN F. HUERAS, AND PAUL A NAGIN." DR. DOBB'S, AUGUST 1980, p. 46. a book review...

EDITOR. "CLUBS AND NEWSLETTERS." BYTE, AUGUST 1980, p. 226. lists a free Pascal newsletter from Rational Data Systems, 245 W. 55th St., New York, NY 10019.

EDITOR. "THE KEYPRESS FUNCTION." THE APPLE ORCHARD, WINTER 1980, p. 65. the program illustrates the use of KEYPRESS as an externally linked routine.

EDITOR. "NEED TO GET A TEXT FILE TO A PRINTER IN PASCAL?" THE HARVEST NORTHWEST SUBURBAN APPLE USERS GROUP, OCTOBER 1980, p. 8. takes a text file and puts it to the printer in letter form for a specified number of printouts.

EDITOR. "PASCAL ON THE PET (REVIEW OF ABACUS SOFTWARE)." COMPUTE, FEBRUARY 1981, pp. 124-125. a software review...

EDITOR. "A REVIEW OF 'PASCAL' BY PAUL CHIRLIAN." INTERFACE AGE, FEBRUARY 1981, p. 116. a book review...

EDITOR. "PASCAL MICROENGINE: WESTERN DIGITAL." INTERFACE AGE, FEBRUARY 1981, pp. 48-52. a hardware review...

EDITOR. "PASCAL ANIMATION PACKAGE AND PASCAL 1.1 UPDATE KIT." APPLE SHOPPE, MAY/JUNE 1981, pp. 2-3. announcements.

EDITOR. "COMPARISON OF C AND PASCAL." BYTE, JUNE 1981, p. 358. a review...

EDITOR. "A REVIEW OF 'PROGRAMMING FOR POETS: A GENERAL INTRODUCTION USING PASCAL.' BY RICHARD CONWAY, JAMES ARCHER, AND RALPH CONWAY." ONCOMPUTING, SPRING 1981, pp. 34-36. a book review...

EDITOR. "LOOKIT." APPLE ORCHARD, SPRING 1981, p. 43. displays complete 128-character Turtlegraphics character set. originally from Harvest Feb 1981.

EDITOR. "A REVIEW OF 'APPLE PASCAL: A HANDS ON APPROACH' BY ARTHUR LUEHRMANN AND HERBERT PECKHAM." USUS NEWS, FEBRUARY 1982, p. 26. 'although written for the Apple...it is also very readable and useful for the reader who wants to gain an understanding of UCSD Pascal.'

EISENBACH, SUE. "THE COMPLETE PASCAL." PERSONAL COMPUTER WORLD, SEPTEMBER TO DECEMBER 1979. 1. WHY PASCAL? 2. FUNDAMENTALS: ACTION AND DATA 3. CONTROL STRUCTURES: LOOPS 4. DATA STRUCTURES: SIMPLE DATA TYPES, ARRAYS AND SETS. a series of articles...

EISENBERG, J. D., AND HERTZFELD, A. J. "INSIDE THE SILENTYPE FIRMWARE." THE APPLE ORCHARD, WINTER 1980, pp. 43-52. an interface for accesing the lower-level routines to print character sets or special graphics.

ELKINS, JIM. "APPLE SPECIAL INTEREST GROUP." USUS, SPRING 1981, pp. 61-63. gives the purpose of this SIG.

ENDER, PHILIP B. "PASCAL ZAP." CALL -A.P.P.L.E., JANUARY 1981, pp. 47-49. this program allows access to any block on the disk, including the directory and deleted files.

EVANS, AL. "SIDE BY SIDE: PASCAL AND BASIC." CREATIVE COMPUTING, NOVEMBER 1981, pp. 158-163 [5 pp.] compares a makemenu program written in BASIC and Pascal.

EVER, JACOB. "BASIC BEATS PASCAL." CREATIVE COMPUTING, NOVEMBER 1981, pp. 166-172 [4 pp.]. 'the system aspects of BASIC were the determining factors in choosing it over Pascal.'

FEESER, JEFFREY. "WORD PROCESSOR EVALUATION." CALL -A.P.P.L.E., NOVEMBER/DECEMBER 1981, pp. 54-58 [3 pp.]. a review of Powertext.

FELDMAN, MICHAEL B. "INFORMATION HIDING IN PASCAL: PACKAGES AND POINTERS." BYTE, NOVEMBER 1981, pp. 493-498 [4 pp.]. discusses a complex-number data type for Pascal.

FELT, HARLAN. "PAYMAR LOWER CASE MODIFICATION." CIDER PRESS, APRIL 1980, p. 10. a hardware modification.

FLETCHER, DENNIS. "PASCAL POWER USERS LOVE IT, VENDORS ARE GETTING THE MESSAGE, AND STANDARDS ARE ON THE WAY." DATAMATION, JULY 1979, pp. 142-145. 'Pascal is what PL/1 should have been.'

FLORES, IVAN. "MORE IMPROVEMENTS." BYTE, SEPTEMBER 1980, pp. 18-20 [2 pp.]. comparing BASIC and Pascal programs for finding prime numbers. "PASCAL – AT NO CHARGE!" NIBBLE, VOL. 2, NO. 4, 1981, pp. 41-43. the program prints uppercase letters following the "±" character.

FLORINI, JAMES R. "LOWER CASE IN APPLE PASCAL – AT NO CHARGE!" NIBBLE, VOL. 2, NO. 4, 1981, pp. 41-43. the program prints uppercase letters following the " " character.

FLORINI, JAMES R. "PASCAL GRAPHICS IN A FLASH." MICROCOMPUTING, FEBRUARY 1982, pp. 70-71. a routine that prints out the Apple graphics screen in ten minutes or less.

FLORINI, JAMES R. "A REVIEW OF 'APPLE PASCAL: A HANDS-ON APPROACH' BY ARTHUR LUEHRMANN AND HERBERT PECKMAN, AND A REVIEW OF 'PASCAL PROGRAMMING FOR THE APPLE' BY T. G. LEWIS." MICROCOMPUTING, APRIL 1982, pp. 180-182 [2 pp.]. 'my ony complaint about "Apple Pascal: A Hands-on Approach" is that it should have been published two years ago... (Lewis's book) is an excellent sequel to Hands-on.'

FLORINI, JAMES R. "TURNING ON WITH PASCAL." NIBBLE, VOL. 3, NO. 2, 1982, pp. 59-65 [2 pp.]. helps the beginner get into the system.

FOSTER, CHARLIE. "PASCAL WITH A Z80." INTERFACE AGE, NOVEMBER 1980, pp. 60-62 [2 pp.]. his success with Pascal on his CP/M version.

FRICKE, VICTOR. "PASCAL TUTORIAL, PART 1." MICRO, NOVEMBER 1981, pp. 13-20. an article...

FRICKE, VICTOR. "PASCAL TUTORIAL, PART 2." MICRO, DECEMBER 1981, pp. 57-60. an article...

FRIEDMAN, PAUL. "PASCAL FOR THE BASIC PROGRAMMER PART 1." ONCOMPUTING, SPRING 1981, pp. 50-59 [9 pp.]. an intro article; compares a compound interest program in both BASIC and Pascal.

FRIEDMAN, PAUL. "PASCAL FOR THE BASIC PROGRAMMER PART 2." ONCOMPUTING, SUMMER 1981, pp. 48-53. the second of a two-part intro article. compares an insertion sort in BASIC and Pascal.

GABRIELSON, MIKE. "A PASCAL BIBLIOGRAPHY." DR. DOBB'S JOURNAL, FEBRUARY 1979, pp. 29-30. an un-annotated bibliography mostly for the computer scientist. lists 63 articles not listed here. the same quality bibliography as found in Grogono's text.

GABRIELSON, MIKE. "BRINGING UP UCSD PASCAL WITHOUT CP/M." DR. DOBB'S JOURNAL, APRIL 1979, pp. 26 an article...

GAGNE, JIM. "GETTING THE WONDERS OF UCSD PASCAL GOING ON AN S-100 SYSTEM." 3RD WEST COAST COMPUTER FAIRE, NOVEMBER 1978, pp.238-239. he is using Version 1.4.

GAGNE, JIM. "AN INTRODUCTION TO PASCAL A LOOK AT A 'NEW' LANGUAGE." MICROCOMPUTING, JUNE 1980, pp. 68-77 [8 pp.]. an intro article with a sample program called Mathquiz.

GAGNE, JAMES. "A WORD ABOUT SEPARATE PROCEDURES AND SEPARATE UNITS." USUS, AUGUST 1980, pp. 20-21. how these work despite the documentation. USUS is a UCSD Users' Society. 4805 Mercury, Suite A. San Diego, CA 92111.

GAGNE, JAMES. "WIRTHWHILE LANGUAGE (PASCAL)." INFOWORLD, 3:8, pp. 9+. an article...

GAYLORD, SAM. "GENERATE LOWER CASE CHARACTERS WITH PASCAL." PERSONAL COMPUTING, MAY 1981, pp. 65-91 [3 pp.]. 'UCSD Pascal, implemented in Apple's language system, lets you display lower-case characters without costing you a dime extra.'

GILBREATH, JIM. "A HIGH-LEVEL LANGUAGE BENCHMARK." BYTE, SEPTEMBER 1981, pp. 180-198 [9 pp.]. discusses benchmarking with a program doing the sieve of Eratosthenes.

GLASS, ROBERT L. "FROM PASCAL TO PEBBLEMAN... AND BEYOND." DATAMATION, JULY 1979, pp. 146-150. a shop-talk history of the development of Ada.

GRAY, STEPHEN B. "A REVIEW OF 'PASCAL WITH STYLE: PROGRAMMING PROVERBS' BY HENRY F. LEDGARD, JOHN F. HUERAS, AND PAUL A NAGIN." CREATIVE COMPUTING, JUNE 1980, pp. 180-181. 'contains a great deal of helpful information.'

GRAY, STEPHEN B. "A REVIEW OF 'PASCAL: AN INTRODUCTION TO METHODICAL PROGRAMMING' BY WILLIAM FINDLAY AND DAVID A. WATT." CREATIVE COMPUTING, JUNE 1980, p. 183. 'the textbook is intended for use with a first course in programming based on Pascal.'

GRAY, STEPHEN. "A REVIEW OF 'PASCAL' BY PAUL M. CHIRLIAN AND OF "INTRODUCTION TO PASCAL" BY NEILL GRAHAM." CREATIVE COMPUTING, JUNE 1981, pp. 220-221. 'programs are explained in great detail before being presented—one of the several features that make Graham's book of greater value than Chirlian's.'

GRAY, STEPHEN. "A REVIEW OF 'DATA STRUCTURES USING PASCAL' BY AARON M. TENNEBAUM AND MOSHE J. AUGENSTEIN." CREATIVE COMPUTING, DECEMBER 1981, p. 338. 'this may be the best Pascal textbook that also teaches programming (besides data structures); it may also be the only one.'

GREEB, FRED. "PASCAL SPEED COMPARISONS." S-100 MICROSYSTEMS, SEPTEMBER/OCTOBER 1980, p. 48. compares Microsoft BASIC, C-BASIC-2, Microsoft Fortran and UCSD.

GREEN, MARK. "A PORTABLE COMPILER FOR PASCAL-LIKE LANGUAGE." 3RD WEST COAST COMPUTER FAIRE, NOVEMBER 1978, pp. 240-245. discusses the problem of portability with its advantages and disadvantages.

GREENBERG, HARVEY. "IN THE DEPTHS OF THE PASCAL DIRECTORY." CALL -A.P.P.L.E., MAY 1981, pp. 27-28. determines disk capacity without exiting the program; enhances Pascal Zap program by Philip Ender.

GROGONO, PETER. "CASE STATEMENTS AND RELATED TOPICS." BYTE, OCTOBER 1979, pp. 178-182. an article...

GROGONO, PETER. "A REVIEW OF 'STRUCTURED PASCAL' BY JEAN-PAUL TREMBLAY, RICHARD B. BUNT, AND LYLE M. OSPETH." BYTE JANUARY 1981, pp. 300-302 [2 pp.]. describes some flaws in the book.

GUSTAFSON, G. G., JOHNSON, T. A. AND KEY, G. S. "SOME PRACTICAL EXPERIENCES WITH THE PASCAL LANGUAGE." AFIPS CONFERENCE PROCEEDINGS, VOL. 49, 1980, pp. 741-746. the developmental experience of the national OCAN systems center with Pascal and some of their difficulties with Pascal.

HAINES, RON. "SOME NOTES ABOUT THE UCSD ASSEMBLER." APPLE ORCHARD, WINTER 1980, p. 35-39 [2 pp.]. explains the use of local labels and the addressing of variables declared as public.

HARRELL, KEITH. "PASCAL POINTERS AND PRINCIPLES." NIBBLE, NO. 6, 1980, pp. 51-52. a first lesson in Pascal; this is to be a regular column.

HARRELL, KEITH. "PASCAL POINTERS AND PRINCIPLES." NIBBLE, VOL. 2, NO. 1, pp. 63-69 [4 pp.]. this covers procedures and functions and how they can help in writing and debugging Pascal programs; includes a calculator program.

HARRELL, KEITH. "PASCAL POINTERS AND PRINCIPLES." NIBBLE, VOL. 2, NO. 2, pp. 81-93 [4 pp.]. this covers arrays; includes a magazine catalog program.

HARRELL, KEITH. "PASCAL POINTERS AND PRINCIPLES." NIBBLE, VOL. 2, NO. 3, p. 75. this presents some hints for single drive Pascal users.

HEDELMAN, HAROLD. "MODELING THE STRUCTURE OF MAIDENHAIR FERNS." COMPUTER GRAPHICS AND ART FOR 1979, pp. 20-23. a series of graphic studies based on the branching structure of Maidenhair ferns is presented.

HEILMANN, PETER. "EQUIP YOUR APPLE FOR THE CHALLENGE." MICROCOMPUTING, AUGUST 1982, pp. 34-43 [7 pp.]. gives a program to let the Apple perform special math functions in Pascal.

HEINONEN, JARI AND KOTIVUORI, ILMO. "UTILITY EXEC." CALL -A.P.P.L.E., FEBRUARY 1981, pp. 34-36. this program allows the use of control level instructions so that one can jump from one program to another.

HELMERS, CARL. "CONSISTENCY - OR LACK THEREOF (BYTE STANDARDS FOR PASCAL)." BYTE, AUGUST 1978, p. 89. a column...

HELMERS, CARL. "A VISION OF AN INDUSTRY." BYTE, AUGUST 1978, pp. 6-7, 133-141. the experience behind the vision was a day long meeting with Bowles and his associates.

HELMERS, CARL. "ABOUT THE COVER (PASCAL'S TRIANGLE)." BYTE, AUGUST 1978, pp. 16-18 [2 pp.]. a humorous indulgence in Pascal prejudices.

HELMERS, CARL. "A SHORT NOTE ON PASCAL PROGRESS AND OTHER TOPICS." BYTE, JANUARY 1979, p. 6. an announcement of Apple Pascal.

HELMERS, CARL. "ON THE IMPORTANCE OF BACKUPS (INCLUDES A PASCAL UTILITY TO RECOVER FILES)." BYTE, APRIL 1979, pp. 6-an column on a utility program...

HELMERS, CARL. "ERA OF OFF-THE-SHELF PERSONAL COMPUTERS HAS ARRIVED." BYTE, JANUARY 1980, pp. 6-a column of history and the Apple II...

HELMERS, CARL. "A PASCAL CHECKBOOK BALANCING PROGRAM." BYTE, JANUARY 1980, pp. 174-175. the proverbial checkbook program.

HELMERS, CARL. "SEVEN BRIDGES OF KONIGSBERG: DIRECT CURSOR ADDRESSING IN UCSD PASCAL." BYTE, FEBRUARY 1980, pp. 6-10. a column on puzzles...

HELMERS, CARL. "A CAMERA INTERFACE TEST PROGRAM WRITTEN IN PASCAL.' BYTE, MARCH 1980, pp. 6-12, 96-104 [9 pp.]. uses an Apple.

HELMERS, CARL. "COMPUTER-CONTROLLED VIEWING OF THE 1980 ECLIPSE." BYTE, MAY 1980, pp. 6,52-70 [12 pp.]. part 2 of the above, after a successful trip.

HELMERS, CARL. "NUMERICAL PRECISION IN UCSD PASCAL." BYTE, JUNE 1980, p. 17. a letter to the editor asking about six-digit precison.

HELMERS, CARL. "WHO READS BYTE?" BYTE, OCTOBER 1980, pp. 6-14 [4 pp.]. the readership shows a 26% increase in interest in Pascal over the last two years.

HELMERS, CARL. "TOWARD DISPLAY ORIENTED OPERATING SYSTEMS." USUS, SPRING 1981, pp. 35-41. his thesis is that computers with high speed interactive displays should feature menu-oriented systems software.

HEMENWAY, JACK AND TEJA, EDWARD. "PASCAL." EDN, APRIL 5, 1979, pp. 79 an article...

HEWITT, JAY. "DISK I/O IN PASCAL." CALL -A.P.P.L.E., JUNE 1980, p. 48. compares a Pascal program and a similar BASIC program as to disk I/O.

HEYMAN, EDWARD. "A FILE CATALOG SYSTEM FOR UCSD PASCAL." BYTE, MAY 1981, pp. 408-427 [16 pp.]. a search for a file in a 600-entry catalog takes less than a second.

HEYMAN, EDWARD. "FIT—A FEDERAL INCOME TAX PROGRAM IN UCSD PASCAL." BYTE, FEBRUARY 1982, pp. 148-412 [44 pp.]. FIT, among other things, allows entry of tax data for all the lines on form 1040 and schedules A and B.

HOARE, CHARLES ANTONY RICHARD. "THE EMPEROR'S OLD CLOTHES." BYTE, SEPTEMBER 1981, 414-425. 'if only we could learn the right lessons from the successes of the past, we would not need to learn from our failures.'

HOGAN, THOMAS. "A REVIEW OF 'APPLE PASCAL: A HANDS-ON APPROACH' BY ARTHUR LUEHRMANN AND HERBERT PECKHAM." INFOWORLD, 3:22, p. 40. a book review...

HUGARD, JAMES. "PRINTING IN PASCAL." APPLE SHOPPE, JULY/AUGUST 1980, pp. 27-29. 'the problem of directing output to the printer does not seem to be explicitly stated anywhere.'

HUGHES, PHIL. "A REVIEW OF AN INTRODUCTION TO METHODICAL PROGRAMMING BY FINDLAY AND WATT." BYTE, OCTOBER 1980, pp. 320-324 [2 pp.]. 'if you are an instructor, this would be an excellent choice for class.'

HUGHES, PHIL "LUCIDATA P-6800 PASCAL." BYTE, MARCH 1980, p. 184. a software review...

HUGHES, PHIL. "BASIC, PASCAL, OR TINY-C: A SIMPLE BENCHMARKING COMPARISON." BYTE, OCTOBER 1981, pp. 372-375. compares a card-shuffling routine.

HUNT, DANIEL S. "GETTING STARTED IN PASCAL." INTERFACE AGE, NOVEMBER 1980, pp. 56-139 [5 pp.]. a good intro article with 3 programs, Pocketcalc, Comflimit and Numberfix.

HUNT, DANIEL S. "THE GENERAL...A MULTI-PURPOSE COMMUNICATIONS PROGRAM." INTERFACE AGE, OCTOBER 1981, pp.104-107. an article...

HUNT, DANIEL S. "WRITELONG: A PASCAL SIMULATION OF LONG-INTEGER OUTPUT." BYTE, NOVEMBER 1981, pp. 414-415. a program for Pascal versions that do not have long integer conversion.

HUNT, DANIEL S. "LISTING THE DISK DIRECTORY IN CP/M BASED PASCAL." BYTE, JUNE 1982, pp. 497-501. this "getdir" program, written in Pascal/MT, version 3.2 will search a CP/M disk and provide a listing of the disk directory from within an application program.

HYDE, RANDALL. "THE ASSEMBLY LINE: ASSEMBLER MAXI-REVIEWS." CALL -A.P.P.L.E, JANUARY 1980, pp. 18-23. gives two paragraphs on the UCSD adaptable assembler.

HYDE, RANDALL. "MORE ON PASCAL." APPLE COOKBOOK, VOL. 1 NO. 3, 1980, pp. 3-7 [2 pp.]. a few comments on Pascal.

HYDE, RANDALL. "THE APPLE DOCTOR." CALL -A.P.P.L.E., FEBRUARY 1980, p. 43. some comments on interactive files and printer output.

HYDE, RANDALL. "CONNECTING WITH THE UCSD BIOS." THE APPLE ORCHARD, MARCH/APRIL 1980, pp. 25-33. a patch to recognize and use the Computerworld printer interface.

HYDE, RANDALL. "LOCATIONS OF INTEREST TO PASCAL & 6502 USERS." APPLE ORCHARD WINTER 1980, p. 28. gives a memory map and the addresses of console read, write, and init; of printer write and init; of disk write, read, and init; of remote read, write and init.

INFELD, LOU. "APPLE /// PASCAL." CALL -A.P.P.L.E., NOVEMBER/DECEMBER 1981, pp. 45-46. an Apple employee describes his experience with the Apple /// Pascal.

INTERNATIONAL APPLE CORE. "PROGRAM LINEFEED." APPLICATION NOTE, REPRINTED IN MICHIGAN APPLE-GRAM, AUGUST 1980, p. 29. initializes BIOS to filter out any linefeeds sent to printer.

INTERNATIONAL APPLE CORE. "PROGRAM GETREM." APPLICATION NOTE, REPRINTED IN MICHIGAN APPLE-GRAM, AUGUST 1980, p. 30. reads from REMIN and writes to the disk.

INTERNATIONAL APPLE CORE. "PROGRAM TAKE280." APPLICATION NOTE, REPRINTED IN MICHIGAN APPLE-GRAM, AUGUST 1980, pp. 30-31. accepts 280 blocks from REMIN and writes to #5.

INTERNATIONAL APPLE CORE. "PROGRAM TRANSFER." APPLICATION NOTE, REPRINTED IN MICHIGAN APPLE-GRAM, AUGUST 1980, pp. 31-34. sends and receives files or whole volumes over serial line.

INTERNATIONAL APPLE CORE. "PROGRAM FOREIGN." APPLICATION NOTE, RERPRINTED IN MICHIGAN APPLE-GRAM, AUGUST 1980, pp. 35-36. uses an Assembly routine "gettext" and so breaks up big files into smaller ones.

INTERNATIONAL APPLE CORE. "PROGRAM MAIN." APPLICATION NOTE, REPRINTED IN MICHIGAN APPLE-GRAM, AUGUST 1980, p. 37. sets the communications card in a given slot to 110 baud, 8 bits, no parity.

INTERNATIONAL APPLE CORE. "PASCAL LONG INTEGER FIX." APPLICATION NOTE, REPRINTED IN MICHIGAN APPLE-GRAM, AUGUST 1980, pp. 37-38. corrects a stack crash in implementing long integers during a compare operation.

INTERNATIONAL APPLE CORE. "PASCAL HI-RES LOAD/SAVE TO DISK." APPLICATION NOTE, REPRINTED IN MICHIGAN APPLE-GRAM, AUGUST 1980, p. 39. 'this demo program creates a Hi-Res picture in Pascal, then saves it to disk. it is then reloaded and displayed.'

INTERNATIONAL APPLE CORE. "A LIST OF 61 KNOWN PASCAL PROBLEMS." APPLICATION NOTE, MARCH 10, 1980, REPRINTED IN MICHIGAN APPLE-GRAM, AUGUST 1980, pp. 40-41. two to four lines on each problem.

INTERNATIONAL APPLE CORE. "PASCAL UNITS." APPLICATION NOTE, REPRINTED IN MICHIGAN APPLE-GRAM, AUGUST 1980, p. 42. some comments on regular units and intrinsic units.

IRVINE, C. A. "UCSD SYSTEM MAKES PROGRAMS PORTABLE." ELECTRONIC DESIGN, AUGUST 16, 1980, pp. 113-118. 'even moving the whole system to a new processor often takes only hours.'

ISAAK, JIM. "AVOIDING PASCAL'S PITFALLS." MINI-MICRO SYSTEMS, DECEMBER 1980, pp. 143-148 [4 pp.]. 'some of the "holes" in Pascal—legacies of its origin as a teaching, rather than applications—programming, language—will not be filled in... Pascal's worst shortcoming is its lack of separate compilation modules.'

JAMES, WILLIAM. "PASCAL TEXT RECOVERY." CALL -A.P.P.L.E., MAY 1981, pp. 37-40. aids in the recovery of the text files of Pascal programs from a disk whose directory has been destroyed.

JENSEN, KATHLEEN. "WHY PASCAL?" EDU, FALL 1979, pp. 1-4. this intro article is available from Oregon Software. 'as a teacher, Wirth did not want to create "features" in Pascal which he would then have to spend time teaching students not to use.'

JEPPSON, JOHN. "COUNTING WITH COLORS ON THE APPLE ///." SOFTALK, JUNE 1982, pp. 170-177 [6 pp.]. gives a Pascal and BASIC program for the game of life in color.

KALISH, CANDACE E. AND MAYER, MALINDA F. "DIF: A FORMAT FOR DATA EXCHANGE BETWEEN APPLICATIONS PROGRAMS." BYTE, NOVEMBER 1981, pp. 174-206 [16 pp.]. they give a Pascal program that reads data from a DIF file into an array and then displays the data on the terminal.

KAN, MICHAEL K. "PASCAL MEETS INSTANT INSANITY." MICROCOMPUTING, APRIL 1982, pp. 84-87. this is an example of computer problem-solving using structured programming techniques.

KELLNER, JO. "PASCAL OPERAND FORMATS." APPLE ORCHARD, FALL 1980, pp. 38-40. 'or everything you wanted to know about Pascal variables but couldn't get through to the hotline to ask.'

KELLNER, JO AND CHARLIE. "CONVERTING STRINGS TO NUMBERIC VARIABLES." APPLE ORCHARD, WINTER 1980, pp. 59-61. this intrinsic allows for the editing of integers and reals. designed for Version 1.1.

KELLNER, JO. "PASCAL RUN-TIME ERRORS." APPLE ORCHARD, WINTER 1980, p. 62. some comments on the system list option.

KELLNER, JO. "A REPLY TO GENE WILSON." CIDER PRESS, DECEMBER 1980, p. 13. 'UCSD implemented a 32 bit floating point number, based on the proposed IEEE standard.'

KERN, CHRISTOPHER. "THE BDS C COMPILER." BYTE, JUNE 1981, pp. 356-362 [4 pp.]. compares C and Pascal.

KINGDON, R. A. "EXPERIENCE WITH THE UCSD ADAPTABLE SYSTEM." USUS, SPRING 1981, pp. 23-25. the Apple II is compared with the SuperBrain.

KNUTH, DONALD E. "ALGORITHMS." SCIENTIFIC AMERICAN, APRIL 1977, pp. 63-80 [11 pp.]. discusses the algorithms for sequential search, binary search and hashing. an excellent article.

KOLLASCH, DAVE. "TWO PROGRAMS." ADAM & EVE, APPLE I USERS" GROUP, JULY 1980, p. 3. one very useful function converts a string to an integer and the other helpful program controls the Paper Tiger.

KROUSE, TIM. "PASCAL LANGUAGE." ELECTRONIC DESIGN, SEPTEMBER TO DECEMBER 1978, SIX PARTS.

1. "PASCAL ISN'T JUST ONE MORE COMPUTER LANGUAGE. IT PROMISES TO BE SIMPLE, FLEXIBLE AND FAST." SEPTEMBER 13, 1978, pp. 82-86.
2. "POWERFUL STATEMENTS AND A VERSATILE SYNTAX GIVE PASCAL PROGRAM "BODY"." SEPTEMBER 27, 1978, pp. 80-86.
3. "PASCAL'S INPUT AND OUTPUT PROCEDURES ARE POWERFUL, YET EASY TO MASTER." NOVEMBER 8, 1978, pp. 100-104.
4. "VERSATILE GROUPINGS AND USER-DEFINED DATA TYPES MAKE PASCAL REALLY SHINE." NOVEMBER 8, 1978, pp. 106-111.
5. "MOVING BIT PATTERNS OR WORD GROUPS CAN BE A STRUGGLE - BUT NOT IN PASCAL." DECEMBER 6, 1978, pp. 106-111.
6. "WITH A REAL-TIME OPERATING SYSTEM, A PASCAL PROGRAM CAN RUN YOUR TEST SET." DECMBER 20, 1978, pp. 78-81. a full introduction to the language.

KRUTCH, JOHN. "PASCAL DREAM (TRS-80)." 80 MICROCOMPUTING, JUNE 1981, pp. 174-177. an article...

KUHNER, ANITA. "BITS AND PIECES." ADAM & EVE, APPLE II USERS' GROUP. NOVEMBER 1980, p. 5. one trick makes sure that APPLE1 is in drive #4 before ending a program and another clever trick that extracts the date.

LEHMAN, JOHN A. "GEAR-RATIO CALCULATION FOR BICYCLE DERAILLEURS." BYTE, MARCH 1980, pp. 68-70 [2 pp.]. Mundie's article rewrites this BASIC program in Pascal.

LESSER, HARTLEY G. "A REVIEW OF 'APPLE PASCAL: A HANDS-ON APPROACH' BY ARTHUR LUEHRMANN AND HERBERT PECKHAM." BYTE, NOVEMBER 1981, pp. 458-462 [3 pp.]. 'I would jump at the chance to buy a sequel.'

LEVENTHAL, LANCE. "MUC SOFTWARE." DIGITAL DESIGN, VOL. 9 NO. 12, pp. 86-87. an article...

LEWELLEN, TOM K. "A PATCH FOR 80 COLUMN VIDEO BOARDS AND APPLE PASCAL." CALL -A.P.P.L.E., OCTOBER 1980, pp. 51-52. the program allows KEYPRESS and type ahead buffers to work with the Videx and M&R 80 column boards.

LEWIS, MARC. "AN EXPERIMENTAL PASCAL-LIKE LANGUAGE FOR MICROPROCESSORS." WEST COAST COMPUTER FAIRE, 1978, pp. 489-493. an experimental language is described with its novel features discussed.

LIBES, SOL. "BYTELINES. UCSD PASCAL NEWS." BYTE, JUNE 1980, p. 176. notices about the UCSD licenses, a Pascal newsletter, and PUG.

LIBES, SOL. "NEWS AND VIEWS PASCAL." S-100 MICROSYSTEMS, JULY 1980, pp. 10-11. a regular column.

LIBES, SOL. "BYTELINES UCSD PASCAL CONTROVERSY CONTINUES." BYTE, SEPTEMBER 1980, p. 168. licensees charge that UCSD violated the "fair use doctrine" in cancelling their licenses; Apple Computer, Inc. has an uncancellable license.

LIBES, SOL. "UCSD VERSION 4.0." MICROSYSTEMS, MAY 1981, p. 14. an article...

LIEBERMAN, DAVID E. "COMPILE-LOAD-AND-GO USING 'EXEC' FILES." NIBBLE, VOL. 2, NO. 6, 1981, p. 53. gives some ideas about EXEC files.

LIEBERMAN, DAVID E. "PASDIR (PASCAL DIRECTORY LISTER)." NIBBLE, VOL. 2, NO. 7, 1981, pp. 89-95 [3 pp.]. this BASIC program establishes a foundation for reading data from a Pascal diskette and storing the information in a DOS3.3 format.

LIEBERMAN, DAVID E. "EXPAND PASCAL EXEC FILE CAPABILITY." NIBBLE, VOL. 2, NO. 8, 1981, P. 111-123 [4 pp.]. this utility program generates EXEC files which automatically assemble, compile, and link programs.

LIEBERMAN, DAVID E. "BASDIR" (READ DOS 3.3 DIRECTORIES FROM APPLE PASCAL). NIBBLE, VOL. 2, NO. 8, 1981, pp. 111-123 [5 pp.]. this Pascal program establishes a foundation for reading data from a DOS 3.3 diskette under the UCSD Pascal operating system.

LIFFICK, BLAISE W., ED. THE BYTE BOOK OF PASCAL. PETERSBOROUGH, N.H.: BYTE PUBLICATIONS 1979.
PASCAL: A (NEARLY) MACHINE INDEPENDENT SOFTWARE SYSTEM." BYTE, MAY 1978 [4 pp.]. 'it appears to be far more practical to standardize the entire software system than the language processor alone.'

MUNDIE, DAVID. "IN PRAISE OF PASCAL." BYTE, AUGUST 1978 [6 pp.]. 'personal computing will never achieve its full potential as long as our state of the art machines are hobbled with a language as far from state of the art as BASIC is.'

FORD, GARY. "COMMENTS ON PASCAL, LEARNING HOW TO PROGRAM, AND SMALL SYSTEMS." BYTE, MAY 1978 [4 pp.]. discusses Wirth's two principal goals for Pascal.

HELMERS, CARL. "IS PASCAL THE NEXT BASIC?" BYTE, DECEMBER 1977 [4 pp.]. comparing the advantages of BASIC and Pascal.

CHUNG, KIN-MAN AND YUEN, HERBERT. "A PROPOSED PASCAL COMPILER." BYTE, AUGUST 1978 [2 pp.]. intro to the 3 part article.

ALPERT, STEPHEN R. "PASCAL, A STRUCTURALL STRONG LANGUAGE." BYTE, AUGUST 1978 [6 pp.]. considers some of the language features of Pascal. gives a Polish "compiler" listing.

FORSYTH, CHARLES H. AND HOWARD, RANDALL J. "COMPILATION AND PASCAL ON THE NEW MICROPROCESSORS." BYTE, AUGUST 1978 [7 pp.]. 'for languages like Pascal, compilation is the preferred method of implementation on hybrid 8 and 16 bit microprocessors.'

SCHWARTZ, ALLAN M. "PASCAL VERSUS BASIC: AN EXERCISE." BYTE, AUGUST 1978 [10 pp.]. compares a Pascal version of the game Mastermind with one of BASIC.

BOWLES, KEN. "PASCAL VERSUS COBOL: WHERE PASCAL GETS DOWN TO BUSINESS." BYTE, AUGUST 1978 [8 pp.]. 'Pascal provides data structuring facilities generally superior to those of COBOL.'

CHUNG, KIN-MAN AND YUEN, HERBERT. "A 'TINY' PASCAL COMPILER." BYTE, SEPTEMBER TO NOVEMBER 1978 [30 pp.]. a full discussion of the p-code interpreter, the p-compiler and the p-code to 8080 conversion.

LOUIS, DR. B. GREGORY. " 'TINY' PASCAL IN 8080 ASSEMBLY LANGUAGE." pp. 91-93. a comment on the work of Chung and Yuen.

KHERIATY, LARRY. "WADUZITDO: HOW TO WRITE A LANGUAGE IN 256 WORDS OR LESS." BYTE, SEPTEMBER 1978 [9 pp.]. a complete high level language processor that fits in less than 256 bytes on either a 6800 or 8080 based system.

FREY, PETER W. AND ATKIN, LARRY A. "CREATING A CHESS PLAYER." BYTE, OCTOBER 1978 TO JANUARY 1979 [47 pp.]. a full discussion with the program for writing a chess player.

KANISS, ALAN, DICHRISTOFARO, VINCENT AND SANTINI, JOHN. "AN APL INTERPRETER IN PASCAL" pp. 157-162. with program in the appendix.

HELMERS, CARL. "A PASCAL PRINT UTILITY PROGRAM." pp. 163-187. a menu-driven print utility complete with program.

MUNDIE, DAVID A. "AN AUTOMATIC METRIC CONVERSION PROGRAM." pp. 189-195. converts a whole list of metric units.

MUNDIE, DAVID A. "A COMPUTER-ASSISTED DIETING PROGRAM." pp. 197-198. the program estimates how long a given weight loss will take, based on the person's activity level and food energy intake.

LITWIN, LARRY M. "PASCAL GRAPHICS: A SIMPLIFIED WAY FOR A TIGER TO EAT APPLE PIE." NIBBLE, NO. 6, 1980, pp. 21-22. the Pascal algorithm accesses the graphics array directly and sends the proper "bit sequence" to the Paper Tiger.

LITWIN, LARRY M. "PASCAL TEXT PROCESSING." NIBBLE, VOL. 2, NO. 3, pp. 75-79 [3 pp.]. the program processes lower case with the IDS 440 printer.

LLOYD, STEPHEN. "ROM TEST." CIDER PRESS, OCTOBER # 2 1980, pp. 17-19. 'the purpose of the program is to verify proper operation of the ROM on-board the SSM AIO card.'

LLOYD, STEPHEN. "MASTER CATALOG." CIDER PRESS, OCTOBER # 2 1980, pp. 19-21. 'this program creates a master catalog of as many diskette directories as can be written into the catalog file.'

LLOYD, STEPHEN. "ATTACH-BIOS CONSOLE DRIVER." APPLE ORCHARD, FALL 1981, pp. 45-52. provides a type-ahead buffer and stop, flush, and break functions; and supports the shift key mod.

LOEB, TOM. "WRITING THE WRONGS." CALL -A.P.P.L.E., NOVEMBER/DECEMBER 1980, p. 65. a corrected listing for the 1980 Call -A.P.P.L.E. article by Alan B. Winston.

LOUIS, G. "PAPERBYTE BAR CODES WITH INTEGRAL DATA SYSTEMS PRINTERS." BYTE, MAY 1981, pp. 228-232 [3 pp.]. software generation and reading of bar codes is reliable and now inexpensive; the listing is in Tiny Pascal.

LUBAR, DAVID. "THREE ROADS TO PASCAL." CREATIVE COMPUTING, NOVEMBER 1981, pp. 124-126 [2 pp.]. a review of "Apple Pascal—A Hands-On Approach" by Arthur Luehrmann and Herbert Packham; "Pascal Primer" by David Fox and Mitchell Waite; and "Pascal Programming for the Apple" by T. G. Lewis. "Of the three, 'Apple Pascal—A Hands-On Approach' is the best buy for the Apple owner."

MARKOFF, JOHN. "MORE PROGRAMMING FLEXIBILITY PROMISED WITH NEW UCSD P-SYSTEM." INFOWORLD, 3:30, p. 4. an article...

MATSUMOTO, TOM. "PASCAL TUTOR." APPLE COOKBOOK VOL. 1 NO. 1, 1979, pp. 9-10. setting up an algorithm for Fibonacci numbers.

MATSUMOTO, TOM. "PASCAL TURTLE GRAPHICS." APPLE COOKBOOK, VOL. 1 NO. 1, 1979 p. 2. on controlling the turtle head.

MATSUMOTO, TOM. "PASCAL TUTOR." APPLE COOKBOOK, VOL. 1 NO. 2, 1979, pp. 2-4. an intro for the rank beginner on how to use the editor and filer.

MATTHEWS, JOHN B. "CONVERTING APPLE DOS AND PASCAL TEXT FILES." BYTE, APRIL 1982, pp. 447-463. allows the exchange of information between DOS 3.3 and Pascal operating systems

MAUNEY, GENE. "FUN WITH APPLE AND PASCAL (GAME)." COMPUTE, MARCH 1981, pp. 68-70. an article...

MCCARTHY, DAVID PAUL. "PASCAL BIBLIOGRAPHY." CALL -A.P.P.L.E., MAY 1981 pp. 21-26. the second most extensive collection of articles and books on Pascal for the hobbyist. the 1981 bibliography is contained within this 1982 bibliography.

MCCLELLAND, GEORGE. "LOWER CASE INPUT IN PASCAL." MICHIGAN APPLE-GRAM, MAY 1980, p. 20. a reprint from Southeastern Software Newsletter, issue # 14, p. 5. includes the listing.

MCCORD, JIM. "DEAR UCSD PASCAL-ERS." UCSD PASCAL HOBBY NEWSLETTER. NO. 1, 2 AND 3. 5 JANUARY 1980, 20 MARCH 1980, 12 AUGUST 1980, [20 pp.]. all kinds of wonderful tidbits, tips and notices for the hobbyist; the author has seceded to Softech, which hopefully, will do as well.

MCCOY, EARL. "DATA ABSTRACTIONS AND PROGRAM CORRECTNESS (BASIC VS. PASCAL)." BYTE, SEPTEMBER 1979, pp. 166-171. an article...

MACC. "APPLE][NOTE # 1 COMMUNICATING WITH THE MACC UNIVAC 1180/80." JANUARY 1980, pp. 1-8. MACC is the computing center of the University of Wisconsin, Madison.

MACDONALD, DOUG. "RECURSION: SOLVING AGE-OLD MYSTERIES." MICRO-COMPUTING, DECEMBER 1981, pp. 104-108 [4 pp.]. an introduction to recursion with a factorial program in Pascal, Logo, and BASIC.

MANGASARIAN, JEFFREY. "CYRILLIC ANYONE?" CREATIVE COMPUTING, JULY 1982, pp. 120-132 [6 pp.]. this excellent program enables one to change the character set displayed by the Apple to a character set of one's own choice.

MARCIA, DAVID. "INTRODUCTION TO PASCAL." INTERFACE AGE, MAY 1981, pp. 133-134. an article...

MEADOR, LEE. "READ DOS 3.3 FILES FROM PASCAL 1.1." APPLE ORCHARD, SUMMER 1981, pp. 34-44 [8 pp.]. this is a unit to read DOS 3.3 files and a program to convert text files from DOS 3.3 format to Pascal format.

MERRITT, JIM. "PASCAL FROM BEGINNING TO END." CREATIVE COMPUTING SEPTEMBER/OCTOBER 1978, pp. 149-156. an intro article. "Pascal provides an elegant, easy way for you to talk sense to your computer."

MERRITT, JIM. "BUSINESS EDITORIAL: PASCAL IS HERE TO STAY." INTERFACE AGE, MAY 1979, pp. 52 an article...

MERRITT, JIM. "THE PASCAL PATH: FIRST STEPS." SOFTALK, FEBRUARY 1981, pp. 14-15. discusses a compiler vs. an interpreter and the process involved in developing software.

MERRITT JIM. "THE PASCAL PATH: MORE FIRST STEPS." SOFTALK, MARCH 1981, pp. 12-15 [3 pp.]. algorithms, identifiers, a first program, semicolons.

MERRITT, JIM. "THE PASCAL PATH: PASCAL SURVIVAL GUIDE." SOFTALK, APRIL, 1981, pp. 63-68 [5 pp.]. the editor.

MERRITT, JIM. "THE PASCAL PATH: PASCAL SURVIVAL GUIDE: THE REST." SOFTALK, MAY, 1981, pp. 56-59. compiling and execution.

MERRITT, JIM, "THE PASCAL PATH: THE PATH BECOMES A RAILROAD." SOFTALK, JUNE 1981, pp. 74-76. reading syntax charts; gives also a chart for special keystrokes.

MERRITT, JIM. "THE PASCAL PATH: TOOLS OF THE CRAFT, PART ONE." SOFTALK, JULY 1981, pp. 51-56 [5 pp.]. four fundamental data types, literals, constants, enumerated types, and subranges

MERRITT, JIM. "THE PASCAL PATH: TOOLS OF THE CRAFT, PART 2." SOFTALK, AUGUST 1981, pp. 80-86. discusses variables and operators.

MERRITT, "THE PASCAL PATH: TOOLS OF THE CRAFT, PART 3: CONTROL FLOW." SOFTALK, SEPTEMBER 1981, pp. 38-42. discusses comparison operators, precedence and looping statements.

MERRITT, JIM. "THE PASCAL PATH: TOOLS OF THE CRAFT, PART 4: CONTROL FLOW AND DECISION." SOFTALK, OCTOBER 1981, pp. 15-21 [6 pp.]. discusses further the WHILE and FOR loops and introduces the IF statement.

MERRITT, JIM. "THE PASCAL PATH: TOOLS OF THE CRAFT, PART 5." SOFTALK, NOVEMBER 1981, pp. 34-184 [5 pp.]. discusses WRITELN, fieldwidth, and comments.

MERRITT, JIM. "THE PASCAL PATH: TOOLS OF THE CRAFT, PART 6." SOFTALK, DECEMBER 1981, pp. 16-20 [4 pp.]. discusses the CASE statement.

MERRITT, JIM. "THE PASCAL PATH: TOOLS OF THE CRAFT, PART 7: MILESTONES." SOFTALK, JANUARY 1982, pp. 53-58 [4 pp.]. discusses procedures.

MERRITT, JIM. "THE PASCAL PATH: TOOLS OF THE CRAFT PART 8." SOFTALK, FEBRUARY 1982, pp. 167-174 [6 pp.]. discusses procedures parameters, WRITE, and WRITELN.

MERRITT, JIM. "THE PASCAL PATH: TOOLS OF THE CRAFT, PART 9." SOFTALK, MARCH 1982, pp. 32-36 [4 pp.]. discusses functions and the naming of functions and procedures.

MERRITT, JIM. "THE PASCAL PATH: TOOLS OF THE CRAFT, PART 10." SOFTALK, APRIL 1982, pp. 38-47 [5 pp.]. on READ and READLN.

MERITT, JIM. "THE PASCAL PATH: TOOLS OF THE CRAFT, PART 11: CHARACTER INPUT FROM THE KEYBOARD." SOFTALK, MAY 1982, pp. 48-50. discusses reading a character and EOF and EOLN.

MERITT, JIM. "THE PASCAL PATH: TOOLS OF THE CRAFT, PART 12." SOFTALK, JUNE 1982, pp. 146-151 [5 pp.]. discusses advanced input and output, i.e., files.

MERRITT, JIM. "THE PASCAL PATH: TOOLS OF THE CRAFT, PART 13." SOFTALK, JULY 1982, pp. 174-182 [7 pp.]. discusses the input and output with non-text files, interactive files, and output to the printer.

MERRILL, RON.; MERRILL, PAT.; AND HOWARD, BRUCE. "HISTOGRAM ALGORITHM." JOURNAL OF PASCAL AND ADA, MAY/JUNE 1982, pp. 6-9. this article shows how to use and interpret histograms.

MERRILL, RON.; MERRILL, PAT.; AND HOWARD, BRUCE. "UNIFORM RANDOM NUMBER GENERATION AND APPLICATIONS." JOURNAL OF PASCAL AND ADA, MAY/JUNE 1982, pp.10-18. this article introduces several uniform random number generators and tests for evaluating the uniformity and independence of the random number draws.

MERRILL, RON.; MERRILL, PAT.; AND HOWARD, BRUCE. "APPLICATIONS SOFTWARE." JOURNAL OF PASCAL AND ADA, MAY/JUNE 1982, pp. 19-39. this program formats a text with indenting, forming margins, right justifying by filling in extra spaces so that the right margins are even, and placing headings and footer titles on each page.

MERRILL, RON.; MERRILL, PAT.; AND HOWARD, BRUCE. "RELEVANT: CAN FORTH REPLACE PASCAL?" JOURNAL OF PASCAL AND ADA, MAY/JUNE 1982, pp. 40-42. 'Pascal would benefit with an interactive debugger and possible an interpretive capability.'

MICKELSON, LEE. "PICO ADVENTURE (AN ADVENTURE IN PASCAL)." NIBBLE, VOL. 2 NO. 1, 1981, pp. 39-45 [4 pp.]. gives both the structure of an Adventure program and an introduction to Pascal.

MILLER, ALAN. "JRT PASCAL FOR CP/M" INTERFACE AGE, MAY 1981, pp. 106-108. an article...

MILLER, ALAN. "RATFOR: PASCAL CONSTRUCTIONS IN FORTRAN PROGRAMS." INTERFACE AGE, OCTOBER 1981, pp. 100-103. an article...

MILLER, ALAN. "PASCAL FOR CP/M: DIGITAL MARKETING'S PASCAL/M." INTERFACE AGE, SEPTEMBER 1980, pp. 96-103. a software review.

MILLER, ALAN. "SOFTWARE REVIEW: MT MICROSYSTEMS PASCAL/MT+." INTERFACE AGE, JULY 1981, pp. 94-96. evaluating a CP/M version of Pascal for 8080 or Z80 systems.

MODULAR SOFTWARE. "PASCAL REFERENCE CARD." 1980. a handy reference to procedures, functions, p-machine op codes, etc.

MOFFAT, DAVID. "A PASCAL BIBLIOGRAPHY." PASCAL NEWS, NO. 19, SEPTEMBER 1980, pp. 10-22. this is a complete bibliography for the computer scientist, which does not "overlay" with our list of articles, intended primarily for the hobbyist.

MORRIS, ROBERT, AND PERCHIK, JAMES. "RECURSION AND SIDE EFFECTS IN PASCAL." BYTE, MAY 1981, pp. 316-324 [5 pp.]. the focus of the article is the management of variables that result from procedure calls.

MOSHELL, J. M. "ASSEMBLY LANGUAGE PROGRAMMING WITH UCSD PASCAL." COMPUTE, JULY/AUGUST 1980, pp. 52-57. an introduction to the UCSD assembler with a large program example.

MULLIGAN, JOHN P. "PROGRAMMING WITH PASCAL." MICRO, OCTOBER 1980, REPRINTED IN THE BOOK, "MICRO/APPLE 1," CHELMSFORD, MASSACHUSETTS, pp. 143-151. an overview of Pascal with a quicksort listing.

MUNDIE, DAVID. A. "PASCAL VS BASIC." PEOPLES COMPUTER, JANUARY 1978, p. 41. an article...

MUNDIE, DAVID. "ROUND 3: PASCAL COOLLY COUNTERS." RECREATIONAL COMPUTING, SEPTEMBER 1979, p. 28 an article...

MUNDIE, DAVID. "PILOT/P: IMPLEMENTING HIGH-LEVEL LANGUAGE IN A HURRY." BYTE, JULY 1980, pp. 154-170 [9 pp.]. this is a preprocessor that accepts PILOT/P source code and translates it into Pascal source code.

MUNDIE, DAVID. "GETTING INTO A METRIC GEAR." BYTE, AUGUST 1980, p. 18. a program in response to Lehman's article.

MUNDIE, DAVID. "PASCAL AND THE GREAT RACE." BYTE, SEPTEMBER 1980, p. 94. comments on an article in Byte, April 1980, and notes that, in contrast to Pascal, BASIC does not allow for files of arrays.

MUNRO, ALLEN. "THERE'S A POWERFUL WORD PROCESSOR HIDING IN YOUR PASCAL APPLE." SOFTALK, FEBRUARY 1982, pp. 39-46 [5 pp.]. includes a printout program for Pascal text files.

NAREFF, MAX J. "DECIMAL TO ROMAN NUMERAL." CIDER PRESS, JULY 1980, pp. 13-14. uses case statements, MOD, and DIV.

NAREFF, MAX J. "ADDFRACTNS." CIDER PRESS, JULY 1980, pp. 14-15. the program performs addition of two fractions.

NAREFF, MAX J. "CRAWLER." CIDER PRESS, OCTOBER 1980, p. 12. this program is an exercise in controlling the location of output to the screen by tabbing.

NAREFF, MAX J. "WINDCHILL FACTOR." CIDER PRESS, OCTOBER 1980, p. 13. calculates the degree of perceived coldness from ambient temperature and wind velocity.

NAREFF, MAX J. "DEMOFUNCT1:BEGINNER'S NOTES." CIDER PRESS, OCTOBER 1980, pp. 13-14. discusses the choice of a function or a procedure and exemplifies with a program.

NAREFF, MAX J. "PCNTSOLVER:BEGINNER'S NOTES." CIDER PRESS, OCTOBER # 2 1980, pp. 13-14. this program solves percent problems, demonstrating the use of sets in Pascal.

NAREFF, MAX J. "FILER NOTE." CIDER PRESS, DECEMBER 1980, p. 14. how to send the diskette directory to the printer.

NAREFF, MAX J. "BEGINNER'S NOTES AN EVENING AT THE PASCAL INTEREST GROUP." CIDER PRESS, DECEMBER 1980, pp. 15-16. program Cryptogram demonstrates the use of the string intrinsic functions.

NAREFF, MAX J. "BEGINNER'S NOTES A SPLIT-SCREEN DEMONSTRATION." CIDER PRESS, DECEMBER 1980, p. 16. the program demonstrates one method of writing successively to each of the two forty column screens.

NASSI, I. AND SHNEIDERMAN, B. "FLOWCHART TECHNIQUES FOR STRUCTURED PROGRAMMING." ACM SIGPLAN NOTICES VOL. 8 NO. 8, AUGUST 1973, pp. 12-26. a method for modelling simply-ordered structures.

NAYER, ALAN J. "USING ABBREVIATIONS IN APPLE PASCAL." INTERFACE AGE, NOVEMBER 1981, pp. 98-103 [5 pp.]. uses the EXEC file to interpret abbreviations before compiling a

NEEDLE, DAVID. "IEEE ADOPTS PASCAL STANDARD, EXPECTS AGREEMENT ON S-100 BUS SOON." INFOWORLD, 3:22, p. 17. an article...

NELDNER, THOMAS EDWARD. "MORE MAZE BUILDING: A PASCAL PROGRAM TO GENERATE MAZES EFFICIENTLY ON A PRINTER." BYTE, MAY 1982, pp. 274-284 [6 pp.]. refers to David Matuszek's article in BYTE, December 1981, for the theory of mazes.

NORRIS, PAUL. "USING YOUR PRINTER FROM PASCAL." CIDER PRESS, OCTOBER # 2 1980, pp. 14-15. notes the different ways of getting text to the printer. program Printset is a routine for Centronics 737. a second program writes an interactive file to the printer.

NORTH, STEVE. "APPLE PASCAL." CREATIVE COMPUTING, DECEMBER 1980, pp. 43-46 [2 pp.]. shares his impressions of Apple/UCSD and gives an explanation of what a p-machine is.

O'LOUGHLIN, J. "PASCAL CRITIQUE AND A COMMENT." BYTE, DECEMBER 1978, pp. 179-180. a letter from a reader concerning the coverage of Pascal in Byte with a response by Carl Helmers.

OREGON SOFTWARE. "WHAT'S THE DIFFERENCE BETWEEN BASIC AND PASCAL?," BYTE, AUGUST 1980, p. 69. a clever ad comparing the different approaches to drawing a circle.

OVERGAARD, MARK. "UCSD PASCAL: A PORTABLE SOFTWARE ENVIRONMENT FOR SMALL COMPUTERS." AFIPS CONFERENCE PROCEEDINGS, VOL. 49, 1980, pp. 747-754. discusses independence from the host processor and host peripherals.

PARSONS, RONALD G. "UCSD PASCAL TO CP/M FILE TRANSFER PROGRAM." DR. DOBB'S, AUGUST 1979, pp. 12-16. with a 4 and ½ page listing.

PARSONS, RONALD G. "UCSD PASCAL TERMINAL PARAMETERS." DR. DOBB'S, FEBRUARY 1980, pp. 34-35. a program in which the keybord cursor keys, the screen cursor movement characters, etc. may be defined to the system.

PAULSEN, ARNE. "MORE SIGNIFICANT DIGITS FOR PASCAL." BYTE, OCTOBER 1980, p. 294. a 36-decimal digit precision is available for some machines.

PHILLIPS, THOMAS. "TINY PASCAL SOURCE CREATOR." BYTE, JULY 1979, pp. 231-232. a utility program for the North Star...

POSA, JOHN. "MICROCOMPUTER MADE FOR PASCAL." ELECTRONICS, OCTOBER 12, 1978, AND REPRINTED IN CREATIVE COMPUTING, FEBRUARY 1979, p. 76. 'Western Digital Corp. has designed a mircocomputer around a language, instead of the other way around.'

POSA, JOHN. "PASCAL BECOMES SOFTWARE SUPERSTAR." ELECTRONICS, OCTOBER 12, 1978, AND REPRINTED IN CREATIVE COMPUTING, FEBRUARY 1979, pp. 113-115. 'within eight months, Pascal was running on the 8080, and Bowles was stunned. . ."we've got something here and we better let the world know about it".'

POSA, JOHN. "PROGRAMMING MICROCOMPUTER SYSTEMS WITH HIGH-LEVEL LANGUAGES." ELECTRONICS, JANUARY 18, 1979, pp. 105-112. Pascal is popular for good reasons.

POSA, JOHN. "PASCAL PEOPLE UNHAPPY OVER STANDARD." ELECTRONICS, FEBRUARY 15, 1979, p. 96. ANSI, BSI, ISO, and even IEEE are in the act, as attempts to settle differences between academicians and industrial users are unavailing.

POWERS, DAVID E. "PASCAL FOR THE TRS-80." CREATIVE COMPUTING, FEBRUARY 1980, pp. 24-28 [4 pp.]. observations on implementing Pascal on any micro.

PROGRAMMA INTERNATIONAL. "CLARITY PASCAL VERSION 1.0." Clarity Tiny Pascal is a subset of Pascal inspired by Chung & Yuen's "Tiny Pascal compiler".

PUCKETT, DALE. "PASCAL REVIEW." "68" MICRO JOURNAL, NOVEMBER 1979, pp. 14 an article...

PUCKETT, DALE. "LUCIDATA PASCAL: A 68XX COMPILER." INFOWORLD, 3:8, pp. 22-23. an article...

RAVEN-JENSEN, S. "ROUND 2: BASIC VS PASCAL VS BASIC." RECREATIONAL COMPUTING, MAY 1979, pp. 14 an article...

REESE, BOB. "PATCHY PASCAL." CREATIVE COMPUTING, MARCH 1982, pp. 156-157. discusses that the Apple Pascal monitor can be patched or modified in any manner; includes program.

REEVE, LARRY, C. "POLYBYTES UPDATE." MICROCOMPUTING, JULY 1982, p. 38. some corrections concerning Shoemaker's review.

REINTJES, PETER B. "NETWORK TOOLS: IDEAS FOR INTELLIGENT NETWORK SOFTWARE." BYTE, OCTOBER 1981, pp. 140-174 [13 pp.]. includes modules for a dialer function, a prompt function, and a converse function in Pascal.

REITZ, RANDY. "NORTH STAR TOPICS." S-100 MICROSYSTEMS, MAY/JUNE, 1980, pp. 18-22 [4 pp.]. a general purpose permuted keyword index program.

RITTER, TERRY. "VARIETIES OF THREADED CODE FOR LANGUAGE IMPLEMENTATION." BYTE, SEPTEMBER 1980, pp. 206-227 [13 pp.]. 'continued development of direct-threaded code structures could result in a language representation that would look more like Pascal p-code than threaded code.'

ROADS, C. "MACHINE TONGUES IV." COMPUTER MUSIC JOURNAL, MARCH 1979, pp. 8-13. a brief history of Pascal, some general and specific features of the language and a list of some existing compilers.

ROADS, C. "AN INTRODUCTION TO COMPUTER MUSIC: HISTORY AND FUNDAMENTALS." RECREATIONAL COMPUTING, MAY 1980, pp. 4-an article...

ROBERTS, HENRY. "A.P.P.L.E. DOCTOR." CALL -A.P.P.L.E., OCTOBER 1981, pp. 51-52. a short comparison of BASIC and Pascal.

ROBERTS, HENRY. "A.P.P.L.E. DOCTOR." CALL -A.P.P.L.E., JUNE 1982, pp. 73, 77. answers questions on the transfer of Pascal files to BASIC, printers, floating point numbers, etc.

ROBERTS, WILLIAM L. "NAME THAT TYPE." MICROCOMPUTING, FEBRUARY 1982, pp. 80-82. explains types in Pascal and techniques for using them.

ROBERTSON, PETER D. "SOME CONTRARY OPINION (PASCAL)." BYTE, APRIL 1979, pp. 243-245 [2 pp.]. letter from reader criticizing Pascal and praising BASIC.

ROBINSON, SCOTT G. "MICROMODEM SUPPORT IN APPLE PASCAL." BYTE, JULY 1981, pp. 308-324 [9 pp.]. Pascal support of the standard operational features of the Micromodem II—an alternate solution to that of Thomas H. Wotecki in February 1981 Byte.

ROGERS, PAUL L. "A REVIEW OF INTRODUCTION TO PASCAL BY WELSH AND ELDER." ONCOMPUTING, FALL 1980, p. 34. "superior in organization." should be supplemented with Ledgard's book.

ROSING, MIKE, AND MCLAURIN, KEITH. "PASCAL INTERNALS." CALL -A.P.P.L.E., MARCH/APRIL, 1981. covers in depth the boot process, how to use disk I/O, the directory, how p-code interpreter works, and some useful Pascal locations. gives a disassembler program also.

RUSSELL, P. TIM. "TRUNCATION AND ROUNDING." THE APPLE SHOPPE, MAY/JUNE 1980, pp. 24-25. two useful points on some undocumented features.

SAND, PAUL A. "REVIEWS OF THE PASCAL INTEREST GROUP LIBRARY DISCS." INSIDE WASHINGTON APPLE PI, pp. 37-39. describes the programs available on library disk PIG1.

SAND, PAUL A. "THREE PASCAL 'FEATURES'." APPLE ORCHARD, MAY-JUNE 1982, pp. 55-58 [3 pp.]. discusses three quirks of the Apple][Pascal: the MOD function, real number input, and real number output.

SCHMIDT, DEAN. "PERIODIC TABLE." CREATIVE COMPUTING, NOVEMBER 1981, p. 184. an Apple Pascal program that produces the Periodic Table of Elements on the screen is available by writing to the author.

SCHMIDT, ULRICH. "LETTERS: MORE ON APPLE PASCAL UNITS." BYTE, JULY 1982, pp. 26-28 [2 pp.]. some comments on Tonken's article in the February Byte

SCHRODT, PHILLIP A. "MICROCOMPUTERS IN THE STUDY OF POLITICS: PREDICTING WARS WITH THE RICHARDSON ARMS-RACE MODEL." BYTE, JULY 1982, pp. 108-134 [14 pp.]. a Pascal program gives insight into arms races and other two-party conflicts.

SCHWARTZ, DANA J. "HUFFIN (PASCAL TO DOS)." CALL -A.P.P.L.E., OCTOBER 1981, pp. 13-15. converts a Pascal file to DOS 3.3.

SEDLET, STEVEN, AND DUST, JONATHAN. "LINKING A PASCAL MICROENGINE TO A CYBER 170." BYTE, NOVEMBER 1981, pp. 472-489 [17 pp.]. this program enables the Microengine to log on to a Cyber and provides for the transfer of files between both machines.

SHEPARD, BILL. "LOW RESOLUTION GRAPHICS IN PASCAL." APPLE ORCHARD, SPRING 1981, pp. 80-90 [9 pp.]. a complete unit that translates BASIC's low resolution functions into Pascal.

SHEPARD, BILL. "A CORRECTED PAGE 82 OF THE PROGRAM OF LOW RESOLUTION GRAPHICS IN PASCAL." APPLE ORCHARD, FALL 1981, pp. 62-63. corrections for the earlier program.

SHEPARD, BILL. "HARDWARE INDEPENDENT CONSOLE IN PASCAL." APPLE ORCHARD, JULY/AUGUST 1982, pp. 56-70 [9 pp.]. fills the need for a more generalized console input and output capability than is currently available.

SHILLINGTON, KEITH. "STRUCTURE: THE KEY TO PASCAL'S PROBLEM-SOLVING POWER." DATAMATION, JULY 1979, pp. 151-152. K.S. worked at UCSD.

SHOEMAKER, D.C. "LUCIDATA PASCAL: POLYBYTES CONVERTS AN SWTP PACKAGE TO HEATH'S HDOS." MICROCOMPUTING, APRIL 1982, pp. 203-204. Lucidata Pascal is a subset of the ISO standard Pascal; "a truly remarkable value."

SHOEMAKER, D.C. "LUCIDATA PASCAL: THE BEST PASCAL FOR HEATH GETS EVEN BETTER." MICROCOMPUTING, JULY 1982, pp. 159-160. version 3.8 has great improvements; one improvement is that the data type, pointer, has been added.

SITES, RICHARD L. AND PERKINS, DANIEL P. "UNIVERSAL P-CODE DEFINITION VERSION [0.5]." DEPARTMENT OF ELECTRICAL ENGINEERING AND COMPUTER SCIENCES. pp. 1-40. reproduced by: National Technical Information Information Service U. S. Department of Commerce Springfield, VA 22161

SJOWALL, T. "CP/M TO UCSD PASCAL FILE CONVERSION." DR. DOBB'S, VOL. 5, NO. 9, pp. 16-19. an article...

SKJELLUM, ANTHONY. "MORE FEATURES FOR CP/M." MICROSYSTEMS, MAY 1981, pp. 16-18 an artile...

SLATER, MICHAEL. "APPLE PASCAL COMPILER." CIDER PRESS, APRIL 1980, p. 9. (*$L LISTFILE*) generates a code file, but it may get lost. He gives 3 solutions.

SMITH, BRIAN. "FUN WITH PASCAL." APPLE SHOPPE, VOL. 1 NO. 5, 1980, pp. 7-8. a short program, which prints out the ASCII characters, to illustrate some basics of programming in Pascal.

SMITH, DAVID E. "APPLE PASCAL." APPLE SHOPPE, VOL. 1 NO. 4, pp. 17-22. compares Pascal and BASIC with a program which plots the sine, cosine and tangent functions.

SMITH, STEPHEN P. "CONCERNING PASCAL: A HOMEBREW COMPILER PROJECT." BYTE, APRIL, 1978, pp. 150-151. the status of his pet project.

SMOLIN, ROCKY. "A REVIEW OF 'PASCAL PRIMER'." INTERFACE AGE, OCTOBER 1981, p. 154. a book review...

SMOLIN, ROCKY. "A REVIEW OF 'PASCAL PROGRAMS FOR SCIENTISTS AND ENGINEERS'." INTERFACE AGE, DECEMBER 1981, p.134. a book review...

SOFTECH. "SOME NEWS." PASCAL UPDATE NEWS, APRIL 1980, pp. 1-2. may be a successor to McCord's Hobby Newsletter.

SOKOL, DAN. "PASCAL—PEEKS & POKES." CIDER PRESS, MAY 1980, p. 10. the program is designed for the System.Library.

SOKOL, DAN "SAMPLE SUBROUTINE FOR KEYPRESS." CIDER PRESS, MAY 1980, p. 10. a subroutine for recognizing KEYPRESS despite Sup-R-Terminal etc.

SOKOL, DANIEL D. "PASCAL PEEK & POKE." APPLE SHOPPE, JULY/AUGUST 1980, pp. 7-8. the utility with explanation.

SOKOL, DANIEL D. "NOTES ON ABSOLUTE LOCATION INTERFACES TO APPLE PASCAL." BYTE, SEPTEMBER 1980, pp. 324-325. two programming quickies are presented. the first functions as a PEEK and POKE as in BASIC. the second is an Assembly-language linkage.

SOKOL, DAN. "COMPUTER-AIDED DRAFTING WITH APPLE PASCAL." BYTE, JULY 1981, pp. 388-429 [29 pp.]. special routines link the Apple Graphics Tablet to UCSD Pascal to aid in drawing schematics.

SOMMER, JOHN. "BASIC AND PASCAL SQUARE OFF." MICROCOMPUTING, APRIL 1982, pp. 140-143 [3 pp.]. 'but for those of us who have been spoiled by the ease of writing and debugging BASIC programs and the performance of Microsoft's Compiled Basic, the motive for change is not so great.'

STEIN, HERBERT. "A HOMEBREW PASCAL COMPILER." BYTE, AUGUST 1978, pp. 46-47. lists some of his difficulties.

STIEGLER, MARC. "PASCAL I/O INTERFACING MADE EASY." MICROCOMPUTING, MAY 1982, pp. 94-96. the author developed a Pascal mechanism for tone generation on the C8P.

STORK, JAMES. "DRAWING WITH UCSD PASCAL AND THE HIPLOT PLOTTER." BYTE, OCTOBER 1981, PP. 214-246 [14 pp.]. a plotting program with the Houston Instrument Hiplot for graphs, characters, etc.

SUE, JEFFREY. "PASCAL NOTES." CIDER PRESS, APRIL 1980, p. 9-10. discusses one-disk blues among other things.

SUE, JEFFREY. "PRODUCT REVIEW." CIDER PRESS, DECEMBER 1980, p. 14. 'the only disadvantage I can find is that P.I.T.S. handles only text files.'

SWAINE, MICHAEL. "DIFFERENT LANGUAGES SOLVE THE SAME PROBLEM: PASCAL." INFOWORLD 3:29, p. 21. an article...

SWEET, JERRY N. "CHEDIT: A GRAPHICS-CHARACTER EDITOR." BYTE, MAY 1982, pp. 426-444 [10 pp.]. define your own character set for Apple Pascal.

TATE, AUSTIN. "SYSTEMS PROGRAMMING TECHNIQUES IN PASCAL." USUS, SPRING 1981, pp. 26-30. these techniques are for the preparation of communications software from UCSD to EMAS.

THURLOW, DENNIS. "PASCAL." 80 MICROCOMPUTING, APRIL 1981, p. 31. an article...

THURLOW, DENNIS. "UCSD PASCAL COMPILER (TRS-80)." 80 MICROCOMPUTING, OCTOBER 1981, pp. 40-41. an article...

THURLOW, DENNIS. "A REVIEW OF 'INTRODUCTION TO PASCAL: INCLUDING UCSD PASCAL'." 80 MICROCOMPUTING, NOVEMBER 1981, p. 28. a book review...

TODD, ALLEN W. "SIXTEEN SECTOR DISK COPY." THE APPLE SHOPPE, MAY/JUNE 1981, pp. 17-22. program Universal copy is supposed to copy any standard Apple 16-sectored Pascal, FORTRAN, or DOS diskette.

TONKENS, ROSS. "LETTERS: MORE ON APPLE PASCAL UNITS." BYTE, JULY 1982, p. 28. the admission of a minor error in Tonken's article in the February Byte.

TONKENS, ROSS M. "APPLE/UCSD PASCAL 1.1: A USER'S EVALUATION." CREATIVE COMPUTING, NOVEMBER 1981, p. 77. a review of the new version.

TONKENS, ROSS M. "A GUIDED TOUR OF APPLE PASCAL UNITS AND LIBRARIES." BYTE, FEBRUARY 1982, pp. 225-244 [12 pp.]. includes two sample units: one that provides PEEKing and POKEing, and another that accesses the date; also there is a startup program that displays a color test pattern.

TONKENS, ROSS M. "KINETIC COLOR GRAPHIC ART FOR THE PASCAL EQUIPPED APPLE][." CREATIVE COMPUTING, FEBRUARY 1982, pp. 98-108 [5 pp.]. the program produces a fast, continuously evolving color graphics display based on the algorithms published by Louis Ceza.

TRAMMEL, ROBERT E. "STORING PASCAL HI-RES SCREENS ON DISK." CALL -A.P.P.L.E., MAY 1981, pp. 57-59. the program demonstrates a technique for storing and recalling high-resolution pages to and from disk storage under complete Pascal program control.

TYRO, A. "DISCOVERING PASCAL." CIDER PRESS, APRIL 1980, p. 9. demonstrates exponentiation by use of EXP and LN.

TYRO, A. "PASCAL—'LINELIMIT'." CIDER PRESS, MAY 1980, p. 11. a Pascal translation of BASIC's PEEK (37) with an immediate update.

VAN DEVENTER, HERBERT C. "PROGRAM PEEKDEMO." ADAM & EVE, APPLE II USERS' GROUP, APRIL 1981, pp. 2-5 [2 PP.]. a very clear explanation of the PEEK and POKE functions in Pascal; well annotated with 5 bibliographical references.

VAUGHAN, CLAUDIA M. "BRIDGING THE GAP." CALL -A.P.P.L.E., FEBRUARY 1980, pp. 36-37. compares an Applesoft menu as to how it might appear in Pascal.

VAUGHAN, CRAIG. "PASCAL LOWER CASE WITH DAN PAYMAR'S CHIP." THE BEST OF CIDER PRESS 1978-1979, p. 33. the program modifies BIOS.

VAUGHAN, CRAIG. "KEEPING ON TOP OF THE APPLE." CALL -A.P.P.L.E., FEBRUARY 1980, pp. 32-33. chats on about Micromodems, etc.; a program modifies BIOS to work with Paymar's lower-case adapter.

VAUGHAN, CRAIG AND MEADOR, LEE. "MODIFYING PASCAL TO WORK WITH THE PAYMAR LC ADAPTER." APPLE ORCHARD, SPRING 1981, p. 47. this is a lower-case patch for Pascal Version 1.1.

WAITE, MITCHELL, AND FOX, DAVID. "ADDENDUM TO A BOOK REVIEW." INFOWORLD, JUNE 7, 1982, p. 31. praises Wortman's review.

WALDMAN, CYE H. "TURBO-CHARGED APPLE? A FIRST LOOK AT THE MILL." USUS NEWS, FEBRUARY 1982, pp. 21-22. gives benchmarks for the 6809 on the Apple.

WALKER, BILL. "SORTING WITH BINARY TREES." BYTE, OCTOBER 1980, pp. 96-263 [19 pp.]. gives a Pascal program for sorting a binary tree and much more.

WALLACE, BRUCE. "USING PAGE TWO WITH APPLE PASCAL TURTLE GRAPHICS." BYTE, MAY 1981, p. 122. 'it turns out to be fairly simple to use the unit Turtlegraphics on either page.'

WALLS, KEITH S. "THE FANTASTIC NEW WORLD OF APPLE PASCAL." CALL -A.P.P.L.E., JANUARY 1980, p. 25. gives a program for lower-case Pascal with the Paymar chip.

WAYNE, PHIL. "LANGUAGE LAB." APPLE SHOPPE, VOL. 1 NO. 3, 1979, pp. 11-17 [5 pp.]. the author has written a comprehensive Pascal that retains compatability with the Apple DOS; Apscalle is to be released by Programma.

WAYNE, PHIL. "PASCAL WORKSHOP HOW TO PATCH THE PASCAL BIOS TO CHANGE YOUR I/O SYSTEM!" APPLE SHOPPE, VOL. 1 NO. 5, 1980, pp. 20-22. a utility to dump or modify any byte in any Pascal file on the disk; with this patch-up kit one can get lowercase with the Paymar board.

WEEMS, CHIP. "AN INTRODUCTION TO PROGRAMMING IN PASCAL." WEST COAST COMPUTER FAIRE, 1978, pp. 494-505. an intro on the beginner's level.

WEEMS, CHIP. "DESIGNING STRUCTURED PROGRAMS." BYTE, AUGUST 1978, pp. 143-154. an article...

WICKHAM, KENNETH. "PASCAL IS A 'NATURAL'." IEEE SPECTRUM, MARCH 1979, pp. 35-41. a serious evaluation of Pascal for the micro.

WILBUR, JOHN. "PASCAL NOTE FOR THE SUP-R-TERMINAL." INTERNATIONAL APPLE CORE, APPLICATION NOTE, REPRINTED IN MICHIGAN APPLE-GRAM, AUGUST 1980, p. 29. a solution to a KEYPRESS problem.

WILLIAMS, GREGG. "A REVIEW OF STRUCTURED PROGRAMMING AND PROBLEM-SOLVING WITH PASCAL." BYTE, JUNE 1979, pp. 201-202. 'demonstrates the necessity of firm grounding in design and implementation of programs.'

WILSON, GENE. "SINGLE DRIVE." THE BEST OF CIDER PRESS 1978-1979, pp. 32-33. a discussion of the workability of the single drive system in Pascal.

WILSON, GENE. "PASCAL/MT+ NUTS AND BOLTS." APPLE ORCHARD, MARCH/APRIL 1982, pp. 70-71. some notes for one wishing to use Pascal MT+ on an Apple.

WINSTON, ALAN B. "THE MULTI LINGUAL APPLE." PEEKING AT CALL -A.P.P.L.E., VOL. 2, 1979, pp. 188-190. discusses his first impressions of certain features like linking, data structures, Turtlegraphics, etc.

WINSTON, ALAN B. "THE MULTI LINGUAL APPLE." CALL -A.P.P.L.E., FEBRUARY 1980, pp. 35-36 AND CALL -A.P.P.L.E., MARCH/APRIL 1980, pp. 28-29. discusses lower-case, single drive systems and gives some simple machine language subroutines.

WIRTH, NIKLAUS. "PROGRAM DEVELOPMENT BY STEPWISE REFINEMENT." COMMUNICATIONS OF THE ACM, VOL. 14 NO. 4, APRIL 1971, pp. 221-227. a discussion of design decisions and the decomposition of tasks into subtasks and of data into data structures.

WIRTH, NIKLAUS. "AN ASSESSMENT OF THE PROGRAMMING LANGUAGE PASCAL." IEEE TRANSACTIONS ON SOFTWARE ENGINEERING, VOL. SE-1, NO. 2, JUNE 1975, pp. 192-198 a discussion of data type, sequential-file structure and type union.

WIRTH, NIKLAUS. "COMMENT ON A NOTE ON DYNAMIC ARRAYS IN PASCAL." SIGPLAN NOTICES, NO. 11, JANUARY 1976, pp. 37-38. 'the absence of dynamic arrays is clearly the most frequently cited shortcoming of Pascal.'

WO, DR. "CYCLOIDS: EXPLORING THE CONCENTRIC LAYERS OF APPLE-PASCAL." APPLE ORCHARD, SUMMER 1981, pp. 53-55. this program draws Blaise Pascal's characterization of a cycloid, i.e. the path described by a point on a circle as it rolls along a straight line.

WO, DR. "PUFFIN: BLAISE GOES BOTH WAYS." CALL -A.P.P.L.E., NOVEMBER/DECEMBER 1981, pp. 13-42 [16 PP.]. this is a DOS-to-Pascal file converter.

WO, DR. "CYCLOIDS: BACKING UP DIRECTORIES OR 'I NEVER SMOKE BETWEEN CIGARETTES!'" APPLE ORCHARD, WINTER 1981/1982, pp. 38-55, [6 pp.]. this program provides some measure of protection against directory disastors.

WO, DR. "BLAISE AWAY! A PRIMER ON PASCAL POINTERS." INSIDE WASHINGTON APPLE PI, pp. 29-44 [3 pp.]. 'pointers permit direct addressing of absolute blocks of memory, a trick which makes saving Hi-Res graphics images to disk a triviality.' includes program.

WO, DR. "BLAISE AWAY! DAN PAYMAR MEETS M. PASCAL: LOWER CASE INPUT FOR YOUR PASCAL APPLE." INSIDE WASHINGTON APPLE PI, pp. 30-32. his method for implementing lowinput is to incorporate it into the procedure SYSGEN.

WO, DR. "FOOLING THE COMPILER OR HOW TO KNOW WHERE YOU'RE POINTING." INSIDE WASHINGTON APPLE PI, pp. 32-34. includes a further application of saving and recalling graphics.

WO, DR. "BLAISE AWAY: THE CASE OF THE DISAPPEARING DIRECTORY OR PICKING APPLE'S BRAIN." INSIDE WASHINGTON APPLE PI, pp. 35-37. this program allows the writing and reading of the directory.

WO, DR. "TAKING A FLING AT A FILER OR REINVENTING A BIG WHEEL." INSIDE WASHINGTON APPLE PI, pp. 42-49. shares his efforts to duplicate some of the functions of the system filer: a library UNIT, "filer".

WO, DR. "BLAISE AWAY! SPRINT PLANTING: SEEDS FOR A TEXT FORMATTER." INSIDE WASHINGTON APPLE PI, pp. 50-54. the program is a simple line oriented text formatter with some error checking.

WO, DR. "WILL THE REAL APPLE PASCAL PLEASE STAND UP!" APPLE ORCHARD, MAY-JUNE 1982, pp. 75-80 [4 pp.]. reviews the notion of portability of APPLE][Pascal, Version 1.1, Apple /// Pascal, and UCSD Pascal, Version IV.

WOODHEAD, ROBERT J. "APPLE PASCAL CROSS-REFERENCE." BYTE, OCTOBER 1981, pp. 419-429 [10 pp.]. a modified version of APPLE ///:CROSSREF program, which is ultimately the algorithm of Niklaus Wirth.

WORTMAN, LEON. "A REVIEW OF 'PASCAL PRIMER' BY DAVID FOX AND MITCHELL WAITE." INFOWORLD, APRIL 19, 1982, p. 63. 'I heartily recommend this book to you if you want to make the change over from BASIC to Pascal.'

WORTMAN, LEON. "A REVIEW OF 'PASCAL: AN INTRODUCTION TO METHODICAL PROGRAMMING' BY FINDLAY & WATT." INFOWORLD, APRIL 26, 1982, pp. 41-43 [2 pp.]. 'this excellent, easy-to-read, fairly advanced book on Pascal is now in its second edition. the first was printed in 1978.'

WOTEKI, THOMAS H. "A PASCAL LIBRARY UNIT FOR THE MICROMODEM II." BYTE, FEBRUARY 1981, pp. 106-136 [16 pp.]. presents a complete package of remote communications programs using the Micromodem running under Apple Pascal.

WOTEKI, THOMAS H. AND SAND, PAUL A. "FOUR IMPLEMENTATIONS OF PASCAL." BYTE, MARCH 1982, pp. 316-356 [20 pp.]. compares Pascal/Z, Pascal/M, Pascal/MT+, and UCSD Pascal; includes a Primes program by Knuth, a program that determines floating-point precision, and a benchmark program.

WURZEL, BILL. "THE LANGUAGE SYSTEM – THE APPLE GROWS UP." THE APPLE ORCHARD, MARCH/APRIL 1980, pp. 74-77. short comments on the various systems of Apple Pascal.

YARNALL, W. M. "LINEAR PROGRAMMING TECHNIQUES IN PASCAL." S-100 MICROSYSTEMS, MARCH/APRIL 1980, PP. 14-27 [12 pp.]. 'this is the first part of a two-part article on linear programming in Pascal. linear programming provides a means for solving problems with numerous constraints that often make solutions non-obvious.'

YOUNG, CHRIS. "DOS/BIOS DIRECTORY AND FILE CONVERSION IN NORTH STAR UCSD PASCAL, PART II." MICROSYSTEMS, NOVEMBER 1981, pp. 40-47. an article...

A BIBLIOGRAPHY OF PASCAL BOOKS

REFERENCE MANUALS

Apple Corporation. APPLE PASCAL REFERENCE MANUAL. Cupertino, CA: Apple, 1979 [312 pp.].

Apple Corporation. APPLE PASCAL OPERATING SYSTEM REFERENCE MANUAL. Cupertino, CA: Apple, 1980 ($25.00) [298 pp.].

Apple Corporation. APPLE PASCAL LANGUAGE REFERENCE MANUAL. Cupertino, CA: Apple, 1980 ($20.00) [209 pp.].

Jensen, Kathleen and Wirth, Niklaus. PASCAL USER MANUAL AND REPORT [2nd ed]. New York, NY: Springer-Verlag, 1978 ($7.90) [167 pp.].

Regents of U of C. UCSD PASCAL VERSION II.0 A PRODUCT FOR MINI AND MICRO-COMPUTERS USERS' MANUAL. San Diego, CA: Softech, 1980 ($25.00) [440 pp.].

INTRODUCTORY TEXT BOOKS

Alagic, Saud and Arbib, Michael A. THE DESIGN OF WELL-STRUCTURED AND CORRECT PROGRAMS. New York, NY: Springer-Verlag, 1978 ($14.80) [292 pp.].

Atkinson, Laurence. PASCAL PROGRAMMING. Chichester: John Wiley & Sons, 1981 ($21.00) [428 pp.].

Bachmann, Karl Heinz. DIE PROGRAMMIERUNGS-SPRACHEN PASCAL UND ALGOL 68. Berlin, DDR: Akademie-Verlag, 1976 [220 pp.].

Barron, D. W., editor. PASCAL: THE LANGUAGE AND ITS IMPLEMENTATION. New York, NY: John Wiley & Sons, 1981 ($35.00) [301 pp.].

Borgerson, Mark J. A BASIC PROGRAMMER'S GUIDE TO PASCAL. New York, NY: John Wiley & Sons, 1982 ($9.95) [118 pp.].

Bowen, Kenneth. SPEAKING PASCAL. Rochelle Park, NJ: Hayden, 1981 ($11.95) [236 pp.].

Bowen, Kenneth A. SPEAKING PASCAL: A COMPUTER LANGUAGE PRIMER. Rochelle Park, NJ: Hayden, 1982 ($11.95) [236 pp.].

Bowles, Kenneth L. MICROCOMPUTER PROBLEM SOLVING USING PASCAL. New York, NY: Springer-Verlag, 1977 ($9.80) [563 pp.].

Bowles, Kenneth L. BEGINNER'S MANUAL FOR THE UCSD PASCAL. Software System. New York, NY: McGraw Hill Paperbacks, 1980 ($11.95) [204 pp.]. (also available with Apple][diskette from San Diego, CA: Softech 1980 ($20.00))

Campbell, Roy Harold and Miller, Thomas John. A PATH PASCAL LANGUAGE. Urbana, IL: Dept of Computer Science, University of Illinois, 1978 [20 pp.].

Chernicoff, Stephen. PASCAL LANGUAGE MANUAL. Science Research Associates, Inc., 1978 ($5.50) [142 pp.].

Cherry, George William. PASCAL PROGRAMMING STRUCTURES: AN INTRODUCTION TO SYSTEMATIC PROGRAMMING. Reston, VA: Reston Publishing Company, 1980 ($12.95) [314 pp.]

Chirlian, Paul M. PASCAL. Matrix Publishers, 1980 ($12.95) [200 pp.].

Clark, Randy and Koehler, Stephen. THE UCSD PASCAL HANDBOOK. Englewood Cliffs, NJ: Prentice-Hall, 1982 ($15.95) [356 pp.].

Coleman, Derek. A STRUCTURED PROGRAMMING APPROACH TO DATA. MacMillan Press, 1978 ($12.10) [222 pp.].

Conway, Richard Walter; Gries, David; and Zimmerman, E. Carl. Foreward by Niklaus Wirth. A PRIMER ON PASCAL. Cambridge, MA.: Winthrop Publishers, 1976 ($13.95) [433 pp.] 2nd ed. 1981 ($11.95) [440 pp.].

Conway, Richard; Archer, James; and Conway, Ralph. PROGRAMMING FOR POETS: A GENTLE INTRODUCTION USING PASCAL. Cambridge, MA: Winthrop Publishers, 1980 ($12.00) [352 pp.].

Cooper, Doug. INTRODUCTION TO PASCAL FOR SCIENTISTS. New York, NY: John Wiley & Sons, 1981 [260 pp.].

Cooper, Doug and Clancy, Michael. OH! PASCAL. New York, NY: W. W. Norton, 1982 ($15.95) [476 pp.].

Davidson, Gregory. PRACTICAL PASCAL PROGRAMS. Berkeley, CA: Osborne/McGraw/Hill, 1982, ($15.99) [205 pp.].

Davis, Henry. PASCAL NOTEBOOK. VOLUME I: INTRODUCTION TO PASCAL. Beaverton, OR: Dilithium Press, 1980 ($9.95) [150 pp.]. VOLUME II: THE PASCAL COMPILER. Beaverton, OR: Dilithium Press, 1980 ($9.95) [150 pp.]. VOLUME III: COMPILER WRITING IN PASCAL. Beaverton, OR: Dilithium Press, 1980 ($9.95) [150 pp.].

Eisenbach, Susan and Sadler, Christopher. PASCAL FOR PROGRAMMERS. New York, NY: Springer-Verlag, 1981 ($12.00) [201 pp.].

Findlay, William and Watt, David A. PASCAL: AN INTRODUCTION TO METHODICAL PROGRAMMING. Potomac, MD: Computer Science Press, 1978 ($11.95) [306 pp.].

Fox, David and Waite, Michael. PASCAL PRIMER. Indianopolis, IN: Sams Books, 1981 ($16.95) [206 pp.].

Graham, Neill. INTRODUCTION TO PASCAL. St. Paul, MN: West Publishers, 1980 ($10.95) [243 pp.].

Grant, Charles W. and Butah, John. INTRODUCTION TO UCSD PASCAL SYSTEMS. Berkeley, CA: Sybex, 1981 ($14.95) [250 pp.].

Grogono, Peter. PROGRAMMING IN PASCAL. Reading, MA: Addison-Wesley, 1978 ($10.95) [1st ed 359 pp.] [2nd ed 1980 363 pp.].

Grogono, Peter. PROGRAMMING IN PASCAL WITH PASCAL—1000. Reading, MA: Addison-Wesley, 1980 ($13.95) [379 pp.].

Heiserman, David L. PASCAL. Summit, PA: Tab Books, 1980 ($9.95) [350 pp.].

Hergert, Douglas and Kalash, Joseph T. APPLE PASCAL GAMES. Berkeley, CA: Sybex, 1981 ($14.95) [371 pp.].

Hume, J.N.P. and Holt, Richard C. PROGRAMMING IN STANDARD PASCAL. Reston, VA: Prentice-Hall, 1980 ($16.95) [389 pp.].

Hume, J.N.P. and Holt, Richard C. UCSD PASCAL: A BEGINNER'S GUIDE TO PROGRAMMING MICROCOMPUTERS. Reston, VA: Prentice-Hall, 1982 ($12.95) [346 pp.].

Jones, William B. PROGRAMMING CONCEPTS: A SECOND COURSE. Englewood Cliffs, NJ: Prentice-Hall, 1982 ($19.95) [336 pp.].

Kaucher, Edgar; Klatte, Rudi; u. Ulrich, Christian. HOHERE PROGRAMMIERSPRACHEN ALGOL, FORTRAN, PASCAL IN EINHEITLICHER UND UBERSICHTLICHER DARSTELLUNG. Manheim, DDR: Bibliographisches Institute, 1978 [258 pp.].

Katzan, Harry. INVITATION TO PASCAL. New York, NY: Petrocelli, 1982 ($17.50) [233 pp.].

Kenedy, Michael and Solomon, Martin B. PASCAL: PROGRAM DEVELOPMENT WITH TEN INSTRUCTION SUBSETS (TIPS) AND STANDARD PASCAL. Englewood Cliffs, NJ: Prentice-Hall, 1982 ($17.95) [560 pp.].

Kieburtz, Richard B. STRUCTURED PROGRAMMING AND PROBLEM-SOLVING WITH PASCAL. Englewood Cliffs, NJ: Prentice-Hall, 1978 ($12.95) [365 pp.].

Koffman, Elliot B. PROBLEM SOLVING AND STRUCTURED PROGRAMMING IN PASCAL. Reading, MA: Addison & Wesley, 1981 ($13.95) [483 pp.].

Koffman, Elliot B. PASCAL: A PROBLEM SOLVING APPROACH. Reading, MA: Addison & Wesley, 1982 [470 pp.].

Ledgard, Henry F.; Hueras, John F.; and Nagin, Paul A. PASCAL WITH STYLE: PROGRAMMING PROVERBS. Rochelle Park, NJ: Hayden, 1979 ($6.95) [210 pp.].

Ledgard, Henry and Singer, Andrew. ELEMENTARY PASCAL. New York, NY: Vintage Books, 1982 ($12.95) [266 pp.].

Lewis, T. G. PASCAL PROGRAMMING FOR THE APPLE. Reston, VA: Reston Publishing, 1981 ($17.95 cloth, $12.95 paper) [234 pp.].

MacEwen, Glenn H. INTRODUCTION TO COMPUTER SYSTEMS: USING THE PDP-11 AND PASCAL, New York, NY: McGraw-Hill, 1980 ($19.95) [462 pp.].

McGregor, James J., and Watt, Alan H. SIMPLE PASCAL. Computer Science Press, 1981 ($10.95) [182 pp.].

Miller, Alan. PASCAL PROGRAMS FOR SCIENTISTS AND ENGINEERS. Berkeley, CA: Sybex, 1981 ($25.00 cloth, $16.95 paper) [250 pp.].

Moore, Lawrie. FOUNDATIONS OF PROGRAMMING WITH PASCAL. New York, NY: John Wiley & Sons, 1982 ($49.95) [238 pp.].

Peckham, Herbert D. and Luehrmann, Arthur. APPLE PASCAL. New York, NY: McGraw-Hill, 1981 ($14.95) [430 pp.].

Prather, Ronald E. PROBLEM SOLVING PRINCIPLES: PROGRAMMING WITH PASCAL. Englewood Cliffs, NJ: Prentice-Hall, 1982 ($19.95) [368 pp.].

Price, David. PASCAL: A CONSIDERATE APPROACH. Englewood Cliffs, NJ: Prentice-Hall, 1981 ($9.95) [197 pp.].

Rohl, J. S. and Barrett, H. J. PROGRAMMING VIA PASCAL. Cambridge: Cambridge University Press, 1980 ($15.95) [327 pp].

Schneider, G. Michael; Weingart, Steven W.; and Perlman, David M. AN INTRODUCTION TO PROGRAMMING AND PROBLEM SOLVING WITH PASCAL. New York, NY: John Wiley & Sons, 1978 ($14.95) [394 pp.].

Schneider, G. M. ADVANCED PROGRAMMING AND PROBLEM SOLVING WITH PASCAL. New York, NY: John Wiley & Sons, 1981 ($25.95) [506 pp.].

Stocks, Arthur Ian. THE PASCAL-11 PROGRAMMING SYSTEM. Urbana, IL: Dept. of Computer Science, University of Illinois. [107 pp.].

Tiberghien, Jacques. THE PASCAL HANDBOOK. Berkeley, CA: Sybex, 1980 ($14.95) [473 pp.].

Tremblay, Jean-Paul and Blunt, Richard B. STRUCTURED PASCAL. New York, NY: McGraw-Hill, 1980 ($9.95) [421 pp.].

Webster, C. A. G. INTRODUCTION TO PASCAL. London, England: Heyden, 1976 [129 pp].

Welsh, Jim and Elder, John. INTRODUCTION TO PASCAL. Englewood Cliffs, NJ: Prentice-Hall, 1979 ($14.95) [282 pp].

Wilson, I. R. and Addyman, A. M. A PRACTICAL INTRODUCTION TO PASCAL. New York, NY: Springer-Verlag, 1979 ($7.95) [148 pp.].

Zaks, Rodnay. INTRODUCTION TO PASCAL (INCLUDING UCSD PASCAL). Berkeley, CA: Sybex, 1980 ($12.95) [320 pp.].

DATA STRUCTURES AND ADVANCED BOOKS

Brinch Hansen, Per. THE ARCHITECTURE OF CONCURRENT PROGRAMS. Englewood Cliffs, NJ: Prentice-Hall, 1977 ($28.50).

Donohue, James Edward. COMPLEMENTARY DEFINITIONS OF PROGRAMMING LANGUAGE SEMANTICS. New York, NY: Springer-Verlag, 1976 [172 pp.].

Hartmann, A. C. A CONCURRENT PASCAL COMPILER FOR MINICOMPUTERS. New York, NY: Springer-Verlag Lecture Notes in Computer Science. No. 50, 1977.

Herschel, Rudolf u. Pieper, Friedrich. PASCAL:SYSTEMAT. DARST. VON PASCAL U. CONCURRENT PASCAL FUR D. ANWENDER. Wien, Oesterreich: Oldenbourg, 1979 [248 pp.].

Horowitz, Ellis, and Sahni, Sartaj. FUNDAMENTALS OF DATA STRUCTURES. Potomac, MD: Computer Science Press, 1976 ($19.95) [564 pp.].

Knuth, Donald E. THE ART OF COMPUTER PROGRAMMING [2nd ed]. Reading, MA: Addison-Wesley, 1973 ($23.50) [634 pp.].

Lewi, J. A PROGRAMMING METHODOLOGY IN COMPILER CONSTRUCTIONS, PART 1: CONCEPT. North-Holland, 1979 [308 pp.].

Nori, K. V.; Ammann, U.; Jensen, K.; Nageli, H. H.; and Jacobi, Ch. THE PASCAL (P) COMPILER: IMPLEMENTATION NOTES. 1974.

Tenenbaum, Aaron M. and Augenstein, Moshe J. DATA STRUCTURES USING PASCAL. Englewood Cliffs, NJ: Prentice-Hall ($23.95) [545 pp.].

Wirth, Niklaus. ALGORITHMS + DATA STRUCTURES = PROGRAMS. Englewood Cliffs, NJ: Prentice-Hall, 1976 ($20.95) [366 pp.].

Wirth, Niklaus. REVIDIERTER BERICHT UBER DIE PROGRAMMIERSPRACHE PASCAL. Berlin, DDR: Akademie Verlag, 1976 [48 pp.].

If there be no end to the making of books, then what about magazines!

ADAM & EVE USERS' GROUP 2411 Monroe St. Madison, WI 53711 $12.00 year (monthly)

APPLE COOKBOOK 131 Highland Vacaville, CA 95688 $15.00 year (six times a year) (but going out of business)

APPLE EDUCATION NEWS 10260 Bandley Drive Cupertino, CA 95014 Complimentary to Apple owners.

APPLE ORCHARD INTERNATIONAL APPLE CORE 910 A George Street Santa Clara, CA 95050 $15.00 year (bi-monthly)

THE APPLE SHOPPE P.O. Box 701 Placentia, CA 92670 $12.00 year

BYTE 70 Main St. Peterborough NH 03458 (800) 258 5485 $19.00 year (monthly)

CIDER PRESS SAN FRANCISCO APPLE CORE 1515 Sloot Blvd. Suite 2 San Francisco, CA 94132

CALL -A.P.P.L.E. 304 Main Ave. S. Suite 300 Renton, WA 98055 $45.00 first year $20.00 thereafter (monthly)

COMPUTE! P. O. Box 5406 Greensboro, NC 27403

COMPUTER DESIGN 11 Goldsmith St. Littleton, MA 01460

CREATIVE COMPUTING P.O. Box 789-M Morristown, NJ 07960 (800) 631 8112 $20.00 year (monthly)

DATAMATION 666 Fifth Ave. New York, NY 10103 $36.00 year (monthly)

DR. DOBB'S JOURNAL Peoples Computer Co. 1263 E. Camino Real P. O. Box E Menlo Park, CA 94025 $21.00 year (monthly)

EDN ELECTRONIC DESIGN NEWS 270 St. Paul Street Denver, CO 80206 $30.00 year (22 x)

ELECTRONICS 1221 Avenue of the Americas New York, NY 10020

FROM THE CORE CAROLINA APPLE CORE P.O. Box 31424 Raleigh, NC 27622 $12.00 year (monthly)

INSIDE WASHINGTON APPLE PI (P.O. Box 34511, Washington, DC 20034)

INTERFACE AGE 16704 Marquardt Ave. Cerritos, CA 90701 $18.00 year (monthly)

JOURNAL OF PASCAL AND ADA (P.O. Box 327, Payson, Utah 84651. $14.00 a year (six issues))

PASCAL NEWS Pascal User's Group P. O. Box 4406 Allentown, PA 18104 $10.00 year (quarterly)

PERSONAL COMPUTER WORLD 14 Rathbone Place London WIP IDE, England 8.00 pounds year (monthly)

PERSONAL COMPUTING 50 Essex St. Rochelle Park, NJ $18.00 year (monthly)

RECREATIONAL COMPUTING 1263 El Camino Real Menlo Park, CA 94025 $12.00 year (bi-monthly)

SOFTALK 11021 Magnolia Boulevard North Hollywood, CA 91601 For one year, complimentary to Apple owners.

MICRO P.O. Box 6502 Chelmsford, MA $18.00 year (monthly)

MICROCOMPUTING 80 Pine St. Peterborough, NH 03458 $25.00 year (monthly)

MICHIGAN APPLE-GRAM P.O. Box 551 Madison Heights, MI 48071 $12.00 year (ten times a year)

NEWSLETTER SOUTHEASTERN SOFTWARE 6414 Derbyshire Drive New Orleans, LA 70126 $10.00 year (ten times a year)

NIBBLE S.P.A.R.C. P.O. Box 325 Lincoln, MA 01773 $17.50 year (eight times a year)

NSAUG 650 Pompano Ln. Palatine, IL 60067 $12.00

ONCOMPUTING 70 Main St. Peterborough, NH 03458 (800) 258 5485 $8.50 year (quarterly)

Interactive, Goof-Proof Keyboard Input

Ron DeGroat

```
(***************************)
(* Listing #2: KYBD DEMO *)
(*                      *)
(* by Ron De Groat      *)
(***************************)

{$V-}
PROGRAM KYBDDEMO;

USES KYBDSTUFF;


VAR ALPHABET  : SETOFCHAR; {Type defined in KYBDSTUFF}
    FLOAT_PT  : REAL;
    INT_NUM,
    HEX_VAL    : INTEGER;
    HEXWORD    : STRING[2];
    ALFASTRING  : STRING[10];
    CH          : CHAR;

BEGIN

  REPEAT
    WRITELN('*** HIT ANY KEY TO CONTINUE DEMO ***');
  UNTIL KEYPRESS;
  READ(KEYBOARD,CH); {To clear keypress}

  PAGE(OUTPUT);
  PROMPTAT(0,'TRY TO INPUT ILLEGAL DATA.');

  ALPHABET:=['A'..'Z'];
  PROMPTAT(4,'INPUT ALFA STRING (LENGTH<=3): ');
  GETSTRING(ALFASTRING,ALPHABET,3);

  WRITELN;
  INT_NUM:=GETINTEGER('INTEGER (-1<I<100): ',100,-1);

  WRITELN;
  FLOAT_PT:=GETFPNUM('FLOATING PT NUM (0.1<FP<9.999): ',
                                          9.999,0.1);
  WRITELN;
  HEX_VAL:=GET_HEX_VAL('HEX ADDR: ',4);
  INTTOHEX(HEXVAL,HEXWORD);
  WRITELN('HEX VALUES RETURN AS INTEGER: ',HEXVAL);
  WRITELN('BUT CAN BE CONVERTED TO HEX:  ',HEXWORD);

  WRITELN;
  HEX_VAL:=GETHEXVAL('HEX BYTE:  ',2);
  WRITELN('HEX VALUE: ',HEX_VAL);

END.
```

Bad input is probably the most frequent and bothersome user problem in Apple Pascal. This article describes how to make keyboard input virtually goof-proof by preventing invalid data from ever entering a program. Beyond that, the routines presented here (in Listing #1) make keyboard input more interactive by carefully checking each key for legality as it is pressed.

In Apple Pascal, when a program is waiting for numeric input, an execution error ('BAD INPUT FORMAT') occurs if an alphabetic character is accidentally entered. The computer politely informs the user to 'PRESS [SPACE] TO CONTINUE', whereupon, the system responds in a most unfriendly manner — it re-initializes itself.

Obviously, the system does not take execution, or run-time, errors lightly. It reacts with the most emphatic action it can muster. In fact, the idea behind the emphatic action is that execution errors should not occur at all. Pascal was designed with built-in safeguards which tend to prevent run-time errors from happening. Usually, if a program compiles without error, it will also execute without error. The major exception involves errors caused by unexpected keyboard input.

Unfortunately, most programs require input from humans via the keyboard. Since most humans are error-prone at times, and since Pascal is so intolerant of execution errors, it is extremely important to have keyboard input routines which filter out as much illegal data as possible. The simplest approach would check each input line for legality when the carriage return is pressed. A more interactive approach would check each key for legality when it is pressed.

```
(*****************************************)
(*                                       *)
(* Listing #1: KYBDSTUFF                 *)
(*                                       *)
(* Written by Ron DeGroat   July, 1981   *)
(*                                       *)
(*****************************************)

{$S+,V-}
UNIT KYBDSTUFF; INTRINSIC CODE 25 DATA 26;

{Removing 'INTRINSIC...26;' makes the unit regular.
 Regular units may be explicitly linked with the Linker.
 Intrinsic units must be installed in the SYSTEM.LIBRARY.}


INTERFACE

TYPE SETOFCHAR = SET OF CHAR; {Must be declared for parameter list}

{The following commands may be used by the host program in WRITE statements}
{These variable identifiers must not be redeclared in the host program      }

VAR CR,          {Carriage return}
    BS,          {Back space      }
    EOL,         {Erase to end of line}
    EOS,         {Erase to end of screen}
    BELL:CHAR;   {Sound bell}

FUNCTION  GET_CHAR(OKSET:SETOFCHAR):CHAR;
PROCEDURE GETSTRING(VAR S:STRING; OKSET:SETOFCHAR; MAXLEN:INTEGER);
FUNCTION  GET_HEX_VAL(PROMPT:STRING; MAXLEN:INTEGER):INTEGER;
FUNCTION  HEX_TO_INT(HEXSTR:STRING):INTEGER;
PROCEDURE INT_TO_HEX(INT:INTEGER; VAR HEX_STR:STRING);
FUNCTION  FP_NUM(FP_STR:STRING):REAL;
FUNCTION  GET_FP_NUM(PROMPT:STRING; MAXVAL,MINVAL:REAL):REAL;
FUNCTION  GET_INTEGER(PROMPT:STRING; MAXVAL,MINVAL:INTEGER):INTEGER;
PROCEDURE PROMPTAT(LINE:INTEGER; MESSAGE:STRING);
FUNCTION  KEYPRESS:BOOLEAN;


IMPLEMENTATION

VAR HEXDIGIT      :PACKED ARRAY[0..15] OF CHAR;


(**********************************************)
(* GETS CHARACTER IN OKSET, ALL OTHERS BEEPED. *)
(**********************************************)

FUNCTION GET_CHAR((OKSET:SETOFCHAR):CHAR);

VAR CH    :CHAR;
    GOOD  :BOOLEAN;

BEGIN
  REPEAT
    READ(KEYBOARD,CH);
    IF EOLN(KEYBOARD) THEN CH:=CR;
    GOOD:=CH IN OKSET;
    IF NOT GOOD THEN WRITE(BELL)
      ELSE IF CH IN [' '..CHR(125)]
             THEN WRITE(CH);
  UNTIL GOOD;
  GET_CHAR:=CH;
END;


(***********************************************************)
(* GETS STRING WITH MAXIMUM LENGTH AND CHARACTERS IN OKSET *)
(***********************************************************)
```

```
PROCEDURE GETSTRING(VAR S:STRING; OKSET:SETOFCHAR;
                                  MAXLEN:INTEGER);
VAR S1          :STRING[1];
    STEMP       :STRING;
    LEN         :INTEGER;
    FIRSTCHAR   :BOOLEAN;
    LASTCHAR    :BOOLEAN;
    GETSET      :SETOFCHAR;

BEGIN
 S1:=' '; STEMP:='';
 IF MAXLEN<1 THEN MAXLEN:=1
 ELSE IF MAXLEN>255 THEN MAXLEN:=255;
 REPEAT
  LEN:=LENGTH(STEMP);
  FIRSTCHAR:=(LEN=0);
  LASTCHAR:=(LEN=MAXLEN);

  IF FIRSTCHAR THEN GETSET:=OKSET
  ELSE IF LASTCHAR THEN GETSET:=[CR,BS]
       ELSE GETSET:=OKSET+[CR,BS];

  S1[1]:=GETCHAR(GETSET);

  IF S1[1] IN OKSET THEN STEMP:=CONCAT(STEMP,S1)
  ELSE IF S1[1]=BS THEN
    BEGIN
     WRITE(BS,' ',BS);
     DELETE(STEMP,LEN,1);
    END;
  UNTIL S1[1]=CR; WRITELN;
 S:=STEMP;
END;


(**********************************)
(* PLACE MESSAGE AT SPECIFIED LINE *)
(**********************************)

PROCEDURE PROMPTAT(LINE:INTEGER; MESSAGE:STRING);
BEGIN
 GOTOXY(0,LINE);
 WRITE(MESSAGE,EOL);
END;


(*********************************)
(* CONVERT INTEGER TO HEX STRING *)
(*********************************)

PROCEDURE INT_TO_HEX((INT:INTEGER; VAR HEX_STR:STRING));

VAR HIBYTE,LOBYTE  :INTEGER;

BEGIN
 HEX_STR:='0000';

 IF INT<0 THEN
   BEGIN
     INT:= INT+32767+1;;
     HIBYTE:= (INT DIV 256) +128;
   END
 ELSE
   HIBYTE:= INT DIV 256;
   LOBYTE:= INT MOD 256;

 HEXSTR[1]:= HEXDIGIT[HIBYTE DIV 16];
 HEXSTR[2]:= HEXDIGIT[HIBYTE MOD 16];
 HEXSTR[3]:= HEXDIGIT[LOBYTE DIV 16];
 HEXSTR[4]:= HEXDIGIT[LOBYTE MOD 16];

 WHILE (HEXSTR[1]='0') AND (LENGTH(HEXSTR)>1) DO DELETE(HEXSTR,1,1);

END;
```

Another feature that would enhance keyboard input is the ability to backspace and edit a value before it is committed to the program by a carriage return. In Apple Pascal, backspacing is supported for STRING input, but not for REAL and INTEGER input. To get around this problem, all data would have to be read in as a string and then converted to its appropriate numerical value. To summarize, a good input routine would filter out illegal data to prevent execution errors, check keys pressed individually to make program response more interactive, and read numbers as strings to permit backspacing.

Getting floating point numbers (PROCEDURE GETFPNUM) is the most complicated input routine because wide variation is possible in the floating point format. For example, the first character may be in the set ['0'..'9', '-', '.'], but after that the negative sign is not allowed. Only one decimal point is accepted and a maximum length is also set. In addition, maximum and minimum numerical values are defined. With all these constraints, it is easy to prevent most input-related execution errors from occurring.

When the intrinsic unit shown in Listing #1 is compiled and installed in the SYSTEM.LIBRARY, it can be conveniently used by any Pascal program with a 'USES KYBDSTUFF' declaration (in the same way that the intrinsic units, TURTLEGRAPHICS or APPLESTUFF, are used). In addition to the convenience, intrinsic units are good for saving disk space because they only exist on disk in the SYSTEM.LIBRARY. But sometimes intrinsic units are not appropriate. For example, if a program must be self-contained and independent of the SYSTEM.LIBRARY, a regular unit should be used. Or, when memory is limited and only one or two routines are needed, it is more efficient to simply copy the required routines directly into the text of the program.

The KYBDDEMO shown in Listing #2 demonstrates how to use KYBDSTUFF. The KYBDDEMO also allows the user to test the effectiveness of the input routines. The fastest way to make these routines absolutely fool-proof is through user feedback. Any suggestions for enhancement from the readers would be greatlv appreciated.

The routines shown in Listing #1 make keyboard input highly interactive and goof-proof. These input routines can be used to make user-friendly programs that are virtually immune to execution errors.

GETCHAR is the most general and useful of these routines. It checks each character for legality as it is typed in. Only characters in the OKSET are accepted. Other characters are not allowed, and a bell is sounded to warn the user that he is attempting to input illegal data. Since each character is checked individually, user input becomes completely interactive. GETCHAR is used by the other routines to get strings, hex values, integers and floating point numbers.

Currently the most serious bottleneck in computer advancement concerns software, not hardware. Perhaps a lesson can be learned about software development from the hardware world.

In electronics, the integrated circuit revolutionized electronic circuit design by modularizing basic electronic circuits. With the IC as the basic building block, complex electronic devices became less expensive and easier to build. Even simple circuits were improved by the efficient, plug-in chips available.

In computers, a similar revolution is needed in software design. Efficient, well-constructed software building blocks would greatly simplify and enhance program development. High-quality, plug-in modules with universal application could be used to eliminate a lot of duplicated effort and replace a score of mediocre routines with finely tuned, standardized procedures. With good building blocks, a second-rate programmer could turn out first-rate programs.

```
(************************************)
(* CONVERT HEX STRING TO INTEGER *)
(************************************)

FUNCTION HEX_TO_INT((HEXSTR:STRING):INTEGER);

VAR I,NUM,DIGIT   :INTEGER;

BEGIN
 NUM:=0;
 FOR I:=1 TO LENGTH(HEXSTR) DO
 BEGIN
   DIGIT:=SCAN(16,=HEXSTR[I],HEXDIGIT);
   NUM:=NUM*16+DIGIT;
  END;
 HEX_TO_INT:=NUM;
END;

(********************************************)
(* GET HEX NUMBER AND RETURN INTEGER VALUE *)
(********************************************)

FUNCTION GET_HEX_VAL((PROMPT:STRING; MAXLEN:INTEGER):
                                           INTEGER);
VAR HEXSET   :SETOFCHAR;
    HEX_STR  :STRING;

BEGIN
  WRITE(PROMPT,EOL);
  HEXSET:=['0'..'9','A'..'F'];
  IF MAXLEN>4 THEN MAXLEN:=4;
  GETSTRING(HEX_STR,HEXSET,MAXLEN);
  GET_HEX_VAL:=HEX_TO_INT(HEX_STR);
END;


(************************************************)
(* CONVERT FLOATING PT. STRING TO REAL VALUE *)
(************************************************)

FUNCTION FP_NUM((FP_STR:STRING):REAL);

VAR POWER,SIGN,I      :INTEGER;
    NUM               :REAL;

BEGIN
  IF FP_STR[1]='-' THEN
    BEGIN
      SIGN:=-1;
      DELETE(FP_STR,1,1);
    END
  ELSE SIGN:=1;

  POWER:=POS('.',FP_STR);
  IF POWER<>0 THEN
    BEGIN
      DELETE(FP_STR,POWER,1);
      POWER:=LENGTH(FP_STR)-POWER+1;
    END;

  NUM:=0;
  FOR I:=1 TO LENGTH(FP_STR) DO
    NUM:=10*NUM+(ORD(FP_STR[I])-ORD('0'));
  FP_NUM:=SIGN*NUM/PWROFTEN(POWER);

END;
```

```
(*****************************************)
(* USED BY GET_FP_NUM AND GET_INTEGER *)
(*****************************************)

FUNCTION GET_NUM(MAXVAL,MINVAL:REAL; PT_OK:BOOLEAN):REAL;

VAR FIRSTCHAR, LASTCHAR    :BOOLEAN;
    NUMSET, GETSET, OKSET  :SETOFCHAR;
    NUM_STR_TEMP           :STRING[10];
    S1                     :STRING[1];
    LEN, MAXLEN            :INTEGER;
    NUM                    :REAL;

BEGIN
  NUMSET:=['0'..'9'];
  IF MINVAL<0 THEN OKSET:=NUMSET+['-'] ELSE OKSET:=NUMSET;
  IF PT_OK THEN MAXLEN:=8 ELSE MAXLEN:=7;
  S1:=' '; NUM_STR_TEMP:='';

  REPEAT
    LEN:=LENGTH(NUM_STR_TEMP);
    FIRSTCHAR:=(LEN=0);
    LASTCHAR:=(LEN=MAXLEN);

    IF PT_OK THEN OKSET:=OKSET+['.']
    ELSE OKSET:=OKSET-['.'];

    IF FIRSTCHAR THEN GETSET:=OKSET
    ELSE
      IF LASTCHAR THEN GETSET:=[CR,BS]
      ELSE GETSET:=OKSET+[CR,BS]-['-'];

    S1[1]:=GET_CHAR(GETSET);
    IF S1='.' THEN PT_OK:=FALSE;

    IF S1[1] IN OKSET THEN
      BEGIN
        NUM_STR_TEMP:=CONCAT(NUM_STR_TEMP,S1);
        IF S1[1] IN NUMSET THEN
          BEGIN
            NUM:=FP_NUM(NUM_STR_TEMP);
            IF (NUM>MAXVAL) OR (NUM<MINVAL) THEN
              BEGIN
                WRITE(CHR(7));
                WRITE(BS,' ',BS);
                DELETE(NUM_STR_TEMP,LEN+1,1);
              END;
          END;
      END

    ELSE IF S1[1]=BS THEN
      BEGIN
        IF POS('.',NUM_STR_TEMP)=LEN THEN
          PT_OK:=TRUE;
        WRITE(BS,' ',BS);
        DELETE(NUM_STR_TEMP,LEN,1);
      END;

   UNTIL S1[1]=CR; WRITELN;

   GET_NUM:=FP_NUM(NUM_STR_TEMP);

END; {GET_NUM}
```

It is hoped that the routines presented here will set a trend in Apple computer circles towards the development of standardized software tools with universal application. Good tools make life easier and produce better programs.

```
(******************************************************************)
(* GETS FLOATING PT. NUMBER BETWEEN SPECIFIED MAX AND MIN VALUES *)
(******************************************************************)

FUNCTION GET_FP_NUM{(PROMPT:STRING; MAXVAL,MINVAL:REAL):REAL};

VAR POINT_OK:BOOLEAN;

BEGIN
  WRITE(PROMPT,EOL);
  POINT_OK:=TRUE;
  GET_FP_NUM:=GET_NUM(MAXVAL,MINVAL,TRUE);
END;

(**************************************************************)
(* GETS INTEGER NUMBER BETWEEN SPECIFIED MAX AND MIN VALUES *)
(**************************************************************)

FUNCTION GET_INTEGER{(PROMPT:STRING; MAXVAL,MINVAL:INTEGER):INTEGER};

VAR POINT_OK:BOOLEAN;

BEGIN
  WRITE(PROMPT,EOL);
  POINT_OK:=FALSE;
  GET_INTEGER:=TRUNC(GET_NUM(MAXVAL,MINVAL,FALSE));
END;


(****************************************)
(* PASCAL VERSION OF KEYPRESS FUNCTION *)
(* MAY NOT WORK WITH EXTERNAL CONSOLE  *)
(****************************************)

FUNCTION KEYPRESS{:BOOLEAN};

TYPE BYTE=0..255;
     PA=PACKED ARRAY[0..1] OF BYTE;

VAR MEMREF:RECORD CASE BOOLEAN OF
             TRUE: (ADDR:INTEGER);
             FALSE:(BYTE:^PA);
            END;
    RPTR,WPTR,KEYBD:BYTE;

BEGIN
    MEMREF.ADDR:=-16384;  (*KEYBD INPUT PORT*)
    KEYBD:=MEMREF.BYTE^[0];

    MEMREF.ADDR:=-16616;  (*BUFFER COUNTERS*)
    RPTR:=MEMREF.BYTE^[0];  (*INPUT *)
    WPTR:=MEMREF.BYTE^[1];  (*OUTPUT*)

    KEYPRESS:=(KEYBD > 127) OR (RPTR <> WPTR);

END;

BEGIN          {MAIN PROGRAM}

  CR:=CHR(13);    {ctl-M}
  BS:=CHR(8);     {ctl-H}
  EOL:=CHR(29);   {ctl-]}
  EOS:=CHR(11);   {ctl-K}
  BELL:=CHR(7);
  HEXDIGIT:='0123456789ABCDEF';

END.
```

Terminal Independent Screen Control

Roy Bollinger

BEING a Software Engineer for better than 18 years and being dedicated to the humanization of software interfaces, I found my new Apple Pascal language system lacking in full screen cursor control. Since I am firmly convinced that the Apple is an excellent machine, I knew that full screen cursor control must be possible, I just had to find out how.

While reading the Apple Pascal Reference Manual, I found a section titled

4.3 SYSTEM RECONFIGURATION : SETUP.CODE

starting on page 240. I decided that since all of this information was required to run the Apple in a terminal independent manor, this is where I must begin my investigation. Within that section I found a subsection titled

4.3.4 VIDEO SCREEN CONTROL CHARACTERS

starting on page 246. Now I knew I had struck pay dirt, for contained within this section were all of the full screen controls I wanted.

The first thing I did was use a file dump program, similar to the one described in the October issue of *Call -A.P.P.L.E.*, to dump the MISCINFO file that is generated by the SETUP.CODE program. Next, I ran SETUP.CODE and answered each of the questions requiring a numeric answer with sequential positive integers starting with one. Then I dumped the resulting MISCINFO file and compared the results with the original dump. From this I was able to determine where SETUP.CODE placed each of the answers in the MISCINFO file. Table 1 lists the results of that comparison.

Next, I ran SETUP.CODE a number of times, answering each of the true–false prefix questions in order. From this I was able to determine where SETUP.CODE placed each of the prefix flags in the MISCINFO file. The results are also listed in table 1.

Armed with this information, I decided to generate a PASCAL UNIT which would contain procedures that would allow programmers the use of full screen cursor control. Listing 1 is a listing of that UNIT.

The value of using the contents of the MISCINFO file to obtain full screen cursor control is that no matter what terminal you use, if you have the proper MISCINFO file installed, you will always be able to use the CRT utilities described in Listing 1 with no software modifications. Additionally, the sameCRT utilities are usable with the new Apple FORTRAN system.

```
(*$s+*)
unit crtutilites;

interface
   var
      LUNMISCINFO : file;

   procedure CURSORHOME;
   procedure CURSORUP;
   procedure CURSORDOWN;
   procedure CURSORLEFT;
   procedure CURSORRIGHT;
   procedure CLEARSCREEN;
   procedure CLEARLINE(LINENUMBER : integer);
   procedure ERASEOL;
   procedure ERASEOS(LINENUMBER : integer);
   procedure DISPLAY(VTAB,HTAB : integer; LINEOFTEXT : string);
   procedure PROMPT(VTAB : integer; PROMPTLINE : string);

implementation
   const
      BLOCKSIZE = 512;

   type
      CRTCOMMAND = (LEADIN, UP, RIGHT, ERASEEOL, ERASEEOS, HOME,
                    LEFT, CLEARS, CLEARL, DOWN);

      INPUTBUFFER = record
                       MISCINFO : packed array[1..BLOCKSIZE] of char,
                    end;

   var
      LOWERVTAB, UPPERVTAB,
      LOWERHTAB, UPPERHTAB,
      NUMOFBLOCKS,
        PREFIXCONTROL : integer; (* variable containing 8 one bit flags that *
                                  * determine whether or not the crt command *
                                  * must be prefixed by the lead in command  *)
```

```
    CRTCONTROL   : packed array [CRTCOMMAND] of char;
    PREFIXED     : packed array [CRTCOMMAND] of boolean;
    INPUTPOINTER: ^INPUTBUFFER;
    HEAPPOINTER : ^integer;

procedure CURSORHOME;
   begin
      if PREFIXED[HOME] then
         unitwrite(1,CRTCONTROL[LEADIN],1);
      unitwrite(1,CRTCONTROL[HOME],1);
   end;

procedure CURSORUP;
   begin
      if PREFIXED[UP] then
         unitwrite(1,CRTCONTROL[LEADIN],1);
      unitwrite(1,CRTCONTROL[UP],1);
   end;

procedure CURSORDOWN;
   begin
      if PREFIXED[DOWN] then
         unitwrite(1,CRTCONTROL[LEADIN],1);
      unitwrite(1,CRTCONTROL[DOWN],1);
   end;

procedure CURSORLEFT;
   begin
      if PREFIXED[LEFT] then
         unitwrite(1,CRTCONTROL[LEADIN],1);
      unitwrite(1,CRTCONTROL[LEFT],1);
   end;

procedure CURSORRIGHT;
   begin
      if PREFIXED[RIGHT] then
         unitwrite(1,CRTCONTROL[LEADIN],1);
      unitwrite(1,CRTCONTROL[RIGHT],1);
   end;


procedure CLEARSCREEN;
   begin
      if PREFIXED[CLEARS] then
         unitwrite(1,CRTCONTROL[LEADIN],1);
      unitwrite(1,CRTCONTROL[CLEARS],1);
   end;

procedure ERASEOL;
   begin
      if PREFIXED[ERASEEOL] then
         unitwrite(1,CRTCONTROL[LEADIN],1);
      unitwrite(1,CRTCONTROL[ERASEEOL],1);
   end;

procedure CLEARLINE;
  begin
     if LINENUMBER < LOWERVTAB then
        LINENUMBER := LOWERVTAB
     else if LINENUMBER > UPPERVTAB then
        LINENUMBER := UPPERVTAB;
     GOTOXY(0,LINENUMBER);
     ERASEOL;
  end;

procedure ERASEOS;
   begin
      if LINENUMBER < LOWERVTAB then
         LINENUMBER := LOWERVTAB
      else if LINENUMBER > UPPERVTAB then
         LINENUMBER := UPPERVTAB;
      if PREFIXED[ERASEEOS] then
         unitwrite(1,CRTCONTROL[LEADIN],1);
      unitwrite(1,CRTCONTROL[ERASEEOS],1)
   end;
```

```
procedure DISPLAY;
   begin
      if VTAB < LOWERVTAB then
         VTAB := LOWERVTAB
      else if VTAB > UPPERVTAB then
         VTAB := UPPERVTAB;
      if HTAB < LOWERHTAB then
         HTAB := LOWERHTAB
      else if HTAB > UPPERHTAB then
         HTAB := UPPERHTAB;
      GOTOXY(HTAB,VTAB);
      WRITE(OUTPUT,LINEOFTEXT);
   end;

procedure PROMPT;
   begin
      if VTAB < LOWERVTAB then
         VTAB := LOWERVTAB
      else if VTAB > UPPERVTAB then
         VTAB := UPPERVTAB;
      GOTOXY(0,VTAB);
      WRITE(OUTPUT,PROMPTLINE);
      ERASEOL;
   end;

begin (* unit initialization *)
   RESET(LUNMISCINFO,'*SYSTEM.MISCINFO');
   MARK(HEAPPOINTER);
   NEW(INPUTPOINTER);
   with INPUTPOINTER^ do
      begin
         NUMOFBLOCKS := BLOCKREAD(LUNMISCINFO,MISCINFO,1);
         CLOSE(LUNMISCINFO);

         PREFIXCONTROL := ORD(MISCINFO[73]);

         CRTCONTROL[LEADIN    ] := MISCINFO[63];
         CRTCONTROL[UP        ] := MISCINFO[68];
         CRTCONTROL[RIGHT     ] := MISCINFO[67];
         CRTCONTROL[ERASEEOL  ] := MISCINFO[66];
         CRTCONTROL[ERASEEOS  ] := MISCINFO[65];
         CRTCONTROL[HOME      ] := MISCINFO[64];
         CRTCONTROL[LEFT      ] := MISCINFO[69];
         CRTCONTROL[CLEARS    ] := MISCINFO[72];
         CRTCONTROL[CLEARL    ] := MISCINFO[71];
         CRTCONTROL[DOWN      ] := CHR(10);

         PREFIXED[LEADIN    ] := false;
         PREFIXED[UP        ] := ODD(PREFIXCONTROL        );
         PREFIXED[RIGHT     ] := ODD(PREFIXCONTROL div   2);
         PREFIXED[ERASEEOL  ] := ODD(PREFIXCONTROL div   4);
         PREFIXED[ERASEEOS  ] := ODD(PREFIXCONTROL div   8);
         PREFIXED[HOME      ] := ODD(PREFIXCONTROL div  16);
         PREFIXED[LEFT      ] := ODD(PREFIXCONTROL div  32);
         PREFIXED[CLEARS    ] := ODD(PREFIXCONTROL div  64);
         PREFIXED[CLEARL    ] := ODD(PREFIXCONTROL div 128);
         PREFIXED[DOWN      ] := false;

         LOWERVTAB := 0;
         UPPERVTAB := ORD(MISCINFO[75]);
         LOWERHTAB := 0;
         UPPERHTAB := ORD(MISCINFO[77]);
      end;
   RELEASE(HEAPPOINTER);
end.
```

Table 1. MISCINFO File Description

Byte	Reference	Value	Description
1- 62			Does not seem to be created by SETUP.CODE
63	4.3.4 246	0	Lead in to screen
64	4.3.4 247	25	Move Cursor Home
65	4.3.4 246	11	Erase to end of line
66	4.3.4 247	29	Erase to end of screen
67	4.3.4 247	28	Move cursor right
68	4.3.4 247	31	Move cursor up
69	4.3.4.247	8	Backspace
70			Unknown
71	4.3.4 247	0	Erase line
72	4.3.4 247	12	Erase screen
73	4.3.4 246		Prefix flags for video screen control characters bit 0 - Move cursor up bit 1 - Move cursor right bit 2 - Erase to end of line bit 3 - Erase to end of screen bit 4 - Move cursor home bit 5 - Backspace bit 6 - Erase screen bit 7 - Erase line
74			Unknown
75	4.3.2 243	24	Screen height
76			Unknown
77	4.3.2 243	79	Screen width
78			Unknown
79	4.3.3 245	15	Key to move cursor up CTRL-O
80	4.3.3 245	12	Key to move cursor down CTRL-L
81	4.3.3 245	8	Key to move cursor left CTRL-H
82	4.3.3 245	21	Key to move cursor right CTRL-U
83	4.3.3 245	3	Key to end file CTRL-C
84	4.3.3 244	6	Key for flush CTRL-F
85	4.3.3 244	0	Key for break
86	4.3.3 244	19	Key for stop CTRL-S
87	4.3.3 245	8	Key to delete character CTRL-H
88	4.3.2 243	63	Nonprinting character ?
89	4.3.3 245	24	Character to delete line CTRL-X
90	4.3.3 246	27	Editor escape key ESC
91	4.3.3 244	0	Lead in from the keyboard
92	4.3.3 246	3	Editor "accept" key CTRL-C
93-512			Does not seem to be created by SETUP.CODE

Pascal Disk Directory Structure

Allen W. Todd

HAVE you ever wanted to directly access the directory of a Pascal diskette from within a program? This would be simple if only you knew: 1) where the directory is located; and 2) what the structure of the diskette directory is. The answer to the first question is fairly easily deduced. If you have used the Pascal filer to obtain E)xtended directory listings of your diskettes, you see that the first user file begins on block 6. This leaves blocks 0 ---) 5 as a likely place to find the directory. In fact, the directory occupies blocks two through five, while blocks zero and one are reserved for the second stage boot-strap routines. The actual structure of the directory is less easily seen, but once revealed, becomes elegantly simple. The structure of a U.C.S.D. Pascal disk directory is shown by the declarations show in Table I.

Thus a Pascal directory consists of from 0 to 77 variant records of type 'direntry'. Directory entries are stored sequentially beginning on block 2 of each diskette. Each direntry is a variant record with two possible variants. The actual variant of a given record is determined by its tag field. For direntry the tag field is dfkind (filetype). Therefore if the filetype is either 'volume' or 'secure' then the direntry contains information about the entire diskette volume. This volume entry is the first entry in the directory (direntry[0]) and contains the information in Table II.

An example of how to use this information is shown in the listing of FUNCTION getdirectory. This is a function that attempts to read the directory from volume number 'dunit'. If getdirectory finds a Pascal directory on 'dunit', it returns a pointer to the directory and updates the string variable 'vname' to contain the name of the found volume. If the directory cannot be read or is not a valid directory, getdirectory returns a nil pointer and does not update 'vname'. Once you know that a valid directory has been read, you may use the returned pointer to access any directory information desired.

TABLE I

```
TYPE
 vid        = string[7];          (Volume Name)
 fid        =string[15];          (File Name)
 daterec    =PACKED RECORD        (Date Record (16 Bits))
               mo:    1..12;
               day:   1..31;
               year:  0..99;
             END;
 filekind   = (vol,               (Disk Volume Entry)
               badfile,           (File Containing Bad Blocks)
               code,              (Code File, Machine Executable)
               text,              (Text File, Human Readable)
               info,              (Information File, For Debugger)
               data,              (Data File)
               graf,              (Graphics Vectors)
               foto,              (Graphics Screen Image)
               secure);           (Security, not used)

 direntry     = RECORD
dfirstblock   : INTEGER;          (First Block of File)
dlastblock    : INTEGER;          (Last Block of File)
CASE dfkind: filekind OF          (File Type)
      vol,secure:                 (Volume Entry Variant)
    (dvid       : vid;            (Volume Name)
     deovblk    : INTEGE          (Number of Blocks)
     dfilenum   : INTEGE          (Number of Files)
     ddummy     : INTEGE          (Dummy)
     dlastboot  : daterec);       (Date Last Booted)
  badfile,code,text,info,dat
 graf, foto:                      (File Entry Variant)
    (dfid       : fid;            (File Name)
     dlastbyte  : 1..512;         (EOF Byte)
     daccess    : daterec)        (Date Last Accessed)
 END;  (direntry)
 directory = ARRAY[0..77] O
  direntry; (Max. 77 Entries i
 Directory)
```

TABLE II

Field	Data Type	Typical Value
First Block of Volume Entry	Integer	0
Last Block of Volume Entry	Integer	6
Entry Type (filekind)	Integer	0 or 8
Volume Name	String[7]	'APPLE1'
Number of Blocks on Volume	Integer	280
Number of Files on Volume	Integer	0..76
Dummy (space filler)	Integer	0
Date Last Booted	Daterec	(any date)

The remaining directory entry records contain information for each individual file contained on the diskette. Table III

TABLE III

Field	Data Type	Typic Value
First Block of File	Integer	6..279
Last Block of File	Integer	6..279
Entry Type (filekind)	Integer	1..7
File Name	String[15]	'SYSTEM APPLE'
Number of Bytes in Last Block	Integer	512
Date Last Modified	Daterec	(any date)

```
PROGRAM DIR;

TYPE
   pointer = ^directory;
   vid = string[7];
   fid = string[15];
   daterec = PACKED RECORD
                mo:    1..12;
                day:   1..31;
                year:  0..99;
              END;
   filekind = (vol, badfile, code, text, info, data, graf, foto, secure);
   direntry = RECORD
                 dfirstblock: INTEGER;
                 dlastblock:  INTEGER;
                 CASE dfkind: filekind OF
                    vol, secure: (dvid:       vid;
                                  deovblk:    INTEGER;
                                  dfilenum:   INTEGER;
                                  ddummy:     INTEGER;
                                  dlastboot:  daterec);
                    badfile, code, text, info, data, graf, foto:
                                 (dfid:       fid;
                                  dlastbyte:  1..512;
                                  daccess:    daterec)
                 END;
   directory = ARRAY[0..77] OF direntry;

VAR
   dirptr: ^directory;
   I, device: INTEGER;
   volname: string;

FUNCTION getdirectory (dunit: INTEGER; VAR vname: string):pointer;

BEGIN
   getdirectory:= NIL;
   new(dirptr);
   {$I-}
   unitread (dunit,dirptr^,sizeof(directory),2);
   {$I+}
   IF ioresult = 0
      THEN WITH dirptr^[0] DO
         BEGIN
            IF (dfkind IN [vol,secure])
               AND (dfirstblock=0)
               AND (dlastblock=6)
               THEN
                  BEGIN
                     vname:=dvid;
                     getdirectory:=dirptr;
                  END;
         END; {with}
   END; {getdirectory}

BEGIN {main program}
   write('Get directory from device number: ');
   readln(device);
   IF getdirectory(device,volname)=NIL
   THEN writeln('Can''t find directory')
   ELSE BEGIN
           writeln(volname,':');
           FOR I:= 1 TO dirptr^[0].dfilenum DO
             WITH dirptr^[I], daccess DO
                BEGIN
                  WHILE length(dfid)<15 DO dfid:=concat(dfid,' ');
                  writeln(dfid,dlastblock-dfirstblock:4,
                          mo:4,'/',day:2,'/',year:2,dfirstblock:5);
                END;
        END;
END.
```

Text File Header Page

Alan J. Nayer

MANY users of the Apple Pascal Operating System and language are acquainted with the format in which TEXT files are stored. Most probably, those in particular who have written programs or used the Editor as a word processor are familiar with the general design of a text file.

This article presupposes the reader's general knowledge of the text file format, as well as an understanding of the Environment parameters in the Pascal Editor. To refresh one's memory of the former, I suggest reading or rereading the brief section on text files in the Apple Pascal Operating System Reference Manual (page 266 in the current edition). The manual does not elaborate on the header page of the text file though, and I would like to delve more deeply into this area.

Text files are made up of pages, where a page consists of two contiguous blocks on disk, or 1,024 bytes since each block contains 512 bytes. Text files always consist of an integral number of pages, thus the characteristic that they always occupy an even number of blocks on disk. The first page is the header page, the majority of which is unused and is filled with binary zeros by the operating system; in fact, only about one-eighth of these 1,024 bytes contains useful information.

This data makes up the Environment of the text file, that part which can be viewed or modified via the S(et command of the Editor. A list of these items is in figure 1.

The first significant set of data begins at byte 4 (Note: all offsets are from byte 0; byte 4 then is actually the fifth byte of the header page). The ten markers, numbered 0 through 9, which may be set to mark specific positions in the text file are stored here, one immediately after the other. The name of marker 0 spans bytes 4 through 11, marker 1 from 12 through 19, and so on. Markers are entered from the Editor and are padded with spaces or truncated as necessary to form an eight-character name.

The Editor relates each marker name with the specific byte address at which the cursor resides at the time the command is entered. For example, if the cursor is at the first byte of the data portion of the text at the time a marker is set, the marker address would be 1. These marker addresses are stored as two-byte integers, starting at byte 94 of the header page. As expected, the first marker address (at bytes 94–95) refers to the first marker name (at bytes 4–11), and this relationship continues through marker 9.

Three words of boolean data immediately follow the marker addresses, though only the high-order bit is significant in each. These three boolean values are used to denote on/off conditions for, respectively, the Auto indent, Filling, and Token default options in the Environment.

Next, three two-byte integer fields delimit the margins of the text; these variables are, in order, the Left margin, Right margin, and Para margin. The Command character is stored in the next two bytes, in character format.

The last two items are dates; first is the date the text file was created, followed by the date it was last updated. Both dates are set by the system from the system date, and are stored in the truly packed format that is used throughout the operating system. The month, day, and year are stored respectively in the first 4, next 5, and last 7 bits of the word.

Listing 1 is a program called TEXTINFO that will interrogate the text header page of any text file and display and/or print the pertinent data.

DATA	STRT BYTE	END BYTE	LEN	FORMAT	NOTES
Marker names	4	83	80	packed char	10 occurrences, each element is 8 bytes
Marker addr's	94	113	20	integer	10 occurrences, each element is 2 bytes
Auto indent	114	115	2	boolean	only hi-order bit used
Filling	116	117	2	boolean	only hi-order bit used
Token def	118	119	2	boolean	only hi-order bit used
Left margin	120	121	2	integer	
Right margin	122	123	2	integer	
Para margin	124	125	2	integer	
Command ch	126	127	2	char	
Date created	128	129	2	packed int	
Month					first 4 bits
Day					next 5 bits
Year					last 7 bits
Date updated	130	131	2	packed int	
Month					first 4 bits
Day					next 5 bits
Year					last 7 bits

Figure 1: The pertinent data in the Pascal text file's header page

I then attempted to use the BLOCKREAD input function to access the first block of the header page, and this worked satisfactorily. Since a full 512-byte block is the smallest unit that can be read by a BLOCKREAD, FILLER3 had to be appended to the definition of HEADER to pad it to the length of a block.

Though not directly related to the topic of discussion, the method used to display output on the screen or write it to the printer may prove useful in many applications. Procedure WRITEINFO handles this task with the use of only one file, OUTPUTFILE, which is declared as an INTERACTIVE file. The parameter passed to this procedure is a string – either "CONSOLE:" or "PRINTER:" – that directs the routine to use the appropriate device for output.

Those who perform much word processing using the Pascal Editor may find a hardcopy catalog of the Environment information (particularly the dates and margination data) of all their text files a helpful tool.

The program requests the text file name – the suffix .TEXT will be supplied by the program – and the destination of the output; it may be sent to the screen, the printer, or both. A response of just a carriage return to either query will prematurely end the program.

Output to the screen or printer is essentially in the same format. Figure 2 shows two samples. The first displays the data retrieved from the header page of a Pascal program in which neither the Environment nor markers were set; the system default options prevailed. The second sample shows the data taken from a text file I used during word processing – in fact, it is this article, which I created in the Pascal Editor. Several of the Environment options were changed from their default values, and two markers were set.

I believe the program is fairly self-documenting, though a few points are noteworthy. The Pascal record type HEADER represents the data stored in the first block of the text header page. FILLER1 and FILLER2 are needed to pass by unused areas. FILLER3 serves a unique purpose in allowing the data to be accessed via a BLOCKREAD and the decision to use this I/O function deserves further explanation.

I tried to use the more straightforward method of reading the data into HEADER without the FILLER3 definition (its length was 132 bytes) by declaring a file of type HEADER, and then added the code to read the first record with a GET statement. However, the data retrieved by this GET was from the second page of the text file, that page which contains the start of the actual text data. Apparently, the operating system does not ignore in this instance the fact that the file is actually a text file, even though the file declaration states that the file is of type HEADER and not TEXT.

```
         Text file: *TEXTINFO.TEXT

Auto indent = True          Filling = False
Token def = True              Command ch = ^

Left margin = 0          Right margin = 79
            Para margin = 5

Date created = 13-Aug-81
Date updated = 28-Sep-81

    Marker name      Marker address
           no markers used
```

```
              Text file: ARTICLE.TEXT

Auto indent = False          Filling = True
Token def = True               Command ch = ^

Left margin = 8          Right margin = 73
             Para margin = 8

Date created = 23-Sep-81
Date updated = 2-Oct-81

         Marker name      Marker address
   0      FIGURE1             9398
   1      FIGURE2            10789
```

Figure 2: Two sample outputs from TEXT_INFO

```
{------------------------------------------------------------------}
{      LISTING #1:  TEXT_INFO                                       }
{                                                                   }
{          This program interrogates the Pascal TEXT file header    }
{          and displays and/or prints the Environment parameters    }
{                                                                   }
{      Written by Alan J. Nayer                  September, 1981    }
{------------------------------------------------------------------}

PROGRAM TEXT_INFO;

TYPE DATE=                   { format in which system stores dates      }
        PACKED RECORD
          MONTH  : 0..12;
          DAY    : 0..31;
          YEAR   : 0..100
        END;

     HEADER=                 { format of text file's first header block  }
        PACKED RECORD
          FILLER1      : PACKED ARRAY[0..3] OF CHAR;
          MARKER       : PACKED ARRAY[0..9,0..7] OF CHAR;
          FILLER2      : PACKED ARRAY[0..9] OF CHAR;
          MARKER_ADDR  : PACKED ARRAY[0..9] OF INTEGER;
          AUTO_INDENT  : PACKED ARRAY[0..15] OF BOOLEAN;
          FILLING      : PACKED ARRAY[0..15] OF BOOLEAN;
          TOKEN_DEF    : PACKED ARRAY[0..15] OF BOOLEAN; program
          LEFT_MARGIN  : INTEGER;
          RIGHT MARGIN : INTEGER;
```

```
        PARA_MARGIN : INTEGER;
        COMMAND_CH  : CHAR;
        DATE_CREATED: DATE;
        DATE_UPDATED: DATE;
                         { filler3 pads the header record to        }
                         { 512 bytes for the blockread              }
        FILLER3     : PACKED ARRAY[0..379] OF CHAR
      END;

VAR TEXT_HDR          : HEADER;
    IN_FILE_NAME      : STRING;
    MONTH_NAMES       : STRING[36];
    CR,FF,CLEAR_EOL,BEL,NUL,DESTINATION
                      : CHAR;
    GOOD_DEST,SCREEN,PRINTER
                      : SET OF CHAR;
{-----------------------------------------------------------------------}

PROCEDURE INITIALIZATION;

BEGIN
  CR:=CHR(13);
  FF:=CHR(12);
  CLEAR_EOL:=CHR(29);
  BEL:=CHR(7);
  NUL:=CHR(0);
  MONTH_NAMES:='JanFebMarAprMayJunJulAugSepOctNovDec';
  SCREEN:=['S','B','s','b'];
  PRINTER:=['P','B','p','b'];
  GOOD_DEST:=SCREEN+PRINTER
END;  { initialization }

PROCEDURE GET_INPUT_FILE;

VAR TFILE       : FILE;    { treat the text file as an untyped file    }
                           { so we can read the first header block     }
    NUM_BLOCKS  : INTEGER;
    GOOD_FILE   : BOOLEAN;

BEGIN
  WRITELN(FF,'TEXT INFO');
  REPEAT                   { until input file is successfully read     }
    GOTOXY(0,5);
    WRITE('Name of text file (.TEXT will be added):',CR,CLEAR_EOL);
    READLN(IN_FILE_NAME);
    IF IN_FILE_NAME='' THEN EXIT(PROGRAM) ELSE   { <RET> exits program  }
      IN_FILE_NAME:=CONCAT(IN_FILE_NAME,'.TEXT');
    GOTOXY(0,23);
                                                                  {$I-}
    RESET(TFILE,IN_FILE_NAME);
    GOOD_FILE:=IORESULT=0;
    IF NOT GOOD_FILE THEN WRITE('Can''t find ',IN_FILE_NAME,
                                  CLEAR_EOL,BEL) ELSE
    BEGIN                  { if file was opened successfully,          }
                           { attempt to read the first header block    }
      NUM_BLOCKS:=BLOCKREAD(TFILE,TEXT_HDR,1);
                                                                  {$I+}
      IF (NUM_BLOCKS<>1) OR (IORESULT<>0) THEN
      BEGIN
        WRITE('Can''t read ',IN_FILE_NAME,BEL,CLEAR_EOL);
        EXIT(PROGRAM)
      END ELSE WRITE(IN_FILE_NAME,' opened and read',CLEAR_EOL);
      CLOSE(TFILE,LOCK)
    END
  UNTIL GOOD_FILE
END;  { get_input_file }

PROCEDURE GET_OUTPUT_FILE;

BEGIN
  GOTOXY(0,10);
  WRITELN('Send the output to the:');
  WRITELN('S(creen':15,CR,'P(rinter or':19,CR,'B(oth':13);
  WRITE('choice: ');
  REPEAT
    READ(KEYBOARD,DESTINATION);
    IF EOLN(KEYBOARD) THEN EXIT(PROGRAM)
  UNTIL DESTINATION IN GOOD_DEST;
  WRITE(DESTINATION)
END;  { get_output_file }
```

```
PROCEDURE T_OR_F(BOOL:BOOLEAN; VAR TR_FL:STRING);

BEGIN
  IF BOOL THEN TR_FL:='True ' ELSE TR_FL:='False'
END;  { t_or_f }


PROCEDURE CONV_DATE(DATE_PARAM:DATE; VAR EXPANDED_DATE:STRING);

VAR S1,S2,S3 : STRING[3];

BEGIN
  WITH DATE_PARAM DO
  BEGIN
    STR(DAY,S1);
    STR(YEAR,S3);
    S2:=COPY(MONTH_NAMES,MONTH*3-2,3);
    EXPANDED_DATE:=CONCAT(S1,'-',S2,'-',S3)
  END
END;  { conv_date }


PROCEDURE WRITE_INFO(OUT_FILE_NAME:STRING);

VAR OUTPUT_FILE    : INTERACTIVE;  { This file will be assigned to       }
                                   { either the console: or printer:     }
    STRNG1,STRNG2  : STRING;
    MARKER_NUM     : INTEGER;

BEGIN
  REWRITE(OUTPUT_FILE,OUT_FILE_NAME);
  IF OUT_FILE_NAME='CONSOLE:' THEN WRITELN(OUTPUT_FILE,FF);
  WRITELN(OUTPUT_FILE,'Text file: ':20,IN_FILE_NAME,CR,CR);
  WITH TEXT_HDR DO
  BEGIN
    T_OR_F(AUTO_INDENT[0],STRNG1);
    T_OR_F(FILLING[0],STRNG2);
    WRITELN(OUTPUT_FILE,'Auto indent = ',STRNG1,
            'Filling = ':16,STRNG2);
    T_OR_F(TOKEN_DEF[0],STRNG1);
    WRITELN(OUTPUT_FILE,'Token def = ',STRNG1,
            'Command ch = ':22,COMMAND_CH,CR);
    WRITELN(OUTPUT_FILE,'Left margin = ',LEFT_MARGIN:2,
            'Right margin = ':22,RIGHT_MARGIN:2);
    WRITELN(OUTPUT_FILE,'Para margin = ':26,PARA_MARGIN,CR);
    CONV_DATE(DATE_CREATED,STRNG1);
    CONV_DATE(DATE_UPDATED,STRNG2);
    WRITELN(OUTPUT_FILE,'Date created = ',STRNG1,CR,
            'Date updated = ',STRNG2,CR);
    WRITE(OUTPUT_FILE,'Marker name':16,'Marker address':19);
                           { if the first byte of the marker name is    }
                           { chr(0), there is no marker                 }
    IF MARKER[0,1]=NUL THEN WRITE(OUTPUT_FILE,CR,
                                   'No markers used':27) ELSE
      FOR MARKER_NUM:=0 TO 9 DO
        IF MARKER[MARKER_NUM,1]<>NUL THEN
          WRITE(OUTPUT_FILE,CR,MARKER_NUM:3,MARKER[MARKER_NUM]:12,
                MARKER_ADDR[MARKER_NUM]:14)
  END;
  IF OUT_FILE_NAME='PRINTER:' THEN WRITELN(OUTPUT_FILE,CR,CR)
END;  { write_info }


BEGIN  { main }
  INITIALIZATION;
  GET_INPUT_FILE;
  GET_OUTPUT_FILE;
  IF DESTINATION IN SCREEN THEN WRITE_INFO('CONSOLE:');
  IF DESTINATION IN PRINTER THEN WRITE_INFO('PRINTER:');
END.
```

Pascal Date Procedure

David A. Geddes and Ron DeGroat

Have you ever wanted to keep date information current on files created as part of your Pascal turnkey program (SYSTEM.STARTUP)? Normally, it is necessary to go to the Filer and change the date before calling up the program. This, of course, defeats the purpose of a turnkey program. It also means that the Filer must be on the disc.

In an effort to overcome this problem I started poking around in the Pascal system and eventually wrote the self-contained PROCEDURE GETDATE (shown in Listing #1). The PROGRAM DATEDEMO demonstrates how GETDATE may be used in a turnkey program. If placed in the SYSTEM.STARTUP, DATEDEMO allows the user to easily set the date everytime the disk is booted.

GETDATE first looks at the date stored on disc and asks if it should be changed. Changes are made in the same way as the Filer Date option except that the month may also be input as an integer. If a change is specified by the user, both the disc and memory are updated so that new files will contain the new date. The date (whether updated or not) is returned in string form by GETDATE as a variable parameter (see GETDATE procedure heading). The CONST DATELOC (the location of the date in memory) is correct for Pascal version 1.1. Those using version 1.0 should change DATELOC to -22254.

Caution should be exercised the first time this procedure is used. It should be tested on discs that are well backed up because an error could do terrible things to your disc.

This work was simplified and helped along by Philip Ender's 'PASCAL ZAP' which appeared in the January, 1981 issue of Call-A.P.P.L.E. Also, some of the ideas involving pointers and records were gleaned from Christopher Anson's POKE routine in the Jul-Aug 1980 Call-A.P.P.L.E.

```
(*********************************************)
(* Listing #1: Demonstration of GETDATE     *)
(*                                           *)
(* Written by: David Geddes and Ron DeGroat *)
(*             May, 1981                     *)
(*********************************************)

PROGRAM DATEDEMO;

VAR DATE:STRING;

PROCEDURE GETDATE(VAR DATE:STRING);

{ Gets date and allows for update similar to the  }
{ D(ate option in the Filer.  The date (in string }
{ form) is returned in the variable parameter.    }

CONST MONTHS='**JanFebMarAprMayJunJulAugSepOctNovDec';

      DATELOC=-21992;  { -22254 for version 1.0 }

TYPE DATEREC = PACKED RECORD
                 MM : 0..12;
                 DD : 0..31;
                 YY : 0..99;
               END; {daterec}

     MEMDATEREC = RECORD CASE INTEGER OF
                    1:(DATE:^DATEREC);
                    2:(LOC : INTEGER);
                  END; {memdaterec}

VAR DISKBLK2:RECORD
               XXX     : PACKED ARRAY[0..19] OF CHAR;
               VOLDATE : DATEREC;
               ZZZ     : PACKED ARRAY[22..511] OF CHAR;
             END;

    NEWDATE     :DATEREC;
    MEMDATE     :MEMDATEREC;
    DD,MM,YY    :INTEGER;
    CHANGE      :STRING;
    DONE        :BOOLEAN;


FUNCTION INT(NUM:STRING):INTEGER;

{ Converts string to integer, works only for pos. values.}

VAR I,X:INTEGER;

BEGIN {int}
  X:=0;
  FOR I:=1 TO LENGTH(NUM) DO
    X:=10*X+(ORD(NUM[I])-ORD('0'));
  INT:=X;
END; {int}


PROCEDURE CHANGEDATE;

{ Changes date to user's specification }

CONST UCMONTHS='**JANFEBMARAPRMAYJUNJULAUGSEPOCTNOVDEC';
      LCMONTHS ='**janfebmaraprmayjunjulaugsepoctnovdec';

VAR DASH:INTEGER;
    MONPART:STRING;
    NEWDATE:DATEREC;
```

```
PROCEDURE SETDATE;

{ Sets date on disk and in memory. }

BEGIN
  DISKBLK2.VOLDATE:=NEWDATE;
  UNITWRITE(4,DISKBLK2,512,2,0);
  MEMDATE.LOC:=DATELOC;
  MEMDATE.DATE^:=NEWDATE;
END; {setdate}


BEGIN {changedate}

{ Change day? }

   DASH:=POS('-',CHANGE);
   CASE DASH OF
     0:DD:=INT(CHANGE);
     1:DD:=DISKBLK2.VOLDATE.DD;
     2,3:DD:=INT(COPY(CHANGE,1,DASH-1));
   END;
   IF (DD<1) OR (DD>31) OR (DASH>3)
   THEN NEWDATE.DD:=DISKBLK2.VOLDATE.DD
   ELSE NEWDATE.DD:=DD;
   IF DASH=0 THEN CHANGE:=''
   ELSE DELETE(CHANGE,1,DASH);

{ Change month? }

   DASH:=POS('-',CHANGE);
   IF DASH>0 THEN MONPART:=COPY(CHANGE,1,(DASH-1))
   ELSE IF LENGTH(CHANGE)>0 THEN MONPART:=CHANGE
        ELSE MONPART:='';
   CASE LENGTH(MONPART) OF
     0:MM:=DISKBLK2.VOLDATE.MM;
     1,2:MM:=INT(MONPART);
     3:MM:=POS(MONPART,MONTHS) DIV 3+POS(MONPART,UCMONTHS)
           DIV 3+POS(MONPART,LCMONTHS) DIV 3;
   END;
   IF (MM<1) OR (MM>12)
   THEN NEWDATE.MM:=DISKBLK2.VOLDATE.MM
   ELSE NEWDATE.MM:=MM;

{ Change year? }

   IF (DASH>0) AND (LENGTH(CHANGE)>DASH) THEN
     BEGIN
       DELETE(CHANGE,1,DASH);
       YY:=INT(CHANGE)
     END
   ELSE YY:=DISKBLK2.VOLDATE.YY;
   IF (YY<0) OR (YY>99)
   THEN NEWDATE.YY:=DISKBLK2.VOLDATE.YY
   ELSE NEWDATE.YY:=YY;

   SETDATE; {on disk and in memory}

END; {changedate}


PROCEDURE GETVOLDATE(VAR DATE:STRING);

VAR DAY,YEAR:STRING;

BEGIN
  UNITREAD(4,DISKBLK2,512,2,0);
  WITH DISKBLK2.VOLDATE DO
    BEGIN
      STR(DD,DAY);
      STR(YY,YEAR);
      DATE:=CONCAT(DAY,'-',COPY(MONTHS,3*MM,3),'-',YEAR);
    END;
END; {getvoldate}

BEGIN {The heart of GETDATE}
  REPEAT
    GETVOLDATE(DATE);
    WRITELN('Today is: ',DATE); {Volume Date}
    WRITE('New date? ');
    READLN(CHANGE);
    DONE:=(LENGTH(CHANGE)=0);
    IF NOT DONE THEN CHANGEDATE;
  UNTIL DONE;
  GETVOLDATE(DATE);
END; {getdate}

BEGIN {datedemo}
  GETDATE(DATE);
  WRITELN;
  WRITELN(DATE);
END. {datedemo}
```

Enhanced Console Driver

Chris Wilson

As you undoubtedly know, there are several graphic characters which can't be generated directly from the Apple][keyboard. The table below lists all of the ASCII graphic characters. The characters which can't be generated by the keyboard (other than the lower-case letters) are underlined.

!"#$%&'()* + ,-./0123456789
:;<=>?

@ABCDEFGHIJKLMNOPQRST
UVWXYZ[\]— ∧ =

'abcdefghijklmnopqrstuvwxyz{:}"

The console driver in this article is an enhancement of the standard Pascal 1.1 console driver. It not only allows you to directly enter these additional characters from the keyboard, but also provides better lower-case keyboard support than the standard driver.

The ATTACHUD and SYSTEM. ATTACH programs from the Pascal 1.1 BIOS package (available from International Apple Core, 910-A George St., Santa Clara, CA 95050, $7.50) are required to install the enhanced driver.

My driver is an adaption of Randy Hyde's "Lazer Systems' Input Editor," which was designed to work with BASIC and DOS.

The driver works by filtering input characters read through the standard driver. Write, initialization, and status calls go straight to the standard driver.

Escape sequences are used to control the enhanced driver. One set of escape sequences is used to control lower-case entry and a second set is used to perform entry of the additional graphic characters.

Since the standard driver is still used to handle the actual keyboard input and to provide type ahead, lower-case entry must first be enabled in the standard driver by typing Ctrl-E. (Note: the Ctrl-E, Ctrl-W, Ctrl-R, and Ctrl-T characters are handled by the standard driver read routine.)

The enhanced driver implements a software shift key and a shift-lock (or caps-lock) mode. You start out in lower-case mode (as soon as you type that Ctrl-E mentioned above). To upshift a single character you simply prefix it with escape (ESC). Thus to upshift "a" you type "ESC a," similar to "SHIFT a" at a typewriter. This convention is simpler than the two key Ctrl-W prefix which the standard driver requires for up-shifting. To place the keyboard in caps-lock mode, type "ESC ESC." To return to lower-case mode, simply type "ESC ESC" again.

So much for lower-case entry support. Escape sequences are also used to enter the additional graphic characters. The table below summarizes this set of escape sequences:

ESC 1 or !	→ :	{chr(124)}
ESC 2 or "	→ ~	{chr(126)}
ESC 3 or #	→ del	{chr(127)}
ESC 7 or '	→ '	{chr(96)}
ESC 8 or (	→ {	{chr(123)}
ESC 9 or)	→ }	{chr(125)}
ESC , or <	→ [	{chr(91)}
ESC . or >	→]	{chr(93)}
ESC - or =	→ —	{chr(95)}
ESC / or ?	→ \	{chr(92)}
ESC <space>	→ ESC	

Since ESC is being used to control all these driver functions, there needs to be a way to input an ESC character to programs such as the Editor. Simply type "ESC <space>" to input an ESC character.

When you run ATTACHUD to build the data file for SYSTEM. ATTACH, answer its questions as shown below:

Enter name of attach data file: ATTACH.DATA

Will you ever use the (2000.3FFF hex) Hi-Res page? N

Will you ever use the (4000.5FFF hex) Hi-Res page? N

What is the name of this driver? This must be the .PROC name in its assembly source (RETURN to exit program): CONSOLE

Which unit numbers should refer to this device driver?

Unit number (RETURN to abort program): 1

Do you want this unit to be initialized at boot time? Y

Do you want another unit number to refer to this device driver? Y

Unit number (RETURN to abort program): 2

Do you want this unit to be initialized at boot time? N

Do you want another unit number to refer to this device driver? N

Do you want this driver to start on a certain byte boundary? N

Do you want to attach another driver? N

```
; Copyright (c) 1982 by Chris Wilson
;
; The special escape sequences supported
; by this enhanced console driver are
; listed in the table below:
;
;    ESC 1 or !   -> |     {chr(124)}
;    ESC 2 or "   -> ~     {chr(126)}
;    ESC 3 or #   -> del   {chr(127)}
;    ESC 7 or '   -> `     {chr(96)}
;    ESC 8 or (   -> {     {chr(123)}
;    ESC 9 or )   -> }     {chr(125)}
;    ESC , or <   -> [     {chr(91)}
;    ESC . or >   -> ]     {chr(93)}
;    ESC - or =   -> _     {chr(95)}
;    ESC / or ?   -> \     {chr(92)}
;    ESC <space>  -> ESC
;    ESC ESC      -> {caps-lock toggle}
;    ESC a        -> A
;     :  :        -> :
;    ESC z        -> Z
;
; The SYSTEM.ATTACH program is used to
; install this driver.
;
;

INDIRECT .EQU   002
JVAFOLD  .EQU   0EE
ACJVAFLD .EQU   0E2

         .PROC  CONSOLE

         JMP    CONCKHDL ;SYSTEM.ATTACH will patch the start of CONCK
                         ;to jump here
         STA    TEMP1    ;All read, write, init, and stat calls will
                         ;jump here
         STY    TEMP1+1
         PLA             ;Save caller's return address
         STA    RETURN
         PLA
         STA    RETURN+1
         TXA             ;Use X-reg to determine the type of call
         BEQ    READ
         CMP    #1
         BEQ    WRITE
         CMP    #2
         BEQ    INIT
         CMP    #4
         BEQ    STATUS
         LDX    #3       ;No such I/O command
         JMP    RET

RETURN   .WORD 0
TEMP1    .WORD 0
ROUTINE  .WORD 0

READ     ;Code for a read
         LDA    RDRTN+1  ;Fix up stack so that the standard read routine
         PHA             ;returns to READRTN so that we can filter
         LDA    RDRTN    ;keyboard characters
         PHA
         LDY    #1       ;offset to address of the standard read routine
         BNE    GET1     ;in the copy of the jump vector made by
                         ;SYSTEM.ATTACH

WRITE    ;Code for a write
         LDY    #4
         BNE    GET
```

```
INIT        ;Code for init

            ;First patch bios jump vector so that write, init, and
            ;status calls go direct to the standard console routines
            LDA    0C08B      ;Fold in interpreter
            LDY    #4
            JSR    FIXUP      ;Write
            LDY    #7
            JSR    FIXUP      ;Init
            LDY    #43.
            JSR    FIXUP      ;Status

            ;Now undo the patch to the standard CONCK routine (made by
            ;SYSTEM.ATTACH) which causes it to branch to the start of
            ;this driver
            LDY    #55.       ;Get address of original CONCK
            LDA    @ACJVAFLD,Y
            STA    INDIRECT
            INY
            LDA    @ACJVAFLD,Y
            STA    INDIRECT+1
            LDY    #0
            LDA    #08        ;PHP
            STA    @INDIRECT,Y
            INY
            LDA    #48        ;PHA
            STA    @INDIRECT,Y
            INY
            LDA    #8A        ;TXA
            STA    @INDIRECT,Y
            LDA    0C083      ;Fold in bios

            LDY    #7
            BNE    GET

STATUS      ;Code for status
            LDY    #43.

GET         LDA RETURN+1      ;Fix up stack so that standard driver
            PHA               ;routine returns directly to caller
            LDA RETURN
            PHA

GET1        ;ACJVAFLD contains a pointer to the copy of the
            ;jump vector made by SYSTEM.ATTACH before
            ;it was modified to attach this driver
            LDA    @ACJVAFLD,Y
            STA    ROUTINE
            INY
            LDA    @ACJVAFLD,Y
            STA    ROUTINE+1
            LDY    TEMP1+1    ;Restore registers
            LDA    TEMP1
            JMP    @ROUTINE ;Go to the standard driver routine

FIXUP       LDA    @ACJVAFLD,Y
            STA    @JVAFOLD,Y
            INY
            LDA    @ACJVAFLD,Y
            STA    @JVAFOLD,Y
            RTS

RDRTN       .WORD READRTN-1
ESRTN       .WORD ESCRTN-1
CAPSLOCK    .BYTE 0

TABLE1      .ASCII "123789,.-/"
            .ASCII "!"
            .BYTE  022
            .ASCII "#'()<>=?"
            .ASCII " "
TABLE2      .BYTE  07C,07E,07F,060,07B,07D,05B,05D,05F,05C
            .BYTE  07C,07E,07F,060,07B,07D,05B,05D,05F,05C
            .BYTE  01B
TBLSIZE     .EQU   *-TABLE2
```

```
READRTN  CMP  #01B       ;ESC?
         BEQ  ESCKEY
         LDY  CAPSLOCK   ;Capslock set?
         BNE  CHKLC
         CMP  #041       ;No, upper case?
         BCC  RET
         CMP  #05A+1
         BCS  RET
         ORA  #020       ;Yes, force to lower case
         JMP  RET
CHKLC    CMP  #061       ;Lower case?
         BCC  RET
         CMP  #07A+1
         BCS  RET
         AND  #0DF       ;Yes, force to upper case
         JMP  RET
ESCKEY   LDA  ESRTN+1    ;Fix up stack so that standard read
         PHA             ;routine returns to ESCRTN
         LDA  ESRTN
         PHA
         LDY  #1
         JMP  GET1

ESCRTN   LDY  #TBLSIZE
CONVLOOP CMP  TABLE1,Y   ;Check character after ESC to see if it's
         BEQ  CHANGE     ;one of the magic ones
         DEY
         BPL  CONVLOOP
         JMP  NOTSPCL
CHANGE   LDA  TABLE2,Y   ;Yes, substitute corresponding character
         JMP  RET        ;in TABLE2

NOTSPCL  CMP  #01B       ;ESC?
         BNE  NOTESC
         LDA  CAPSLOCK   ;Yes, toggle capslock
         EOR  #0FF
         STA  CAPSLOCK
         JMP  READ       ;Get next character

NOTESC   CMP  #061       ;Lower case?
         BCC  RET
         CMP  #07A+1
         BCS  RET
         AND  #0DF       ;Yes, shift to upper case

RET      TAY             ;Save A-reg
         LDA  RETURN+1   ;Fix up stack so that we can return to
         PHA             ;original caller
         LDA  RETURN
         PHA
         TYA             ;Restore A-reg
         RTS

CONCKHDL PHP             ;Save state of machine
         PHA
         TXA
         PHA
         TYA
         PHA
         CLC             ;Get address of CONCK
         LDY  #55.
         LDA  @ACJVAFLD,Y
         ADC  #6         ;Bump by 6 because of the patch made by
                         ;SYSTEM.ATTACH
         STA  ROUTINE
         INY
         LDA  @ACJVAFLD,Y
         ADC  #0
         STA  ROUTINE+1
         JMP  @ROUTINE

         .END
```

A Structured Record for the DOS VTOC

Paul W. Mosher

Breaking programming habits formed in several years of learning BASIC has not been easy for me in my efforts to get more at home with Pascal. Reviewing my Pascal scratchings to date, I have to admit that many of them are literal translations of ideas which I thought out "in BASIC." In particular, the idea of using "structured data types" has been slow to filter into my collection of useful techniques even though it represents one of the main advances of Pascal-type languages over some more old-fashioned languages like BASIC. I am not alone, however, since many published Pascal programs and routines seem to have the same avoidance of "structured data types."

As a learning experience for myself, as well as a possible start toward writing some DOS 3.3 utilities in Pascal, I tried to figure out a way of building a structured data type to represent the VTOC of a DOS 3.3 disk. You should understand that the results of the accompanying program could be obtained without using the structured record just as you would do in BASIC. However, the use of a structured record makes the program much simpler to understand and probably much shorter. In nine short lines a disk map is drawn showing free and used sectors, and a single statement computes the number of free sectors on the disk!

A Piece of the Real World

The aim of using a structured data type is to create an abstract representation of part of the "real world." Ideally, the data are described in the program in such a way that the "meaning" of the data is clearly reflected to someone reading the program. In the case of this article, the part of the "real world" is the sequence of 256 bytes in sector 0 on track 17 of a DOS 3.3 disk. To follow my description of the structured record, look on pages 132–133 of the DOS 3.3 (or 3.2) manual.

The table listed there gives the meaning of the bytes in the VTOC sector. You will immediately see that these bytes stand for a variety of different things. For example, bytes $1 and $2 each stand for a single number describing the track and sector to examine for the start of the disk catalog. By contrast, bytes $36 and $37 are to be treated together as a single number representing the number of bytes in each sector of the disk.

Bytes $30–$33 are supposed to be thought of as an array of 32 single bits. Further down the table, that very same kind of 32 bit array is repeated over and over 35 times (140 bytes) from $38 through $C3 to form the Disk Bit Map. Each bit in this array of 1120 bits stands for a single sector on the disk (half are spares); a 1 indicating that the sector is free and a 0 indicating that it is in use. It would be silly to refer to these 140 bytes as decimal or hexidecimal numbers because the "meaning" is in the individual bits. By the same token, there would be no point in referring to $36 and $37 separately because the "meaning" in these bytes is a single number. It is the attempt to refer to each section of the 256 bytes in a way appropriate to "what it is" that is behind the structured record.

To complicate matters, you can see from the DOS manual that there are a number of "unused" bytes scattered throughout the 256 bytes of the sector. The structured record, which will be the template or pattern for 256 bytes in the Apple memory into which we will read the VTOC sector, has to take account of the unused bytes to get everything in the right place.

Representing the VTOC as an Abstract Structure

In order to make the description clearer, I have listed the Pascal program with line numbers and will refer to the lines by these numbers (see listing). The plan will be to designate 256 bytes in terms of a series of named variables (fields) which represent, by their name and TYPE, the meaning of the VTOC.

We start (line 9) by defining a type "byte" as an integer (subrange type) between 0 and 255. An array of such "Bytes" would use up 2 actual memory bytes each, because an integer is stored in two bytes, no matter what range of values it is allowed to take. The high order byte would be wasted. However, in a PACKED ARRAY or PACKED RECORD the Pascal system will use the minimum amount of room needed to store a variable of a given type which, of course, for a number within the range of the type "byte" would be a single byte.

In the definition of the Packed Record called VTOC_structure in lines 16–34 we can make a variable of type Byte correspond to one memory byte. The record begins this way with Unused_A (line 17) which stands for the unused byte $0 at the start of the VTOC sector. The next three bytes are actual integer values of the type "byte" which have meaning and are given names in lines 18–20.

The two unused bytes in $4 and $5 are represented by a Packed Array of bytes, containing 2 bytes, of course. I chose to number them to correspond to their positions in the record but could have called them [0..1] instead. Notice that this packed array starts on an even numbered byte of the record. I mention this because the Pascal system thinks in terms of "words," or two byte groups, and all packed arrays have to start on a word boundary even if this means that a byte gets wasted when putting one packed thing inside another packed thing. (See the Apple Pascal Language Reference Manual, pp. 17–18).

The next byte, $6, stands for the volume number and is named (see line 22). Following the volume number comes a series of 32 unused bytes ($7-$26). I first tried to represent them by a "Packed Array [0..31] of Byte" but the system went berserk for the reason mentioned in the previous paragraph! The packed array found itself starting in byte $8 leaving byte $7 empty and everything in the record after that was in the wrong place. My solution was to fill byte $7 singly in line 23, then fill the next 31 bytes with a packed array. That didn't work either!

Putting an odd number of bytes in a packed array starting on a "word" boundary, of course, made the array end in the middle of a word. The system then allocated the remainder of *that* word to the array causing a similar problem as before. (See the Apple Pascal Language Reference Manual, p. 16.) The solution that works (lines 24 & 25) is to define an array of 30 bytes and then declare the 32nd byte separately. From here to $30 things are pretty straight forward.

The 4 bytes starting at $30, however, stand for 32 separate bits rather than numbers, and so here we need a new way to describe these 4 bytes which will allow us to refer to the 32 bits one at a time.

A bit for each sector in a track plus 16 additional unused bits make up the bit map for each track on the disk (see bottom of page 133 in the DOS manual). The collection of all the bit maps for the tracks make up the bit map for the entire disk. I defined a single sector_bit (line 10) as a type of variable which can have only two possible values: "In_use" or "Free." By listing the values in this order, rather than (Free, In_use), the value of 0 gets associated with "In_use" and 1 gets associated with "Free" just as on the disk.

Now (line 11) the bit map of a whole track, the "Track_bit_map," can be defined as an array of 32 sector_bits. Just like the type Boolean, the type "Sector_bit" can only have two values so it takes only one bit to represent it in a packed array. The entire 32 sector_bits fit into just 4 bytes in a Packed Array [0..31] of Sector_bit. This is similar to the 4 bytes on the disk!

Sadly, however, the DOS VTOC bytes are in the wrong order so that the bit represented by Track_bit_map[6] actually stands for sector 14 and so forth. (See the bottom of p. 133 in the DOS manual.) In my program, I handled the problem with a mapping function when I needed to address the bit for a particular sector. If there is a more "natural" or aesthetic way to set up this part of the record, to index the bits in the order of their meaning, I couldn't think of it and would be grateful to anyone who has a clearer solution to offer. The problem looks like this:

	First of 4 bytes								Second of 4 bytes							
Array position:	0	1	2	3	4	5	6	7	8	9	10	11	12	13	14	15
Sector represented:	8	9	10	11	12	13	14	15	0	1	2	3	4	5	6	7

Of course bits 16–31, contained in the third and fourth bytes, are not used. Line 28 uses the type Track_bit_map to fill in the 4 bytes.

Bytes $34 and $35 in the DOS manual description are again straight forward and represented by lines 29 and 30. Now bytes $36 and $37 are to be treated as a single integer value and are arranged just the way the Pascal system would arrange an integer variable. Therefore, in line 31 the field "Bytes_per_sec" is declared as an integer type.

Starting at byte $38 of the disk sector, the next 140 bytes are a map of the entire disk showing which sectors are in use. In line 12, the type "Disk_bit_map" is defined as a packed array of 35 Track_bit_maps. Using this data type allows all 140 bytes to be defined in the field shown in line 32.

Using the New Type to Make a Variable

Now that a new data type, "VTOC_structure," has been described, an actual variable of this type can be declared (Line 42). This variable, named VTOC, will be a 256 byte area of memory into which the VTOC of a disk can be read. The fields within the VTOC are then simply referenced by designations like "VTOC.Volume_number" without any other programming! Even a single bit within the bit map can be referred to as "VTOC.bit_map[track, sector]." Of course, it would be the bit for the wrong sector because of the problem mentioned above. To handle this latter problem the function "Mapping_of( )" (lines 47–52) was added to map the bit array onto the correct sector numbers. Now the reference "VTOC.bit_map [track, mapping_of(sector)]" will give the correct bit.

Using the Structured Data

The program, itself, is simply a demonstration of some ways to use the VTOC variable. In the four lines 58, 59, 65, and 66 the VTOC of the DOS 3.3 disk is read into the VTOC record variable by first reading the block containing track 17, sector 0 into a buffer (line 65) and then moving the first 256 bytes of the buffer into the VTOC (line 66). Lines 89 to 98 print a used-sector map of the disk while lines 103 to 108 count and print out the number of free sectors on the disk.

```
Program VTOC_READ;

CONST
  VTOC_block      = 136;  (* Lower half of this block is VTOC sector  *)

TYPE
  Sector          = 0..15;
  Track           = 0..34;
  Byte            = 0..255;
  Sector_bit      = (In_use, free);
  Track_bit_map   = Packed Array[0..31] of Sector_bit;
  Disk_bit_map    = Packed Array[0..34] of Track_bit_map;
  Blockbuffer     = Packed Array[0..511] of byte;
```

```
  VTOC_structure= Packed Record
             Unused_A       :    Byte;
             Dir_sec_start  :    Byte;
             Dir_Trk_start  :    Byte;
             Dos_Release    :    Byte;
             Unused_B       :    Packed Array [4..5] of byte;
             Volume_number  :    Byte;
             Unused_C       :    Byte;
             Unused_D       :    Packed array [8..37] of byte;
             Unused_E       :    Byte;
             Max_TS_Pairs   :    Byte;
             Unused_F       :    Packed array [40..47] of byte;
             Mask_bytes     :    Track_bit_map;
             Tracks_on_disk :    Byte;
             Secs_per_track :    Byte;
             Bytes_per_sec  :    Integer;
             Bit_map        :    Disk_bit_map;
             Unused_G       :    Packed array [196..255] of byte;
   End;  (* VTOC structure  *)


VAR
  Unit_num,
  Block,
  Free_spaces    :  Integer;
  Dummy          :  Char;
  VTOC           :  VTOC_structure;
  Input_buffer   :  Block_buffer;
  Sec_num        :  Sector;
  Trk_num        :  Track;

    Function Mapping_of (To_be_mapped : Sector) : Sector;
        Begin
          If To_be_mapped < 8
             then Mapping_of :=  To_be_mapped + 8
             else Mapping_of :=  To_be_mapped - 8
        End;



Begin  (* MAIN PROGRAM  *)

  Unit_num := 5;  (* I used drive 2, slot 6 for the DOS 3.3 disk  *)
  Block    := VTOC_block;

(* -------------------------------------------------------------------
   Read the block containing the VTOC sector into the Input Buffer and then
   move the first 256 bytes of the input buffer into the VTOC variable
   ------------------------------------------------------------------- *)
  Unitread (Unit_num, Input_buffer, 512, Block);
  Moveleft (Input_buffer[0], VTOC, 256);


(* -------------------------------------------------------------------
   Print out some information about the VTOC
   ------------------------------------------------------------------- *)
  Writeln('Directory starts at sector :', VTOC.Dir_sec_start );
  Writeln('Directory starts at track  :', VTOC.Dir_trk_start );
  Writeln('DOS release number is      :', VTOC.DOS_release   );
  Writeln('DISKETTE volume number     :', VTOC.Volume_number );
  Writeln('Maximum T/S pairs in sector:', VTOC.Max_TS_pairs  );
  Writeln('Number of tracks on disk   :', VTOC.Tracks_on_disk);
  Writeln('Number of sectors per track:', VTOC.Secs_per_track);
  Writeln('Number of bytes per sector :', VTOC.Bytes_per_sec );
  Writeln('SIZE OF "VTOC" variable    :', SIZEOF(VTOC)       );
  Writeln;
  Write(' << press any key for disk map and free space >>');
  Read(Dummy); Writeln;
```

```
(* -----------------------------------------------------------------
   Draw a map of disk showing sectors in use
   ----------------------------------------------------------------- *)
  For Sec_num := 0 to 15 do
    begin
     Write(Sec_num:2,': ');
     For Trk_num := 0 to 34 do
       If VTOC.bit_map[ Trk_num, Mapping_of(Sec_num) ] = free
            then write('.')
            else write('*');
      Writeln;
    end; (* For sec_num loop *)
  Write('     ');For Trk_num := 0 to 34 do write (Trk_num MOD 10);Writeln;

(* -----------------------------------------------------------------
   Compute number of free sectors on disk and print it out
   ----------------------------------------------------------------- *)
  Free_spaces := 0;
  For Trk_num := 0 to 34 do
    for Sec_num := 0 to 15 do
      if VTOC.bit_map[Trk_num, Sec_num] = free
        then Free_spaces := Free_spaces + 1;
  Writeln ('     Free Space on Disk = ', Free_spaces, ' Sectors');

End.
```

```
PAGE  1                NUMBERED LISTING OF PROGRAM TO READ VTOC                30-DEC-1981
-----------------------------------------------------------------------------------------

Program VTOC_READ;

CONST
  VTOC_block     = 136;  (* Lower half of this block is VTOC sector  *)

TYPE
  Sector         = 0..15;
  Track          = 0..34;
  Byte           = 0..255;
  Sector_bit     = (In_use, free);
  Track_bit_map  = Packed Array[0..31] of Sector_bit;
  Disk_bit_map   = Packed Array[0..34] of Track_bit_map;
  Blockbuffer    = Packed Array[0..511] of byte;


  VTOC_structure= Packed Record
                   Unused_A       :    Byte;
                   Dir_sec_start  :    Byte;
                   Dir_Trk_start  :    Byte;
                   Dos_Release    :    Byte;
                   Unused_B       :    Packed Array [4..5] of byte;
                   Volume_number  :    Byte;
                   Unused_C       :    Byte;
                   Unused_D       :    Packed array [8..37] of byte;
                   Unused_E       :    Byte;
                   Max_TS_Pairs   :    Byte;
                   Unused_F       :    Packed array [40..47] of byte;
                   Mask_bytes     :    Track_bit_map;
                   Tracks_on_disk :    Byte;
                   Secs_per_track :    Byte;
                   Bytes_per_sec  :    Integer;
                   Bit_map        :    Disk_bit_map;
                   Unused_G       :    Packed array [196..255] of byte;
    End;  (* VTOC structure  *)


VAR
  Unit_num,
  Block,
  Free_spaces     :  Integer;
  Dummy           :  Char;
  VTOC            :  VTOC_structure;
  Input_buffer    :  Block_buffer;
  Sec_num         :  Sector;
  Trk_num         :  Track;
```

```
   Function Mapping_of (To_be_mapped : Sector) : Sector;
       Begin
         If To_be_mapped < 8
            then Mapping_of :=  To_be_mapped + 8
            else Mapping_of :=  To_be_mapped - 8
       End;
```

[PAGE 1]

PAGE 2 NUMBERED LISTING OF PROGRAM TO READ VTOC (CONTINUED) 30-DEC-1981

```
Begin  (* MAIN PROGRAM  *)

  Unit_num := 5;  (* I used drive 2, slot 6 for the DOS 3.3 disk  *)
  Block    := VTOC_block;

(* ---------------------------------------------------------------------
   Read the block containing the VTOC sector into the Input Buffer and the
   move the first 256 bytes of the input buffer into the VTOC variable
   --------------------------------------------------------------------- *)
  Unitread (Unit_num, Input_buffer, 512, Block);
  Moveleft (Input_buffer[0], VTOC, 256);


(* ---------------------------------------------------------------------
   Print out some information about the VTOC
   --------------------------------------------------------------------- *)
  Writeln('Directory starts at sector :', VTOC.Dir_sec_start );
  Writeln('Directory starts at track  :', VTOC.Dir_trk_start );
  Writeln('DOS release number is      :', VTOC.DOS_release   );
  Writeln('DISKETTE volume number     :', VTOC.Volume_number );
  Writeln('Maximum T/S pairs in sector:', VTOC.Max_TS_pairs  );
  Writeln('Number of tracks on disk   :', VTOC.Tracks_on_disk);
  Writeln('Number of sectors per track:', VTOC.Secs_per_track);
  Writeln('Number of bytes per sector :', VTOC.Bytes_per_sec );
  Writeln('SIZE OF "VTOC" variable    :', SIZEOF(VTOC)       );
  Writeln;
  Write(' << press any key for disk map and free space >>');
  Read(Dummy); Writeln;


(* ---------------------------------------------------------------------
   Draw a map of disk showing sectors in use
   --------------------------------------------------------------------- *)
  For Sec_num := 0 to 15 do
    begin
     Write(Sec_num:2,': ');
     For Trk_num := 0 to 34 do
       If VTOC.bit_map[ Trk_num, Mapping_of(Sec_num) ] = free
          then write('.')
          else write('*');
       Writeln;
    end; (* For sec_num loop *)
  Write('    ');For Trk_num := 0 to 34 do write (Trk_num MOD 10);Writeln;

(* ---------------------------------------------------------------------
   Compute number of free sectors on disk and print it out
   --------------------------------------------------------------------- *)
  Free_spaces := 0;
  For Trk_num := 0 to 34 do
    for Sec_num := 0 to 15 do
      if VTOC.bit_map[Trk_num, Sec_num] = free
        then Free_spaces := Free_spaces + 1;
  Writeln ('    Free Space on Disk = ', Free_spaces, ' Sectors');

End.
```

```
SAMPLE PROGRAM OUTPUT
---------------------
Note: output of version listed here goes to console screen


Directory starts at sector :17
Directory starts at track  :15
DOS release number is      :3
DISKETTE volume number     :100
Maximum T/S pairs in sector:122
Number of tracks on disk   :35
Number of sectors per track:16
Number of bytes per sector :256
SIZE OF "VTOC" variable    :256

 << press any key for disk map and free space >>
 0: ************.*...*.***........*....
 1: ************.*...*.***........*....
 2: ************.*...*.***........*....
 3: **************...*.***.*......*....
 4: **************..******.*...*..*....
 5: **************..******.*...*..*....
 6: **************..******.*...*..*....
 7: **************..******.*...*..*....
 8: **************..********...*..*....
 9: **************..*********..*..*..*.
10: *************************..*.**..*.
11: *************************..*.******
12: ***********************************
13: ***********************************
14: ***********************************
15: ***********************************
    01234567890123456789012345678901234
    Free Space on Disk = 143 Sectors
```

Pascal Techniques Hardware Interfacing

Chris Wilson

The purpose of this article is to explain some of the techniques which can be used to write Pascal programs which directly interface with external hardware devices without the need for special assembly language support routines. The Hayes Associates Micromodem II is used for the purpose of example, and this article includes both an interface UNIT for the Micromodem and a terminal program.

I was inspired to write the interface UNIT contained in this article after reading the article by Thomas H. Woteki in the February 1981 issue of BYTE. His interface UNIT is a mixture of Pascal PEEKs and POKEs along with special assembly language support routines. It seemed to me that Pascal was powerful enough to avoid the need for all of the assembly language routines as well as most of the PEEKs and POKEs.

The two things which are crucial to my approach are the memory-mapped I/O structure of the Apple II and the existence of packed RECORDS in Pascal.

The 6502 microprocessor in the Apple II does not have special instructions for communicating with external hardware devices (external to the 6502 itself). Instead a technique called memory-mapped I/O is used. This technique simply means that each hardware device appears to be one or more memory locations. All of the normal 6502 instructions which reference memory are then used to communicate with the external hardware devices. In the case of the Apple II, the address range from $C000 to $CFFF is reserved for memory-mapped I/O.

The first step then in writing a program to interface with an external hardware device such as the Micromodem, is to examine the memory-mapped I/O structure for that device. Table one shows this structure for the Micromodem as explained in the owner's manual.

Table 1: Memory-mapped Micromodem I/O structure (for slot 2)

ADDRESS	READ	WRITE
$C0A5	Modem Status	Modem Control
$C0A6	ACIA Status	ACIA Control
$C0A7	Receive Data	Transmit Data

It is important to notice that the Micromodem has three read-only memory locations and three write-only locations sharing the same memory addresses. For example, a write to address $C0A6 will update the ACIA control register, but a read to the same address will return the value of the ACIA status register and not the current contents of the ACIA control register. Thus a program must keep a separate copy of the current contents of any write-only registers whose values it needs to know. (Note: ACIA stands for Asynchronous Communications Interface Adapter and refers to the Motorola MC6850 chip used in the Micromodem.)

```
(*$S+,I-,R-*)

(*$C COPYRIGHT 1981 BY CHRIS WILSON *)

UNIT MICROMODEM; INTRINSIC CODE 23 DATA 24;

INTERFACE

  USES APPLESTUFF;

  TYPE
    BAUDRATE = (LOW, HIGH);
    MODE = (ANSWER, ORIGINATE);

  FUNCTION RINGING: BOOLEAN;
  FUNCTION CARRIER: BOOLEAN;
  FUNCTION RCVRFULL: BOOLEAN;
  FUNCTION TRANSEMPTY: BOOLEAN;
  FUNCTION DCERROR: BOOLEAN;
  FUNCTION ESCAPE: BOOLEAN;

  PROCEDURE WAIT(TIME: INTEGER);
  PROCEDURE INITCOMM(WORDSELECT: INTEGER);
  PROCEDURE SETMODE(MD: MODE);
  PROCEDURE SETRATE(BR: BAUDRATE);
  PROCEDURE SETWORD(WORDSELECT: INTEGER);
  PROCEDURE ENABLETRANSMIT;
  PROCEDURE DISABLETRANSMIT;
  PROCEDURE DISCONNECT;
  PROCEDURE WAITFORCARRIER;
  PROCEDURE DIAL(NUMBER: STRING);
  PROCEDURE AUTOANSWER;
  PROCEDURE BREAK;
  PROCEDURE PUTREM(CH: CHAR);
  PROCEDURE GETREM(VAR CH: CHAR);
```

```
IMPLEMENTATION

  TYPE
    WORD = PACKED ARRAY [0..1] OF CHAR;
    STATUSWORD = PACKED RECORD
      FILLER1: 0..127;
      RINOT: BOOLEAN;     (* RING INDICATOR *)
      RDRF: BOOLEAN;      (* RECEIVE DATA REGISTER FULL *)
      TDRE: BOOLEAN;      (* TRANSMIT DATA REGISTER EMPTY *)
      DCDNOT: BOOLEAN;    (* CARRIER DETECT NOT *)
      CTSNOT: BOOLEAN;    (* CTS NOT *)
      FE: BOOLEAN;        (* FRAMING ERROR *)
      OVRN: BOOLEAN;      (* RECEIVER OVERRUN *)
      PE: BOOLEAN;        (* PARITY ERROR *)
      IRQ: BOOLEAN        (* INTERRUPT REQUEST *)
      END;
    CONTROLWORD = PACKED RECORD
      BRS: BAUDRATE;      (* BIT RATE SELECT; 1 = 300 BAUD *)
      TXE: BOOLEAN;       (* TRANSMITTER ENABLE *)
      MODES: MODE;        (* MODE SELECT; 1 = ORIGINATE *)
      CTS: BOOLEAN;       (* CONTROLS CTS *)
      ST: BOOLEAN;        (* SELF TEST *)
      FILLER1: 0..3;
      OH: BOOLEAN;        (* OFF HOOK *)
      CDS: 0..3;          (* COUNTER DIVIDE SELECT *)
      WS: 0..7;           (* WORD SELECT *)
      TC: 0..3;           (* TRANSMIT CONTROL *)
      RIE: BOOLEAN        (* RECEIVE INTERRUPT ENABLE *)
      END;

  VAR
    CONTROL: CONTROLWORD;
    MODEM: PACKED RECORD
      CASE INTEGER OF
      0: (ADDRESS1: INTEGER;
          ADDRESS2: INTEGER);
      1: (CONTROL: ^ CONTROLWORD;
          DATAOUT: ^ WORD);
      2: (STATUS: ^ STATUSWORD;
          DATAIN: ^ WORD)
      END;

  FUNCTION RINGING;
        (*=======*)

  (* TEST RING INDICATION *)

  BEGIN
  RINGING := NOT MODEM.STATUS^.RINOT;
  END;

  FUNCTION CARRIER;
        (*=======*)

  (* TEST FOR PRESENCE OF CARRIER *)

  BEGIN
  CARRIER := NOT MODEM.STATUS^.DCDNOT;
  END;

  FUNCTION RCVRFULL;
        (*========*)

  (* TEST RECEIVE DATA REGISTER FULL *)

  BEGIN
  RCVRFULL := MODEM.STATUS^.RDRF;
  END;
```

The control and status registers are divided into various fields as shown in table two. The notation used in the table is "[S:W]" where "S" is the most significant bit of the field and "W" is the width of the field in bits. Bit seven is the most significant bit of each byte.

Table 2: Micromodem register format

Modem Control:
- [7:1] - Off Hook
- [6:2] - [unused]
- [4:1] - Self Test
- [3:1] - Clear To Send
- [2:1] - Mode Select
- [1:1] - Transmitter Enable
- [0:1] - Bit Rate Select

Modem Status:
- [7:1] - Ring-Indicator Not
- [6:7] - [unused]

ACIA Control:
- [7:1] - Receive Interrupt Enable
- [6:2] - Transmit Control
- [4:3] - Word Select
- [1:2] - Counter Divide Select

ACIA Status:
- [7:1] - Interrupt Request
- [6:1] - Parity Error
- [5:1] - Receiver Overrun
- [4:1] - Framing Error
- [3:1] - Clear-To-Send Not
- [2:1] - Data-Carrier-Detect Not
- [1:1] - Transmit Data Register Empty
- [0:1] - Receive Data Register Full

Once the memory-mapped I/O structure of the hardware device is known, a decision has to be made as to how to access the various bits and pieces of the hardware's memory locations from Pascal.

As mentioned above, one approach is to define Pascal PEEK and POKE routines which are used to manipulate the memory locations of interest and then use DIV and MOD to isolate fields within bytes. This approach is simple but has the disadvantage of being obscure when it comes to setting and testing bits as well as slow if lots of DIVs and MODs are used. In time critical applications like pulse dialing the Micromodem, a special assembly language routine is used.

The approach used in this article is to define Pascal packed RECORDs which exactly map onto the actual structure of the hardware memory locations. This approach is slightly more difficult than the other, but it has the advantage of being very clear to follow and very fast, since the Pascal interpreter will do shifting and Masking to isolate fields, instead of multiplies and divides. In order to use this approach, you must understand how the compiler allocates fields within RECORDS, and how words are actually stored in memory.

The basic unit of storage in Pascal is the 16-bit word. The bits in a word are numbered from 15 to zero, where bit 15 is the most significant bit. The packing of fields into words is partially explained in the Apple Pascal Language Reference Manual starting on page 17.

What is not explained is that fields are allocated starting at bit zero and continuing toward bit 15 until either 1) the current word is full, 2) the next field is too big to fit in the remainded of the current word, or 3) the next field is either an ARRAY or a RECORD.

Furthermore, fields within a list such as "A, B, C: BOOLEAN" are allocated in reverse order (i.e. "C" will be the first field allocated) and consecutive ARRAY elements in a packed ARRAY are allocated from left to right (i.e. starting with bit zero). All of this is complicated by the fact that the Apple II is a byte swapped machine, which means that the two bytes in a word are reversed in memory as shown in table three.

```
FUNCTION TRANSEMPTY;
        (*==========*)

(* TEST TRANSMIT DATA REGISTER EMPTY *)

BEGIN
TRANSEMPTY := MODEM.STATUS^.TDRE;
END;

FUNCTION DCERROR;
        (*=======*)

(* TEST FOR DATA-COMM ERROR *)

VAR
  CH: CHAR;
  COPY: STATUSWORD;

BEGIN
COPY := MODEM.STATUS^;
WITH COPY DO
  IF PE OR OVRN OR FE OR CTSNOT OR DCDNOT THEN
    BEGIN
    DCERROR := TRUE;
    (* CLEAR RECEIVER *)
    CH := MODEM.DATAIN^[0];
    END
  ELSE
    DCERROR := FALSE;
END;

FUNCTION ESCAPE;
        (*======*)

(* TEST FOR KEYBOARD ESCAPE *)

CONST
  ESC = 27;

VAR
  CH: CHAR;

BEGIN
IF KEYPRESS THEN
  BEGIN
  READ(KEYBOARD,CH);
  ESCAPE := (CH = CHR(ESC));
  END
ELSE
  ESCAPE := FALSE;
END;
```

Table 3: Memory representation of a Pascal word

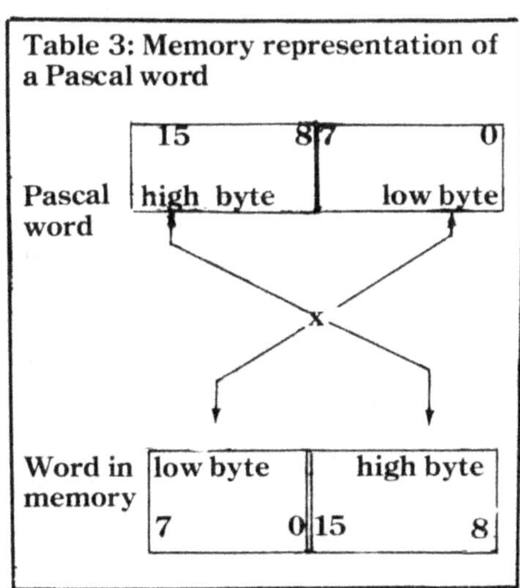

With the information discussed so far, it is possible to construct a Pascal interface definition for the Micromodem. Table four is an extract from the Micromodem UNIT which shows the definitions I used.

STATUSWORD is a definition of the read-only modem and ACIA status registers at $C0A5 and $C0A6. CONTROLWORD is a definition of the write-only modem and ACIA control registers at the same addresses. The comments show the field allocation done by the compiler.

Notice the strategic use of filler fields to make sure everything is allocated correctly. I also avoid using lists of the form "A, B, C: BOOLEAN" so that I don't have to worry about which item the compiler allocates first.

The variable CONTROL is used to keep a copy of the current contents of the write-only control registers. Any time a control field is updated, the field in CONTROL is changed first and then the entire control word is copied to MODEM.CONTROL."

```
PROCEDURE INITCOMM; (* WORDSELECT: INTEGER *)
         (*========*)

(* RESET AND INITIALIZE ACIA *)

VAR
  WAIT: INTEGER;

BEGIN
CONTROL.CDS := 3;  (* MASTER RESET *)
MODEM.CONTROL^ := CONTROL;
WAIT := 0;
REPEAT
  WAIT := SUCC(WAIT)
UNTIL NOT(CARRIER) OR (WAIT > 5000);
WITH CONTROL DO
  BEGIN
  BRS := HIGH;
  TXE := FALSE;
  MODES := ORIGINATE;
  CTS := TRUE;
  ST := FALSE;
  FILLER1 := 0;
  OH := FALSE;
  CDS := 1;
  WS := WORDSELECT MOD 8;
  TC := 0;
  RIE := FALSE;
  END;
MODEM.CONTROL^ := CONTROL;
END;

PROCEDURE SETMODE; (* MD: MODE *)
         (*=======*)

(* SET THE MODE *)

BEGIN
CONTROL.MODES := MD;
MODEM.CONTROL^ := CONTROL;
END;

PROCEDURE SETRATE; (* BR: BAUDRATE *)
         (*=======*)

(* SET THE BAUD RATE *)

BEGIN
CONTROL.BRS := BR;
MODEM.CONTROL^ := CONTROL;
END;

PROCEDURE SETWORD; (* WORDSELECT: INTEGER *)
         (*=======*)

(* SET THE WORD LENGTH, PARITY, AND STOP BITS *)

BEGIN
CONTROL.WS := WORDSELECT MOD 8;
MODEM.CONTROL^ := CONTROL;
END;

PROCEDURE ENABLETRANSMIT;
         (*==============*)

(* TURN ON THE MODEM TRANSMITTER *)

BEGIN
CONTROL.TXE := TRUE;
MODEM.CONTROL^ := CONTROL;
END;
```

The initialization portion of the UNIT sets the ADDRESS1 and ADDRESS2 fields of MODEM to point to the appropriate memory locations for the Micromodem.

Table 4: Pascal interface definitions for the Micromodem

```
TYPE
  WORD = PACKED ARRAY [0..1]
    OF CHAR;
  STATUSWORD = PACKED RECORD
    FILLER1: 0..127;        (* [6:7] *)
    RINOT: BOOLEAN;         (* [7:1] *)
    RDRF: BOOLEAN;          (* [8:1] *)
    TDRE: BOOLEAN;          (* [9:1] *)
    DCDNOT: BOOLEAN;        (* [10:1] *)
    CTSNOT: BOOLEAN;        (* [11:1] *)
    FE: BOOLEAN;            (* [12:1] *)
    OVRN: BOOLEAN;          (* [13:1] *)
    PE: BOOLEAN;            (* [14:1] *)
    IRQ: BOOLEAN            (* [15:1] *)
    END;

CONTROLWORD = PACKED RECORD
    BRS: BAUDRATE;          (* [0:1] *)
    TXE: BOOLEAN;           (* [1:1] *)
    MODES: MODE;            (* [2:1] *)
    CTS: BOOLEAN;           (* [3:1] *)
    ST: BOOLEAN;            (* [4:1] *)
    FILLER1: 0..3;          (* [6:2] *)
    OH: BOOLEAN;            (* [7:1] *)
    CDS: 0..3;              (* [9:2] *)
    WS: 0..7;               (* [12:3] *)
    TC: 0..3;               (* [14:2] *)
    RIE: BOOLEAN            (* [15:1] *)
    END;

VAR
  CONTROL: CONTROLWORD;
  MODEM: PACKED RECORD
    CASE INTEGER OF
    0: (ADDRESS1: INTEGER;
       ADDRESS2: INTEGER);
    1:(CONTROL: ^CONTROLWORD;
       DATAOUT: ^WORD);
    2: (STATUS: ^STATUSWORD;
       DATAIN: ^WORD)
    END;
```

One additional thing is needed: a Pascal wait routine which can be used to delay for a specified number of milliseconds. The one I use is listed below. It was derived by adding statements such as "DUMMY := 0" to the FOR loop until 10,000 iterations of the loop took exactly 10 seconds to execute as timed on a stop watch. It is accurate within a few percent.

```
PROCEDURE WAIT(TIME: INTEGER);
(* = = = = *)

(* WAIT "TIME" MILLISECONDS *)

VAR
     I,
     DUMMY: INTEGER;

BEGIN
FOR I := 1 TO TIME DO
     BEGIN
     DUMMY := 0;
     DUMMY := 1;
     DUMMY := 2;
     END;
END;
```

I hope you have found this article instructive. Study of the interface UNIT for the Micromodem should clear up any confusion as to how various constructs are used. You may also find the trick of saving and restoring the Apple text pages and X, Y cursor location in the terminal program of interest.

```
PROCEDURE DISABLETRANSMIT;
        (*===============*)

(* TURN OFF THE MODEM TRANSMITTER *)

BEGIN
CONTROL.TXE := FALSE;
MODEM.CONTROL^ := CONTROL;
END;

PROCEDURE PICKUP;
        (*======*)

(* PLACE PHONE OFF-HOOK *)

BEGIN
CONTROL.OH := TRUE;
MODEM.CONTROL^ := CONTROL;
END;

PROCEDURE HANGUP;
        (*======*)

(* PLACE PHONE ON-HOOK *)

BEGIN
CONTROL.OH := FALSE;
MODEM.CONTROL^ := CONTROL;
END;

PROCEDURE DISCONNECT;
        (*==========*)

(* BREAK CONNECTION *)

VAR
  CH: CHAR;
  WAIT: INTEGER;

BEGIN
DISABLETRANSMIT;
HANGUP;
WAIT := 0;
WHILE CARRIER AND (WAIT < 5000) DO
  BEGIN
  WAIT := SUCC(WAIT);
  CH := MODEM.DATAIN^[0];
  END;
END;

PROCEDURE WAIT; (* TIME: INTEGER *)
        (*====*)

(* WAIT "TIME" MILLISECONDS *)

VAR
  I,
  DUMMY: INTEGER;

BEGIN
FOR I := 1 TO TIME DO
  BEGIN
  DUMMY := 0;
  DUMMY := 1;
  DUMMY := 2;
  END;
END;

PROCEDURE WAITFORCARRIER;
        (*==============*)

(* WAIT FOR CARRIER *)

VAR
  CH: CHAR;
  WAIT: INTEGER;

BEGIN
WRITELN('WAITING FOR CARRIER...');
ENABLETRANSMIT;
WAIT := 0;
REPEAT
  WAIT := SUCC(WAIT);
  CH := MODEM.DATAIN^[0]
UNTIL CARRIER OR ESCAPE OR (WAIT > 30000);
IF NOT CARRIER THEN
  DISCONNECT;
END;

PROCEDURE DIAL; (* NUMBER: STRING *)
        (*====*)

(* DIAL THE INDICATED NUMBER *)

VAR
  CH: CHAR;
  I,
  J,
  DIGIT: INTEGER;
```

```
BEGIN
IF NOT(CONTROL.OH) AND (LENGTH(NUMBER) <> 0) THEN
  BEGIN
  WRITELN('<ESC> ABORTS AUTO DIAL');
  WRITE('PREPARING TO DIAL...');
  SETMODE(ORIGINATE);
  PICKUP;
  WAIT(1400);
  WRITELN('OK');
  WRITE('DIALING...');
  FOR I := 1 TO LENGTH(NUMBER) DO
    BEGIN
    IF ESCAPE THEN
      BEGIN
      WRITELN('>>> ABORTED <<<');
      DISCONNECT;
      EXIT(DIAL);
      END;
    WRITE(NUMBER[I]);
    IF NUMBER[I] IN ['0'..'9'] THEN
      BEGIN
      DIGIT := ORD(NUMBER[I])-ORD('0');
      IF DIGIT = 0 THEN
        DIGIT := 10;
      WAIT(600);
      FOR J := 1 TO DIGIT DO
        BEGIN
        HANGUP;
        WAIT(61);
        PICKUP;
        WAIT(39);
        END;
      END
    ELSE IF NUMBER[I] = '*' THEN
      WAIT(2000);
    END;
  WRITELN;
  WAITFORCARRIER;
  END;
END;

PROCEDURE AUTOANSWER;
          (*==========*)

(* WAIT FOR RING & THEN ANSWER THE PHONE *)

BEGIN
IF NOT CONTROL.OH THEN
  BEGIN
  WRITELN('<ESC> ABORTS AUTO ANSWER');
  REPEAT
    WRITE('WAITING FOR RING...');
    REPEAT
      IF ESCAPE THEN
        BEGIN
        WRITELN;
        WRITELN('>>> ABORTED <<<');
        DISCONNECT;
        EXIT(AUTOANSWER);
        END
    UNTIL RINGING;
    WRITELN('OK');
    SETMODE(ANSWER);
    PICKUP;
    WAITFORCARRIER
  UNTIL CARRIER;
  END;
END;
```

```
PROCEDURE BREAK;
        (*=====*)

(* SENDS BREAK FOR 250 MILLISECONDS *)

VAR
  CH: CHAR;

BEGIN
CONTROL.TC := 3;
MODEM.CONTROL^ := CONTROL;
WAIT(250);
CONTROL.TC := 0;
MODEM.CONTROL^ := CONTROL;
(* NOW CLEAR ERRORS *)
WAIT(10);
CH := MODEM.DATAIN^[0];
END;

PROCEDURE PUTREM; (* CH: CHAR *)
        (*======*)

(* SEND CHAR TO THE MODEM *)

VAR
  WAIT: INTEGER;

BEGIN
IF MODEM.STATUS^.TDRE THEN
  MODEM.DATAOUT^[0] := CH
ELSE
  BEGIN
  WAIT := 0;
  WHILE CARRIER AND NOT(TRANSEMPTY) AND (WAIT < 5000) DO
    WAIT := SUCC(WAIT);
  IF TRANSEMPTY THEN
    MODEM.DATAOUT^[0] := CH;
  END;
END;

PROCEDURE GETREM; (* VAR CH: CHAR *)
        (*======*)


(* GET CHAR FROM THE MODEM *)

VAR
  WAIT: INTEGER;

BEGIN
IF MODEM.STATUS^.RDRF THEN
  CH := MODEM.DATAIN^[0]
ELSE
  BEGIN
  WAIT := 0;
  WHILE CARRIER AND NOT(RCVRFULL) AND (WAIT < 5000) DO
    WAIT := SUCC(WAIT);
  IF RCVRFULL THEN
    CH := MODEM.DATAIN^[0];
  END;
END;

(* ========== INITIALIZATION ========== *)

BEGIN
MODEM.ADDRESS1 := -16219;
MODEM.ADDRESS2 := -16217;
END.
```

```
(*$S+*)

(*$C COPYRIGHT 1981 BY CHRIS WILSON *)

(* NUMEROUS IMPROVEMENTS MADE AT THE SUGGESTION OF BILL GORD *)

PROGRAM TERMINAL;

USES APPLESTUFF, MICROMODEM;

CONST
  BADCH = '?';
  DCERRORCH = '!';

TYPE
  LINE = STRING[100];

VAR
  CTRLB,
  CTRLX,
  NUL,
  BEL,
  BS,
  LF,
  CR,
  ESC,
  DEL,
  ANSWR: CHAR;
  XMITDELAY,
  WORDSELECT: INTEGER;
  BR: BAUDRATE;
  WAITFORLF,
  HALFDUPLEX: BOOLEAN;
  DISPLAYABLE: PACKED SET OF CHAR;

FUNCTION PEEK(ADDRESS: INTEGER): INTEGER;
       (*====*)

TYPE
  WORD = PACKED ARRAY [0..1] OF 0..255;
  FREEUNION = RECORD
    CASE INTEGER OF
    0: (ADDR: INTEGER);
    1: (VALUE: ^ WORD)
    END;

VAR
  MEMORY: FREEUNION;

BEGIN
MEMORY.ADDR := ADDRESS;
PEEK := MEMORY.VALUE^[0];
END;

PROCEDURE UPCHAR(VAR CH: CHAR);
         (*======*)

BEGIN
IF CH IN ['a'..'z'] THEN
  CH := CHR(ORD('A')+(ORD(CH)-ORD('a')));
END;

PROCEDURE UPSTRING(VAR S: STRING);
         (*========*)

VAR
  I: INTEGER;

FUNCTION UPCHAR(CH: CHAR): CHAR;
  BEGIN
  IF CH IN ['a'..'z'] THEN
    UPCHAR := CHR(ORD('A')+(ORD(CH)-ORD('a')))
  ELSE
    UPCHAR := CH;
  END;
```

```
BEGIN
FOR I := 1 TO LENGTH(S) DO
  S[I] := UPCHAR(S[I]);
END;

PROCEDURE BELL;
          (*====*)

BEGIN
(* SHORT BELL TO AVOID MISSING ANYTHING *)
NOTE(24,2);
END;

PROCEDURE DISPLAY(CH: CHAR);
          (*=======*)

BEGIN
IF CH = BEL THEN
  BELL
ELSE IF CH = CR THEN
  WRITELN
ELSE IF CH IN DISPLAYABLE THEN
  WRITE(CH)
ELSE IF CH < ' ' THEN
  WRITE('^',CHR(ORD('@')+ORD(CH)))
ELSE
  WRITE(BADCH);
END;

PROCEDURE TEACH;
          (*=====*)

BEGIN
GOTOXY(0,3);
WRITELN('THIS PROGRAM TURNS THE APPLE ][ INTO');
WRITELN('A SMART TERMINAL.  WHILE YOU ARE CON-');
WRITELN('NECTED TO THE REMOTE COMPUTER, ALL OF');
WRITELN('THE STANDARD PASCAL CONTROL COMMANDS');
WRITELN('(E.G. CTRL-A, CTRL-@, CTRL-F) WILL WORK');
WRITELN('AS THEY NORMALLY DO, INCLUDING THE');
WRITELN('LOWERCASE COMMANDS.');
WRITELN;
WRITELN('SPECIAL KEYS IN TERMINAL MODE:');
WRITELN;
WRITELN('<CTRL-B> SENDS BREAK TO THE REMOTE');
WRITELN('         COMPUTER.');
WRITELN;
WRITELN('<CTRL-X> SENDS DEL (RUBOUT) TO THE');
WRITELN('         REMOTE COMPUTER.');
WRITELN;
WRITELN('<ESC>    ENTERS ESCAPE MODE WHICH');
WRITELN('         ALLOWS PROGRAM OPTIONS TO BE');
WRITELN('         CHANGED, ETC.');
END;

PROCEDURE SETUP;
          (*=====*)

VAR
  CH: CHAR;

PROCEDURE SETBAUDRATE;
          (*===========*)

VAR
  RATE: INTEGER;

BEGIN
GOTOXY(0,5);
IF BR = HIGH THEN
  WRITELN('CURRENT BAUD RATE: 300')
ELSE
  WRITELN('CURRENT BAUD RATE: 110');
WRITELN;
WRITE('BAUD RATE: ');
READLN(RATE);
```

Pascal Speed-Up Software for The Mill 6809 Board

Michael Christensen

[Beginners may wish to read the companion background section before reading this review.]

What kind of CPU does the Apple have?

There are only a hand full of popular CPU's that can be found in most of the small computers. Because the kind of CPU a microcomputer has tells a lot about the nature of the machine, small computers are often classified by their CPU. The Apple's CPU is called a "6502," and thus the Apple is said to be "a 6502 machine," suggesting that all 6502 machines have much in common. The Z-80, 6502, 8080, and 6809 are good examples of well known and widely used 8-bit microprocessors. All CPUs are given obscure names in order to comply with the industry-wide practice of intimidating the uninitiated.

Can the Apple use any other CPUs?

Microsoft has a card that plugs into the Apple to convert the Apple from a 6502 machine to a Z-80 machine. Since the greatest body of software for microcomputers has been written for the Z-80, and because the Z-80 is the most widely used CPU in small computers, this product significantly widens the range of applications for Apple users.

There are also 8088 and 68000 boards now becoming available for the Apple. The Mill offers a 6809 CPU for the Apple to work with its 6502 CPU.

Which CPU is best?

Comparing CPUs is difficult, because each has different merits and demerits in different applications. Generally though, the 6502 is relatively fast and sometimes relatively awkward to program; the Z-80 is relatively slow but is often considered relatively nice to program. The 6809 is becoming increasingly popular, largely because it is very versatile and easy to program. All of these CPU's are "8-bit" (they transfer eight "binary digits" with each "clock cycle").

The Mill
Stellation II
The Lobero Bldg., P.O. Box 2342
Santa Barbara, CA 93120

The Mill

THE Mill is a firmware board that plugs into the slot of your choice in the Apple, creating a multiprocessing environment by taking control of the system with it's resident 6809 CPU, and allowing the Apple's own 6502 CPU to run at 20% of its normal speed. That's right — both CPUs are running at the same time.

It is evident that there are at least five ways you can apply the power of The Mill:

1. multiprocessing applications
2. writing and executing 6809 machine code
3. speeding up BASIC programs
4. speeding up Pascal programs
5. running 6809 applications made or modified for the Apple.

The Speed-Up Kit

The scope of this article is limited to the fourth application listed above, speeding up Pascal programs. This feature is facilitated with two add-on packages from Stellation: The Pascal Speed-Up Kit for The Mill (to allow Pascal to use the Mill's 6809 CPU) and the separate Floating Point Package that can be used to improve the Speed-Up Kit's treatment of floating point numbers.

Both packages are software based. The Speed-Up Kit modifies the file SYSTEM.APPLE on your boot disk. A program is run only once, and then you transfer the new SYSTEM. APPLE file to the disks you like; thereafter The Mill is virtually invisible. The new SYSTEM.APPLE file occupies the same number of blocks on disk that the old one did. The resulting interpreter uses a now slower 6502 to execute all 6502 code encountered in the code stream, and uses the 6809 to execute all of the P-code encountered. The 6809 P-code interpreter is significantly faster than the 6502's, and with both CPUs running you get a faster machine (sometimes).

Benchmarks indicate that the board does produce substantial increases in speed, although not nearly as much as you might expect from The Mill's advertisements. Stellation Two, the manufacturer, has been advertising a 30% to 300% faster P-machine. This is essentially correct, but it may also be a point of confusion. Your P-machine may be that much faster, but Pascal programs are a mix of P-code and 6502, so your programs often won't be 30-300% faster. I was unable to make any program execute over 60% faster, and found that some programs without The Floating Point Package actually executed slower with The Mill than without. The demonstration program that is provided with the kit runs 60% faster than it would without The Mill.

The pattern is somewhat predictable: programs that use a lot of P-code will run faster, and programs that use a lot of 6502 code will run slower. Anything in Pascal with a lot of input/output will make heavy use of the 6502. TURTLEGRAPHICS, APPLESTUFF and LONG-INTEGERS are all units written in 6502 code, and you may not expect routines therein to run faster with The Mill.

Floating Point

Almost all of the poor performers of The Speed-Up Kit's modified interpreter were math routines. Stellation Two consequently added software to improve this situation (i.e. the Floating Point Package).

If you do not use The Floating Point Package with The Speed-Up Kit, then the 6502 will be used for floating point operations instead of the 6809. Since the 6502 is running at only 20% of its normal speed, floating point routines will be slower than they would if the Mill weren't employed at all.

Within the Pascal language, there were some fine increases in speed in places you are most likely to use. Procedure calls, passing variables, loops, addition, multiplication, string intrinsics — all of these are employed frequently by most programs, and all did very well.The speed of many of the intrinsics will in practice vary depending on the size and characteristics of the parameters passed to them.

Special Features

When you execute the Speed-Up Kit software to modify Pascal, you can specify the slot number you'd like to have The Mill in. You also have the opportunity to have a little window appear on the screen all the time if you want; a window that tells you if the 6809 or the 6502 was last invoked. The window, located in the top right corner of the left text page, is continually flashing back and forth between "6809" and "6502," giving you a rough idea how much the 6502 is being used. Continually printing this window does not slow the machine down significantly. The window can be very helpful, and can be turned off when unwanted by revising the SYSTEM.APPLE file with the software provided.

Ease Of Use

Simplicity is definitely a characteristic here. I haven't seen much other hardware that was simpler to take advantage of. Really, you just plug the thing in, run a program, transfer a file or two, and then forget about it. If all you want to do is speed-up your Pascal programs, you won't have to spend a lot of time learning how to use this card.

Reliablility and Compatibility

The CPU is, after all, the "brain" of your computer; with any brain transplant I would expect complications. The compatiblity totally surprised me — none of my software had to be modified at all to execute with The Mill.

The Mill and Pascal seem to get along quite well. I did note that certain extremely large programs seem to suffer stack overflows early; presumably there is not quite as much memory left in the system after the Speed-Up Kit has been applied. The software also conflicted with a certain solid-state disk drive I was testing, although this only occurred when the Mill was displaying the 6502/6809 window on the screen.

Documentation

It's important to note that the documentation I received was both preliminary and weak. Content was acceptable to good, but there seemed to me to be a lack of material for beginnings. The format (stapled photocopies) was not up to current commercial standards. There was very little detailed information about The Speed-Up Kit, although I suppose the software is simple enough that little detail is required.

The kit I used also had a 6809 assembler and a very readable book by Lance Leventhal called "6809 Assembly Language Programming".

Details On The Benchmarks

Several Pascal language intrinsics, units and programs were placed in simple REPEAT loops with 1000 to 10,000 iterations. Loop time was subtracted and then iterations were divided out to produce the approximate number of milliseconds required for a single iteration. A Mountain Hardware Apple Clock was used to time the language intrinsics from within the software, while the programs and operating system listed at the bottom of Table 1 were timed manually.

The results are provided in Table 1, ranked by percent increase in speed provided by The Mill. Hopefully these benchmarks will provide users of The Mill with some objective criteria both for when to use The Mill and which intrinsics to take advantage of when The Mill is going to be used.

Conclusions

I recommend you buy The Mill, The Speed-Up Kit and The Floating Point Package to improve you Pascal system only under certain circumstances. If you have a specific application that is slower than you desire and you believe that a 10-40% improvement in speed will be worth the initial investment, then the Mill may be just what you need. Also, you should look for a low cost software solution first ('low cost" means cheaper than the board and its software). It is generally a poor idea to buy hardware to solve problems that can be improved in software; this is especially important if this is software you are planning to market. For some applications it could be worth the money, but for other applications it may provide only marginal improvement at best. You must examine your needs and decide for yourself.

A few people might also benefit from employing the 6809 in their development projects without the use of the Speed-Up software. It may be possible (although I have not fully explored this avenue) to link 6809 code directly into Pascal programs.

If you were planning to use The Mill to speed-up compiling or housekeeping, forget it. The compiler and the filer both seem to run at virtually the same speed with The Mill as without. But if you do a lot of work in the editor, you may be interested to know that The Mill improved speed there about 30-40%.

I hope no one will expect their Pascal programs to run 30-300% faster with The Mill after reading Stellation Two's advertising. P-code, yes. Whole programs, no. Hopefully Stellation Two will make some effort to clear this confusion up and rethink their advertising strategy. Someone has designed and implemented a good tool for the Apple, and it would be tragic for it to be brushed aside because people misunderstand its capabilities. For my own personal applications, I anticipate an overall speed increase of 10-40% for the average Pascal program with The Mill and the Speed-Up Software. This kind of improvement in performance could in certain cases be very valuable.

I have only evaluated The Mill with the Pascal Speed-Up Software and Floating Point Package in this review. There are at least four other applications of The Mill: multiprocessing, writing 6809 assembly language programs, speeding up BASIC programs. and running 6809 programs tailored for the Apple — all are areas I have not examined and which may deserve your consideration.

(continued from first page)

A new generation of "16-bit" single chip CPUs is emerging in the marketplace, delivering greater speed and the ability to directly address more memory (like the 8086, the 68000 and the Z8002). Recently, "32-bit" processors have become became available to computer manufacturers. This new technology is already translating into better speed and easier memory management for personal computers.

What is Pascal?

Pascal is a computer language, just like BASIC and FORTRAN are computer languages. It helps the programmer communicate with his machine faster and get his work done faster and better. The flavor of Pascal that comes with the Apple is UCSD Pascal Version II.1. In order to make Pascal easier to move from one CPU to another CPU, the operating system that this Pascal runs under makes use of something called a "P-code interpreter".

What is an interpreter?

The Apple's 6502 CPU can only execute binary 6502 machine code. It can't execute things written in other computer languages like Pascal or BASIC. It needs a translator for each language it wants to run. Sometimes the translating is done while the program is being run, in which case we call the translator an "interpreter." In order for the Apple to execute BASIC programs, a BASIC interpreter must be present somewhere in memory to translate the BASIC code into 6502 machine code so the Apple can understand it.

What is P-Code?

In Pascal, there are two translators used. The first translator, the "Pascal compiler," compacts the Pascal language into a special intermediate language called "P-code" (the P stands for "pseudo"). The P-code file is stored on disk until it's time to execute the program. When the program is executed, the P-code is loaded into memory and translated into binary 6502 machine code by the second translator, called the "P-code interpreter." This P-code interpreter is loaded into memory whenever you boot Pascal, but it is not stored permanently in the Apple — instead it is stored on diskette, so it can be easily modified and updated.

What is floating point?

"Floating point" refers to numbers with a decimal point. Numbers without decimals or fractions (like 1, 5, -13, or 25) are called "integers." Numbers such as 1.1, 1.414, -25.00 are called "real" numbers. "Floating point" numbers are real numbers. Operations involving floating point numbers are more complex and considerably slower than operations for integers.

INTRINSIC TESTED	NORMAL (msecs)	MILL (msecs)	MILL % CHANGE	MILL WITH FP UPDATE	MILL FP % CHANGE
Abs	0.60	0.80	-25.00	0.30	100.00
Addition	0.20	0.10	100.00	0.20	0.00
Atan (arc tangent)	110.50	113.40	-2.56	61.40	79.97
BlockRead	7.00	5.00	40.00	5.00	40.00
BlockWrite	129.00	170.00	-24.12	81.00	59.26
Concat	8.50	6.70	26.87	6.70	26.87
Copy	4.30	3.30	30.30	3.30	30.30
Cos (cosine)	36.90	40.00	-7.75	18.70	97.33
Division (integer)	1.10	0.90	22.22	0.90	22.22
Division (real)	6.10	6.90	-11.59	3.90	56.41
Exp	31.50	32.50	-3.08	17.10	84.21
FillChar	0.90	0.90	0.00	0.90	0.00
For loop	0.60	0.40	50.00	0.40	50.00
Function call	1.20	0.90	33.33	0.90	33.33
Get	6.00	4.00	50.00	4.00	50.00
Gotoxy	14.30	12.50	14.40	12.50	14.40
If..Then	0.10	0.10	0.00	0.10	0.00
Insert / Delete	5.70	4.10	39.02	4.10	39.02
Length	0.40	0.30	33.33	0.30	33.33
Ln (natural log)	33.30	34.70	-4.03	18.90	76.19
Log (common log)	37.10	38.30	-3.13	21.10	75.83
Mark / Release	0.40	0.30	33.33	0.30	33.33
MemAvail	0.50	0.80	-37.50	0.40	25.00
Mod	1.20	1.00	20.00	0.90	33.33
Multiplication	1.10	0.30	266.67	0.30	266.67
Page (clears screen)	170.00	170.00	0.00	170.00	0.00
Pass parameter	1.50	0.70	114.29	0.60	150.00
Pass var parameter	1.00	0.60	66.67	0.70	42.86
Pos	7.60	5.80	31.03	5.70	33.33
Procedure call	0.80	0.50	60.00	0.60	33.33
Put	10.00	8.00	25.00	8.00	25.00
PwrOfTen	0.40	0.70	-42.86	0.30	33.33
Repeat loop	0.60	0.40	50.00	0.40	50.00
Reset	411.00	345.00	19.13	345.00	19.13
Rewrite	1212.00	1204.00	0.66	1204.00	0.66
Round	0.80	1.10	-27.27	0.60	33.33
Scan	2.10	1.70	23.53	1.70	23.53
Seek	326.00	226.00	44.25	226.00	44.25
Segment call	199.00	199.00	0.00	201.00	-1.00
Sin (sine)	39.20	42.00	-6.67	21.10	85.78
SizeOf	0.10	0.10	0.00	0.10	0.00
Sqr	2.30	2.60	-11.54	1.00	130.00
Sqrt	6.30	6.80	-7.35	6.80	-7.35
Str	2.70	3.30	-18.18	3.30	-18.18
Subtraction	0.20	0.20	0.00	0.10	100.00
Trunc	0.80	1.10	-27.27	0.60	33.33
Write	28.00	25.00	12.00	22.00	27.27
Writeln	67.00	65.00	3.08	60.00	11.67

APPLE'S-EYE VIEW

BY
JIM HILGER

JUST TURNED ON HIS APPLE II.

JUST READ THE REFERENCE MANUAL.

JUST GOT A LONG PROGRAM TO LOAD FROM CASSETTE.

ACCIDENTALLY HIT RESET.

STAYED UP ALL NIGHT PLAYING STAR TREK

CAN'T GET A LONG PROGRAM TO LOAD FROM ANYWHERE.

GOT A PROGRAM TO RUN ON THE THIRD ATTEMPT.

GOT A PROGRAM TO RUN ON THE SECOND ATTEMPT.

GOT A PROGRAM TO RUN ON THE FIRST ATTEMPT.

TRIED TO INSTALL HOME-BREW HARDWARE.

NEWLY PURCHASED $100 SOFTWARE PACKAGE PRINTED ONE LINE AND HUNG.

FRIEND'S TWO-YEAR-OLD CHILD SPILLS ROOT BEER ON FLOPPY DISKETTES.

Inverse, Flash and Lowercase Display

David Lieberman

IN the March–April 1981 issue of *Call –A.P.P.L.E.*, Ron DeGroat offered a nifty patch for SYSTEM.APPLE which enabled Pascal to display lower case characters using the Paymar Lower Case Adapter. I spoke with him about this patch, and told him my only objection was the permanency of the modification to SYSTEM.APPLE. In fact, recognizing this drawback, he mentions in his article that the user might consider dedicating a diskette for his/her lower case application.

After speaking with Ron, I came up with the equivalent machine language patch that modifies the *SYSTEM.APPLE* code that resides in the RAM card. No modification to the disk is necessary. The patch can be removed simply by doing a cold start.

If you want the patch inserted each time you boot your system, a call to the Lca procedure can be included in your System Startup file. Figure 1 illustrates an example Pascal program which calls the subroutine that writes the patch into BIOS. Figure 2 illustrates the machine language routine which performs the modifications. Note: the "pseudo-upper case" feature of Pascal is inhibited. You cannot display upper-case characters in inverse using the Ctrl-R command while the Paymar patch is in place.

If you wish to display inverse or flashing characters, however, figure 2 also includes three procedures for doing this. To display text in inverse for example, one might use the following sequence:

```
Gotoxy(0,4);
Inverse;
Write ("THIS MESSAGE IS IN
INVERSE");
Normal;
```

The only restriction you must observe is that lower case characters cannot be displayed in inverse or flashing modes. Attempts to display lower case characters in inverse or flashing produces nonsense characters.

The Program LcaPatch demonstrates how Lca may be used to obtain true lowercase display with a lowercase adapter. The user should be warned that this fix is only good for Pascal 1.1 and that other patches and modifications to the *BIOS* (Basic Input/Output System) could result in conflicts.

If the properly compiled and linked code for LcaPatch is renamed *SYSTEM.STARTUP*, the Lca patch will be invoked everytime the system is booted. Since no permanent changes are made, this patch is relatively safe. To disable lowercase display, change the name of *SYSTEM.STARTUP* to something else and re-boot.

Fig. 1

```
Program LcaPatch;

Procedure Lca;  External;

(* Lca must be linked in to LcaPatch *)

Begin
  Lca;
  Gotoxy(8,8);
  Write('Pascal 1.1 with lowercase display');
End.
```

Fig. 2

```
        .PROC    INVERSE          ;NO PARAMETERS

;PROCEDURE INVERSE;
;------------------
;
;THE NEXT THREE SUBROUTINES PROVIDE PASCAL
;WITH THE ABILITY TO DISPLAY INVERSE,
;NORMAL, OR FLASHING CHARACTERS IN THE
;NORMAL APPLE TEXT WINDOW.  INVERSE DISPLAYS
;CHARACTERS IN BLACK ON WHITE VIDEO.
;
        LDA      0C083            ;SELECT 2ND 4K BANK
        LDA      0C083            ;WRITE ENABLE
        LDA      #00
        STA      0DAB0            ;CLEAR BITS 6 & 7
        LDA      0C088            ;SELECT 1ST BANK & WRITE PROTECT
        RTS
;
;
        .PROC    NORMAL           ;NO PARAMETERS
```

```
;PROCEDURE NORMAL;
;-----------------
;
;NORMAL DISPLAYS CHARACTERS IN WHITE ON BLACK
;VIDEO
;

        LDA      0C083
        LDA      0C083
        LDA      #80
        STA      0DAB0         ;SET BIT 7
        LDA      0C088
        RTS
;
;
        .PROC    FLASH         ;NO PARAMETERS
;
;PROCEDURE FLASH;
;----------------
;
;FLASH DISPLAYS CHARACTERS BLINKING
;BETWEEN INVERSE AND NORMAL MODES.
;
         LDA     0C083
         LDA     0C083
         LDA     #40
         STA     0DAB0         ;SET BIT 6
         LDA     0C088
         RTS

        .PROC LCA

;THIS PROCEDURE MODIFIES PASCAL 1.1 BIOS IN
;MEMORY SO THAT LOWERCASE CHARACTERS CAN BE
;DISPLAYED WITH A LOWERCASE ADAPTER.  THIS
;FIX WILL ONLY WORK FOR PASCAL 1.1.

;WRITTEN BY DAVE LIEBERMAN 12-JUN-81

ADDR1   .EQU 0DAAB
RAMON   .EQU 0C083
RAMCLR  .EQU 0C088

        LDA RAMON       ;SELECT 2ND 4K BANK
        LDA RAMON       ;WRITE-ENABLE

        LDA #176.       ;SUPPRESS UC CONVERSION
        STA ADDR1
        LDA #02.
        STA ADDR1+1
        LDA #0          ;DISABLE PSEUDO UC
        STA ADDR1+239.

        LDA RAMCLR      ;SELECT 1ST BANK
        RTS

        .END
```

FROM THE VERY CORE OF APPLE

A Pascal Character Editor

Dean Rosenhain

In Apple Pascal, there are two commands specifically designed to place text on the hi-res screen — WCHAR and WSTRING. The character set used by these commands is stored in a disk data file called SYSTEM.CHARSET. Exact specifications for this 1024 byte file are found on pages 99 and 100 of the APPLE PASCAL LANGUAGE REFERENCE MANUAL. Each character image is stored as eight consecutive bytes in an array of 128 images. The Pascal declaration necessary to create new character sets or edit existing ones, is shown below:

Another way to send characters to the hi-res screen is with DRAWBLOCK, a Turtlegraphics routine thatcopies a bit array from memory onto the screen to form a screen image. Actually WCHAR and WSTRING use DRAWBLOCK. (For more information on bit map display, read Loy Spurlock's article in 'APPLESAUCE', Vol. 1 no. 7 (Oct. 1979) which was reprinted in Call-APPLE, Jan. 1980.)

To show how DRAWBLOCK can be used to display characters, suppose SYSTEM.CHARSET has been retrieved from disk and placed in an array called CHARACTERS (with a declaration like that given above).

```
TYPE
     BITS = 0.7;
     BYTE = SET OF BITS;
     CHARIMAGE = PACKED ARRAY[0..7] OF BYTE;
     CHARSET = PACKED ARRAY[0..127] OF CHARIMAGE;
VAR  CHARACTERS:CHARSET;
     CHARFILE :FILE OF CHARSET
```

```
PROGRAM CHARED;
(**************************************)
(*                                    *)
(*         HI-RES CHARACTER           *)
(*              EDITOR                *)
(*           VERSION 2.2.1            *)
(*                                    *)
(*      BY... Dean  Rosenhain         *)
(*                                    *)
(**************************************)

USES TURTLEGRAPHICS;

TYPE BITS = 0..7;
     BYTE = SET OF BITS;
     CHARIMAGE= PACKED ARRAY[0..7] OF BYTE;
     CHARSET= PACKED ARRAY[0..127] OF CHARIMAGE;

VAR  CURRENTSET:CHARSET;
     CURRENTCH :CHARIMAGE;
     CHARFILE  :FILE OF CHARSET;
     DISKIO,I,OLD,H,V,OLDH,OLDV:INTEGER;
     CHOICE:CHAR;
     ONE:BOOLEAN;

PROCEDURE PRINTAT(X,Y:INTEGER; S:STRING);
BEGIN
  MOVETO(X,Y);
  WSTRING(S);
END;

PROCEDURE INPUT(X,Y:INTEGER;VAR S:STRING);

(* This procedure allows input of        *)
(* strings on the graphics screen. The   *)
(* ability to backspace over mistakes    *)
(* is supported.                         *)


VAR TEMP  :STRING;
    S1    :STRING[1];
    CH    :CHAR;
BEGIN
   TEMP:='';
   S1:=' ';
   MOVETO(X,Y);
   REPEAT
      READ(KEYBOARD,CH);
      IF CH IN ['!'..'Z'] THEN
      BEGIN
        WCHAR(CH);
        S1[1]:=CH;
        TEMP:=CONCAT(TEMP,S1);
      END
      ELSE
        IF (ORD(CH)=8) AND (LENGTH(TEMP)>0) THEN
        BEGIN
          DELETE(TEMP,LENGTH(TEMP),1);
          MOVETO(TURTLEX-7,Y);
          WCHAR(' ');
          MOVETO(TURTLEX-7,Y);
        END;
```

```
    UNTIL CH=CHR(32);
    S:=TEMP;
 END;

PROCEDURE SHOWCHAR(NUM:INTEGER);
VAR X,Y:INTEGER;
BEGIN
   X:=10*(NUM MOD 16)+5;
   Y:=150-(NUM DIV 16)*10;
   DRAWBLOCK(CURRENTSET[NUM],1,0,0,7,8,X,Y,10);
END;

PROCEDURE DISPLAYSET;
VAR NUM:INTEGER;
BEGIN
    FOR NUM:= 0 TO 127 DO
      SHOWCHAR(NUM);
END;

PROCEDURE DISKERROR(ERR:INTEGER);
VAR S:STRING;
 TIME:INTEGER;
BEGIN
   CHARTYPE(5); (* INVERSE MODE *)
   IF ERR IN [6,7,10] THEN
    PRINTAT(10,2,'bad filename, not available.')
   ELSE
     BEGIN
       STR(ERR,S);
       S:=CONCAT('disk error # ',S);
       PRINTAT(10,2,S);
     END;

   WRITELN(CHR(7));
   FOR TIME:= 1 TO 3000 DO (* nothing *);
   CHARTYPE(10);   (* Normal mode *)
   WRITELN(CHR(7));
   PRINTAT(10,2,'                                    ');
END;

PROCEDURE FILEIN;
VAR FILENAME:STRING;
BEGIN
     INPUT(101,27,FILENAME);
     PRINTAT(101,27,'                     ');
     IF LENGTH(FILENAME)=0 THEN EXIT(FILEIN);
     IF FILENAME='*' THEN FILENAME:='SYSTEM.CHARSET';
(*$I-*)
     RESET(CHARFILE,FILENAME);
     DISKIO:=IORESULT;
     IF DISKIO<>0 THEN DISKERROR(DISKIO)
     ELSE
     BEGIN
       CURRENTSET:= CHARFILE^;
       CLOSE(CHARFILE,LOCK);
       DISPLAYSET;
       PRINTAT(90,160,'                    ');
       PRINTAT(90,160,FILENAME);
     END;
(*$I+*)
END;

PROCEDURE FILEOUT;
VAR FILENAME:STRING;
BEGIN
  INPUT(101,12,FILENAME);
  PRINTAT(101,12,'                     ');
  IF LENGTH(FILENAME)<1 THEN EXIT(FILEOUT);
  IF FILENAME='*' THEN FILENAME:='SYSTEM.CHARSET';
(*$I-*)
  REWRITE(CHARFILE,FILENAME);
  DISKIO:=IORESULT;
  IF DISKIO=0 THEN
```

To put the character 'A' in the middle of the graphics screen would require:

DRAWBLOCK(CHARACTERS [65],1,0,0,7,8,140,90,10)

Where the source of the image is 'CHARACTERS[65]' with 65 being the ASCII code for 'A'. As can be seen from the declarations above, CHARACTERS[65] is one 8-byte CHARIMAGE. The other parameters define the following:

- '1' = THE NUMBER OF BYTES USED BY EACH ROW OF DOTS IN THE IMAGE.
- '0' = THE NUMBER OF DOTS, OR BITS, TO BE SKIPPED IN THE ROW BEFORE COPYING.
- '0' = THE NUMBER OF VERTICAL DOTS TO BE SKIPPED.
- '7' = THE WIDTH OF THE IMAGE, IN DOTS.
- '8' = THE HEIGHT OF THE IMAGE, IN DOTS.
- '140' = THE 'X'-COORDINATE FOR THE BOTTOM-LEFT CORNER OF THE IMAGE.
- '90' = THE 'Y'-COORDINATE FOR THE BOTTOM-LEFT CORNER.
- '10' = THE 'MODE' OF DISPLAY.

The mode parameter is a powerful option that specifies the way an image is drawn on the screen (for more details, see manual). Sixteen different modes allow such things as inverse display (mode=5). If a mode of 6 (Exclusive-Or) is used to draw a string on graphics and then redraw it at the same location, the string will be erased, but the original underlying image will be restored. A mode of 10 is the standard default — 'copy bytes directly to the screen'.

If it wasn't for the DRAWBLOCK procedure, it would be difficult (and slow) to display character sets unless they were the SYSTEM.CHARSET. The DRAWBLOCK procedure allows a program to use several character sets at once. Without too much difficulty, one could construct larger characters and adjust the parameters of DRAWBLOCK to display them. Of course, to remain interchangable with SYSTEM.CHARSET, the character sets must conform with the declarations given above.

The character set editor presented here is designed for simple use. Although the listing is moderately self-documenting, it is worthwhile to mention some of the characteristics of the program and its operation. When the program starts, procedure SETUP displays the current character set (which should, initially, be random dots). Procedure MENU1 then displays some of the commands available. The other command menu (procedure MENU2) is made visible by typing a space. Procedure INPUT echoes the keyboard to the TURTLEGRAPHICS screen. A filename of '*' may be used in place of 'SYSTEM.CHARSET'. Procedure FILEIN does the transfer and captures all disk errors. Procedure FILEOUT is the companion procedure for saving sets to disk.

The character to be edited is chosen by moving a square 'cursor' (procedure HILITE) with the keys 'W,A,S,Z'. Grab shows the character on the right of the screen in an expanded format. The keys 'I,J,K,M' are used to move the plotting crosshairs. 'Y' plots and 'N' clears the current point. Push puts the altered character back into the character set at the location of the HILITE cursor.

After you create and save your custom character set to disk, you may want to change its name to SYSTEM.CHARSET so that it will be used by the TURTLEGRAPHICS routines, WCHAR and WSTRING. To do this, enter the Filer and Change the name of the SYSTEM.CHARSET to something else. For example:

Change?APPLE1:
SYSTEM.CHARSET
To?APPLE1:
OLD.CHARSET

Then rename your new characterset 'SYSTEM.CHARSET' so that it will be recognized by the system. For example:

Transfer?MYDISK:MYSET
To?APPLE1:SYSTEM.-
CHARSET

Or if the new set is already on the destination disk:

Change?:MYSET
To?SYSTEM.CHARSET

From then on, your own character set will be loaded and used by the TURTLEGRAPHICS routines.

```
    BEGIN
      CHARFILE^:=CURRENTSET;
      PUT(CHARFILE);
      CLOSE(CHARFILE,LOCK);
      PRINTAT(90,160,'                    ');
      PRINTAT(90,160,FILENAME);
    END
  ELSE DISKERROR(DISKIO);
(*$I+*)
END;

PROCEDURE HILITE(LETTER:INTEGER; COLOR:SCREENCOLOR);
VAR I:INTEGER;
BEGIN
  PENCOLOR(NONE);
  MOVETO(10*(LETTER MOD 16)+3,149-(LETTER DIV 16)*10);
  PENCOLOR(COLOR);
  TURNTO(0);
  FOR I:=1 TO 4 DO
  BEGIN
    MOVE(10); (*draw a square *)
    TURN(90);
  END;
  PENCOLOR(NONE);
END;

PROCEDURE CROSSHAIR(X,Y:INTEGER);
BEGIN
  PENCOLOR(NONE);
  MOVETO(201+X*10,83+Y*10);
  TURNTO(0);
  PENCOLOR(REVERSE);
  MOVE(4);
  PENCOLOR(NONE);
  MOVETO(203+X*10,81+Y*10);
  TURNTO(90);
  PENCOLOR(REVERSE);
  MOVE(4);
  PENCOLOR(NONE);
END;

PROCEDURE EXPAND(CH:CHARIMAGE);
VAR ROW,DOT:0..7;
BEGIN
  FOR ROW:= 0 TO 7 DO
    FOR DOT:= 0 TO 6 DO
     BEGIN
       MOVETO(200+DOT*10,80+ROW*10);
       IF DOT IN CH[ROW] THEN WCHAR(CHR(1))
        ELSE WCHAR(' ');
     END;
END;  (* EXPAND *)

PROCEDURE CLEARFIELD;
VAR ROW:0..7;
BEGIN
  FOR ROW:=0 TO 7 DO
    CURRENTCH[ROW]:=[];
  EXPAND(CURRENTCH);
END;
```

```
PROCEDURE SETUP;
VAR J:INTEGER;
BEGIN
    INITTURTLE;

    PRINTAT(0,180,'Pascal SYSTEM.CHARSET Editor version 2');
    PRINTAT(155,170,'by D. Rosenhain');
    PRINTAT(0,160,'Current Set:'); (* NONE *)

    DISPLAYSET;

    OLD:=0; I:=0;
    HILITE(I,WHITE);

    MOVETO(199,79); (* DRAW SQUARE *)
    PENCOLOR(WHITE);
    MOVETO(268,79);
    MOVETO(268,159);
    MOVETO(199,159);
    MOVETO(199,79);
    PENCOLOR(NONE);

    FOR J:= 1 TO 7 DO (* DRAW GRID *)
    BEGIN
        MOVETO(199,79+J*10);
        PENCOLOR(WHITE);
        MOVETO(268,79+J*10);
        PENCOLOR(NONE);
    END;

    FOR J:= 1 TO 6 DO
    BEGIN
        MOVETO(199+J*10,79);
        PENCOLOR(WHITE);
        MOVETO(199+J*10,159);
        PENCOLOR(NONE);
    END;

    CLEARFIELD;

    H:=0; V:=0;
    CROSSHAIR(H,V);
    OLDH:=H; OLDV:=V;
    ONE:=TRUE;

    CHARTYPE(5);
    PRINTAT(0,60,'Commands:');
    CHARTYPE(10);
    PRINTAT(90,60,'(space) for more....');
END;
```

```
PROCEDURE MENU1;
BEGIN
    VIEWPORT(0,279,0,59);
    FILLSCREEN(BLACK);

    CHARTYPE(5);
    PRINTAT(0,44,'select char:');

    CHARTYPE(10);
    PRINTAT(0,30,'W: up');
    PRINTAT(0,20,'Z: down');
    PRINTAT(0,10,'A: left');
    PRINTAT(0, 0,'S: right');

    CHARTYPE(5);
    PRINTAT(100,44,'To edit:');

    CHARTYPE(10);
    PRINTAT(100,30,'I: up');
    PRINTAT(100,20,'M: down');
    PRINTAT(100,10,'J: left');
    PRINTAT(100, 0,'K: right');
    PRINTAT(175,40,'Y: plot');
    PRINTAT(175,30,'N: no plot');
    PRINTAT(175,20,'C: clear');
    PRINTAT(175,10,'G: grab');
    PRINTAT(175, 0,'P: push');
    VIEWPORT(0,279,0,191);
END;

PROCEDURE MENU2;
BEGIN
    VIEWPORT(0,279,0,59);
    FILLSCREEN(BLACK);
    MOVETO(0,40);
    PRINTAT(0,40,'Q:exit  T:save set  R:load set');
    PRINTAT(10,24,'File to load:....................');
    PRINTAT(10,9,'File to save:....................');
    VIEWPORT(0,279,0,191);
END;

BEGIN  (* MAIN PROGRAM *)
    SETUP;
    MENU1;
    REPEAT
       READ(KEYBOARD,CHOICE);
       CASE CHOICE OF
       ' ':BEGIN
             IF ONE THEN MENU2
                    ELSE MENU1;
             ONE:= NOT ONE;
           END;
```

```
          'A':I:= (I+128-1) MOD 128;

          'S':I:= (I+1) MOD 128;

          'Z':I:= (I+16) MOD 128;

          'W':I:= (I+128-16) MOD 128;

          'G':BEGIN
                CURRENTCH:=CURRENTSET[I];
                EXPAND(CURRENTCH);
                CROSSHAIR(H,V);
              END;

          'C':BEGIN
                CLEARFIELD;
                CROSSHAIR(H,V);
              END;

          'P':BEGIN
                CURRENTSET[I]:=CURRENTCH;
                SHOWCHAR(I);
              END;

          'R':BEGIN
                IF ONE THEN MENU2;
                FILEIN;
                ONE:=FALSE;
              END;

          'T':BEGIN
                IF ONE THEN MENU2;
                FILEOUT;
                ONE:=FALSE;
              END;

          'Y':BEGIN
                CURRENTCH[V]:=CURRENTCH[V]+[H];
                MOVETO(200+H*10,80+V*10);
                WCHAR(CHR(1));
                CROSSHAIR(H,V);
              END;

          'N':BEGIN
                CURRENTCH[V]:=CURRENTCH[V]-[H];
                MOVETO(200+H*10,80+V*10);
                WCHAR(' ');
                CROSSHAIR(H,V);
              END;

          'I':V:=(V+1) MOD 8;

          'M':V:=(V+8-1) MOD 8;

          'J':H:=(H+7-1) MOD 7;

          'K':H:=(H+1) MOD 7;

        END(* CASE *);

        IF CHOICE IN ['I','J','K','M'] THEN
        BEGIN
          CROSSHAIR(OLDH,OLDV);
          CROSSHAIR(H,V);
          OLDH:=H; OLDV:=V;
        END;

        IF CHOICE IN ['W','A','S','Z'] THEN
        BEGIN
          HILITE(OLD,BLACK);
          HILITE(I,WHITE);
          OLD:=I;
        END;

     UNTIL CHOICE='Q';
  END.
```

Artillery

David Miller

LONG, long ago, when the computer first came into being, it was occasionally put to work for less than peaceful purposes. Its human overlords used it to calculate trajectories for projectiles (commonly known as "shells") that were belched forth by large, noisy cylinders (guns). To the misfortune of the targets (buildings, tanks, etc.), yesterday's computers performed the tedious calculations quickly and accurately. Today's computers, while they aren't playing Space Invaders, provide even more advanced missile and ballistics control.

Of course, all of this can be scaled down slightly from the real world to that of the home computer. What was once a war game can be transformed into a computer game; suddenly, the effects are somewhat less lethal, and damage is inflicted only on the loser's pride. The game I am referring to is one that flourishes on the screens of small computers under names such as BALLISTICS, SHOOT, PIE LOB, etc. Two opponents alternately shoot over some sort of obstacle to blow each other up by specifying the power and angle of elevation of their shots. Difficulties include changing position, terrain, and wind, not to mention the fiend on the other side of the mountain! After seeing several fascinating battles being waged, I decided to write my own version of the game. It proved to be a difficult, but enjoyable, task. Eventually, the program was to go through several stages of development, each presenting a new set of challenges.

My first ARTILLERY game was born about 3 years ago, and I wrote it in DEC BASIC-PLUS on a DEC PDP 11/70 system. Because none of the terminals had graphics capability, I was forced to use the text screen as a pseudo-graphical display. To make life easier, I sketched a wall for an obstacle using a column of "I"s and drew a ground line of "=" signs along the bottom of the screen. Each player was represented by a "+" sign along the ground, and the block cursor was moved with direct cursor addressing to simulate the travelling projectile. As a game, it was exciting to play, and was extremely popular among the computer games contingent. Just goes to show that a game doesn't have to use graphics to be a success.

Version 2 came along a few months later, when I translated the original program into APPLESOFT and added hi-resolution graphics. I left the basic arrangements the same, drawing the ground and wall in color and using shape tables to create a pair of tanks representing the players. However, I soon decided to start a major rewrite and draw some hilly terrain to add spice to the game. At the same time, it would be possible to translate the game into Pascal (which I would soon be updating my system to) and make use of the more advanced TURTLEGRAPHICS. Pascal would let me structure the program much more efficiently, would run faster and would produce a more readable result, thanks to the use of long variable names. It soon proved possible to add even more exciting effects, such as colorful explosions and sound, and the result was to become a definitive Pascal version of the game.

So, version 3 was born, my first programming effort in Pascal. I worked out an algorithm to produce hills of various sizes and shapes on the screen, and then experimented with the different random factors used to create scenarios for each round. The result is a much more enjoyable game to play, although the first two versions were extremely popular both at home and at school. I'm sure it will be hard for the addicts to resist the challenge of the new enhancements! In this article, I'd like to describe the game of ARTILLERY, the fine points of strategy for its play, and some possible changes the reader might like to make. First, however, let's see how to go about setting up a game like ARTILLERY and how to transform it into a functioning program.

Planning Artillery from the Ground up

Basically, what will be required is a little knowledge of physics and the equations of motion. We'll be simulating the trajectory of a moving body, given a set of initial conditions. The X and Y positions of the players will be randomly set each round, along with the wind and its direction. That leaves two factors for each of the players to input, velocity and angle. The basic equations needed to describe the motion of the projectile are as follows:

(1) Y = Y0 + V0*T + G*T∧2/2

and

(2) X = X0 + V0*T + A*T∧2/2

Where Y0 and X0 are the initial player positions. The V0's in the two equations are different, specifying the initial velocity of the shot in the Y and X directions, respectively. The single input velocity is converted into the two values by using the angle that was given (which must be converted from degrees to radians before it can be used with Pascal's transcendental functions). The X velocity is the original velocity multiplied by the COSINE of the angle, and the Y velocity is the original velocity multiplied by the SINE of the angle. Thus, the angle is used to break a single problem down into 2 separate problems, which when combined will yield a trajectory.

"T" stands for time, which will be started at 0 and ticked off in arbitrary increments. Small time increments will produce trajectory points that are very close together, increasing the accuracy of the game and at the same time slowing the apparent motion of the projectile. You might want to change this increment in the program to speed things up. "G" is the acceleration of gravity, approximately 32.2 ft/sec$\pm$2, that causes a rising body to slow down and a falling body to pick up speed (remember Newton and his Apple? Pun intended!). It is needed to describe the vertical motion of the projectile, since any object will have a downwards acceleration of G whenever it is freely rising or falling. "A" in the second equation stands for horizontal acceleration, but the term can be dropped out since there is no acceleration in the X direction for a trajectory problem. The X equation must be modified slightly to take the wind into account; the wind factor is considered as an additional horizontal velocity to be either added to or subtracted from the horizontal velocity of the projectile.

Now that we can describe the motion of the shot (using FUNCTIONs in the Pascal program), we'll need to draw a majestic hill on the screen. Anyone familiar with trigonometry will recall the shape of a sine wave. If you're not mathematically inclined, imagine two hills, side by side, with their bases touching. Then, rotate the hill on the right about its base until it is upside down, sort of a mirror image, and you'll have an idea of what a sine wave looks like. Here, we can use the portion of the sine wave that lies above the x axis (the normal hill on the left) as an "outline" for our computer mountain. To change the height, we simply multiply the function by a number, in effect increasing its amplitude. An algorithm to produce the hill is implemented in the DRAWSCREEN procedure of ARTILLERY. The ground on either side of the hill can be filled in by extending the plot to the edge of the screen while we're drawing.

Once the terrain is drawn, it's time to put the players on the screen. As I was writing the Pascal program, I wondered what to use in place of the original tanks, as Pascal lacks BASIC's shape table capability. *Suddenly, inspiration hit — instead of drawing little tanks, why not use the apple provided in the TURTLEGRAPHICS character set? Adding a slightly deranged twist to a game is usually a good idea. The thought of a pair of apples belching shots at each other over a mountain is more than hilarious and proved to be an excellent innovation. Also, it became a simple matter to make the apple explode when hit, as flashing it back and forth between the inverse and normal character modes produced a dramatic effect.

So, we've drawn the terrain (using randomly generated numbers to specify hill height, position, width, etc.) and dropped our two apples onto the ground, one on each side of the hill, again using random numbers to specify the X position of each on the screen. The SCREENBIT function will be used to see whether or not an apple has hit the ground, and we can then set the initial Y position accordingly. How do we input the values for velocity and angle? The easiest way is to remove part of the graphics screen and use the bottom of the normal text display; in other words, we want to use page 1 of hi-resolution graphics as it is normally implemented in BASIC. Unfortunately, Pascal doesn't provide the programmer with mixed graphics and text. The answer is to make use of a POKE procedure to POKE the text window open, the same way it can normally be done from BASIC. Once we have the four lines of text available at the bottom of the screen, we can use the usual WRITE and READLN statements to prompt for and receive input. But wait a minute, there's one more problem!

When Pascal uses READLN to input a real variable, it won't let you use the left arrow to backspace over it and make corrections before hitting RETURN. To avoid confusion, the best thing to do is to input the entire line as a string, separate it into two sub-strings by noting the position of the comma, and *then* convert each sub-string to a real variable. In BASIC, this could easily be accomplished using the VAL function. Pascal, however, doesn't have one, so I decided to make use of a nifty little VAL function, written for Pascal, that appeared in the May 1981 issue of CALL -A.P.P.L.E. By inserting it near the top of the program, we can provide very convenient input for the numbers.

**EDITOR'S NOTE — Actually, bit arrays are Pascal's equivalent to BASIC's shape tables. For an example see "A PASCAL CHARACTER EDITOR" elsewhere in this issue.*

After all the data is in, the final step is to animate the moving shot, the task of procedure PLOTTRAJECTORY. The initial conditions are set, and functions XPOSITION and YPOSITION calculate the position of the shell for each tick of the clock. First we check to make sure the shot will be between the left and right edges of the screen. Next, we use the SCREENBIT function to find out if it will hit something. If not, we draw and erase a tiny box at the coordinate of the shot and click the speaker.

Note the use of the color REVERSE to keep the plot from affecting the stats at the top of the screen. This process continues until the shot either goes off the side of the screen or hits something, in which case we check the last position of the projectile to see if an apple has been hit. Action can be taken accordingly, such as exploding the loser's apple and cratering the ground on impact.

Finally, we have the basic shell of a functioning ARTILLERY program. Each procedure was written separately and tested to decrease the time spent waiting for everything to compile. Once all were working properly, they were pasted together from the Pascal editor and controlled by the main program. Afterwards, additional procedures for a countdown, title page, instructions, etc. were separately tested and merged in. Of course, many glitches in syntax and logic appeared during the programming, but a little persistence took care of them. Finally, after all the desired effects were added, and the game had been tested and fine tuned, it was ready to take on the world. So, without further delay, let's get on to the game!

How to Type in Artillery

Very simply, go into the Pascal editor and start typing! The comments can be left out if you'd like to save some time, but they may prove invaluable later on. The left and right curly brackets can be replaced wherever they appear by "(*" and "*)", respectively, if you don't have Pascal 1.1 and lack the ability to use lower case from the editor. In general, any lower case that appears in the listing (instructions, program strings, etc.) may be typed in as upper case. Also, you'll note my frequent use of the underscore in long variable names.

This serves to make them more readable, and was done using the techniques described in "Moving the Heap to get Special Characters" from the June 1981 issue of *Call -A.P.P.L.E.* Because the underscore is ignored by the Pascal compiler, and is not normally available on the Apple's keyboard, it may be removed from variables with no ill effects.

The listing, as given, is about 14K long, and approaches the memory limits of the editor (which is why it isn't more extensively commented). Note that the swapping option of the compiler is turned on at the top of the listing due to the size of the program. Failure to include the top line of "{$S+" will result in a compile time error. Finally, observe that the units TURTLEGRAPHICS, APPLE-STUFF, and TRANSCEND are all used by ARTILLERY. The files SYSTEM.LIBRARY and SYSTEM. CHARSET (for printing text on the graphics screen) must be on-line during compilation! The easiest way to proceed is to type ARTILLERY in as the work file on APPLE1:. Once it's complete, update the workfile, leave the editor, and compile, with APPLE1: in drive 1 and APPLE2: in drive 2. When everything runs correctly, enter the filer and S)ave the workfile and codefile onto another disk under a different name.

Playing the Game

Artillery starts off with a colorful title page and a query for instructions. A response of "Y" will produce two pages of helpful notes on the text screen. Next, each player will be asked to type in his or her name (if you use lower case, it will be printed during play by the TURTLE-GRAPHICS character set). Anything beyond the first 10 characters will be cut off, since the names must fit properly in the top portion of the graphic display. Once the names are in, you are given the option of playing with or without wind. Perhaps it would be easier for rookies to play the first few games without wind in order to get a feel for the proper velocities and angles to use. But it soon becomes possible to score on the first or second shot most of the time, and you'll find that the wind adds an element of extreme challenge and unpredictability.

Now the fun begins. The text screen disappears, to be replaced by the graphics screen where some sort of green mountain is being created from the ground up. Then a little apple will quietly float to the ground on the left of the hill, crunching slightly with the impact, to be followed by its opponent on the other side. Finally, the names of the players, and their respective scores, will appear in the top corners of the screen, with the wind and its direction displayed in the top center. Underneath the mountain, the prompt "V,A " will appear on the side of the player who is to shoot, asking for the velocity and angle of the shot. Let's see how a typical game might be played...

— A Scenario —

The first player eyes his opponent and notes that, for this round, there is no wind at all. He realizes the importance of the first shot; due to the present calm, and the fact that both happen to be on the same ground level, the same pair of inputs that will destroy his foe will also destroy him! With but a moment's calculation, he fires — "5.8,56" — and holds his breath as a ticking white dot emerges from his stem and arcs towards the silently waiting apple across the screen. Alas! A groan escapes as his shell falls just a hair short, the explosion cratering the ground immediately in front of his rival. With a chortle of glee, the enemy increases the power slightly, returns the shot — "5.9,56" — and watches triumphantly as the hurtling projectile falls inevitably towards our hero's apple. The explosion is magnificent as the unhappy fruit flashes in agony, emitting a series of dying wails. The top of the screen clears, and a brief, musical countdown flashes as both attempt to regain their composure for the next round...

Their anticipation is rewarded as a gigantic mountain blossoms in the middle of the screen. It appears that conditions have worsened; a gale force wind of 37 is blowing from right to left. Our hero, on the left side of the screen, once again has the first shot, as his unlucky apple had just been destroyed (whoever gets hit goes first). With the wind whipping in his face, he uses more power and a lower angle to compensate, and fires — "8.4,43." The shot skims over the mountain and craters the ground just beyond his opponent. The enemy, in turn, raises his angle almost to the vertical, relying on the wind to carry his shot, and uses just enough power to clear the top of the mountain. "7,89" — and both wait expectantly as the dot disappears merrily off the top of the screen, ticking all the while. At last it emerges, but carries too far and disappears off the left side of the screen. Our hero, for once in a commanding position, reduces his velocity slightly and destroys his foe.

And so it goes, round after round, until both give up in exhaustion. The enemy types "5,-9" and the graphics screen disappears, to be replaced by the final score and a sign heralding the victor. Although they could start another game, it's time to give the apple a little rest, and they retire in the assurance that they will return again to fight another day.

Some Closing Comments and Suggestions

I'd like to encourage the readers to make further improvements and add some more bizarre twists to ARTILLERY. Why not experiment with different constants for gravity, and fight on the moon or perhaps another planet? Modify the program so that a shooter can blow himself up (won't happen with the present version). Experiment with different ranges for random numbers in procedure SETUP to personalize the game. Or try writing an external procedure in assembly language for better sound effects and explosions. The INCLUDE option of the compiler can be used to break the program into smaller pieces if it grows too large for the editor to handle. In any case, I'd welcome any intelligent suggestions and comments from those concerned.

Lastly, I'd like to mention a problem I encountered with the SCREENBIT function. When I first started dropping apples from the sky, they would occasionally continue right on through the ground, presumably ending up somewhere in China. There was no apparent reason for this, and it took me several hours to solve the problem. It seems that, due to the way the hi-resolution screen works, SCREENBIT occasionally won't detect a COLOR if only a single horizontal point is specified. Once I checked the point *and* the point next to it, everything worked fine, and the apples planted themselves perfectly every time. This probably wouldn't have happened if the ground was white rather than green.

But a snowball fight between two apples just would have been too much to swallow...

```
{$S+}

PROGRAM ARTILLERY;

{$C Copyright 1981 by David Miller }
{$C 79 Hawley Ave, Port Chester,   }
{$C N.Y. 10573  (914)-939-8955     }

USES TURTLEGRAPHICS, APPLESTUFF, TRANSCEND;


CONST
        GRAVITY      = 32.2 ;
        PI           = 3.14159;
        BOTTOM       = 32;
        WINDOW       = -16301;
TYPE
        BYTE = 0..255;
        PAB  = PACKED ARRAY[0..1] OF BYTE;
        MULTITYPE = RECORD
                 CASE INTEGER OF
                    1 : (INT:INTEGER);
                    2 : (PTR:^PAB);
                    3 : (DPTR:^INTEGER)
                 END;
        LEVEL_OF_PLAY = (EASY,HARD);
VAR
        CH                : CHAR;
        LEFT_PLAYER,
        RIGHT_PLAYER      : STRING[10];
        WIND_DIRECTION    : STRING[12];
        HIT,LEFT_SHOT,
        RIGHT_SHOT,
        CONTACT           : BOOLEAN;
        DIFFICULTY        : LEVEL_OF_PLAY;
        WIND,
        LEFT_SCORE,
        RIGHT_SCORE,
        HILL_POSITION,
        HILL_HEIGHT,
        HILL_WIDTH,
        HILL_LEFT,
        HILL_RIGHT,
        LEFTEL,
        RIGHTEL,
        LEFT_POSITION,
        RIGHT_POSITION    : INTEGER;
        SINE, COSINE,
        VELOCITY,
        WIND_FACTOR,
        ANGLE             : REAL;


PROCEDURE POKE(ADDR:INTEGER;VALUE:BYTE);
VAR LOCAL:MULTITYPE;
BEGIN
  LOCAL.INT := ADDR;
  LOCAL.PTR^[0] := VALUE
END; { POKE }


FUNCTION RAND(LOW, HIGH:INTEGER):INTEGER;
VAR MX, Z, D:INTEGER;
BEGIN
  Z    := HIGH - LOW+1;
  MX   := (MAXINT-HIGH+LOW) DIV Z+1;
  MX   := MX*(HIGH-LOW)+(MX-1);
  REPEAT
    D    := RANDOM
  UNTIL D <= MX;
  RAND   := LOW+D MOD Z
END; { RAND }
```

```
FUNCTION VAL(OPER:STRING):REAL;
VAR IL,I:INTEGER;
NUM :SET OF CHAR;
    VL  :REAL;
    CH  :CHAR;
BEGIN
  NUM:=['.','-','+','0'..'9'];
  VL:=0; IL:=LENGTH(OPER); VAL:=0;
  IF IL=0 THEN EXIT(VAL);
  FOR I:=1 TO IL DO
  BEGIN
    CH:=OPER[I];
     IF NOT (CH IN NUM) THEN I:=IL+1
     ELSE
      IF (CH<>'.') AND (CH<>'-') AND (CH<>'+')
      THEN VL:=VL*10+ORD(CH)-48;
  END;
  IF POS('.',OPER)>0 THEN
     VL:=VL/PWROFTEN(IL-POS('.',OPER));
     CH:=OPER[1];
     IF CH='-' THEN VL:=-VL;VAL:=VL;
END; { VAL }


FUNCTION AT(ROW, COL:INTEGER):CHAR;
BEGIN
  GOTOXY(COL, ROW);
  AT := CHR(4);
END; { AT }


PROCEDURE CONVERT;
CONST FACTOR=13;
BEGIN
  VELOCITY := VELOCITY * FACTOR;
  SINE     := SIN(ANGLE*PI/180);
  COSINE   := COS(ANGLE*PI/180);
END; { CONVERT }


{ Draw a fancy opening page for the program      }
{ on the hi-res screen. Prompt for instructions. }


PROCEDURE SPLASHPAGE;
VAR TOPX,TOPY,BOTX,BOTY,
    I, J : INTEGER;

  PROCEDURE POSITION(ROW,COLUMN:INTEGER);
  BEGIN
    PENCOLOR(NONE);
    MOVETO(COLUMN*7-2,184-ROW*12);
  END; { HI-RES POSITION }

  PROCEDURE BOX(COLOR:SCREENCOLOR;UPPERX,UPPERY,LOWERX,LOWERY:INTEGER);
  BEGIN
    PENCOLOR(NONE); TURNTO(0); MOVETO(UPPERX,UPPERY);
    PENCOLOR(COLOR);
    MOVETO(LOWERX,UPPERY);MOVETO(LOWERX,LOWERY);
    MOVETO(UPPERX,LOWERY);MOVETO(UPPERX,UPPERY);
  END; { BOX }

BEGIN { SPLASHPAGE }
  INITTURTLE;
  TOPX:=0;TOPY:=191;BOTX:=279;BOTY:=0;
  FOR I:=1 TO 11 DO
    BEGIN
      FOR J:=1 TO 2 DO
        BEGIN
          BOX(BLUE,TOPX,TOPY,BOTX,BOTY);
          TOPX:=TOPX+1; BOTX:=BOTX-1;
          TOPY:=TOPY-1; BOTY:=BOTY+1;
        END; { J LOOP }
      TOPX:=TOPX+2; BOTX:=BOTX-2;
      TOPY:=TOPY-2; BOTY:=BOTY+2;
    END; { I LOOP }
```

```
  POSITION(5,16); WSTRING('ARTILLERY');
  POSITION(6,19); WSTRING('by:');
  POSITION(7,15); WSTRING('David Miller');
  { Draw 4 Apples in display corners. }
  POSITION(4,11); WCHAR(CHR(1)); POSITION(4,29); WCHAR(CHR(1));
  POSITION(11,11);WCHAR(CHR(1)); POSITION(11,29);WCHAR(CHR(1));
  POSITION(9,15); WSTRING('Do you want');
  POSITION(10,14); WSTRING('Instructions ?');
  READ(CH);
END; { SPLASHPAGE }


{ Instructions are split into 2 procedures because of }
{ limitations on the size of a procedure (1200 bytes) }


PROCEDURE HELP1;
BEGIN
  TEXTMODE;
  PAGE(OUTPUT);
  WRITELN('Welcome to ARTILLERY, a battle to the');
  WRITELN('death between two ferocious players. The');
  WRITELN('object is simple: to blast your opponent');
  WRITELN('off the screen !!! That sounds like fun,');
  WRITELN('doesn''t it? Please read on...');
  WRITELN;
  WRITELN('Each game consists of a number of diff-');
  WRITELN('ferent "rounds", in which you and your');
  WRITELN('antagonist will alternate taking shots');
  WRITELN('at each other, hampered by the various');
  WRITELN('randomly generated terrains. The Apple');
  WRITELN('will produce hills of varying heights');
  WRITELN('and widths, placing them somewhere near');
  WRITELN('the middle of the screen. The height of');
  WRITELN('the terrain on each side of the hill');
  WRITELN('will fluctuate. Each player is a small,');
  WRITELN('bitten apple which magically falls some-');
  WRITELN('where on the screen, one on each side of');
  WRITELN('the hill.');
  WRITELN;
  WRITE  ('Hit any key to go on to the next page.');
  READ(CH);
END; { HELP1 }


PROCEDURE HELP2;
BEGIN
  PAGE(OUTPUT);
  WRITELN('Each of you will shoot by entering the');
  WRITELN('velocity (1-16) and angle (0-140 deg) of');
  WRITELN('elevation of the shot as 2 numbers,to be');
  WRITELN('separated by a comma. They may have dec-');
  WRITELN('imal values. Hopefully, your shot will');
  WRITELN('soar over the hill and destroy your');
  WRITELN('opponent. But there are other problems..');
  WRITELN;
  WRITELN('A random wind is generated for each new');
  WRITELN('round. It varies in intensity from 0 to');
  WRITELN('40 and in direction from left to right.');
  WRITELN('You''ll need to lower your angle to');
  WRITELN('counterract a strong wind blowing in');
  WRITELN('your face, and raise your angle when the');
  WRITELN('wind is behind you. In fact, you might');
  WRITELN('even have to shoot backwards !!!');
  WRITELN;
  WRITELN('To end the game, enter -9 for the angle.');
  WRITELN('Good luck, & may the best Apple win !!!');
  WRITELN;
  WRITE  ('Hit any key to start the game...');
  READ(CH);
END; { HELP2 }


{ Input the player names for display at the top }
{ of the graphics screen. Makes sure that each  }
{ does something other than hitting RETURN.     }
```

```
PROCEDURE GET_NAMES;
BEGIN
  TEXTMODE;
  PAGE(OUTPUT);
  WRITELN(AT(7,8),'Please enter your names:');
  WRITELN(AT(8,8),'========================');
  REPEAT
    WRITE(AT(10,8),'Player 1 ? ');
    READLN(LEFT_PLAYER);
  UNTIL LENGTH(LEFT_PLAYER)>0;
  REPEAT
    WRITE(AT(11,8),'Player 2 ? ');
    READLN(RIGHT_PLAYER);
  UNTIL LENGTH(RIGHT_PLAYER)>0;
  WRITE(AT(13,11),'Play with wind ?');
  GOTOXY(60,10); READ (CH);
  IF (CH='N') OR (CH='n') THEN DIFFICULTY:=EASY
    ELSE DIFFICULTY:=HARD;
  WRITE(AT(15,8),'[ Hit any key to start ]');
  GOTOXY(60,10);
  READ(CH);
END; { GET_NAMES }


{ Display final games stats, option to start }
{ another game with different opponents.     }


PROCEDURE END_GAME;
BEGIN
  TEXTMODE;
  PAGE(OUTPUT);
  WRITELN(AT(6,14),'Final Score:');
  WRITELN(AT(7,14),'============');
  WRITELN(AT(9,14),LEFT_PLAYER,':',LEFT_SCORE);
  WRITELN(AT(10,14),RIGHT_PLAYER,':',RIGHT_SCORE);
  IF LEFT_SCORE>RIGHT_SCORE THEN WRITELN(AT(12,14),LEFT_PLAYER,' WINS!')
   ELSE
   IF RIGHT_SCORE>LEFT_SCORE THEN WRITELN(AT(12,14),RIGHT_PLAYER,'WINS!')
   ELSE WRITELN(AT(12,14),'Tie Game!');
  WRITE(AT(14,14),'Another game ? '); READ(CH);
END; { ENDGAME }


{ Set all random variables for the next round  }
{ of play, including wind, hill, and player    }
{ positions. The ranges for random numbers can }
{ be altered, within limits, to fine-tune the  }
{ game to your own personal preference.        }


PROCEDURE SETUP;
BEGIN
  PAGE(OUTPUT);
  HIT := FALSE;
  RANDOMIZE;
  WIND           := RAND(0,40);
  WIND_FACTOR    := WIND * 1.2;
  IF RAND(0,10)  <= 5 THEN
   WIND_DIRECTION:= '<-To Left--' ELSE
   WIND_DIRECTION:= '--To Right->';
  HILL_HEIGHT    := RAND(50,140);
  HILL_POSITION  := RAND(100,170);
  HILL_WIDTH     := RAND(45,140);
  HILL_LEFT      := HILL_POSITION - (HILL_WIDTH DIV 2);
  HILL_RIGHT     := HILL_POSITION + (HILL_WIDTH DIV 2);
  LEFTEL         := RAND(10,3*HILL_HEIGHT DIV 5);
  RIGHTEL        := RAND(10,3*HILL_HEIGHT DIV 5);
  LEFT_POSITION  := RAND(10,HILL_LEFT-10);
  RIGHT_POSITION := RAND(HILL_RIGHT+10,269);
END; { SETUP }


{ Take the random vars from SETUP and draw the   }
{ hill on the screen. A sine wave is used to     }
{ generate the hill, with the height being used }
{ as the amplitude of the function.             }
```

```
PROCEDURE DRAW_SCREEN;
VAR
        LEFT, RIGHT      : INTEGER;
        I, J, MAX        : INTEGER;
        INCREMENT,
        ANGLE,
        DELTA,
        PRESENT_HEIGHT,
        NEXT_HEIGHT      : REAL;
BEGIN
  INITTURTLE;
  MAX       := ABS(HILL_LEFT - HILL_RIGHT) DIV 2;
  INCREMENT := 1.57 / MAX;
  ANGLE     := 0;
  FOR I := 1 TO MAX DO
    BEGIN
      NEXT_HEIGHT := HILL_HEIGHT*SIN(ANGLE+INCREMENT);
      PRESENT_HEIGHT := HILL_HEIGHT*SIN(ANGLE);
      DELTA := NEXT_HEIGHT - PRESENT_HEIGHT;
      LEFT := TRUNC(HILL_LEFT + I);
      RIGHT:= TRUNC(HILL_RIGHT - I);
      IF PRESENT_HEIGHT < LEFTEL THEN LEFT := 0;
      IF PRESENT_HEIGHT < RIGHTEL THEN RIGHT := 279;
      FOR J := 0 TO TRUNC (DELTA) DO
        BEGIN
          PENCOLOR(NONE);
          MOVETO(LEFT,TRUNC(PRESENT_HEIGHT)+J+BOTTOM);
          PENCOLOR(GREEN);
          MOVETO(RIGHT,TRUNC(PRESENT_HEIGHT)+J+BOTTOM);
        END;
      ANGLE := ANGLE + INCREMENT;
    END;
END; { DRAW_SCREEN }


{ Display player names, scores, and wind data }
{ at the top of the screen. A little Apple is }
{ dropped on each side of the hill.           }


PROCEDURE SET_DISPLAY;
CONST
        DELAY =20;
VAR
        WIND_STR,
        SCORE_STR        : STRING;
        I,J,K            : INTEGER;
BEGIN
  I := 184;
  PENCOLOR(NONE);
  CHARTYPE(6);
  WHILE NOT SCREENBIT(LEFT_POSITION,I-1) AND
        NOT SCREENBIT(LEFT_POSITION+1,I-1) DO
    BEGIN
      I := I-1;
      MOVETO(LEFT_POSITION,I);
      WCHAR(CHR(1));
      FOR J := 1 TO DELAY DO;
      MOVETO(LEFT_POSITION,I);
      WCHAR(CHR(1));
    END;
  MOVETO(LEFT_POSITION,I);
  LEFTEL := I;
  WCHAR(CHR(1));
  FOR J:=1 TO 5 DO
    BEGIN
      NOTE(1,1);
      FOR K:=1 TO 60 DO;
    END;
  I := 184;
  WHILE NOT SCREENBIT(RIGHT_POSITION,I-1) AND
        NOT SCREENBIT(RIGHT_POSITION+1,I-1) DO
```

```
      BEGIN
        I := I-1;
        MOVETO(RIGHT_POSITION,I);
        WCHAR(CHR(1));
        FOR J := 1 TO DELAY DO;
        MOVETO(RIGHT_POSITION,I);
        WCHAR(CHR(1));
      END;
    MOVETO(RIGHT_POSITION,I);
    RIGHTEL := I;
    WCHAR(CHR(1));
    FOR J:=1 TO 5 DO
      BEGIN
        NOTE(1,1);
        FOR K:=1 TO 60 DO;
      END;
    IF DIFFICULTY=HARD THEN
      BEGIN
        STR(WIND,WIND_STR);
        MOVETO(112,183); WSTRING(CONCAT('WIND ',WIND_STR));
        MOVETO(98,175); WSTRING(WIND_DIRECTION);
      END;
    STR(LEFT_SCORE,SCORE_STR);
    MOVETO(0,183); WSTRING(CONCAT(LEFT_PLAYER,':',SCORE_STR));
    STR(RIGHT_SCORE,SCORE_STR);
    MOVETO(255-LENGTH(RIGHT_PLAYER)*7,183);
    WSTRING(CONCAT(RIGHT_PLAYER,':',SCORE_STR));
    POKE (WINDOW,0);
  END; { SET DISPLAY }


  { Make a little crater where a missed shot has }
  { hit the ground, clicking to sound the blast. }


  PROCEDURE CRATER(XPOS,YPOS,RADIUS:INTEGER);
  VAR I : INTEGER;
  BEGIN
    PENCOLOR(NONE);
    MOVETO(XPOS,YPOS);
    PENCOLOR(BLACK);
    FOR I:=1 TO 17 DO
      BEGIN
        MOVETO(XPOS,YPOS);
        TURNTO(RAND(0,359));
        MOVE(RADIUS);
        NOTE(1,1);
      END;
  END; { CRATER }


  { Calculate the trajectory points using a pair }
  { of functions, until the SCREENBIT function   }
  { indicates we've hit something. Then check to }
  { see what we've hit. If it's ground, make a   }
  { crater and redraw the Apple. If it's a hit,  }
  { set HIT to true so PLAY will explode it.     }
```

```
PROCEDURE PLOT_TRAJECTORY;
CONST
        SCREEN_LEFT     = 0;
        SCREEN_RIGHT    = 279;
        DELTA           = 0.04;
        HEIGHT_ADJUST   = 9;
VAR
        X, Y, I, CLICK,
        INITIAL_Y,
        INITIAL_X         : INTEGER;
        TIME, XVELOCITY : REAL;

  FUNCTION Y_POSITION (TIME:REAL):REAL;
  BEGIN
    Y_POSITION := INITIAL_Y + (VELOCITY * SINE
    * TIME - (GRAVITY*SQR(TIME)/2));
  END; { Y_POSITION }

  FUNCTION X_POSITION (TIME:REAL):REAL;
  BEGIN
    X_POSITION := INITIAL_X+3+((XVELOCITY * COSINE
    + WIND_FACTOR ) * TIME);
  END; { X_POSITION }

BEGIN { PLOT_TRAJECTORY }
   IF WIND_DIRECTION = '<-To Left--' THEN WIND_FACTOR := - ABS(WIND_FACTOR
  IF LEFT_SHOT THEN
    BEGIN
      INITIAL_Y  := LEFTEL + HEIGHT_ADJUST;
      INITIAL_X  := LEFT_POSITION;
      XVELOCITY  := VELOCITY;
    END
  ELSE
    BEGIN
      INITIAL_Y  := RIGHTEL + HEIGHT_ADJUST;
      INITIAL_X  := RIGHT_POSITION;
      XVELOCITY  := - ABS(VELOCITY);
    END;
  TIME          := 0;
  CONTACT       := FALSE;
  REPEAT
    X  := TRUNC(X_POSITION(TIME));
    Y  := TRUNC(Y_POSITION(TIME));
    IF (X < SCREEN_LEFT) OR (X > SCREEN_RIGHT)
      THEN EXIT (PLOT_TRAJECTORY);
    IF (SCREENBIT(X,Y) OR SCREENBIT(X+1,Y))
       AND (Y<175) THEN CONTACT := TRUE;
    FOR I := 0 TO 1 DO
      BEGIN
        PENCOLOR(NONE);
        MOVETO(X,Y);
        PENCOLOR(REVERSE);
        TURNTO(  0); MOVE(1);
        TURNTO( 90); MOVE(1);
        TURNTO(180); MOVE(1);
        TURNTO(270); MOVE(1);
        TURNTO(360); MOVE(1);
      END;
    NOTE(1,1);
    TIME   := TIME + DELTA;
  UNTIL CONTACT;
  IF ((LEFT_SHOT) AND (X>=RIGHT_POSITION-1) AND
      (X<=RIGHT_POSITION+8) AND (Y<=RIGHTEL+9) AND
      (Y>=RIGHTEL))
  OR ((RIGHT_SHOT) AND (X>=LEFT_POSITION-1) AND
      (X<=LEFT_POSITION+8) AND (Y<=LEFTEL+9) AND
      (Y>=LEFTEL))
  THEN HIT := TRUE;
  IF NOT HIT THEN
    BEGIN
      CRATER(X,Y+2,5);
      PENCOLOR(NONE); CHARTYPE(10);
      IF LEFT_SHOT THEN MOVETO(RIGHT_POSITION.RIGHTEL)
        ELSE MOVETO(LEFT_POSITION,LEFTEL);
      WCHAR(CHR(1)); { Redraw the Apple if slightly damaged }
    END;
END; { PLOT_TRAJECTORY }
```

```
{ Explode by flashing the Apple between inverse }
{ and normal character modes. Include some      }
{ random notes for an interesting sound effect. }


PROCEDURE EXPLODE;
CONST DELAY = 50;
VAR X,Y,I,J : INTEGER;
BEGIN
  PENCOLOR(NONE);
  IF LEFT_SHOT THEN
    BEGIN
      X := RIGHT_POSTION;
      Y := RIGHTEL;
    END
  ELSE
    BEGIN
      X := LEFT_POSITION;
      Y := LEFTEL;
    END;
  FOR I := 1 TO 20 DO
    BEGIN
      CHARTYPE(5);
      MOVETO(X,Y);
      WCHAR(CHR(1));
      NOTE(RAND(1,50),2);
      FOR J:= 1 TO DELAY DO;
      CHARTYPE(10);
      MOVETO(X,Y);
      WCHAR(CHR(1));
      NOTE(RAND(1,50),2);
      FOR J:= 1 TO DELAY DO;
    END;
    CHARTYPE(10);
    MOVETO(X,Y);
    WCHAR(CHR(32));
END; { EXPLODE }


{ Do a musical countdown at the top of the screen }


PROCEDURE COUNTDOWN;
VAR I, CLICK     : INTEGER;
    NUM          : STRING;
BEGIN
  VIEWPORT(0,279,170,191);
  FILLSCREEN(BLACK);
  PENCOLOR(NONE); CHARTYPE(10);
  MOVETO(98,183); WSTRING('COUNTDOWN:');
  FOR I := 50 DOWNTO 0 DO
    BEGIN
      STR(I,NUM); NUM := CONCAT(NUM,'   ');
      MOVETO(168,183); WSTRING(NUM);
      NOTE(I,2);
    END;
  VIEWPORT(0,279,0,191);
END; { COUNTDOWN }


PROCEDURE UPDATE_SCORE;
BEGIN
  IF LEFT_SHOT THEN LEFT_SCORE := LEFT_SCORE +1
  ELSE RIGHT_SCORE := RIGHT_SCORE+1;
END;


{ Controls all procedures for play of a game. }
{ Continues until someone enters an angle of  }
{ -9 to end the game and possibly start again }
```

```
PROCEDURE PLAY;
VAR
        LEFT,
        COMMA     : INTEGER;
        INPUT,
        VEL_STR,
        ANG_STR   : STRING;
BEGIN
  REPEAT
    BEGIN
      LEFT_SHOT := NOT LEFT_SHOT;
      RIGHT_SHOT:= NOT RIGHT_SHOT;
      IF LEFT_SHOT THEN LEFT := 0 ELSE LEFT := 26;
      REPEAT
        WRITE(AT(23,LEFT),'V,A> ');
        READLN(INPUT);
        COMMA:=POS(',',INPUT);
        VEL_STR:=COPY(INPUT,1,COMMA-1);
        ANG_STR:=COPY(INPUT,COMMA+1,LENGTH(INPUT)-COMMA);
        VELOCITY := VAL(VEL_STR); ANGLE := VAL(ANG_STR);
        IF ANGLE = -9 THEN EXIT(PLAY);
      UNTIL (VELOCITY>0)  AND (ANGLE>0) AND
            (VELOCITY<16) AND (ANGLE<140);
      CONVERT;
      PLOT_TRAJECTORY;
    END;
  UNTIL HIT;
  EXPLODE;
  UPDATE_SCORE;
  COUNTDOWN;
END; { PLAY }



BEGIN { Main ARTILLERY Controller }
  SPLASHPAGE;
  IF (CH = 'Y') OR (CH = 'y') THEN
    BEGIN
      HELP1;
      HELP2;
    END;
  REPEAT
    LEFT_SCORE  := 0;
    RIGHT_SCORE:= 0;
    LEFT_SHOT   := FALSE;
    RIGHT_SHOT  := TRUE;
    GET_NAMES;
      REPEAT
        SETUP;
        IF DIFFICULTY=EASY THEN WIND_FACTOR:=0;
        DRAW_SCREEN;
        SET_DISPLAY;
        PLAY;
      UNTIL ANGLE = -9; { END GAME }
    END_GAME;
  UNTIL (CH = 'N') OR (CH = 'n'); { END PROGRAM }
  PAGE(OUTPUT);
END.
```

Pascal Text Formatter

Chris Wilson

Most commercial word processing packages really consist of two programs packaged as one: a screen-oriented editor and a text formatter. Since the UCSD Pascal system has a perfectly good editor, the only thing missing for word processing in Pascal is a text formatter.

In the excellent book Software Tools by Kernighan and Plauger, there are a number of useful utilities, one of which is a text formatter.

I have converted their program FORMAT from Ratfor to Pascal and have made several extensions (as suggested by the authors). My program FORMAT is listed at the end of this article.

Files processed by FORMAT consist of a mixture of command lines which describe the desired appearance of the output and text lines. Any line beginning with a period ('.') is considered to be a command line. Command lines which can't be understood are simply ignored.

The beginning period of a command is followed by a two-chapter command name. In addition, some commands have an optional parameter which must be separated from the command name by at least one space. (Note: command names are converted to upper case before being examined, thus they may be typed in either lower or upper case.)

For example the command

    .in 10

selects an indentation of ten spaces.

There are several ways of specifying the numeric parameter for commands such as indent. The first is to leave it blank which results in a default value (zero in the case of indent)

    .in

The second is simply to specify the desired value directly

    .in 10

```
(*$S+*)

(*$C Copyright (c) 1981 by Chris Wilson *)

PROGRAM FORMAT;

CONST
  HUGE = 1000;
  MAXDEFPOOL = 5000;
  PAGEWIDTH = 80;
  PAGELENGTH = 66;

TYPE
  STRING255 = STRING[255];
  ARGTYPE = (DEFAULTED,RELPLUS,RELMINUS,ABSOLUTE);
  CMDTYPE = (UNKNOWN,DEFINED,BP,BR,CE,DE,EN,FI,FO,
    HE,IND,LS,NE,NF,PL,RM,SO,SP,TI,UL);
  TITLEINFO = RECORD
    EMPTY: BOOLEAN;
    LEFTM,
    RIGHTM: INTEGER;
    LEFTS,
    CENTERS,
    RIGHTS: STRING255
    END;
  ENTRYP = ^ ENTRY;
  ENTRY = RECORD
    NAME: PACKED ARRAY [1..8] OF CHAR;
    LLINK,
    RLINK: ENTRYP;
    TYP: CMDTYPE;
    START,
    LINES: INTEGER
    END;

VAR
  BACKSPACE: CHAR;
  DOTCOUNT,
  LINECOUNT: INTEGER;
  EMITPAGE,
  INCLUDING,
  NONCONSOLE: BOOLEAN;
  INCLUDEFILE,
  SOURCEFILE,
  DESTFILE: TEXT;
  SOURCENAME,
  DESTNAME: STRING;
  FILL: BOOLEAN;
  LSVAL,  (* LINE SPACING *)
  INVAL,  (* INDENT *)
  RMVAL,  (* RIGHT MARGIN *)
  TIVAL,  (* TEMPORARY INDENT *)
  CEVAL,  (* # OF LINES TO CENTER *)
  ULVAL,  (* # OF LINES TO UNDERLINE *)
  CURPAGE,  (* OUTPUT PAGE NUMBER *)
  NEWPAGE,  (* NEXT PAGE NUMBER *)
  LINENO, (* NEXT LINE TO BE PRINTED *)
  PLVAL,  (* PAGE LENGTH IN LINES *)
  M1VAL,  (* TOP MARGIN, INCLUDING HEADER *)
  M2VAL,  (* MARGIN AFTER HEADER *)
  M3VAL,  (* MARGIN AFTER LAST TEXT LINE *)
  M4VAL,  (* BOTTOM MARGIN, INCLUDING FOOTER *)
```

```
     BOTTOM, (* LAST LIVE LINE ON PAGE *)
     OUTW,    (* WIDTH OF TEXT CURRENTLY IN OUTBUF *)
     OUTWDS, (* NUMBER OF WORDS IN OUTBUF *)
     DIR: INTEGER;
     HEADER,
     FOOTER: TITLEINFO;
     HASNUMERICARG: SET OF CMDTYPE;
     INBUF,
     OUTBUF,
     BLANKS255: STRING255;
     UNDERLINE: STRING[2];
     ROOT: ENTRYP;
     POOLINX: INTEGER;
     DEFPOOL: PACKED ARRAY [0..MAXDEFPOOL] OF CHAR;

PROCEDURE COMMAND(VAR BUF: STRING255);
  FORWARD;

PROCEDURE UPSTRING(VAR S: STRING);
        (*========*)

VAR
  I: INTEGER;

BEGIN
FOR I := 1 TO LENGTH(S) DO
  IF S[I] IN ['a'..'z'] THEN
    S[I] := CHR(ORD('A')+(ORD(S[I])-ORD('a')));
END;

FUNCTION MIN(A, B: INTEGER): INTEGER;
       (*===*)

BEGIN
IF A < B THEN
  MIN := A
ELSE
  MIN := B;
END;

FUNCTION MAX(A, B: INTEGER): INTEGER;
       (*===*)

BEGIN
IF A < B THEN
  MAX := B
ELSE
  MAX := A;
END;

PROCEDURE ERROR(S: STRING255);
        (*=====*)

BEGIN
WRITELN;
WRITELN('>>> ',S,' <<<');
CLOSE(DESTFILE,LOCK);
WRITELN(LINECOUNT,' lines');
EXIT(FORMAT);
END;

FUNCTION GETLINE(VAR INBUF: STRING255): BOOLEAN;
       (*=======*)

BEGIN
IF INCLUDING THEN
  IF EOF(INCLUDEFILE) THEN
    BEGIN
    CLOSE(INCLUDEFILE);
    INCLUDING := FALSE;
    GETLINE := GETLINE(INBUF);
    EXIT(GETLINE);
    END
  ELSE
    READLN(INCLUDEFILE,INBUF)
```

The third is to specify the difference (plus or minus) between the desired value and the current value

.in +5
.in -5

FORMAT has two modes of processing text lines: word mode and line mode.

In word mode, text lines are broken up into words which are reformatted into output lines based upon margin considerations. Output lines are right justified by the addition of extra spaces before being written out. This whole process is called filling.

In line mode, text lines are copied from input to output without internal rearrangement, although they are still subject to normal formatting such as indentation, centering, and underlining.

Filling is enabled by default.

The no-fill command disables filling

.nf

and the fill command re-enables it

.fi

If there is a partially collected output line when filling is turned off, the output line is forced out before anything else occurs. This procedure is called a break. Many commands implicitly cause a break and the break command

.br

can be used to explicitly invoke it.

The indent command sets the number of spaces by which subsequent output lines are to be indented (i.e. the left margin)

.in 10

The temporary indent command causes a break and then sets the number of spaces by which the next output line is to be indented

.ti +5

The right margin command sets the right margin

.rm 72

Filling operates between the margins set by the right margin command and either the indent or temporary indent command.

The center command causes a break and then centers subsequent lines until either the specified number of lines have been centered or a center command with a value of zero is encountered.

Thus

.ce
text line

centers one line,

.ce n
text line 1
text line 2
.
.
.
text line n

centers n lines which were counted in advance, and

.ce 500
text line 1
text line 2
.
.
.
text line n
.ce 0

centers n lines which were not counted in advance (assuming n <= 500).

The underline command underlines subsequent lines until either the specified number of lines have been underlined or an underline command with a value of zero is encountered

.ul 2
text line 1
text line 2

It is similiar to center but does not cause a break, so individual words can be underlined in filling mode

text line
.ul
text to be underlined
text line
text line

Centering and underlining can be combined

.ce
.ul
text to be centered & underlined

```
ELSE IF EOF(SOURCEFILE) THEN
  BEGIN
  INBUF := '';
  GETLINE := FALSE;
  EXIT(GETLINE);
  END
ELSE
  READLN(SOURCEFILE,INBUF);
LINECOUNT := SUCC(LINECOUNT);
IF NONCONSOLE THEN
  BEGIN
  DOTCOUNT := SUCC(DOTCOUNT);
  WRITE('.');
  IF DOTCOUNT >= 50 THEN
    BEGIN
    WRITELN;
    WRITE('<',LINECOUNT:4,'>');
    DOTCOUNT := 0;
    END;
  END;
GETLINE := TRUE;
END;

FUNCTION ENTERCMD(CMD: STRING255; CT: CMDTYPE): ENTRYP;
       (*========*)

(* ENTER COMMAND INTO TABLE *)

VAR
  P,
  Q: ENTRYP;
  I: INTEGER;

BEGIN
UPSTRING(CMD);
IF LENGTH(CMD) < 2 THEN
  ERROR(CONCAT('Command name too short: ',CMD));
NEW(P);
WITH P^ DO
  BEGIN
  NAME := '        ';
  MOVELEFT(CMD[1],NAME[1],2);
  LLINK := NIL;
  RLINK := NIL;
  END;
IF ROOT = NIL THEN
  ROOT := P
ELSE
  BEGIN
  I := TREESEARCH(ROOT,Q,P^.NAME);
  IF I = 1 THEN
    Q^.RLINK := P
  ELSE IF I = -1 THEN
    Q^.LLINK := P
  ELSE
    P := Q; (* REDEFINE *)
  END;
P^.TYP := CT;
ENTERCMD := P;
END;
```

```
FUNCTION LOOKUP(VAR TOKEN: STRING255): ENTRYP;
       (*======*)

(* LOOK FOR COMMAND IN TABLE *)

VAR
  P: ENTRYP;
  NAM: PACKED ARRAY [1..8] OF CHAR;

BEGIN
LOOKUP := NIL;
IF LENGTH(TOKEN) >= 2 THEN
  BEGIN
  NAM := '        ';
  MOVELEFT(TOKEN[1],NAM[1],2);
  IF TREESEARCH(ROOT,P,NAM) = 0 THEN
    LOOKUP := P;
  END;
END;

PROCEDURE SETVAL(VAR PARAM: INTEGER; VAL: INTEGER; TYP: ARGTYPE;
        (*======*)   DEFVAL, MINVAL, MAXVAL: INTEGER);

(* SETUP PARAMETER AND CHECK RANGE *)

BEGIN
CASE TYP OF
DEFAULTED:
  PARAM := DEFVAL;
RELPLUS:
  PARAM := PARAM+VAL;
RELMINUS:
  PARAM := PARAM-VAL;
ABSOLUTE:
  PARAM := VAL
END; (* CASE *)
PARAM := MIN(PARAM,MAXVAL);
PARAM := MAX(PARAM,MINVAL);
END;

(*$I FORMAT.1 *)

PROCEDURE HANDLEARGS(VAR S, ARGS: STRING255);
        (*==========*)

(* HANDLE DEFINE INVOCATION ARGUMENTS *)

VAR
  I: INTEGER;
  ARG: STRING255;

PROCEDURE GETARG(N: INTEGER; VAR ARG: STRING255);
  VAR I: INTEGER;
    A: STRING255;
  BEGIN
  A := ARGS;
  WHILE (N > 0) AND (LENGTH(A) > 0) DO
    BEGIN
    IF (A[1] = '''') AND (LENGTH(A) > 1) THEN
      BEGIN
      DELETE(A,1,1);
      I := SCAN(LENGTH(A),='''',A[1]);
      ARG := COPY(A,1,I);
      DELETE(A,1,I);
      IF POS('''',A) = 1 THEN
        DELETE(A,1,1);
      END
    ELSE IF (A[1] = '"') AND (LENGTH(A) > 1) THEN
      BEGIN
      DELETE(A,1,1);
      I := SCAN(LENGTH(A),='"',A[1]);
      ARG := COPY(A,1,I);
      DELETE(A,1,I);
      IF POS('"',A) = 1 THEN
        DELETE(A,1,1);
      END
```

By default, output lines are single spaced. The line space command changes the spacing between consecutive output lines. A line space value of two results in double spacing

.ls 2

The space command causes a break and then produces blank lines until either the specified number has been produced or the bottom of a page is reached

.sp 2

Blank lines produced by setting line space to more than one are generated as a side effect of writing the current output line. Since break writes the current output line if it is non-empty, line space action can always occur as a side-effect of break. It is important to understand this effect since it can result in more blank lines than were anticipated when doing a space command.

To mimimize the need for explicit commands, empty text lines and text lines with leading blanks result in special actions.

An empty line causes a break (with appropriate line spacing for the current output line) and then generates a blank output line (with appropriate line spacing for it).

A non-empty line with leading blanks causes a break and a temporary indent equal to the number of leading blanks.

The need command causes a break and then determines whether the specified number of output lines will fit on the current page and, if not, advances to the next page

.ne 10

Need takes line spacing into account. Thus a need count of ten will automatically be adjusted to 20 when double spacing is selected.

The header and footer commands set up running header and footer titles for subsequent pages

.he /left/center/right/
.fo /left/center/right/

The '/' is any arbitrary delimiter which separates the three parts of a running title. The left part is left justified, the right part is right justified, and the center part is centered. The margins used are those in force at the time the command is processed not the margins which happen to be in force when the title is printed.

```
          ELSE
            BEGIN
            I  := SCAN(LENGTH(A),=' ',A[1]);
            ARG  := COPY(A,1,I);
            DELETE(A,1,I);
            END;
          IF LENGTH(A) > 0 THEN
            BEGIN
            I  := SCAN(LENGTH(A),<>' ',A[1]);
            DELETE(A,1,I);
            END;
         N  := PRED(N);
         END;
      IF N <> 0 THEN
         ARG  := '';
      END;

BEGIN (* HANDLEARGS *)
I  := 1;
WHILE I < LENGTH(S) DO
   BEGIN
   I  := I+SCAN(LENGTH(S)+1-I,='$',S[I]);
   IF I < LENGTH(S) THEN
      IF S[I+1] IN ['1'..'9'] THEN
         BEGIN
         GETARG(ORD(S[I+1])-ORD('0'),ARG);
         DELETE(S,I,2);
         IF LENGTH(S)+LENGTH(ARG) <= 255 THEN
           INSERT(ARG,S,I)
         ELSE
           ERROR('Overflow in define argument substitution');
         I  := I+LENGTH(ARG);
         END
      ELSE
         I  := SUCC(I)
   ELSE
      I  := SUCC(I);
   END;
END;
```

```
FUNCTION COMTYPE(VAR BUF: STRING255; EXPAND: BOOLEAN): CMDTYPE;
        (*=======*)

(* DECODE COMMAND, DELETE FROM BUF *)

VAR
  I,
  J: INTEGER;
  P: ENTRYP;
  S,
  CMDBUF: STRING255;

BEGIN
I := SCAN(LENGTH(BUF),=' ',BUF[1]);
CMDBUF := COPY(BUF,1,I);
DELETE(BUF,1,I);
IF LENGTH(BUF) > 0 THEN
  BEGIN
  I := SCAN(LENGTH(BUF),<>' ',BUF[1]);
  DELETE(BUF,1,I);
  END;
DELETE(CMDBUF,1,1); (* '.' *)
UPSTRING(CMDBUF);
P := LOOKUP(CMDBUF);
IF P = NIL THEN
  COMTYPE := UNKNOWN
ELSE
  WITH P^ DO
    BEGIN
    COMTYPE := TYP;
    IF (TYP = DEFINED) AND EXPAND THEN
      BEGIN
      J := START;
      FOR I := 1 TO LINES DO
        BEGIN
        (* TRICKY CODE INVOLVING LENGTH BYTE OF S *)
        MOVELEFT(DEFPOOL[J],S,1+ORD(DEFPOOL[J]));
        J := J+1+LENGTH(S);
        IF POS('$',S) <> 0 THEN
          HANDLEARGS(S,BUF);
        IF POS('.',S) = 1 THEN
          COMMAND(S)
        ELSE
          TXT(S);
        END;
      END;
    END;
END;
```

A '#' appearing anywhere in one of the title parts will be replaced with the current page number. Any of the parts can be empty

.he '25-Jul-81''Page #'

If the entire parameter is empty, the corresponding title is cleared

.he

The begin page command causes a break, then causes the current page, if any, to be finished (footer action, etc.), and finally begins the next page

.bp

The form

.bp 45

also sets the page number of the next page to the specified value.

The page length command sets the number of lines per page

.pl 66

Table one shows the general page layout including the position of title lines.

Table 1: Page Layout

Line	Function
1	
2	[header line]
3	
4	
5	[1st output line]
6	[2nd output line]
.	.
.	.
.	.
pl-5	[2nd to last output line]
pl-4	[last output line]
pl-3	
pl-2	
pl-1	[footer line]
pl	

The source command allows the inclusion of another file

.so [file-title]

It is similiar to the include file capability of the Pascal compiler.

The final commands are the define and end define commands. These commands allow you to define your own parametric commands consisting of both command and text lines

.de p1
.ne 4
.sp 1
.in 10
.rm 72
.ti +5
.en

Define names must be two characters long just like regular command names. In fact regular command names can be redefined if you like.

Defines are invoked by using the define name as a command

.pl

Within the define text parameters are referred to by the notation '$1', '$2', etc. The number after the dollar sign specifies which parameter is being referred to and must be in the range one to nine. These references do not have to be delimited by spaces

.de f1
.ti 60
$1
.sp 2
Dear $2:
.sp 1
Thank you for your recent submission to Call
-A.P.P.L.E.
entitled:
.ce
.ul
.en

When a parametric define is invoked, the actual paramters are specified following the define name, separated by spaces. If a parameter requires embedded blanks, it can be surrounded by either single or double quotes

.f1 'July 26, 1981' Chris
A Pascal Text Formatting Program

Unspecified parameters are replaced by empty strings. Extra parameters are ignored.

```
FUNCTION GETVAL(VAR BUF: STRING255; VAR TYP: ARGTYPE):INTEGER;
        (*======*)

(* EVALUATE OPTIONAL NUMERIC ARGUMENT *)

VAR
  I: INTEGER;
  CONTINUE: BOOLEAN;

BEGIN
IF LENGTH(BUF) = 0 THEN
  TYP := DEFAULTED
ELSE IF POS('+',BUF) = 1 THEN
  TYP := RELPLUS
ELSE IF POS('-',BUF) = 1 THEN
  TYP := RELMINUS
ELSE
  TYP := ABSOLUTE;
IF TYP IN [RELPLUS,RELMINUS] THEN
  DELETE(BUF,1,1);
I := 0;
CONTINUE := TRUE;
WHILE CONTINUE AND (LENGTH(BUF) > 0) DO
  IF BUF[1] IN ['0'..'9'] THEN
    BEGIN
    I := (I*10)+(ORD(BUF[1])-ORD('0'));
    DELETE(BUF,1,1);
    END
  ELSE
    CONTINUE := FALSE;
GETVAL := I;
END;

PROCEDURE GETTL(VAR BUF: STRING255; VAR TITLE: TITLEINFO);
        (*=====*)

(* SETUP TITLE FROM BUF *)

PROCEDURE GETPART(VAR BUF, S: STRING255);
  VAR I: INTEGER;
    DELIM: STRING[1];
  BEGIN
  IF LENGTH(BUF) > 0 THEN
    BEGIN
    DELIM := COPY(BUF,1,1);
    DELETE(BUF,1,1);
    I := POS(DELIM,BUF);
    IF I = 0 THEN
      BEGIN
      S := BUF;
      BUF := '';
      END
    ELSE
      BEGIN
      I := PRED(I);
      S := COPY(BUF,1,I);
      DELETE(BUF,1,I);
      END;
    END
  ELSE
    S := '';
  END;

BEGIN (* GETTL *)
WITH TITLE DO
  BEGIN
  LEFTM := INVAL;
  RIGHTM := RMVAL;
  GETPART(BUF,LEFTS);
  GETPART(BUF,CENTERS);
  GETPART(BUF,RIGHTS);
  EMPTY := (LEFTS = '') AND (CENTERS='') AND (RIGHTS='');
  END;
END;
```

```
PROCEDURE DEFINE(VAR BUF: STRING255);
        (*======*)

(* DEFINE MACRO *)

VAR
  P: ENTRYP;
  CT: CMDTYPE;
  INBUF: STRING255;

BEGIN
P := ENTERCMD(BUF,DEFINED);
WITH P^ DO
  BEGIN
  START := POOLINX;
  LINES := 0;
  WHILE GETLINE(INBUF) DO
    IF POOLINX+1+LENGTH(INBUF) <= MAXDEFPOOL THEN
      BEGIN
      (* TRICKY CODE INVOLVING LENGTH BYTE OF INBUF *)
      MOVELEFT(INBUF,DEFPOOL[POOLINX],1+LENGTH(INBUF));
      POOLINX := POOLINX+1+LENGTH(INBUF);
      LINES := SUCC(LINES);
      IF POS('.',INBUF) = 1 THEN
        BEGIN
        CT := COMTYPE(INBUF,FALSE);
        IF CT = DE THEN
          ERROR(CONCAT('Nested defines not allowed: ',BUF))
        ELSE IF CT = EN THEN
          BEGIN
          LINES := PRED(LINES);
          EXIT(DEFINE);
          END;
        END
      END
    ELSE
      ERROR(CONCAT('Define pool overflow: ',BUF));
  END;
END;

PROCEDURE COMMAND; (* VAR BUF: STRING255 *)
        (*=======*)

(* PERFORM FORMATTING COMMAND *)

VAR
  VAL,
  NEVAL,
  SPVAL: INTEGER;
  CT: CMDTYPE;
  TYP: ARGTYPE;

BEGIN
CT := COMTYPE(BUF,TRUE);
IF CT IN HASNUMERICARG THEN
  VAL := GETVAL(BUF,TYP);
CASE CT OF
UNKNOWN, DEFINED:
  BEGIN
  END;
BP:
  BEGIN
  IF LINENO > 0 THEN
    SPACE(HUGE);
  SETVAL(CURPAGE,VAL,TYP,SUCC(CURPAGE),-HUGE,HUGE);
  NEWPAGE := CURPAGE;
  END;
BR:
  BRK;
CE:
  BEGIN
  BRK;
  SETVAL(CEVAL,VAL,TYP,1,0,HUGE);
  END;
```

Table two is a summary of the various commands and their defaults.

Table 2: Command Summary

Command	Default	Break
.bp n	n = +1	yes
.br		yes
.ce n	n = 1	yes
.de		yes
.en		no
.fi		yes
.fo	////	no
.he	////	no
.in n	n = 0	no
.ls n	n = 1	no
.ne n	n = 1	yes
.nf		yes
.pl n	n = 66	no
.rm n	n = 80	no
.so		no
.sp n	n = 1	yes
.ti n	n = 0	yes
.ul n	n = 1	no

The FORMAT symbolic is too long to be edited as a single file so it has been broken up into two files: FORMAT.TEXT and FORMAT.1. TEXT, which are listed in that order below.

```
DE:
  BEGIN
  BRK;
  DEFINE(BUF);
  END;
EN:
  ERROR('.en outside of define');
FI:
  BEGIN
  BRK;
  FILL := TRUE;
  END;
FO:
  GETTL(BUF,FOOTER);
HE:
  GETTL(BUF,HEADER);
IND:
  BEGIN
  SETVAL(INVAL,VAL,TYP,0,0,PRED(RMVAL));
  TIVAL := INVAL;
  END;
LS:
  SETVAL(LSVAL,VAL,TYP,1,1,HUGE);
NE:
  BEGIN
  BRK;
  NEVAL := 1; (* IN CASE VAL IS RELATIVE *)
  SETVAL(NEVAL,VAL,TYP,1,0,HUGE);
  NEVAL := NEVAL*LSVAL;
  IF LINENO+PRED(NEVAL) > BOTTOM THEN
    SPACE(HUGE);
  END;
NF:
  BEGIN
  BRK;
  FILL := FALSE;
  END;
PL:
  BEGIN
  SETVAL(PLVAL,VAL,TYP,PAGELENGTH,M1VAL+M2VAL+M3VAL+M4VAL+1,HUGE);
  BOTTOM := PLVAL-M3VAL-M4VAL;
  END;
RM:
  SETVAL(RMVAL,VAL,TYP,PAGEWIDTH,SUCC(TIVAL),255);
SO:
  BEGIN
  UPSTRING(BUF);
  IF BUF = '' THEN
    EXIT(COMMAND)
  ELSE IF POS('.TEXT',BUF) = 0 THEN
    IF BUF[LENGTH(BUF)] <> ':' THEN
      IF BUF[LENGTH(BUF)] <> '.' THEN
        BUF := CONCAT(BUF,'.TEXT')
      ELSE
        DELETE(BUF,LENGTH(BUF),1);
  IF INCLUDING THEN
    ERROR('Nested include files not allowed')
  ELSE
    BEGIN
    INCLUDING := TRUE;
    RESET(INCLUDEFILE,BUF);
    END;
  END;
SP:
  BEGIN
  SPVAL := 1; (* IN CASE VAL IS RELATIVE *)
  SETVAL(SPVAL,VAL,TYP,1,0,HUGE);
  SPACE(SPVAL);
  END;
TI:
  BEGIN
  BRK;
  SETVAL(TIVAL,VAL,TYP,0,0,RMVAL);
  END;
```

```
UL:
  SETVAL(ULVAL,VAL,TYP,1,0,HUGE)
END; (* CASE *)
END;

PROCEDURE INIT;
         (*=====*)

VAR
  P: ENTRYP;

BEGIN
BACKSPACE := CHR(8);
DOTCOUNT := 0;
LINECOUNT := 0;
INCLUDING := FALSE;
FILL := TRUE;
LSVAL := 1;
INVAL := 0;
RMVAL := PAGEWIDTH;
TIVAL := 0;
CEVAL := 0;
ULVAL := 0;
CURPAGE := 0;
NEWPAGE := 1;
LINENO := 0;
PLVAL := PAGELENGTH;
M1VAL := 2;
M2VAL := 2;
M3VAL := 2;
M4VAL := 2;
BOTTOM := PLVAL-M3VAL-M4VAL;
OUTW := 0;
OUTWDS := 0;
DIR := 0;
HEADER.EMPTY := TRUE;
FOOTER.EMPTY := TRUE;
HASNUMERICARG := [BP,CE,IND,LS,NE,PL,RM,SP,TI,UL];
OUTBUF := '';
(*$R-*)
BLANKS255[0] := CHR(255);
(*$R+*)
FILLCHAR(BLANKS255[1],255,' ');
UNDERLINE := '_ ';
UNDERLINE[2] := BACKSPACE;
ROOT := NIL;
POOLINX := 0;
P := ENTERCMD('BP',BP);
P := ENTERCMD('BR',BR);
P := ENTERCMD('CE',CE);
P := ENTERCMD('DE',DE);
P := ENTERCMD('EN',EN);
P := ENTERCMD('FI',FI);
P := ENTERCMD('FO',FO);
P := ENTERCMD('HE',HE);
P := ENTERCMD('IN',IND);
P := ENTERCMD('LS',LS);
P := ENTERCMD('NE',NE);
P := ENTERCMD('NF',NF);
P := ENTERCMD('PL',PL);
P := ENTERCMD('RM',RM);
P := ENTERCMD('SO',SO);
P := ENTERCMD('SP',SP);
P := ENTERCMD('TI',TI);
P := ENTERCMD('UL',UL);
END;
```

```
(* ========== MAIN BODY ========== *)

BEGIN
INIT;
PAGE(OUTPUT);
WRITELN('Format (7/27/81, 7:37 PM)');
WRITELN('Copyright (c) 1981 by Chris Wilson');
WRITELN;
WRITE('Source file: ');
READLN(SOURCENAME);
UPSTRING(SOURCENAME);
IF SOURCENAME = '' THEN
  EXIT(FORMAT)
ELSE IF POS('.TEXT',SOURCENAME) = 0 THEN
  IF SOURCENAME[LENGTH(SOURCENAME)] <> ':' THEN
    IF SOURCENAME[LENGTH(SOURCENAME)] <> '.' THEN
      SOURCENAME := CONCAT(SOURCENAME,'.TEXT')
    ELSE
      DELETE(SOURCENAME,LENGTH(SOURCENAME),1);
WRITE('Destination file: ');
READLN(DESTNAME);
UPSTRING(DESTNAME);
IF DESTNAME = '' THEN
  DESTNAME := 'PRINTER:'
ELSE IF POS('.TEXT',DESTNAME) = 0 THEN
  IF DESTNAME[LENGTH(DESTNAME)] <> ':' THEN
    IF DESTNAME[LENGTH(DESTNAME)] <> '.' THEN
      DESTNAME := CONCAT(DESTNAME,'.TEXT')
    ELSE
      DELETE(DESTNAME,LENGTH(DESTNAME),1);
NONCONSOLE := (POS('CONSOLE:',DESTNAME) = 0)
  AND (POS('SYSTERM:',DESTNAME) = 0)
  AND (POS('#1:',DESTNAME) = 0)
  AND (POS('#2:',DESTNAME) = 0);
EMITPAGE := (POS('PRINTER:',DESTNAME) = 1)
  OR (POS('#6:',DESTNAME) = 1)
  OR NOT NONCONSOLE;
RESET(SOURCEFILE,SOURCENAME);
REWRITE(DESTFILE,DESTNAME);
IF NONCONSOLE THEN
  WRITE('<',LINECOUNT:4,'>');
WHILE GETLINE(INBUF) DO
  IF POS('.',INBUF) = 1 THEN
    COMMAND(INBUF)
  ELSE
    TXT(INBUF);
IF LINENO > 0 THEN
  SPACE(HUGE);
CLOSE(DESTFILE,LOCK);
IF NONCONSOLE THEN
  WRITELN;
WRITELN(LINECOUNT,' lines');
END.
```

```
(* Copyright (c) 1981 by Chris Wilson *)

PROCEDURE SKIP(N: INTEGER);
         (*====*)

(* OUTPUT N BLANK LINES *)

VAR
  I: INTEGER;

BEGIN
FOR I := 1 TO N DO
  WRITELN(DESTFILE);
END;

PROCEDURE PUTTL(VAR TITLE: TITLEINFO; PAGENO: INTEGER);
         (*=====*)

(* PUT OUT TITLE LINE WITH OPTIONAL PAGE NUMBER *)

VAR
  I,
  J: INTEGER;
  S: STRING255;
  PAGES: STRING;

PROCEDURE STR(VAL: INTEGER; VAR S: STRING);
  VAR D, I: INTEGER;
    MINUS: BOOLEAN;
  BEGIN
  MINUS := VAL < 0;
  VAL := ABS(VAL);
  S := '      ';
  I := 6;
  REPEAT
    D := VAL MOD 10;
    VAL := VAL DIV 10;
    S[I] := CHR(ORD('0')+D);
    I := PRED(I)
  UNTIL VAL = 0;
  IF MINUS THEN
    BEGIN
    S[I] := '-';
    I := PRED(I);
    END;
  DELETE(S,1,I);
  END;

PROCEDURE REPLACE(VAR S: STRING255);
  VAR I: INTEGER;
  BEGIN
  REPEAT
    I := POS('#',S);
    IF I <> 0 THEN
      BEGIN
      DELETE(S,I,1);
      INSERT(PAGES,S,I);
      END
  UNTIL I = 0;
  END;
```

```
BEGIN (* PUTTL *)
WITH TITLE DO
  IF NOT EMPTY THEN
    BEGIN
    STR(PAGENO,PAGES);
    IF LEFTM > 0 THEN
      WRITE(DESTFILE,' ':LEFTM);
    I := LEFTM;
    IF LENGTH(LEFTS) > 0 THEN
      BEGIN
      S := LEFTS;
      REPLACE(S);
      WRITE(DESTFILE,S);
      I := I+LENGTH(S);
      END;
    IF LENGTH(CENTERS) > 0 THEN
      BEGIN
      S := CENTERS;
      REPLACE(S);
      J := MAX(((LEFTM+RIGHTM)-LENGTH(S)) DIV 2,0);
      IF I < J THEN
        WRITE(DESTFILE,' ':(J-I));
      WRITE(DESTFILE,S);
      I := J+LENGTH(S);
      END;
    IF LENGTH(RIGHTS) > 0 THEN
      BEGIN
      S := RIGHTS;
      REPLACE(S);
      J := RIGHTM-LENGTH(S);
      IF I < J THEN
        WRITE(DESTFILE,' ':(J-I));
      WRITE(DESTFILE,S);
      END;
    END;
WRITELN(DESTFILE);
END;

PROCEDURE PHEAD;
          (*=====*)

(* PUT OUT PAGE HEADER *)

BEGIN
CURPAGE := NEWPAGE;
NEWPAGE := SUCC(NEWPAGE);
IF EMITPAGE THEN
  PAGE(DESTFILE);
IF M1VAL > 0 THEN
  BEGIN
  SKIP(PRED(M1VAL));
  PUTTL(HEADER,CURPAGE);
  END;
SKIP(M2VAL);
LINENO := M1VAL+M2VAL+1;
END;

PROCEDURE PFOOT;
          (*=====*)

(* PUT OUT PAGE FOOTER *)

BEGIN
SKIP(M3VAL);
IF M4VAL > 0 THEN
  BEGIN
  PUTTL(FOOTER,CURPAGE);
  SKIP(PRED(M4VAL));
  END;
END;
```

```
PROCEDURE PUT(VAR BUF: STRING255);
        (*===*)

(* PUT OUT LINE WITH PROPER SPACING AND INDENTING *)

BEGIN
IF (LINENO = 0) OR (LINENO > BOTTOM) THEN
  PHEAD;
IF TIVAL > 0 THEN
  WRITE(DESTFILE,' ':TIVAL);
TIVAL := INVAL;
WRITELN(DESTFILE,BUF);
SKIP(MIN(PRED(LSVAL),BOTTOM-LINENO));
LINENO := LINENO+LSVAL;
IF LINENO > BOTTOM THEN
  PFOOT;
END;

PROCEDURE BRK;
        (*===*)

(* END CURRENT FILLED LINE *)

BEGIN
IF LENGTH(OUTBUF) > 0 THEN
  PUT(OUTBUF);
OUTW := 0;
OUTWDS := 0;
OUTBUF := '';
END;

PROCEDURE SPACE(N: INTEGER);
        (*=====*)

(* SPACE N LINES OR TO BOTTOM OF PAGE *)

BEGIN
BRK;
IF LINENO <= BOTTOM THEN
  BEGIN
  IF LINENO = 0 THEN
    PHEAD;
  SKIP(MIN(N,(BOTTOM+1)-LINENO));
  LINENO := LINENO+N;
  IF LINENO > BOTTOM THEN
    PFOOT;
  END;
END;

PROCEDURE LEADBL(VAR BUF: STRING255);
        (*======*)

(* DELETE LEADING BLANKS, SETUP TIVAL *)

VAR
  I: INTEGER;

BEGIN
BRK;
IF LENGTH(BUF) > 0 THEN
  BEGIN
  I := SCAN(LENGTH(BUF),<>' ',BUF[1]);
  DELETE(BUF,1,I);
  IF LENGTH(BUF) > 0 THEN
    TIVAL := I;
  END;
END;
```

```
FUNCTION WIDTH(VAR BUF: STRING255): INTEGER;
        (*=====*)

(* COMPUTE WIDTH OF CHARACTER STRING *)

VAR
  I,
  BS,
  COUNT: INTEGER;

BEGIN
IF LENGTH(BUF) > 0 THEN
  BEGIN
  I := SCAN(LENGTH(BUF),=BACKSPACE,BUF[1]);
  IF I = LENGTH(BUF) THEN
    WIDTH := I
  ELSE
    BEGIN
    BS := 1;
    I := I+2;
    COUNT := (LENGTH(BUF)+1)-I;
    WHILE COUNT > 0 DO
      BEGIN
      I := I+SCAN(COUNT,=BACKSPACE,BUF[I]);
      COUNT := (LENGTH(BUF)+1)-I;
      IF COUNT <> 0 THEN
        BEGIN
        BS := SUCC(BS);
        I := SUCC(I);
        COUNT := PRED(COUNT);
        END;
      END;
    WIDTH := LENGTH(BUF)-BS;
    END;
  END
ELSE
  WIDTH := 0;
END;

PROCEDURE SPREAD(VAR BUF: STRING255; NEXTRA, OUTWDS: INTEGER);
        (*======*)

(* SPREAD WORDS TO JUSTIFY RIGHT MARGIN *)

VAR
  I,
  NB,
  NE,
  NHOLES: INTEGER;

BEGIN
IF (NEXTRA > 0) AND (OUTWDS > 1) THEN
  BEGIN
  DIR := 1-DIR;
  NE := NEXTRA;
  NHOLES := PRED(OUTWDS);
  I := 1;
  WHILE NE > 0 DO
    BEGIN
    I := I+SCAN((LENGTH(BUF)+1)-I,=' ',BUF[I]);
    IF DIR = 0 THEN
      NB := (PRED(NE) DIV NHOLES)+1
    ELSE
      NB := NE DIV NHOLES;
    NE := NE-NB;
    NHOLES := PRED(NHOLES);
    INSERT(COPY(BLANKS255,1,NB),BUF,I);
    I := I+NB+1;
    END;
  END;
END;
```

```
PROCEDURE PUTWRD(VAR WRDBUF: STRING255);
         (*======*)

(* PUT A WORD IN OUTBUF; INCLUDES MARGIN JUSTIFICATION *)

VAR
  W,
  LAST,
  LLVAL: INTEGER;

BEGIN
W := WIDTH(WRDBUF);
LLVAL := RMVAL-TIVAL;
IF LENGTH(OUTBUF) > 0 THEN
  BEGIN
  LAST := LENGTH(OUTBUF)+1+LENGTH(WRDBUF);
  IF (OUTW+1+W > LLVAL) OR (LAST > 255) THEN
    BEGIN
    SPREAD(OUTBUF,LLVAL-OUTW,OUTWDS);
    BRK;
    END;
  END;
IF LENGTH(OUTBUF) = 0 THEN
  BEGIN
  OUTBUF := WRDBUF;
  OUTW := W;
  END
ELSE
  BEGIN
  INSERT(' ',OUTBUF,LENGTH(OUTBUF)+1);
  INSERT(WRDBUF,OUTBUF,LENGTH(OUTBUF)+1);
  OUTW := OUTW+1+W;
  END;
OUTWDS := SUCC(OUTWDS);
END;

PROCEDURE CENTER(VAR BUF: STRING255);
         (*======*)

(* CENTER A LINE BY SETTING TIVAL *)

BEGIN
TIVAL := MAX(((RMVAL+TIVAL)-WIDTH(BUF)) DIV 2,0);
END;

PROCEDURE UNDERL(VAR BUF: STRING255);
         (*======*)

(* UNDERLINE A LINE *)

VAR
  I: INTEGER;

BEGIN
I := 1;
WHILE (I < LENGTH(BUF)) AND (I < 254) DO
  BEGIN
  IF BUF[I] <> ' ' THEN
    BEGIN
    INSERT(UNDERLINE,BUF,I);
    I := I+2;
    END;
  I := SUCC(I);
  END;
END;
```

```
FUNCTION GETWRD(VAR INBUF, OUT: STRING255): INTEGER;
       (*======*)

(* GET NON-BLANK WORD FROM INBUF INTO OUT, DELETE FROM INBUF *)

VAR
  I: INTEGER;

BEGIN
IF LENGTH(INBUF) > 0 THEN
  BEGIN
  I := SCAN(LENGTH(INBUF),<>' ',INBUF[1]);
  DELETE(INBUF,1,I);
  END;
IF LENGTH(INBUF) > 0 THEN
  BEGIN
  I := SCAN(LENGTH(INBUF),=' ',INBUF[1]);
  OUT := COPY(INBUF,1,I);
  DELETE(INBUF,1,I);
  GETWRD := I;
  END
ELSE
  BEGIN
  OUT := '';
  GETWRD := 0;
  END;
END;

PROCEDURE TXT(VAR INBUF: STRING255);
        (*===*)

(* PROCESS TEXT LINES *)

VAR
  WRDBUF: STRING255;

BEGIN
IF LENGTH(INBUF) = 0 THEN
  LEADBL(INBUF)
ELSE IF INBUF[1] = ' ' THEN
  LEADBL(INBUF);
IF ULVAL > 0 THEN
  BEGIN
  UNDERL(INBUF);
  ULVAL := PRED(ULVAL);
  END;
IF CEVAL > 0 THEN
  BEGIN
  CENTER(INBUF);
  PUT(INBUF);
  CEVAL := PRED(CEVAL);
  END
ELSE IF LENGTH(INBUF) = 0 THEN
  PUT(INBUF)
ELSE IF NOT FILL THEN
  PUT(INBUF)
ELSE
  WHILE GETWRD(INBUF,WRDBUF) > 0 DO
    PUTWRD(WRDBUF);
END;
```

Glossary

ADDRESS – Memory location, usually expressed in hex.

ALGORITHM – A sequence of steps which may be performed by a program or other process, which will produce a given result.

ALPHABETIC CHARACTER – Any one of the letters A through Z (uppercase and lowercase).

ALPHANUMERIC – Consisting of letters, numbers, and other symbols such as punctuation marks and mathematical symbols.

APPLE – (1) The round fleshy fruit of a Rosaceous tree (Pyrus Malus). (2) A brand of personal computer. (3) Apple Computer, Inc. manufacturer of home computers.

APPLESOFT BASIC – A floating-point BASIC interpreter that is included in ROM. It was the successor to Integer BASIC. See *BASIC*.

ARGUMENT – The value on which a function operates.

ARITHMETIC OPERATOR – An operator, such as +, that combines numeric values to produce a numeric result.

ARRAY – Matrix of variable data. This data is accessed by programs to fulfill a need for table style data in an easy to manage format.

ASCII (American Standard Code for Information Interchange) – A character encoding standard that translates uppercase and lowercase letters and symbolic characters into a 7-bit binary representation having the values 0 to 127. The eighth bit, parity and framing bits are not part of this definition.

ASSEMBLER – A program used to translate as assembly language program into the machine language used by a processor.

ASSEMBLY LANGUAGE – A language similar in structure to machine language, but made up of "mnemonics" and "symbols" that are converted to the machine language of a processor by the assembler. Well-written assembly language programs usually run faster and use less memory than BASIC programs, but they usually take longer to write and longer to test and debug than BASIC programs.

BASE – In number systems, the exponent at which the number system repeats itself; the number of symbols required by that number system.

BASIC (Beginner's All-purpose Symbolic Instruction Code) – A programming language that is designed to be easy to learn and use, and encourage people to use computers for simple problem-solving operations. Originally developed at Dartmouth College.

BINARY – The base 2 number system, composed solely of the numbers 0 and 1.

BINARY FILES – Binary files save machine language programs, binary data (which might be automatically gathered from sensors and generated by analog-to-digital converters), etc. Such material may be of arbitrary length and may include in its body any possible binary combination of bits.

BIT – Abbreviation for "Binary DigIT." Either of the binary digits 0 or 1. See *Byte*.

BLOAD – Binary program load.

BLOCK – Storage methodology used by ProDOS for placing data on a floppy disk. Under ProDOS, a 140K 5.25" floppy disk holds 280 blocks (0~279) of 512 bytes each.

BOOT – The process of starting a computer system ("booting up"). A cold boot is starting the computer after it was off. The operating system (DOS 3.3 or ProDOS) is loaded into memory. A warm boot is a reloading of the operating system without a power-down sequence.

BRANCH – To resume program execution at a new location. GOTO and JMP (jump) are branch instructions.

BRUN – Binary program run. The BRUN command in DOS 3.3 and ProDOS causes a binary program to be loaded into memory and run.

BSAVE – Binary program save. The BSAVE command in DOS 3.3 and ProDOS causes the binary data in some portion of memory to be saved as a disk file.

BUFFER – Large temporary memory storage area.

BUG – A program error, often called "an undocumented feature."

BYTE – The amount of storage required to represent one character. Hexadecimal or Decimal representation of eight binary bits: 0~255 in Decimal, $00~$FF in Hexidecimal. 8 bits = 1 byte. 1,024 bytes = 1K or Kilobyte.

CALL – Executes a machine language subroutine contained within the called memory location and onward. Continues until the program code contains an RTS.

CARRIAGE RETURN – The key used as an end of line or end of input terminator. Also called the RETURN key.

CATALOG – A list of all files stored on a disk, sometimes called a "directory."

CHARACTER – A single byte, letter, digit, or other symbol.

CHIP – Tiny pieces of silicon or germanium containing many integrated circuits that perform specific tasks for a computer.

CODE – (1) A number or symbol used to represent some piece of information in a compact or easily processed form. (2) The statements or instructions that make up a program.

COMPILER – A program which translates a high-level language into the machine code used by a computer.

CONCATENATE – To join together, as in C$ = A$ + B$.

CONDITIONAL BRANCH – A branch that depends on the truth of a condition or the value of an expression.

CONSTANT – A symbol in a program representing a fixed, unchanging value. Compare to "Variable."

CONTROL CHARACTER – A special character created by simultaneously typing the "Control" key and another alpha character. These keys are used in the editor for cursor movement, text formatting, and other specified functions. Control-G can be shown as ^G.

CPU – Central Processing Unit. See *Microprocessor*.

CTRL – The "Control" key.

CURSOR – (1) A marker or symbol that delineates where the next action will take place. (2) A programmer who can't find the reason a program is crashing.

DASH (-) – Command that runs a BASIC, machine, EXEC, or interpreter program in ProDOS only.

DATA – Facts or information used by or in a computer program.

DEBUGGING – The process of detecting and correcting errors in a computer program.

DECIMAL – The base 10 number system, composed of the numbers 0 through 9, inclusive.

DECREMENT – Decrease value in calculated steps.

DEFAULT – Nominal value or condition assigned to a parameter when not otherwise specified by the user.

DELETE – Command that removes a file from its directory.

DELIMITER – Symbol to separate data fields.

DIRECTORY – List of files on diskette or part of a group of files on a hard drive. In ProDOS, each directory has a name rather than the "Slot x, Drive x, Volume x" designation in DOS 3.3.

DISKETTE – A 5.25" or 3.5" disk. Apple II 5.25" floppy disks typically hold 140K, and 3.5" disks typically hold 800K of data.

DOS – Disk Operating System such as DOS 3.3 or ProDOS. The user interface between computer and the applications program. An operating system allows the user to execute programs and perform disk operations.

DUMMY – Data with no significance, "GET A$" is a dummy if used just to halt a program.

EDITOR – Text-editing program that allows text to be entered into a data file and manipulated as desired.

ERROR MESSAGE – Message that notifies the user of an error or problem in the execution of a task or program.

EXECUTE – Perform an action specified by a program or computer operator.

EXPRESSION – A formula in a program describing a calculation to be performed.

FAC – Floating Point Accumulator.

FIELD – Contains data which would not normally subdivide.

FIRMWARE – Those components of a computer system consisting of programs stored permanently in read-only memory. Cards for printers and other devices contain firmware.

FLAG – A data bit used to indicate the state of a device or the result of an operation.

FORMAT – Prepare a blank diskette to receive and store information by dividing its surface into tracks and sectors.

FP (FLOATING POINT) – Floating Point BASIC as included in Applesoft.

HEX – Abbreviation of hexadecimal, the base 16 number system.

HEXADECIMAL – The base 16 number system, composed of the numbers 0 through 9, and A through F. Usually notated with a '$' prefix. Hexadecimal is a useful shorthand for describing the contents of a byte, with each hex digit describing half of a byte.

HEX DUMP – Formatted listing of hex data.

HIGH ORDER – The byte containing the value of the left most two digits of a hex expression.

HI-RES – High-Resolution graphics.

INCREMENT – Increase value in calculated steps.

INITIALIZE – (1) To set to an initial state or value in preparation for some computation.
(2) To prepare a blank disk to receive information by dividing its surface into tracks and sectors.

INPUT – (1) Information transferred into a computer from an external source, such as a keyboard, disk drive, or modem. (2) The act or process of transferring such information.

INTEGER – Number without fractional parts in the range -32768 to +32767.

INTEGER BASIC – The BASIC interpreter for the first Apple II. Succeeded by Applesoft BASIC.

INTERPRETER – A program which translates instructions written in a high level to machine code as the program is executed.

INTERRUPT – (1) To temporarily stop a process. (2) A signal created by either hardware or software to demand the immediate attention of a machine's CPU, there by stopping execution of any code that is being executed by said CPU. (3) In data communications, to take an action at a receiving computer that causes the ending computer to end a transmission.

I/O (Input/Output) – The transfer of information in and out of a computer. Used frequently in connection with peripheral devices.

IRQ – Interrupt requests.

JUMP – Another term for a branch.

KILOBYTE (K or KB) – Used with numbers to denote "kilo" or one thousand. 1K = 1,024 bytes. 64K is 64 times 1,024 bytes, or 65,536 bytes.

LABEL – Symbolic name for an address, often expressed in mnemonic form.

LINEFEED – Moves the cursor on the screen down one line. The ASCII character is Control-J.

LOAD – Command that brings a BASIC program into memory from a file.

LOADER – Program that calls up machine code from mass storage and loads it into memory for execution.

LOCK – Command that protects a file from being accidentally renamed, deleted, or altered.

LOGICAL OPERATOR – An operator, such as AND, that combines logical values to produce a logical result.

LOOP – Section of a program that is executed repeatedly until some condition is met such as an index variable reaching a specified ending value.

LOW ORDER – The byte containing the value of the right most two digits of a hex expression.

LO-RES – Low-Resolution graphics.

L.S.B. – The Less Significant Byte of the two-byte pair.

LSB – Least Significant Bit.

MACHINE LANGUAGE – Data groups which are interpreted as instructions to be executed by the processor. See *Assembly Language*.

MEMORY – See *RAM (Random Access Memory)*.

MEMORY LOCATION – A unit of main memory that is identified by an address and can hold a single item of information of a fixed size. In the Apple II, a memory location holds one byte, or 8 bits of information.

MICROPROCESSOR – A computer processor contained in a single integrated circuit, such as the Apple II's 6502 or 65C02 microprocessor.

MNEMONIC – Symbolic abbreviation containing characters helpful in remember an application or function, such as an assembly language instruction.

MOD – Algorithm which returns the remainder of a division operation (must be simulated in Applesoft BASIC).

MONITOR – (1) A closed-circuit television receiver. (2) A program which allows you to use your computer at a very low level, often with the values and addresses of individual memory locations. Monitor commands are used to communicate with the Monitor.

M.S.B. – The More Significant Byte of the two-byte pair.

MSB – Most Significant Bit.

NIBBLE (or Nybble) – (1) A 4-bit unit of data, or half a byte. (2) One of the best and longest-running magazines for the Apple II and Mac, created by entrepreneur and business expert Mike Harvey.
(3) "What are we going to call this series of bits? How about a bite, but spell it with a 'y'! So what do we call half a byte? A 'nybble', obviously!" (attributed to Werner Buchholz at IBM, circa 1956.)

NULL – Having no value.

OBJECT PROGRAM – The program produced by a compiler or interpreter from a high-level program.

OFFSET – Value, often used with or as an index to locate related data and add to a base value.

OPERATOR – A symbol or sequence of characters such as + or AND, specifying an operation to be performed on one or more values (the operands) to produce a result.

OUTPUT – (1) Information transferred from a computer to some external destination, such as the display screen, a disk drive, a printer, or a modem. (2) The act or process of transferring such information.

PAGE – Each page of memory in Apple II computers consist of 256 bytes. That is to say, $00 to $FF would be one page. A 32K machine would have 128 pages, a 48K machine would have 192 pages, while a 64K machine would contain 256 pages of memory. After the Zero Page ($0000~$00FF), each page is described by the first two digits of its 4 digit hexadecimal address.

PARALLEL – A method of data handling in which all the bits composing a word are transmitted simultaneously.

PARSER – Section of interpreter that formats listing of a BASIC program.

PASCAL – A structured programming language made popular by its designer Niklaus Wirth. Pascal was designed with an emphasis on imperative and procedural programming. Named after the French Mathematician Blaise Pascal, Wirth's Pascal programming language was popular as a high-level language from 1970 to about 1984. It was ported to the Apple II by companies such as Programma International and UCSD among others. Wirth won a Turing Award for the language and it has influenced most other modern day procedural programming languages.

PATH – A specified route to a specific subdirectory used in ProDOS.

PC – Program Counter.

PEEK – BASIC command which returns the decimal value of a specified memory location.

PERIPHERAL – An external device connected to a computer such as a printer, modem, monitor, or disk drive.

POINTER – A register memory location containing the memory address of data or instructions.

POKE – BASIC command which stores a decimal value in a specified memory location.

PR# – Command that sends output to the Apple II slot number specified.

PREFIX – A settable pathname that indicates a directory file.

PROCESSOR – A generic term for that part of computer hardware performing arithmetic and logical operations. See *Microprocessor*.

ProDOS – The major operating system for Apple II computers, that stands for Professional Disk Operating System.

PROGRAM – A sequence of instructions to be followed by the computer to carry out desired operations.

PROMPT – To remind or signal the user that some action is expected, typically by displaying a distinctive symbol, a reminder message, or a menu of choices on the display screen.

QUIT – Exiting a program and returning to the operating system.

RAM (Random Access Memory) – The volatile, temporary storage area in the computer that requires power to maintain its contents.

RAM DRIVE – The use of RAM to emulate a disk drive for temporary drive storage.

READ – To transfer information into the computer's memory from a source external to the computer (such as a disk drive or modem), or into the computers processor from a source external to the processor (such as a keyboard or main memory).

REGISTER – Single RAM memory or microprocessor storage location, usually for temporary use. A, X, Y-Registers and S, P, PC-Registers.

RELATIONAL OPERATOR – An operator, such as >, that compares numeric values to produce a logical result.

RENAME – Change the name of the file.

RESET – A key, which is part of a combination that causes the computer to re-boot a program. To Stop and warm start the computer.

ROM (Read Only Memory) – A memory device from where operating instructions and other programs reside permanently and cannot be altered or added to.

ROUTINE – A program which performs a specified task or function.

RS-232 – A standard voltage interface allowing a serial connection between the computer's communications port and an external device such as a modem or a printer.

RUN – The command to execute a BASIC program.

RWTS – Read-Write Track-Sector. These are the Diskette input / output routines.

SAVE – Command to save the BASIC program currently in memory to a file on disk.

SECTOR – The tracks on Apple 5.25" diskettes are subdivided into sectors. The sector is the smallest unit of information that can be written to, or read from, a diskette at one time. Each sector contains one memory page (256 bytes) of usable information. Each track contains the same number of sectors, so the physical length inches or centimeters of a sector on the outermost track is longer than that of a sector on the innermost track. However, sectors on the outermost track and the innermost track take the same amount of time to pass by the read head.

SERIAL – A method of data handling in which the bits composing a word are transmitted one after the other.

STACK – A section of memory used to hold addresses or data items. The page of 256 memory locations from $0100 to $01FF (decimal 256~511) is called the Apple System Stack, as well as memory Page 1. The Stack is used in conjunction with the S-Register or Stack Pointer to provide positive control of the system in situations where control is passed from one portion of a program to another.

STATEMENT – An instruction line in a high-level language. In BASIC, smallest portion of a program complete in itself. Delimited by a ':' or end of line.

STRING – A group of ASCII characters that are alpha, numeric, punctuation, or control.

SUBROUTINE – A section of frequently used operations in a program which are treated as small separate programs.

SYNTAX – The formal structure of an argument or command.

SYNTAX ERROR – An error which specifies to the user that the structure of the line of BASIC code is improperly formatted or that it is missing a required element such as quotation marks.

TABLE – List of values, words, data, etc. that may be referenced by a program.

TEXT FILE – A file containing an arbitrary string of ASCII characters interspersed with occasional carriage returns to specify the end of a line.

TOKEN – One byte hex representation of a BASIC or other high level language command.

TRACE – A debugging method in which the program is executed one instruction at a time, and sometimes the register contents can be examined after each step.

TRACK – Apple 5.25" diskettes have 35 tracks under DOS 3.3. Each consists of a circular recording path at a fixed distance from the center of the disk. Thus, each is like a very thin, at ring, concentric with all the others. They are numbered from 0 (the outermost track) to 34 (the innermost track).

VAL – Applesoft command that solves the value of a string. Also, the founder of A.P.P.L.E.

VARIABLE – Alphanumeric representation which may assume or be assigned a number of values.

VECTOR – Address to be branched to.

VOLUME – In DOS 3.3 and ProDOS, volume refers to floppy disk and hard drive storage.

VTOC (Volume Table of Contents) – On a 5.25" diskette Sector 0 of Track 17 (the track which is equidistant from the innermost and outermost tracks) is reserved for the VTOC.

WHY – Questions that programmers ask that have no answer.

WINDOW – Portion of screen display blocked off for special use.

WOZ – Steve Wozniak, an Apple Computer Inc. co-founder, inventor of the Apple-1 and Apple II computers, all-around genius, nice guy, über geek, philanthropist, and longtime supporter of the A.P.P.L.E. user group.

WRITE – To transfer information from the computer to a destination external to the computer (such as a disk drive or modem) or from the computers processor (such as main memory).

WWA – *What's Where in the Apple: Enhanced Edition* – a very useful programming reference book, also published by A.P.P.L.E.

www.ingramcontent.com/pod-product-compliance
Lightning Source LLC
Chambersburg PA
CBHW081145180526
45170CB00006B/1939